WOMEN'S RIGHTS

The Struggle for Equality in the Nineteenth and Twentieth Centuries

Nancy E. McGlen

Karen O'Connor

PRAEGER

PRAEGER SPECIAL STUDIES • PRAEGER SCIENTIFIC

Library of Congress Cataloging in Publication Data

McGlen, Nancy E., 1947–
  Women's rights.

  Includes bibliographical references and index.
  1. Feminism—United States—History.   2. Women's
rights—United States—History.   3. Equality—History.
I. O'Connor, Karen.   II. Title.
HQ1426.M395   1983   323.3'4'0973   83-3953
ISBN 0-03-063343-5
ISBN 0-03-063344-3 (pbk.)

Published in 1983 by Praeger Publishers
CBS Educational and Professional Publishing
a Division of CBS Inc.
521 Fifth Avenue, New York, NY 10175 USA

© 1983 by Praeger Publishers

3456789 052 987654321

Printed in the United States of America
on acid-free paper

To Agnes Hall Mead and Elizabeth Mead McGlen - N.E.M.

To Allen and Meghan O'Connor McDonogh - K.O'C.

Contents

List of Tables

List of Figures

Acknowledgments

As in the case in most undertakings of this sort, we are indebted to several individuals, groups, and institutions for their assistance. The librarians at the State University of New York at Buffalo, Niagara University, and Emory University all were very helpful. In addition, the collections at each facilitated our efforts to draw on materials from a wide variety of academic disciplines. Each university also provided assistance and support through its computer facilities. The reactions and comments of students at SUNY Buffalo and Niagara University also proved very useful. Several students at Emory University, including Nancy Rossman, also provided assistance.

Numerous women's organizations and research institutes, including the Center for the American Woman and Politics, Center for Women and Work, the Institute for Social Research at the University of Michigan, the National Women's Political Caucus, the National Organization for Women, the Women's Campaign Fund, and the Women's Research and Education Institute, all provided valuable information. We would also like to acknowledge the Inter-University Consortium for Political and Social Research, the General Mills Corporation, the Louis Harris Association, and the Roper Organization for survey data and/or summaries of survey data that were used throughout the book.

We also are indebted to several of our colleagues and friends who supported us in a variety of ways during the four-year period that this book was in preparation: Judith Baer, Marilyn Chandler, Naomi Lynn, Lynda Watts Powell, Sarah Slavin, Robert Stern, and Richard Tobin all provided us with clippings, references, and/or comments and suggestions concerning women and politics. Jerome Black, Louis La Barber, Sandra McGibbon, Allen McDonogh, G. Bingham Powell, Eliz Sanasarian, Joan Spade, Karen St. Marie, Stephen Wasby, and several anonymous reviewers read all or substantial portions of the various drafts of this manuscript and provided many insightful criticisms and suggestions. We would also like to thank our editor, Lynda Sharp, for her support.

Margaret McDonough at Niagara University provided some typing assistance on earlier drafts. We would like to express our special thanks and appreciation to Linda Boyte at Emory University. Ms. Boyte typed a complete draft as well as the final copy of this manuscript from an embarrassingly messy copy and continued to remain in good humor throughout the entire task.

Both authors would especially like to thank Lee Epstein. She not only read the entire manuscript and offered substantive comments but additionally assisted in reorganizing and editing the final draft. She also was instrumental in updating portions of the data analysis.

And, our final expression of appreciation must go to our families. Our husbands, Joe Gadawski and Allen McDonogh, were exceptionally supportive throughout. And, last, we would like to thank Meghan O'Connor McDonogh, who has shared her first three years with this project.

WOMEN'S RIGHTS

1   Introduction

Women's efforts to gain political, economic, and social equality in America are as old as the United States itself. As early as 1789, Abigail Adams wrote to her husband, John, who was in attendance at the Constitutional Convention:

> In the new code of laws...I desire you would remember the ladies and be more generous and favorable to them than your ancestors. Do not put such unlimited power into the hands of the husbands.... If particular care and attention is not paid to the ladies, we are determined to foment a rebellion, and will not hold ourselves bound by any laws in which we have no voice or representation.[1]

The rebellion predicted by Abigail Adams, however, did not begin for more than half a century.

In 1848, in what is widely recognized as the first major step toward female equality, a woman's rights convention was held in Seneca Falls, a rural village in central New York. Present at that meeting were many women who soon were to become leaders of the first woman's rights movement. Most notable among them were Elizabeth Cady Stanton and Lucretia Mott. Today these women are most remembered for their efforts to secure female suffrage; in 1848, however, their goals were much broader in scope. At the Seneca Falls convention, a Declaration of Sentiments (see Appendix A), modeled after the U.S. Declaration of Independence, was issued. Later, at the same meeting, a series of resolutions calling for the abolition of legal, economic, and social discrimination against women was passed. Both the declaration and resolutions reflected these women's dissatisfaction with contemporary moral codes, divorce and criminal laws, and the limited opportunities for women to obtain an education, participate in the church, and enter careers in medicine, law, and politics. While the agenda of rights for women set forth at the convention has been expanded over the years, women's groups today continue to work toward many of the goals first publicly enunciated at Seneca Falls.

Since 1848, however, the pursuit of women's rights has been intermittent. There have been periods of high activity when pressure for reforms has been keen. Most often, these phases have been followed by years of little organized effort. Analytically, three high points of activity, when actual women's rights movements* existed, can be identified: (1) the early woman's rights movement (1848–1875); (2) the suffrage movement (1890–1925); and (3) the current women's rights movement, which is composed of two distinct branches[2] (1966 to the present).[3]

In this book, we examine these three periods of activity in the context of social movement theory. In Chapter Two, we review social movement theory and develop a set of hypotheses concerning social movement formation and success. In succeeding chapters, we detail the rise and development of the various women's rights movements and the accomplishments of each in three issue areas: politics, economics, and the family. Where appropriate, we trace the development and activities of anti movements that arose to oppose their efforts.** These sections, in turn, have been structured to deal with the several stages of the struggle in each issue area. The first chapter in each section sets out the legal and political efforts undertaken to obtain various rights. Because these efforts were strongly influenced by the characteristics of the women's rights movement of the period, as well as by a number of other political and social variables, an attempt is made to show how these several factors interacted to allow women to achieve (or not to achieve) their goals.

The second chapter of each section focuses on the social changes still needed to obtain the conditions necessary for the full exercise of rights. The transformation of public opinion, especially that of women, toward women's participation in each area is of special interest. This is followed by a discussion of how close women have come to obtaining equality and what barriers (legal and social) remain.

---

*We have chosen to refer to all three periods collectively as those displaying "women's rights" activity. The term "woman's rights," however, is used to refer to the first movement.

**Throughout the book, we will refer to those groups that traditionally espouse "conservative" causes and are usually opposed to change as anti movements, groups, or forces; conversely, we will refer to those that traditionally favor "liberal" causes and change as pro movements, groups, or forces.

While we have separated our discussion of each issue area in this fashion, in practice they are not so neatly divided. Arguments in favor of particular changes often are directed both to those in power and to the members of the affected group. Likewise, certain strategies may be chosen with an eye not only to winning a right but also to converting women outside the movement.

Thus, while we have divided "rights" into three general areas, they often overlap. In fact, efforts to achieve success in one area often have affected progress in the others. This has been particularly true for attempts to alter social mores and practices. For example, changes in social institutions that allow for the fuller exercise of political rights often have influenced participation in the economic or social spheres. As discussed in Chapter 8, this has been particularly true for women and the institution of the family. Changes in marital age, number of children, and other aspects of family life have had important ramifications on political and economic participation.

To provide a perspective on the changes that have occurred in women's political, legal, and societal status, in Chapter 9 we examine the recent attempt of the women's rights movement to secure ratification of the Equal Rights Amendment (ERA). It is our belief that the defeat of the ERA reveals many of the difficulties and problems that must be overcome if the struggle for women's rights is to continue to be pursued by members of a viable movement. The future vitality and success of the current women's movement depend on many known and unknown factors. Lessons learned from the past can help us predict the future, but only with time can we know whether the current movement will succeed where others have enjoyed but limited success.

NOTES

1. Quoted in Eleanor Flexner, *Century of Struggle* (New York: Atheneum, 1974), p. 15.

2. The notion that the present movement has two separate branches is drawn from Jo Freeman, *The Politics of Women's Liberation* (New York: David McKay, 1975).

3. These chronological periods are approximate.

2   Social Movement Theory and Women's Rights

INTRODUCTION

In this chapter, we examine social movement theory to develop a framework for the study of the rise and development of the various women's rights movements and the reasons for their successes and failures. From this foundation, we proceed to develop a set of hypotheses of social movement formation and success. We then survey each movement to provide a preliminary test of our hypotheses.

SOCIAL MOVEMENT THEORY

A social movement has been defined as:

> a set of attitudes and self-conscious action on the part of a group of people directed toward change in the social structure and/or ideology of a society and carried on outside of ideologically legitimated channels or which uses these channels in innovative ways.[1]

At the risk of oversimplification, two kinds of theories have been promulgated to explain the formation of protest groups and social movements. The first, mass society theory, holds that isolated, atomized individuals are highly susceptible to demagogues and other such leaders and will respond to their

4

urgings by spontaneous uprisings that lead to protest movements.[2] Evidence from those who study movements, however, fails to substantiate this view. It is not necessarily the alienated, isolated, nonparticipants in society who lead and form social movements, but rather it is previously organized individuals. This finding has led to a second set of explanations for collective behavior that posits that social movements are most likely to occur when individuals are linked to one another via some kind of social tie.[3]

A refinement of this latter idea, which derives from the notion of a public good, is particularly useful in explaining the development of women's movements in the United States. A public good is defined as a "necessarily shared" good, or alternatively, one that when once provided to a single member of a group, cannot be denied or withheld from other members of the group, *whether they contributed to its provisions or not.*[4] An example of a pure public good is the recently defeated Equal Rights Amendment, which had it been ratified, would have guaranteed equal protection of the laws to all women regardless of their support for its provisions.

The goals of most social movements almost always involve the attainment of some kind of public good(s) for their members. Public goods are to be contrasted with private ones, goods that an individual may obtain on his or her own. The purchase of a home or one woman's admission to medical school, for example, involves private goods.

Building upon the concept of a public good, Mancur Olson developed a theory to explain collective action (or more accurately, the relative absence of collective action) in the pursuit of public goods. Olson believes the problem presented by public goods stems from the fact that while all group members have a common interest in their acquisition, they lack a common interest in paying or working for their attainment. This phenomenon occurs at least in part because any member of the group will reap the rewards of the good once it is provided, whether or not he or she worked to achieve the good. In addition, each individual's benefit is so small relative to the high costs of obtaining this good that it may be irrational to contribute to its attainment. This behavior is especially characteristic of large groups where each individual's contribution alone often appears insignificant or incapable of adding to the likelihood of obtaining the good.

According to Olson, this attribute of public goods deters individuals in large groups from organizing voluntarily for the common goal of the group. Only if individual benefits or sanctions distinct from and in addition to the public good are provided will it "pay" those in large groups to band together and to contribute to the provision of the public good.[5] Without a perception of possible personal benefits, individuals in the affected groups will remain latent parts of the unorganized collectivity.

It should be noted that the private benefits and sanctions necessary to mobilize individuals need not be material ones. They can involve factors such as friendship, altruism, status, or prestige. In other instances, a group may be formed when it is possible to inflict negative sanctions upon individual members of the group who do not contribute. For example, a government's ability to fine or imprison citizens for failure to pay taxes helps explain why people contribute to the provision of public goods such as national defense and welfare.[6]

Olson contends, however, that the likelihood of these individual incentives or sanctions being available to a group is rather remote in most instances. Consequently, members of large, latent groups generally do not organize themselves or expend personal resources to obtain a public good, even when all members desire it.[7] William H. Riker and Peter C. Ordeshook have amplified this point, noting that there is a further reason to suspect large groups will not form associations to work for their common interest: as more people have to be brought together organizational costs increase, often becoming prohibitive.[8] For instance, the expense of simply informing 10,000 people of the need for a particular law may present a stumbling block to the organizing of those who would favor the law should they learn its purpose.

The predicament of large groups can be contrasted with that of small ones in which each person's share of the public good is relatively large and the contribution of each member substantial. Olson considers these conditions as being more conducive to the provisions of the public good.[9] A day-care organization is a good example of a small group. A few women organize for the purpose of securing inexpensive, reliable childcare. Only those women who contribute may use the facility. This kind of action, however, may lead to underprovision of the public good. In the day-care example, for instance, the mothers in the cooperative may have solved their immediate child-care needs, but their actions have not brought about a solution to the provision of adequate national childcare for the larger group—all working mothers. In other words, the larger public good has not been obtained.

Another situation where a public good may be provided without the help of all or even a significant number of members of the group occurs in so-called privileged groups. In these situations, some individuals' share of the public good may be sufficiently large to motivate one or several members who possess sufficient resources to seek the good without the help of others. The efforts of Elizabeth Blackwell and Arabella (Belle) Mansfield, the first female doctor and lawyer, respectively, to practice in the United States, are examples of privileged group efforts. The rights secured were made available to others by the work of these two women acting almost alone. Other examples of privileged group activity can be found in the numerous women's service projects (e.g., law and health clinics, rape victim or battered wives counseling centers, etc.) founded in the 1960s and 1970s. The attainment of rights by privileged groups, however, as in the case of small groups, is likely to be insufficient because the individuals who work to secure the good will attain only as much of it as they need (or can afford). Frequently, this will be less than the group as a whole desires.[10] In the case of medicine and law, Blackwell's and Mansfield's efforts left many barriers to the full participation of women in these fields untouched (professional school quotas, for example), a situation that parallels the cooperative day-care center's failure to solve the problem of all working mothers.

The implication of Olson's analysis for the formation of social movements is clear. Shared oppression or grievances alone are insufficient conditions to produce an organized social movement. Additional private incentives normally are necessary to mobilize individuals to work collectively toward common goals. Furthermore, because the availability of potent private incentives for large groups is unlikely, one might expect social movements to be relatively rare. This is especially true when one is dealing with public goods that may be secured, or at least partially secured, by small or privileged groups. Thus, while Olson's theory helps us to understand why the oppression of women has not given birth to a sustained social movement, given the development of three separate movements from different sources, Olson's theory must be expanded to explain adequately their rise.

Leaders and Organizers

One of the variables in collective protest behavior not dealt with by Olson is the role of leaders and organizers.[11] Most successful protest organizations are led by individuals who devote most of their energies, sometimes even their lives, to "the cause." These persons may provide, through their own time and resources, the necessary wherewithal for organizing the group. Whether it be power, altruism, prestige, or the fear of negative sanctions such as imprisonment or economic retribution, the "leaders" in all social movements at least are *partly* motivated by private rewards separate from the public good.[12]

Leaders differ in other ways from the rank and file of the group, and this also helps explain their unique behavior. Usually they are more future-oriented, better educated, and more affluent.[13] Accounts of the early efforts of Susan B. Anthony and Elizabeth Cady Stanton to secure the vote make it clear that neither woman expected female suffrage to be attained quickly.[14] Many more fainthearted women would have quit where Anthony and Stanton began if they were faced with the prospect of a decades-long battle.

When a socially oppressed group has within its midst individuals who possess important leadership traits, the likelihood of the formation of a protest movement appears to increase considerably. In a sense, the presence of such persons transforms the group from Olson's large, latent group to a quasi-privileged group because one or a few individuals have the resources and motivation to pursue a particular good. And, since by definition, a pure public good is one that "spills over," its benefits may be shared by other group members.

Extragroup Inputs and Preexisting Organizations

While the Olson model is enhanced by the introduction of the leadership dimension, its utility may be further enhanced by the addition of concepts articulated by Anthony Oberschall. Oberschall has identified two other factors that may facilitate the organization of a socially oppressed group. In one instance, resolution of the public goods problem is accomplished by extragroup inputs. More specifically, the influx of outside help or resources from persons or institutions not in the group may become the means to the formation of a social movement.[15] The government, the media, and segments of other movements such as organized labor, often pay for or provide necessary organizational start-up costs. This kind of assistance can be direct or indirect. In the early 1960s, for instance, John F. Kennedy's creation of the President's Commission on the Status of Women brought women from all over the United States together, directly fostering communication among leaders of a potential movement. Almost a decade later, the American news media focused attention on the fledgling movement, indirectly aiding movement leaders' efforts to reach a larger audience.

Building upon preexisting associations is a second method that can facilitate formation of a protest movement.[16] While Olson's model implicitly assumes that the members of a group desiring a public good are unorganized individuals acting alone, this often is not the case. Social clubs, churches, sports groups, and other organizations not expressly designed for protest may be mobilized to do so when they feel threatened or when they perceive the need for some change.

Organizational bases like these are important because they can furnish leadership for the new movements as well as many of the necessary private incentives for their leaders. In addition, through their members, these preexisting organizations can supply potential supporters. These bases can be used further to augment the benefits of the public good by providing the private incentives needed to get people to work for and to support the efforts to solve their collective oppression. The presence of these groups serves as well to reduce initial organizational expense.[17] (This phenomenon can also assist the rise of anti movements. For example, right to life forces have built their base by adding supporters from the Roman Catholic Church and many fundamentalist Protestant sects. These religions believe that abortion is morally wrong. Thus, they perceive that the U.S. Supreme Court's decision legalizing abortion is a threat to their basic teachings.)

Additionally, the existence of many small groups helps to solve another problem pointed out by Olson; namely, in a large group no one individual's contribution alone seems significant or necessary. A member of a small group, especially if the association of which he or she is a member is linked to other small groups, can see more clearly how his or her own effort is being combined with that of others to achieve their common interest. The increased sense of expectation and confidence that this fosters may help sustain the member's activity as well as encourage others to join who previously saw no chance that their own efforts could end the group's oppression. This phenomenon was present during the suffrage movement. During that period, hundreds of varied purpose women's clubs banded together to obtain congressional passage and state ratification of the Nineteenth Amendment. It was their combined efforts that clearly made the difference.

Communications Networks

In addition to the existence of an organizational base, whatever the source, lines of communication among the many small groups or their leaders appear critical. While Oberschall seems to assume the existence of this kind of network, Jo Freeman maintains that such a linkage among like-minded individuals may be essential to the birth of a social movement.[18] Communications among leaders may allow small groups to band together to form a large social movement to pressure for a particular societal change.

Clement E. Vose also has pointed to the importance of a communications network to the success of a protest group. In *Caucasians Only,* a study of the National Association for the Advancement of Colored People's (NAACP) litigation activities, he noted the regular exchange of ideas that took place among black civil rights lawyers and its importance to the success of the NAACP's activities.[19] In that instance, it was a network that resulted, in part, from a shared law school experience at Howard University, then an all-black institution and one of the few schools in the country where a black could receive a legal education. Although many women also attended (sex) segregated schools, they have experienced greater difficulties than blacks in developing an independent communications network. Consequently, they often have relied on other social movement networks to establish their critical, first contacts with potential adherents.

Critical Mobilizing Event(s)

Even where all of these factors are present, something more may be needed before the rise of a new social movement occurs. Generally some kind of "event" must occur to ignite the whole process. Freeman has hypothesized that what is needed is a crisis, a recognition that some action must be taken. She notes that without this crisis, some organizers will need to toil weeks, months, or even years to create a "spontaneous" uprising.[20]

Oberschall notes that the crises, what he terms precipitating conditions, may be a series of events or a single happening that signals to the potential group the possibility of success in achieving its goals. This "event" may be the success of a closely allied social movement or group in achieving one or some of its aims or the granting of certain rights to the potential social movement's members.[21] While limited victories seem important to the birth of the various women's movements, in other cases it has been the failure of existing social movements to take up their cause that has precipitated *independent* action by women to achieve their own rights.

The rise of the first woman's movement appears to combine elements of all these precipitating conditions. While both Lucretia Mott and Elizabeth Cady Stanton were long concerned with women's status, they were not prompted to act independently until after the occurrence of several incidents. For example, they first recognized the need for concerted action in 1840 when they were denied seats at an Anti-Slavery Association meeting (as representatives of a preexisting social movement). It was not, however, until 1848, shortly after the debate and passage of the New York State Married Women's Property Act (a partial victory for women) that the two finally sent out the call for the first woman's rights convention.[22] Years of organizing followed, and truly independent, concerted action did not come until women were abandoned by the abolitionists in the late 1860s. The other women's rights movements also can trace their initial formation to a series of precipitating conditions usually combined with subsequent organizing efforts.

THEORY MODIFICATIONS

The question to be asked at this point is what additional modificatons in the theories discussed above are necessary to explain the rise and/or fall of the various women's movements. Olson's assumption that subjugated groups not only are aware of their oppressed status but also of possible remedies must first be altered. As Oberschall and others have pointed out, awareness of a *common* malaise may be difficult for some groups to attain. When identifiable groups of people enjoy few social ties to one another (either communal or associational), individuals are less likely to realize that their personal trials or difficulties are not individual problems but common ones shared by all who have the same attributes as themselves. This has been a particular problem for women because historically they have been isolated and cut off from one another, without a collective geographical or physical base. Living intimately with men, most women concluded that their frustrations were a function of their own weaknesses or inferiority and not the products of their social condition.[23]

The exact means by which a group of women or any collectivity becomes aware of its common oppression is the least understood part of the social movement process. While the existence of an organizational network helps *spread* the idea, we have only a rough notion of the conditions under which the idea is *born*.

Most theorists seeking to explain the rise in consciousness of an oppressed group stress the importance of changing economic and social conditions, and several different explanations have been offered to explain *how* these conditions affect increased awareness. William H. Chafe posits the theory that periods of high women's movement growth coincided with occasions of economic transformation.[24] He notes, for instance, that in the early nineteenth century, the Industrial Revolution created, for the first time, a middle-class woman who could fit the cultural ideal of what a woman's life and position should be: a mother and wife who devoted all her energies to those roles. Prior to the Industrial Revolution, most women and men held this stereotype even though a woman's economic activity generally almost equalled that of her husband or father.[25] The dislocation engendered by the restriction of middle-class women to the home, Chafe maintains, created a situation of "structural strain" that contributed to the radical protest movement by women in the early nineteenth century.[26] Likewise, he views the increased participation in the labor force by women, especially mothers of children, in the 1950s and 1960s as also producing strain between cultural norms surrounding women's role and actual behavior. This conflict once again helped to foster a "revolt" by women.[27] While Chafe's idea of "structural strain" is useful in understanding the growth of consciousness among women during the 1840s and 1960s, it does not explain why, during the late 1880s, a time of relatively little divergence between cultural ideals and behavior for *middle-class* women, the suffrage movement was born.

Others have hypothesized that economic and cultural trends may be important in the development of a collective consciousness when they give rise to a sense of "relative deprivation" on the part of the oppressed group.[28] According to Ted Gurr,

> Relative deprivation is a condition where there is a perceived discrepancy between men's value expectations and their value capabilities. Value expectations are goods and conditions of life to which people believe they are rightfully entitled. Value capabilities are the goods and conditions they think they are capable of attaining or maintaining, given the social means available to them.[29]

Adopting this notion, Freeman chronicled the conditions of the 1950s and 1960s, which she viewed as producing a feeling among middle-class women that they were not getting their "just desserts" when they compared their status to men with similar training and education. The wide gap they found engendered a deep sense of outrage (relative deprivation) that led many of these women to be the first to join the budding women's movement.[30]

Relative deprivation also can be used to explain the rise of consciousness on the part of women in the nineteenth century. During the Industrial Revolution, middle-class women experienced a declining economic status, both absolutely and relatively, when compared to middle-class men.[31] Moreover, their sense of relative *political* deprivation is clear in the comparisons they often made of their position to that of blacks and working-class men. *Political* deprivation, however, perhaps was most keenly felt by women in the early 1900s as they sought the vote.[32]

There is a problem, however, in using either "cultural strain" or "relative deprivation" to explain a "birth of consciousness." Specifically, in some sense both factors are always present or occur for protracted periods of time. For instance, middle-class women began entering the labor force in large numbers long before the formation of the National Organization for Women (NOW). As Oberschall and Olson's analyses show, economic and social conditions alone will not produce a social movement nor, as Freeman and Chafe are aware, a collective consciousness.

Both Freeman and Chafe observe that an important catalyst in the rise of collective consciousness on the part of at least some women was the direct witnessing of the oppression of another group, blacks.[33] Both the first woman's rights movement and the current women's movement were preceded by a push for equality by black Americans and their supporters. Indeed, many adherents of both of these women's movements were initially active in the abolition or civil rights movements. As Chafe has noted,

> The civil rights movement ... focused attention on the extent to which groups of people were oppressed on the basis of cultural and physical characteristics. As women saw and participated in demonstrations demanding freedom and personal dignity, they perceived, like their abolitionist forerunners, a connection to their own lives and hence the possibility of acting for themselves as a group.[34]

In this context, however, the suffrage movement appears unique. In fact, sentiments of shared oppression with blacks generally were absent. Indeed, at times the speeches and strategies of suffrage movement leaders took on racist overtones (see Chapter 3). At the turn of the century, it was activities of the progressive movement, which sought political and social reforms, that helped middle-class women develop an increasing awareness of their political and social oppression. Faced with the tasks of cleaning up corrupt city governments and remedying deplorable slum conditions, women came to realize that they could do little without the vote.

Women's Unique Status and Public "Bads"

Because most women live with men (husbands or fathers) and adopt their status in society, it may take longer for them as a group to recognize their problems because of that unique position. This situation has not only inhibited an awareness of a common interest, it predictably has produced a segment of the female population that will oppose any changes that could have an impact on its status or position in society. As Chafe has pointed out:

> The diverse social and economic existence experienced by women, in contrast [to blacks], discourages the same degree of collective awareness, giving rise to differing perceptions of the need for change. Although few blacks have anything to lose from a change in race relations, many women benefit from the status quo of sex relations and would have to sacrifice material, as well as psychological, assets were the existing distribution of sex roles altered.[35]

In other words, some women see any wholesale change in the status of women not as a public good but as a public *bad*. For example, many women identify the liberalization of divorce laws as a public good, which makes it easier for all women to end unhappy marriages. Other women, however, see these changes as a public bad, which weakens the family structure and thus all women's positions as mothers and wives.

The disagreement over whether a proposed change is a public bad or public good is often related to a debate concerning whether or not the change is something that all women share equally or one that individual women may or may not partake of at a level they desire. Antidiscrimination employment legislation, for example, is difficult for women to categorize as a universal public bad. Only those women who wish to work are affected by this kind of statutory protection. The affected class can be reduced even further to include only those working women who wish to protest their employers' discriminatory practices. Thus, not all women must partake of the "good." Divorce laws, in contrast, may be perceived by some as a universal public bad because they are viewed as weakening marriage, which may affect the entire social order. As a consequence, some argue that these laws may affect all women whether they wish to be affected or not.[36]

Olson and Oberschall assume that all reforms and rights are pure public goods of which all women must partake equally. The employment discrimination example shows that this is not always the case. Additionally, employment discrimination legislation is not the only instance of a nonuniversal public good. When the Nineteenth Amendment was ratified in 1920, women were not forced to exercise their new right. Some chose to vote or even to run for office, while others did neither. Moreover, many states continued to exclude some classes of women from exercising their right to vote by the imposition of poll taxes and/or literacy tests. In other words, even the Nineteenth Amendment fell short of being a pure public good. Rather, it and other similar goods exhibit "jointness of supply." That is, once they are made available to one person, other persons may or can partake of them but only if they so desire.

Thus, Riker and Ordeshook have identified the following three dimensions by which a public good may be classified:

1. whether it is perceived as a good or bad (for example, civil liberties is a good; air pollution is a bad);

2. whether a person is able to choose the amount he or she wants to use (or totally avoid) (for example, he or she can choose public recreation activities; he or she cannot choose air pollution control); and

3. whether a person can be excluded from consumption via fees, special rules, etc. (for example, individuals can be excluded from public parks, toll roads; generally, they cannot be excluded from national defense).[37]

Summarizing these dimensions, a pure public good is one in which all citizens share equally and which all beneficiaries perceive *as a good.*

The exact placement of any change or right on these dimensions often is a matter of great disagreement among women. For instance, opponents of the Equal Rights Amendment characterized the changes it would have produced as being universal public bads. They argued that if the amendment was ratified, men no longer would be responsible for the support of their wives. In contrast, ERA supporters said that the amendment would have little impact on personal relationships.

Disagreement concerning the characteristics of proposed changes or rights for women and whether such changes are goods or bads or limited or universal in application, produces several additional hurdles to the formation of women's movements not recognized in the Oberschall/Olson analysis. Specifically, not only must a sufficiently large organizing cadre of women become aware of their common oppression and the need for change, but also they must convince other women that the reform will be a public good for them, or at the very least, will not diminish their status or position in society. If all women are not convinced of the positive or voluntary nature of the proposed change, the rise of a countermovement, which may further hinder the group's efforts, is possible.

These countermovements seem most likely to develop when some group of women not only sees the proposed change as a bad but also identifies it as one that will affect all women, even if they are opposed to the change. Thus, because of the particularly threatening aspects of pure public good reforms, leaders of the several women's rights movements often have adopted the strategy of acquiring limited rights (e.g., those where women are free to choose the amount desired).[38] However, if a group of women comes to see a proposed change as a threat to an existing good (and thus characterizes the change as a bad), whether they form a countermovement may depend on the existence of the same conditions as those for social change movements posited above. If these factors are missing or lacking, outside resources to create a foundation and to stage or facilitate the occurrence of a critical mobilizing event or events, are necessary.

Also important is an anti movement group's ability to convince women that the proposed good is actually a bad. This latter step may be easier than the communication process faced by the original pro groups or movements. For example, it often is easier to convince women of the need to continue existing institutions like marriage or the family than to persuade them to support some reform in the *hope* that the change will be better than the existing state of affairs.

Anti movements in the United States are further advantaged by the American constitutional system. When rights necessitating constitutional amendments are at issue, prochange forces must win the support of three-fourths of the nation's state legislatures. (The U.S. Constitution specifically sets out two ways to propose amendments as well as two ways to ratify amendments to the Constitution. Amendments may be proposed either by (1) a 2/3 vote in both Houses of Congress or, (2) a national convention called by Congress at the request of 2/3 of the states' legislatures. Once proposed, amendments can then be ratified either by (1) 3/4 vote of the state legislatures or, (2) ratifying conventions specially called in 3/4 of the states.) In contrast, anti groups need "win" the support of only one-fourth plus one of the nation's state houses to succeed, i.e., block ratification. This makes their task much simpler. For example, while ERA supporters were able to secure approval of the amendment in thirty-five state legislatures (in states where over 75 percent of the U.S. population resides), opponents, although not nearly so numerous or even well organized nationally, were able to block its ratification. When it is an anti group that seeks an amendment, however, it faces the same uphill battle. For example, the Right to Life forces also must obtain approval of thirty-eight state legislatures before U.S. Supreme Court decisions upholding a woman's right to an abortion can be nullified.

HYPOTHESES

Thus, given the above analysis, we hypothesize that a women's movement will occur and develop only when the following minimal conditions are met:

1. an organizational base or outside resources to facilitate its development are present;
2. lines of communication exist among potential leaders;
3. a sense of collective oppression and a recognition of the need for a common solution develop within a sizeable group of women; and,
4. a critical mobilizing event (or events) occurs.

We further hypothesize that the prospects of 1 through 4 occurring are facilitated by the presence of a preexisting social movement. Once the new movement is launched, however, its success can be predicted by the kinds of change sought; i.e., are they pure public goods? Therefore, we additionally hypothesize that the new social movement will reach its goals more easily if the rights sought are not pure public goods. If the rights sought will or are perceived to affect all, the chances of the formation of an anti movement are greater. Thus, the probability of the new movement's ability to secure substantial change is reduced.

APPLICATION OF HYPOTHESES TO THE WOMEN'S RIGHTS MOVEMENTS

The Woman's Rights Movement

Prior to 1800, women in the United States were on a more equal footing with men than their counterparts in other sections of the world in many respects. Often they shared in the family business, and sex roles were less distinct. However, this semblance of equality was largely destroyed by the Industrial Revolution.[39] In its wake, many newly middle-class women found themselves pressured to stay in the home. Some of these women soon developed a sense of political deprivation when working-class and immigrant men were given the franchise as states eased property-owning voting restrictions. Because they were unable to enter a business or profession, these women also looked to their husbands' expanding opportunities in all spheres with an increased sense of loss.[40]

More important, perhaps, to the rise of women's consciousness than these economic and social trends was the abolitionist movement. For the many women active in that cause, it helped spark their recognition that women, as a class, were subject to discrimination. Elizabeth Cady Stanton, Lucy Stone, and many other future leaders of the movement came to see their situation as analogous to that of the black slave they were working to free. Indeed, the debate generated among abolitionists about the role women should play in that cause, a debate that eventually split the movement, no doubt was important in raising the question of women's place in society for even larger segments of the citizenry outside the movement.[41]

Not only the idea of women's oppression, but also the ideology and even some of the goals of the future movement, had their roots in abolitionist theory, especially that espoused by those in the branch headed by William Lloyd Garrison, the editor of *The Liberator,* a leading abolitionist newspaper. The rights of blacks and women to vote and otherwise participate were deemed to follow from the position that all men and women were created equal and thus possessed the same inalienable rights to life, liberty, and the pursuit of happiness.[42]

Early emphasis on women as individuals and citizens led logically to the adoption of strategies designed to promote equal opportunity in all spheres including business, religion, education, medicine, and the family. In fact, women active in the first woman's rights movement regularly held conventions (meetings) throughout the Northeast where they passed resolutions demanding equal property and custody rights, increased access to education, business, and professional opportunities, more liberal divorce laws, the vote, an end to the double moral standard, and equality in the religious sphere.[43]

Communication of the call for women's equality and the subsequent development of the woman's rights movement fits our hypotheses. While others, most notably Mary Wollstonecraft, Frances Wright, Margaret Fuller, and Harriet Martineau, wrote about women's downtrodden position long before Stanton and Anthony, a women's movement did not spring from these early exhortations. Even though a prime topic of discussion during much of the early nineteenth century was a woman's proper role,[44] the absence of an organizational base to spread ideas or upon which a movement could be developed prevented the development of a women's movement.

However, after the 1830s, as an outgrowth of religious revivalism, both men and women were encouraged to work for improved conditions for those less fortunate than themselves.[45] The temperance and abolition movements, both outgrowths of revivalism, attracted large numbers of supporters. While women initially were assigned minor roles in these struggles and the battle over their rights to take action in "political causes" often was heated, they eventually took an active and vocal role, especially among the more liberal, Garrisonian branch of the antislavery movement.

In particular, numerous local and national Female Anti-Slavery societies were formed in the mid-1800s. These groups undertook numerous activities, most notably petition campaigns designed to secure legislation to end slavery.[46] The establishment of these societies brought women together for the first time where they were given the opportunity to develop leadership and political skills. Actions of women, including Angelina and Sarah Grimké, Quaker sisters from South Carolina who traveled throughout the United States lecturing on the evils of slavery, earned for other women the right to speak out on political issues as society's code against women speaking in public was "bent" to accommodate the perceived need for action against slavery.[47]

In addition to supplying the resources and wherewithal for establishing the first women's organizations, the abolitionist movement was critical in other ways to the formation of the first woman's rights movement. For example, it brought together women who later would rise to leadership positions. Additionally, an abolitionist meeting provided the event that galvanized some women to act. When delegates to the International Anti-Slavery Convention in London, England denied female representatives from the United States the right to participate, Stanton and Mott realized that their own position was not much better than those whom they were working to set free. Thus, the two women resolved to call a convention of women to petition for their rights when they returned home. However, both women had families to raise, and it was not until several years later but soon after the passage of the New York Married Woman's Property Act that they convened a meeting in Seneca Falls, believing the time was opportune to press for additional rights.

Friendships among other women active in the abolitionist cause produced a set of linkages, which with the aid of abolition newspapers and yearly conventions, served as a communications network of sorts for the fledgling woman's rights movement until after the Civil War. No independent national woman's rights organization, however, was formed until the late 1860s. In 1869, a dispute arose within the American Equal Rights Association (an antislavery group) concerning its endorsement of the proposed Fifteenth Amendment to the U.S. Constitution. When the Association decided to back the amendment over the protests of several women who believed that the amendment could be detrimental to woman's rights, Stanton and Anthony established the National Woman Suffrage Association (NWSA) whose goal was full equality for women in all spheres of life.[48]

Later, in 1869, another women's group was formed, the American Woman Suffrage Association (AWSA), with the more limited aim of female suffrage. Its members believed that Negro suffrage should rightly come before that of women. Headed by Lucy Stone, the AWSA was far more conservative than the NWSA. In fact, its leaders often tried to disassociate it from the more controversial social and economic demands of the NWSA.

Angered by what they saw as abandonment of the larger cause and the more limited goals of the AWSA, *The Revolution,* a newspaper run by Stanton and Anthony, declared:

> [The American's] plan of campaign is to cut off all the "side issues" and to "stick to the one point": the "side issues" being such trifles as wages, education, property, marriage, and divorce; and the "one point" being the ballot.
>   This is like abandoning one's self to the spoon at breakfast, and forgetting the coffee, sugar, and milk which it is to stir up.[49]

The activity of both the NWSA and the AWSA declined after 1875 and did not really pick up again until the time of their merger in 1890 when they joined to become the National American Woman Suffrage Association. Indeed, after 1875, there was little real further growth in the woman's rights movement as women began increasingly to refer to their movement as the "woman suffrage movement," and not the "woman's rights movement."[50] Thus, while an organizational base developed from the abolition effort and made possible this first woman's movement, the restricted and narrow structure of this base was a key factor in the movement's decline. Once the limits of the abolitionist base had been reached, growth was blocked.

Particularly in the South, many women remained isolated from the woman's movement altogether. At least *initially,* efforts to expand beyond this base were doomed by the dearth of organized women outside the abolitionist cause.[51] The movement's strength was further attenuated by the split of this limited base in 1869 and the subsequent isolation of the Anthony-led branch from abolitionists.[52] The divergent aims of the two resulting associations prevented a unified movement from developing until a common goal and ideology were adopted in 1890.

The success of this first woman's rights protest was rather modest. The property laws of many states were rewritten, adding provisions increasing some rights for married women, but the broader goal of full legal, political, and social equality was not realized. Even the more restricted goal of votes for women was not achieved.

In sum, the rise, development, and demise of the first woman's rights movement support our hypotheses. With few women's associations of any sort prior to the 1830s, demands for equality alone were inadequate to spark a movement. Only after an organizational base was developed as a result of the abolition effort did the idea spread and a "movement" with its own leaders develop. However, this restricted and narrow organizational base was a key factor in the movement's demise. Once its limits had been reached, growth lagged. And, while there was some subsequent organizational development on the part of women as a result of the Civil War, the number of women involved in the movement was never very large.[53]

Moreover, the broad range of changes advocated by Anthony and Stanton, most of those changes far ahead of their time, inevitably led to their lack of major successes. Reforms sought by Stanton, particularly liberalized divorce laws (true public goods), were simply too sweeping for a divided movement with a limited base to achieve.

Although many of the changes sought were true public goods, a countermovement did not arise during this first period. This was largely due to the movement's nonthreatening nature. Quite simply, it was never treated by politicians or other women as a serious political or social movement, which lessened the likelihood of the development of a countermovement. There simply was no "spark" to ignite opponents to action.

The Suffrage Movement
Other social trends helped to foster the second push for equality. Both the temperance and progressive movements were instrumental to the development of the suffrage movement in the late nineteenth and early twentieth centuries. For example, the Women's Christian Temperance Union (WCTU), which was founded in 1874, promoted woman suffrage as early as 1879. Its phenomenal growth to over 200,000 members helped spread the need for suffrage to a large number of women.[54] And, in the North and West, the progressive era gave

birth to the settlement house movement and the National Consumers' and Women's Trade Union Leagues. Both organizations were comprised largely of middle-class women who sought to improve the working conditions of children and women. Eventually, many women active in these organizations came to see the ballot as a prerequisite for their success.

Both the temperance and reform or progressive movements assisted the suffrage cause in ways reminiscent of the abolition movement's help of the woman's rights campaign. First, they implanted the idea of the need for suffrage in many women's minds as well as the ideology to support it. However, unlike woman's rights advocates of the earlier era, suffrage leaders did not seek the vote on the basis of natural rights but rather on grounds of expediency. They claimed that the ballot would enable women to reform society, a task they were particularly suited to *as women*. Suffrage leaders further argued that the inherent incorruptibility of women and their acknowledged superior moral character could be harnessed not only to make better laws, but also to act as a counterforce to lesser classes in cleaning up the nation's urban governments.[55]

This ideology clearly buttressed women's limited demand for the vote. Most supporters of suffrage were avowedly content with their roles as mother and wife. In fact, their position and the logic used to support it were Stanton's ideology in reverse. While she had claimed that motherhood and marriage were only incidental roles for women with respect to any claim for rights, for leaders of the suffrage movement, motherhood and marriage were essential and the articulated bases for the right to vote.

Second, the existence of strong women's organizations, especially the WCTU, helped to spread this idea to women who had been untouched or unconvinced by woman's rights advocates of an earlier time. In particular, the WCTU was especially effective in the South where it was able to cloak the "radical" vote idea under the rubric of temperance. Additionally, the WCTU was responsible for organizing women in a region that had previously seen few women's organizations.

Third, the temperance and reform movements provided training for suffrage leaders. For example, two presidents of the National American Woman Suffrage Association (NAWSA), Anna Howard Shaw and Carrie Chapman Catt, came to the suffrage movement via their activities in the temperance movement. Indeed, an interlocking directorate of sorts developed between the various reform groups and the NAWSA.[56]

The reform and temperance movements alone, however, probably would have been insufficient to produce an effective women's movement were it not for the development of a large organizational base of women that came from the phenomenal growth of women's clubs in the 1880s and 1890s. Middle-class women, freed from many domestic tasks by the development of labor-saving devices, devoted some of their extra time to participation in "self-improvement" groups. The growth of these groups, many of which were literary and reading societies, quickly led to the formation of the General Federation of Women's Clubs (GFWC) in 1890. In that year, the GFWC claimed over 500,000 members; by 1910 its membership had mushroomed to 2 million.

When women in these clubs became involved in social causes as a result of the reform movement, they quickly realized their own inferior *political* position. Thus, in 1914, the GFWC decided to support the suffrage movement, which added the organizational strength necessary for a successful social movement.[57] Other organizations of professional, university, and even working women also began to support woman suffrage and became affiliated with the NAWSA. The result was a powerful movement that was able to mount a "Winning Plan" to coordinate the efforts of thousands of women to lobby for the vote.

Although we have dated the beginning of the suffrage movement as 1890, a unified mass movement probably did not develop until approximately 1915. In fact, in 1890, the newly formed NAWSA adopted the strategy of the older AWSA and attempted to secure votes for women on a state-by-state basis and not via a constitutional amendment. Not surprisingly, between 1890 and 1910, its efforts were rewarded with little success. Led by Anna Howard Shaw, a brilliant orator but inefficient manager, the organization languished.

Real growth in the movement, however, was not evident until after 1910. By then, there were several women's organizations with members who realized the importance of the ballot, whatever their particular cause. As their common malaise was recognized, these women turned to the NAWSA and offered their support for its nonpartisan efforts to secure votes for women. However, a number of critical events were required before the movement actually flourished.

One of the first events that led to the resurgence of the woman suffrage cause was the successes achieved by the closely allied progressive reform movement. For example, in the early 1900s, the National Consumers' League successfully lobbied for protective legislation in Washington, Oregon, and California.[58] The Progressive party also enjoyed legislative victories. Not only was it able to introduce political reforms in many state constitutions (such as the referendum and recall), but it also even gained a majority of seats in some state legislatures.[59]

Many women who supported women suffrage were active in the Progressive party and took part in its political battles. Their efforts were rewarded in some midwestern and western states by their party's support of woman suffrage in several successful state referenda battles. In 1912, the Progressive party even included a woman suffrage plank in its presidential campaign platform, an action that influenced some state organizations to do likewise.[60] These "victories" played a role similar to the effect of the first married woman's property act on the woman's rights movement. Specifically, they generated new discussion and debate concerning suffrage and may have encouraged at least some women to renew and increase their efforts for the ballot.[61]

The second more immediate event that generated debate and interest in suffrage occurred in 1913. In that year, Alice Paul, a militant suffragist who had been active in the British women's campaign for the vote, successfully staged a major parade in support of a national suffrage amendment. As women marched through the streets of Washington, D.C., spectators turned on the peaceful demonstrators. The parade quickly became a violent spectacle that was widely reported.[62] Shortly thereafter, the suffrage amendment was debated on the floor of the U.S. Congress for the first time in twenty-six years. Thus, increasing attention was centered on the ballot. Even the conservative GFWC threw its support behind the amendment, thereby bringing all major national women's organizations into the suffrage effort.

While the Washington march served to bolster the number of women publicly committed to suffrage as well as to focus national attention on the problem, it did not bring about agreement on tactics. Although leaders of the NAWSA had initially given tacit support to Alice Paul's efforts, they continued to cling to the belief that their best strategy was to secure the vote on a state-by-state basis. In 1915, however, a series of defeats of state suffrage referenda in four populous states, New York, Massachusetts, Pennsylvania, and New Jersey, forced them to abandon this policy.[63] These losses were a particularly stunning blow to the NAWSA because New Jersey was the only state in the union ever to have allowed women to vote. (Women voted in New Jersey and in some sections of Virginia during colonial times but were disenfranchised by state constitutions.) Additionally, New York and Massachusetts were the birthplaces of most women active in the first woman's movement and had been the site of prosuffrage activity since the 1840s. The crisis produced by the referenda failures led NAWSA members to realize that their state-by-state strategy was not working. It soon became clear that women needed to organize at the national level and to focus their energies on changing the federal constitution. Thus, when Carrie Chapman Catt was elected president of the NAWSA shortly after the 1915 state elections, she, as the major spokesperson for all prosuffrage organizations, quickly moved to reorganize the group to lobby for a national amendment.[64]

The base of this movement, however, was shaky. While the several constituent organizations agreed on the necessity of the vote, their secondary goals or reasons for wanting the ballot varied. For example, women in the more radical Congressional Union (later called the National Woman's Party), a group headed by Alice Paul, advocated total equality for women, while reform women wanted the vote to clean up cities, to end political machines, and to improve conditions of the poor and working women. In contrast, others saw female suffrage as a way to maintain white (or native-born) superiority. Thus, while different interests helped to mobilize women to work for the vote, once suffrage was attained, loyalties to individual associations and aims took precedence and the movement quickly disintegrated.

In addition, unlike the first woman's movement, an anti movement sought to prevent suffrage movement success. Opponents regularly attempted to tie woman suffrage to the demise of the family and to the Roman Catholic Church, which was very unpopular in white, Anglo-Saxon communities. (Many believed that priests exercised tremendous influence over their female parishioners and thus would be able to tell women how to vote.) For example, a leaflet of the Man Suffrage Association charged that suffragists were "opposed to the doctrine that the family is the unit of society and the state."[65] Opponents of suffrage used leaflets such as these, referendum elections, and litigation to attempt to stop ratification of the amendment. However, these actions were unsuccessful. By 1920, a majority of Americans had come to view suffrage not as a life-style endangering activity but rather as a reasonable demand.

The Current Women's Movement

After the demise of the suffrage movement, there was little organized protest activity by women until the 1960s. In that decade, a new women's rights movement arose from two distinct sources. This has led many to refer to the resultant activity as stemming from separate "branches" of the same movement.[66] The "older" branch of the movement, so named because it developed first and generally drew older supporters, includes the National Organization for Women (NOW), the National Women's Political Caucus (NWPC), and the Women's Equity Action League (WEAL), among others. Often called "feminists" or liberal feminists, the prime focus of those in the older branch has been amelioration of legal and economic discrimination in the workplace.

The "younger" branch, sometimes called "radical feminists" or "liberationists," is composed of the many small radical or socialist feminist groups that arose around the United States with little or no national coordination. Each group engages in a variety of local community activities without much organized *national* political activity.[67] The goal or goals of these younger-branch groups is some form of significant alteration in the social, economic, and/or political systems of the United States. While the eventual end point of development may be a merger of the older and younger branches (as was the case in the first woman's movement), for the purpose of testing our hypotheses, each is considered separately.

As in the nineteenth century, the evolution of both branches of the new women's protest movement was preceded and aided by other social movements. The civil rights struggle, in particular, like the abolitionist movement before it, instilled in many women's minds common recognition that their grievances were a product of a cultural and economic structure that kept both blacks and women alike from full equality. Women who participated in efforts for black equality began to ask for those same rights for themselves. They were quick to note that the stereotypical image that blacks were "happy in their place" had a parallel in the "feminine mystique." This latter phrase was coined by Betty Friedan in 1963 to describe what she saw as the dominant philosophy of the 1950s. According to Friedan, the feminine mystique held that women could find their true fulfillment only in the roles of mother and wife. She claimed that this myth, buttressed and maintained by the media, advertisers, and social scientists, resulted in a general feeling of dissatisfaction on the part of many women when they failed to find housework gratifying. Friedan believed this could be remedied by giving women the chance to participate equally with men within the *existing* system. These demands for *equality now* paralleled the integrationist phase of the civil rights movement. Feminists, including Friedan, like many black leaders, did not urge the overthrow of existing social, economic, or political structures; they merely wanted to join and participate equally with white men.

The ideologies, goals, and even many of the strategies of reform adopted by the older branch closely paralleled those adopted by black integrationists. NOW was even modeled after the NAACP. It tried to secure fuller rights for women by working within the "system." It resorted to conventional political lobbying and like the NAACP, NOW and several other women's rights branch groups quickly turned to litigation to secure greater rights for women.

In contrast, the ideology of the liberationists or younger branch has drawn more heavily on the black power stage of the civil rights movement. Some liberationists, for example, espouse the idea of separatism of women from men. The slogan "Black is Beautiful" and the technique of "telling it like it is" to increase awareness of black oppression became models for the motto "Sisterhood is Powerful" and the introduction of consciousness-raising groups designed to convince women of their common oppression.[68]

Although the civil rights movement led some women to recognize their oppression and also provided some ideological elements, it does not appear to have played a *direct* role in supplying the leaders or followers of either branch of the women's movement. Although a number of women who were active in the Southern civil rights movement had key roles in the development of the younger branch, the majority of leaders of both branches gained their experience elsewhere.[69] Moreover, black women generally have not had major leadership roles in either branch. Public opinion polls, however, continue to show high levels of support for women's issues among black women, perhaps providing a latent group ready to be organized.[70]

The counterculture and student and antiwar movements appear to have played a more decisive role for the younger or liberationist branch than did the movement for black rights. In fact, it was from these three movements that many of the leaders, organizers, followers, and core of the ideology that formed the basis of the radical women's protest came. Women in Students for a Democratic Society (SDS) were among the first to recognize that their own activity was in strong contradiction to the goals of equality that group was seeking for others. The first manifesto of SDS women, for example, compared their status with that of the colonial people in the Third World.[71] Thus, the roots of the idea brought the beginning of a theory about the causes and solutions to women's collective oppression.

Therefore, in contrast to women in the older branch, radicals view the "system" (economic, political, and social) as corrupt and therefore in need of replacement. This idea follows directly from the position held by those of the counterculture and student protest movement. The related notion that participation in or cooperation with the system would only prolong the day before it could be overthrown, and thus should be avoided, is a main reason why these women have adopted their particular organizational structure and policy goals. For example, some radicals find the cause of women's plight in a Marxist analysis of the existing economic class system. They argue that women and all other downtrodden groups will achieve freedom and equality only after they overthrow this system and it is replaced with a socialist regime. Others reject this Marxist analysis as incomplete. Women, they argue, cannot expect equality in a socialist state because the source of oppression goes deeper. While they retain the class analogy, they posit the theory that the sex-based class system is the most fundamental division in society and until it is replaced, women will be subjugated.[72] Still other younger-branch women, socialist feminists, see women's oppression as derived from *both* the patriarchal social structure and the capitalist economic system. Hence, they believe both sets of institutions must be overthrown before women will be free.[73] Thus, having briefly outlined the origins and structures of the "new" idea of women's oppression, the question now becomes, how did this idea (or really ideas as it burst forth in two separate places) become the basis for the two branches of the women's movement.

The Younger Branch of the Women's Rights Movement. As they were in the first woman's rights movement, the notion of oppression and many basic elements of the ideology and program of the younger branch (especially the view that the existing social, economic, and/or political system(s) must be replaced) were directly traceable to established protest movements. Its leaders and followers were drawn primarily from the civil rights movement, counterculture, and student protest movements. Participation in these movements led many women to see that it was now the time to press for major changes concerning the role of women in the social system. As it was for Mott and Stanton earlier, the event that galvanized them to act was the failure of established movements to incorporate demands for female equality into their programs.

As early as 1964, a few women began to realize that their own positions in radical organizations were those of second-class citizens.[74] At an SDS meeting held the next year, "catcalls, storms of ridicule and verbal abuse," were hurled at women who broached the women's issue. Later, women who introduced a women's rights plank at the SDS annual meeting in 1966 "were pelted with tomatoes and thrown out of the convention."[75] These responses convinced many women of the need to form their own groups.

The final, major "crisis" came in 1967 at the National Conference for a New Politics (NCNP) held in Chicago, Illinois. A major schism occurred there when New Left women realized that the convention was unwilling to address any women's issues. When Jo Freeman and Shulamith Firestone went to the podium to demand that women's issues be addressed, Firestone was patted on the head and told to "Calm down, little girl," as they were further informed that the convention would not deal with their "trivial" complaints.[76] Freeman went on to found a radical women's group in Chicago; Firestone did the same in New York City.

Subsequently, often without knowledge of what was happening in other areas, women began to hold meetings in cities across the United States. This new idea of women's liberation was spread mainly through the existing infrastructure and communications network of the student movement and counterculture. SDS women and those from other New Left groups in particular, were well suited to the task of organizing the women's groups that sprung up in many parts of the country.[77] The development of a new form of organization, the consciousness-raising group, allowed these women to spread the idea even more effectively that the problems they experienced were not the result of individual failures or situations but instead had roots in the dominant culture and thus were common to all women.

While the number of small groups skyrocketed from 1969 to 1972, their growth was largely uncoordinated. Papers and newsletters like *Notes from the First Year* and *Voice of the Women's Liberation Movement* were attempts to fill this void but generally failed on account of their insufficient funds and lack of workers.[78] And, while some local groups were successful, larger projects or national efforts generally were unsuccessful when attempted. Thus, while consciousness-raising groups effectively promoted the idea of women's common oppression, they often did not serve to mobilize women for political action.

An additional problem faced by the radicals stemmed from their refusal to form organizations with a traditional leadership structure. Rather, they often opted for a "lot" or rotating system of leadership in order to provide all members with a chance to participate equally in the governance of the group. Indeed, women who appeared to take on a leadership or spokesperson role often eventually were ostracized by others in the collective. Thus, these kinds of problems prompted Freeman to note that by 1972, the younger branch was in a serious state of fragmentation and dissolution.[79] According to her, this branch,

> [a] product of the counterculture and New Left...had within a few short years expanded to the boundaries of that culture, transformed and/or integrated most of its organizations and institutions, and then turned in on itself *as it had no place else to go.*[80] [emphasis added]

In 1975, Freeman maintained that any further growth in the younger branch would require expansion beyond the counterculture. While this task has been difficult, the existence of the continually changing number and variety of local women's self-help centers and other such activity indicates some continued vitality in this branch.

Interestingly, however, much of the recent activity at the local level by those previously active in this branch has been undertaken in concert with organizations or members drawn from the older branch of the movement. Additionally, these activities appear to be oriented more toward working within the system than toward its overthrow. Many younger-branch women, frustrated by the limited accomplishments of their small groups, have joined NOW or other older-branch organizations. They have brought with them many of the ideas and theories of radical feminism and thus have had a significant impact on the direction and ideology of the older branch. This continued assimilation of younger-branch women into NOW and other older-branch groups, coupled with evidence of increased cooperation between groups from both branches, may signal the beginnings of unification.[81]

In sum, the growth and development of the younger branch of the movement once again appear to support our hypotheses. Women active in the New Left or black power struggle movements were more easily mobilized once they realized their common oppression. When the New Left failed to recognize and, in fact, ridiculed the legitimate claims of its female members, several women were galvanized to form their own groups. The success of these groups, however, has been hindered by their limited base and the nature of their goals—overthrow of the social, economic, and political systems.

In pursuing these far-ranging changes, younger-branch women seek many true public goods. However, they have failed to develop the requisite base necessary to the successful accomplishment of their goals. Therefore, given how unlikely the adoption of their proposals appears, strong, organized opposition has not arisen to thwart their efforts except in the area of reproductive freedom.

The Older Branch of the Women's Rights Movement. Development of the older branch was not nearly so dependent on any other single social movement. While it drew many of its ideas, programs, and strategies from the integrationist phase of the civil rights movement, for the most part older-branch leaders and followers were not active in that movement. Instead, its evolution was made possible by leaders drawn from other organizations not expressly designed for social protest as well as by the influx of substantial outside resources.

The United States has been characterized as a nation of "joiners." Men and women alike belong to numerous organizations ranging from social clubs and religious associations to unions and business groups. Middle-class women in particular have been and continue to be exceptionally active in community- and church-affiliated organizations.[82] Many of these groups have single-sex memberships and thus have given women the opportunity to develop leadership and organizational skills. While prior to the 1960s, few women's organizations were politically active, some groups, most notably the League of Women Voters and the National Federation of Business and Professional Women (BPW), long were active in the legislative arena. Although these groups provided a potential leadership base for a social movement, conditions for the formation of a protest movement were missing. Leadership potential needed to be galvanized to act. A catalyst needed to be forthcoming to make women aware of their plight and of the need to pressure for a common solution.

Several events occurred to resolve this problem. The advent of the civil rights movement along with the publication of Betty Friedan's book, *The Feminine Mystique,* helped disseminate the idea of group oppression to women across the United States. An additional important factor was the influx of outside resources in the form of organizational aid. For example, in 1961, President Kennedy established a President's Commission on the Status of Women. Many governors soon followed his lead and state commissions eventually were established in all fifty states. Most commission members were women who possessed leadership skills learned from their long association with labor, a political party, or one of several established groups such as the BPW. In addition, many of these commissions produced reports that documented, often for the first time, the extent of discrimination against women and their lack of opportunities and rights.

As Freeman has noted, the work of these commissions was critical to the development of the older branch in several ways. It established a communications network among many politically active women who would be its potential leaders, and it further implanted in the minds of these women not only that they as a group were discriminated against but also that something had to be done to ameliorate the situation.[83]

As with the other women's movements, a number of limited victories, such as the passage of the Equal Pay Act of 1963 and the Civil Rights Act of 1964, also may have encouraged women to believe that the time to press for change was at hand. But the "event" that finally mobilized some commission women to take action was the Equal Employment Opportunity Commission's

(EEOC) failure to enforce provisions of the 1964 Civil Rights Act that prohibited sex discrimination in employment. When it became clear that the bylaws of the Third National Conference of Commissions on the status of Women prohibited conference attendees from passing a resolution demanding that the EEOC treat sex-discrimination complaints seriously, a number of the women present decided to form their *own* independent pressure group—the National Organization for Women. Most of NOW's original members were commission members, and its leadership was drawn almost exclusively from the commission's ranks.

Unlike founders of the younger branch, these women were well trained as leaders, but there were few organizers among them.[84] Thus, NOW's growth initially was slow. One study found that most women who joined NOW before 1969 learned of it through friends, their work in volunteer organizations like BPW, or the political parties—organizations whose members had played a significant role in the state and federal commissions.[85]

While other women's rights organizations were formed after NOW, often because of some women's disagreement with NOW over tactics, the formation of many of these new organizations as well as the increasing political activity of existing women's groups were accomplished by women connected with NOW or the various commissions on the status of women. For example, professional women, including a group of federal government employees, formed associations to lobby for better treatment for women in their fields. In addition, several existing women's organizations, among them the BPW and the Young Women's Christian Association (YWCA), began to take a more active position with respect to women's rights. Thus, little *new* ground was broken in terms of reaching beyond this organizational base until 1970. Indeed, the movement may have failed when the limits of this base were reached had it not been for an additional free resource—publicity.

Early in 1970, the national media began to focus on the women's movement. *The New York Times, Newsweek, New York Magazine,* and the national television networks all devoted time or space to women's issues. According to Freeman, "The cumulative impact of the series of stories was tremendous. Within the short space of a few months the movement went from a struggling new idea to a national phenomenon."[86] When NOW organized a strike to commemorate the fiftieth anniversary of the ratification of the Nineteenth Amendment, extensive reporting of the event further helped to familiarize millions of American women with the existence of the women's movement.[87] Practically overnight, NOW's membership burgeoned as its ideas were carried to a nationwide audience. The publication of *Ms.* in 1972 and the fanfare surrounding it also spread the word of the new movement even further.

Many of NOW's new members were housewives, young mothers, or white-collar and clerical workers, and generally they were not as old as the women who had founded it.[88] To integrate these new members and to accommodate their interests, consciousness-raising sessions were formed within many NOW chapters. These groups provided individual benefits in the form of psychological support and at the same time mobilized these members to join in the effort to achieve the common goal—equality for all women. These newcomers were augmented by the addition of some members of the younger branch who were disenchanted with the lack of progress being accomplished in that quarter. While this increase in size created some problems for NOW, the restricted organizational base problem that hampered the earlier woman's rights movement and the younger branch apparently had been overcome.

The media attention that aided development of the older branch, however, also contributed to the development of an anti movement. By the mid-1970s, some women came to perceive additional rights for women as a threat to their way of life. The Equal Rights Amendment and legalization of abortion were viewed as particularly ominous changes. Using the organizational base of religious and other conservative groups, Phyllis Schlafly and others created a countermovement that blocked passage of the Equal Rights Amendment and may pose a serious threat to the attainment of a number of goals of both branches of the women's rights movement. However, as in the suffrage movement, where the organizational base was unable to sustain it after passage of the Nineteenth Amendment, the diverse organizational base of the Stop-ERA movement may prove too fragile to continue effective sustained efforts. Moreover, the success of this group has resulted in the influx of even more women into NOW. By 1982, membership had risen to 220,000.[89]

Thus, each women's movement supports our theory of group mobilization. Each was preceded by another social protest or reform movement that served to introduce the notion of oppression based on cultural and physical characteristics. This idea was then seized upon by a few women, usually those active in a previous movement, and generalized to their own condition.

The recognition by a few of their common problem, however, did not lead automatically to the formation of a social movement. This occurred only when the women who first recognized the need for change had an organizational base by which to spread the idea and upon which to build the protest. If this organizational base was lacking, as it was in the period before 1840, or if it was too narrow because the changes sought were too far ranging to attract many adherents, as it was in the early woman's rights movement or in the radical branch, the movement failed to materialize or faltered once its limits were reached. The only possible exception to this rule is the older branch of the current movement, which has been able to go beyond its initial, rather limited, base because of free media publicity and organizational assistance from the government. Even in this case, however, development would not have been possible were it not for previously organized women from other voluntary associations and those recruited from the younger branch.

While an overly narrow organizational base explains the stagnation of two of the attempts to mount lasting, independent movements, the demise of the suffrage phase is traceable to an overly diverse organizational base. There, although agreement on a single issue—the ballot—attracted a large number of supporters, suffragists lacked an agreed upon set of second priorities. Thus, once their goal was attained, women activists returned to their individual pursuits or to involvement in the association (with its own goals), which initially drew them into the movement.

The nature of the organizational base, therefore, not only helps explain whether a movement will form and develop but also its ideology, goals, and to some extent, its strategies. The ideology that defines the nature, causes, and solutions of women's condition clearly differed among the three movements. In each instance, the variations were clearly traceable to the origins of the idea of oppression itself. Women in the abolition movement and those influenced by the civil rights movement identified their position with that of black men. In both cases, the goal of equality in the existing political and economic system was borrowed from the black struggle and adopted by women. Additionally, the strategies used in the struggles for black rights also initially were utilized by women; abolitionists circulated petitions and called for a constitutional amendment and so did members of the early women's groups in the 1800s. When the cause of civil rights appeared to falter in the legislative arena, the NAACP launched a litigation strategy to obtain rights through the courts. This is also a tactic that many women's organizations began to use in the 1970s.[90]

The ideologies of both the suffrage and the younger branch also have had roots in other social protests. Suffrage leaders, influenced by the idea of the progressive movement, especially the notions of "political capacity" and the inherent goodness of native-born, middle-class individuals, stressed their own qualifications for the vote and their superiority to immigrant men. They sought no other changes in the roles of the sexes that could affect the family or prevailing social norms. Likewise, those in the younger branch, introduced to the idea of the corruptness of the present political, economic, and social system by the radical and student movements, merely extended that idea to include the overthrow of institutions and structures subjugating women.

In sum, when the conditions of the hypotheses are met, a social movement will form. Its development, growth, and success will depend, however, not only on the nature of the organizational base and the other factors noted above but also on a number of other conditions exogenous to the affected group. One of the most important outside factors is the formation of anti groups or movements.

ANTI MOVEMENTS

As earlier noted, some women's rights activists have faced very real threats to their success, particularly when they seek pure public goods—the development of viable anti movements when rights activists appear close to attaining their goals. All social movements can expect to encounter resistance from those in power positions, but women's rights advocates have faced an additional source of conflict—resistance and sometimes organized opposition from some women who oppose change. For example, there have been varying degrees of organized female opposition to woman suffrage, to the ERA, and to reproductive freedom. While antisuffrage forces were defeated, Stop ERA forces were very successful. However, it remains to be seen whether or not right to life forces will curtail a woman's right to a safe, legal abortion or even access to contraceptive devices (see Chapter 8).

The development of all three anti movements followed the process outlined above. However, because anti groups usually seek to preserve the status quo, this usually has meant that they may be smaller in size or have only a regional base and still be successful. Anti forces, particularly when a constitutional amendment is at issue, need only to be well organized in order to block ratification, while those who seek change need far wider support for their goals. Additionally, history reveals it is often easier to convince people to preserve what exists than to bank on an uncertain future. Thus, women's rights groups often have faced an uphill battle. For example, once anti-ERA forces clouded what the amendment would do by labeling it as a public bad, women's movement supporters were unable to secure ratification even though the amendment was favored by a majority of the American public.

According to the hypotheses offered above, a countermovement is most likely to form when the proposed change is perceived by some to be a pure public bad that necessitates changes that may adversely affect life-styles and in which all will be compelled to partake. If a change is not perceived by some as one that would directly diminish their own social status, opposition groups have tended not to form. Equal pay legislation, for example, initially met with no organized female opposition largely because only those women who wanted to work outside the home would be affected.

The need to make the proposed change appear to be a pure public bad helps to explain a main strategy of organizers of anti movements. Their leaders have attempted (sometimes successfully) to associate the proposed change with such universal "bads" as the end of society, the family, motherhood, the differences between the sexes, or the protected status of women. For instance, in a speech to the Georgia Association Opposed to Woman Suffrage, the audience was warned:

> Woman suffrage, if universally and generally adopted, in a social and political system like ours, would be most unfortunate.... It would

eventually lead to the ruin of American homelife; the destruction of the moral code, the lowering of woman's power and influence, and the final undoing of our government. The women who ask it are simply the unconscious agents of God's worst enemies.

This scheme is wicked woman's emancipation, and good woman's ruination.[91]

More recently, Stop ERA forces were particularly successful in their efforts to tie the amendment to the compulsory drafting of women and the legalization of homosexuality and homosexual marriages and to the abolition of protective labor laws, alimony, economic support of wives by husbands, sex-segregated toilets, social security benefits, and even marriage. *The Phyllis Schlafly Report,* a leading anti-ERA monthly, answered the question, "Who will profit from the ERA?" by proclaiming, "Women will lose, families will lose, society will lose."[92]

The right to life movement, also, has attempted to expand the issue at hand.[93] Its leaders have linked the right of women to control their own bodies to genocide, euthanasia, the end of organized religion and again, the demise of motherhood, the family, and society.

As is the case with pro movements, the formation and development of anti movements require more than simple recognition of the "problem." An organizational base or outside monies or resources to develop a base have also proven necessary to success. In the case of anti movements, money always has been particularly critical. Forces opposed to the Nineteenth Amendment were especially dependent on funds and organizational support from liquor interests. As early as 1881, the National Brewers' Association opposed woman suffrage because of its fear that giving the vote to women would lead to prohibition. On the basis of a self-imposed assessment of several cents per barrel, the Brewers' Association raised millions of dollars to support antisuffrage campaigns at the state and federal level. Besides the liquor interests, there is evidence that the meat-packing, cotton manufacturing, railroad, mining, and other big business interests made contributions (often secretly) to fuel the antisuffrage forces.[94]

considerable speculation, it seems clear that many right-wing groups, including the John Birch Society, Manion Forum Trust Fund, the Parker Chiropractic Research Foundation, the insurance industry, and Schlafly's own Eagle Trust Fund, have contributed at least some monies to these anti-ERA groups.[95] Similarly, right to life forces apparently have relied on funds from many right-wing groups as well as upon the Roman Catholic Church and conservative Protestant denominations in the South.[96]

While outside funding has played an important role in the foundation of many of the anti groups, each also has had an organizational base, although sometimes quite limited. The antisuffrage force base included many of the business groups and associations listed above as contributors as well as several urban political machines, and, in the South, the Democratic Party.[97] These associations provided a foundation for a communications network as well as many of the antisuffrage leaders and followers.[98] Although rather restricted, this organizational base was able to defeat many state suffrage referenda. In fact, on the federal level, it was able to nearly stop state ratification of the Nineteenth Amendment by spending large amounts of money to influence voters and legislators. Its task was made easier by the natural animosity of many politicians to the suffragists' cause.[99] Anti-ERA organizations have drawn members from the John Birch Society, the American party, Pro-America, and Women for Constitutional Government. Phyllis Schlafly's ties with the conservative wing of the Republican party and the readership of her newsletter have contributed to the base of the movement as well. The Morman and fundamentalist churches also have been sources of antiwomen's rights supporters.[100]

The right to life forces have, perhaps, the most extensive organizational base. In addition to many of the above right-wing groups, the Catholic, Mormon, fundamentalist Protestant, Seventh-Day Adventists, and Orthodox Jewish religions all are vehemently opposed to abortion. Because the success of the antiabortion forces probably hinges on their ability to gain a constitutional amendment banning abortion, mobilization of this large base will be critical.

As was true with the pro movements, a crisis or series of crises also appeared important to mobilization of anti forces. For all three examined here, a crisis had been triggered by approaching success, or in the case of abortion, the actual success, of the pro forces. Antisuffrage groups, for instance, did not mobilize effectively until after a few suffrage victories at the state level. Many of their most determined battles came in the last states needed for ratification of the Nineteenth Amendment.[101] Similarly, no real opposition surfaced to the ERA until after congressional passage. Indeed, twenty-two states had ratified the amendment before Schlafly formed Stop ERA.[102] And, Right to Life forces, caught off guard by the Supreme Court's 1973 decision, which struck down restrictive abortion laws,[103] lost no time in building a strong countermovement.

Thus, development of these anti movements followed a pattern very similar to that of pro movements. Each identified the change sought or achieved by women's rights supporters as a pure public bad. Each already had or quickly developed an organizational base and communications network (generally limited) among leaders, often with the help of outside resources. Last, all were sparked to action by a crisis in the form of the success (or approaching success) of forces advocating change. And, more importantly, the effectiveness of these anti forces often is central to the success of prowomen's rights movements, as we discuss in the following chapters.

ADDITIONAL FACTORS AFFECTING SUCCESS OF SOCIAL MOVEMENTS

Of paramount importance to a movement's success in securing public goods are its abilities to form and grow. As we have seen in at least one instance, the absence of an extensive organizational base limited the ability of the early woman's rights movement to achieve many of its more ambitious goals.

The simple development of a movement, however, does not ensure that it will achieve its aims. The ideology of the movement may lead to the adoption of goals or strategies that are doomed to failure. The radical feminists' call for the overthrow of the system (a pure public bad for nearly all citizens) or Elizabeth Cady Stanton's *Woman's Bible* exemplify these problems.* The triumph of any strategy, however, will probably depend most heavily on forces outside the control of the leaders and members of the movement. As we shall see in the chapters that follow, the social climate, the political institutions, the reaction of those in power, and the existence of counter-movements all influence the choice and success of any particular strategy and often the associated movement. Victory in achieving new rights or changes, however, is only one of the steps necessary for equality. Because most of the goals sought by women have been less than pure public goods, even after they are secured many barriers to their full exercise generally remain. In fact, three main obstacles to sexual equality generally persist even after a right is secured. First, the persistence of cultural attitudes, especially among some women, that the new right or freedom is not appropriate activity for women keeps many of them from exercising that right. For example, many of the women who accepted the argument that suffrage would destroy the home did not vote after they were enfranchised. Second, some women may not know how or may be otherwise unprepared to practice their new rights. Equal pay for equal work is useful only if women have the know-how, education, or desire to secure a job held or salary earned by men. Third, overt or covert legal or illegal sanctions may impair the ability of many if not all from using their new rights. To cite but one example, even after the passage of the Nineteenth Amendment, black women in the South were barred from voting by poll taxes, literacy tests, and Jim Crow laws. Thus, the struggle for equality involves not only the mounting

---

*The *Woman's Bible,* 2 vols. (New York: European Publishing Company, 1895 and 1898), consisted of articles, edited by Stanton, designed to refute the arguments that women, according to the Bible, were the inferior sex and should not be granted political, economic, and other social rights.

of a social movement and decisions about appropriate strategies to convince those in power to grant particular rights but also the struggle to change the views of the affected group, the rest of society, and society's institutions.

NOTES

1.   Roberta Ash, *Social Movements in America* (Chicago: Markham Publishing Company, 1972), p. 1.

2.   William Kornhauser, *The Politics of Mass Society* (New York: Free Press, 1959).

3.   Authors who have pointed out the importance of preexisting groups to the development of social movements include Maurice Pinard, "Mass Society and Political Movements: A New Formulation," *American Journal of Sociology* 73 (May 1968):682–690 and James Coleman, *Community Conflict* (New York: Free Press, 1957).

4.   The notion of public good first was introduced by Paul Samuelson in "The Pure Theory of Public Expenditure," *Review of Economics and Statistics* 36 (November 1954):387–390. This definition does not preclude the possibility that some individuals may not want to partake of the good or that other individuals or conditions may make use of the good difficult or costly. Indeed, the importance of these possibilities plays a central role in our discussion of public good and the attainment of women's rights.

5.   Mancur Olson, *The Logic of Collective Action* (New York: Schocken Books, 1971), chap. 1.

6.   Ibid., chap. 3. See also, Robert Cameron Mitchell, "National Environmental Lobbies and the Apparent Illogic of Collective Action," in Clifford S. Russell, ed., *Collective Decision Making: Applications from Public Choice Theory* (Baltimore: Johns Hopkins University Press, 1979), p. 100 for a list of various incentives.

7.   Olson, *Collective Action*, pp. 62–63.

8.   William H. Riker and Peter C. Ordeshook, *An Introduction to Positive Political Theory* (Englewood Cliffs, N.J.: Prentice Hall, 1973), p. 73.

9.   Olson, *Collective Action*, pp. 22–36.

10.   Ibid., pp. 36–43.

11.   The following section draws heavily on Anthony Oberschall, *Social Conflict and Social Movements* (Englewood Cliffs, N.J.: Prentice Hall, 1973).

12.   Ibid., pp. 146–178 and Richard E. Wagner, "Pressure Groups and Political Entrepreneurs: A Review Article," in *Papers on Non-Market Decision Making*, vol. I (1966), pp. 162–170.

13.   Riker and Ordeshook, *Positive Political Theory*, pp. 75–77.

14.   Karen O'Connor, *Women's Organizations' Use of the Courts* (Lexington, Mass.: Lexington Books, 1980), chap. 3.

15.   Oberschall, *Social Conflict*, p. 115.

16.   Ibid., p. 117.

17.   Anne N. Costain argues that preexisting organizations can also be useful because of their contacts with and knowledge about government officials when a social

movement turns its attention toward government activity. "Representing Women: The Transition From Social Movement to Interest Group," *The Western Political Quarterly* 34 (March 1981):100–113.

18. Jo Freeman, *The Politics of Women's Liberation* (New York: David McKay, 1975), p. 48. She terms these like-minded groups cooptable.

19. Clement E. Vose, *Caucasions Only* (Berkeley: University of California Press, 1959).

20. Freeman, *Women's Liberation,* p. 49.

21. Oberschall, *Social Conflict,* pp. 137–140.

22. Elizabeth Cady Stanton, Susan B. Anthony, and Matilda Joslyn Gage, eds., *History of Woman Suffrage,* vol. I, 1848–1861 (Rochester, New York: Charles Mann, 1881), p. 67 (hereafter, HWS I).

23. Betty Friedan, *The Feminine Mystique* (New York: Dell, 1963). For a thorough, insightful discussion of this problem, see also, Helen Mayer Hacker, "Women as a Minority Group," *Social Forces* 30 (October 1951):60.

24. William H. Chafe, "Looking Backward in Order to Look Forward," in Juanita M. Kreps, ed., *Women and the American Economy: A Look to the 1980s* (Englewood Cliffs, N.J.: Prentice Hall, 1976), pp. 8–15.

25. William H. Chafe, *Women and Equality: Changing Patterns in American Culture* (New York: Oxford University Press, 1977), pp. 15–22.

26. Ibid., p. 41.

27. Ibid., p. 94.

28. See, for example, Freeman, *Women's Liberation,* p. 17.

29. Ted Robert Gurr, *Why Men Rebel* (Princeton, N.J.: Princeton University Press, 1970), p. 13.

30. Freeman, *Women's Liberation,* pp. 28–32.

31. Gerda Lerner calls this "revolutions of rising expectations." For example, she notes that the rise of the first woman's movement "depended on a class of educated women with leisure." It was these educated women who often found themselves with little to do with their eduation who became leaders of the movement. *The Majority Finds Its Past: Placing Women in History* (Oxford: Oxford University Press, 1979), pp. 32–33.

32. Ibid., p. 33 and Aileen S. Kraditor, *The Ideas of the Woman Suffrage Movement 1890–1920* (New York: Columbia University Press, 1971), pp. 106–107.

33. Freeman, *Women's Liberation,* pp. 27–28 and Chafe, *Women and Equality,* p. 102.

34. Chafe, *Women and Equality,* p. 96.

35. Ibid., p. 83.

36. For a somewhat similar point, see Joyce Gelb and Marian Lief Palley, "Women and Interest Group Politics: A Comparative Analysis of Federal Decision-Making," *Journal of Politics* 41 (May 1979):362–392.

37. Riker and Ordeshook, *Positive Political Theory,* pp. 260–261.

38. See Denton E. Morrison, "Uphill and Downhill Battles and Contributions to Collective Action," in Clifford S. Russell, ed., *Collective Decision Making,* pp. 130–133 for a similar point about threatened goods versus new goods.

39. We should note that there is a growing debate about just how great the equality of women was during the colonial era. See Mary Beth Norton, "The Myth of

the Golden Age," in Carol Ruth Berkin and Mary Beth Norton, eds., *Women of America, A History* (Boston: Houghton Mifflin, 1979), pp. 37–47. But see Lerner, *Majority Finds Its Past*, for a discussion of women's accomplishments during that period.

40.   However, it was during this period, according to Carl N. Degler, that the concept of separate spheres for women developed in which women gladly embraced the notion that, at least in the home, they were important. *At Odds: Women and the Family in America from the Revolution to the Present* (New York: Oxford University Press, 1980).

41.   See Keith E. Melder, "The Beginning of the Women's Rights Movement in the United States, 1800–1842" (Ph.D. dissertation, Yale University, 1964).

42.   In fact, Buhle and Buhle credit women with being instrumental to the adoption of notions, including inherent rights, found in the Declaration of Independence. Mari Jo and Paul Buhle, eds., *The Concise History of Woman Suffrage* (Urbana: University of Illinois Press, 1978), pp. 77–78.

43.   See Judith Papachristou, *Women Together: A History in Documents of the Women's Movement in the United States* (New York: Alfred A. Knopf, 1976), pp. 41–62 for documents illustrating this point.

44.   In addition to the abolitionist movement, several social trends in the early nineteenth century contributed to this debate. Most notable were the Romantic movement and Protestant revivalism. Both raised questions about women's proper sphere and the changing economic conditions already mentioned above. See Melder, "The Beginnings of the Women's Rights Movement," pp. 432–438.

45.   Chafe, *Women and Equality*, p. 24.

46.   Melder, "The Beginnings of the Women's Rights Movement," chaps. 5 and 6. See also, Ellen Carol DuBois, *Feminism and Suffrage: The Emergence of an Independent Women's Movement in America, 1848–1869* (Ithaca, N.Y.: Cornell University Press, 1978), pp. 21–40.

47.   See generally, Gerda Lerner, *The Grimké Sisters from South Carolina: Pioneers for Woman's Rights and Abolition* (New York: Schocken books, 1967).

48.   An earlier organization of women, the New England Woman Suffrage Association, formed in November 1868, was in many ways not a women's organization but an effort by Republicans and abolitionist men to counter the efforts of Stanton and Anthony. DuBois, *Feminism and Suffrage*, pp. 164–172.

49.   "Shall We Go a Solitary Path?" *The Revolution*, November 24, 1870.

50.   DuBois, *Feminism and Suffrage*, p. 54.

51.   See ibid., chaps. 4 and 5, for a discussion of Anthony and Stanton's generally unsuccessful attempts to organize working women and to link the suffrage cause with that of the fledgling labor movement.

52.   DuBois, *Feminism and Suffrage*, p. 164, argues that the split was a good thing as it resulted in two separate groups seeking new recruits. While this may be true for the suffrage cause, it seems to have hurt the struggle for women's rights beyond the vote.

53.   Eleanor Flexner, *Century of Struggle* (New York: Atheneum, 1974), chap. 7.

54.   Anne Firor Scott, "The 'New Woman' in the New South," in Jean E. Friedman and William G. Shade, eds., *Our American Sisters: Women in American Life and Thought,* 2nd ed. (Boston: Allyn and Bacon, 1976), pp. 190–192.

55. Kraditor, *Ideas of Woman Suffrage*, pp. 43–53.

56. William H. Chafe, *The American Woman: Her Changing Social, Economic and Political Role, 1920–1970* (New York: Oxford University Press, 1972), p. 16.

57. Ibid., pp. 16–17.

58. Clement E. Vose, *Constitutional Change* (Lexington, Mass.: Lexington Books, 1972), pp. 161–178.

59. Papachristou, *Women Together*, p. 169.

60. Alan P. Grimes, *The Puritan Ethic and Women Suffrage* (New York: Oxford University Press, 1967), p. 101.

61. Robert E. Wesser, "Woman Suffrage, Prohibition, and the New York Experience in the Progressive Era," in Milton Plesur, ed., *An American Historian: Essays to Honor Selig Adler* (Buffalo: SUNY Buffalo Press, 1980), pp. 140–141.

62. Papachristou, *Women Together*, p. 172–173.

63. Eileen L. McDonagh and H. Douglas Price, "Who Opposed Women's Suffrage: An Analysis of State Referenda Voting, 1910–1918," paper delivered at the 1982 Annual Meeting of the American Political Science Association.

64. Lois Banner, *Women in Modern America: A Brief History* (New York: Harcourt Brace Jovanovich, 1974), pp. 120–127.

65. Quoted in Vose, *Constitutional Change*, p. 51.

66. Freeman, *Women's Liberation*, pp. 49–50.

67. Ibid., pp. 103–146.

68. Marlene Dixon, "The Rise of Women's Liberation," in Betty and Theodore Roszak, eds., *Masculine-Feminine* (New York: Harper and Row, 1969), p. 191.

69. Although see Judith Hole and Ellen Levine, *Rebirth of Feminism* (New York: Quadrangle Books, 1971), pp. 114–122 and Sara M. Evans, *Personal Politics: The Roots of Women's Liberation in the Civil Rights Movement and the New Left* (New York: Random House, 1980).

70. Claire Knoche Fulenwider, *Feminism in American Politics: A Study of Ideological Influence* (New York: Praeger Publishers, 1980), pp. 63–65.

71. Gayle Graham Yates, *What Women Want: The Ideas of the Movement* (Cambridge, Mass.: Harvard University Press, 1975), p. 7.

72. Yates, *What Women Want*, pp. 87–94. See also, Shulamith Firestone, *The Dialectic of Sex: The Case for Feminist Revolution* (New York: Bantam Books, 1970).

73. Zillah R. Eisenstein, ed., *Capitalist Patriarchy and the Case for Socialist Feminism* (New York: Monthly Review Press, 1978), pp. 22–35.

74. Additionally, women in the Student Nonviolent Coordinating Committee (SNCC) circulated a paper and staged a sit-in to protest the position of women in that organization. Stokley Carmichael, a SNCC leader, was reported to have remarked in response, "The only position for women in SNCC is prone." Quoted in Sara M. Evans, "Tomorrow's Yesterday: Feminist Consciousness and the Future of Women," in Berkin and Norton, eds., *Women of America*, p. 402.

75. Quoted in Hole and Levine, *Rebirth of Feminism*, p. 112.

76. Ibid., pp. 113–114.

77. Freeman, *Women's Liberation*, pp. 61–62.

78. Ibid., pp. 109–111.

79. Ibid., pp. 142–143.

80. Ibid., p. 143.

81. See Fulenwider, *Feminism in American Politics,* pp. 15–16 where she concludes the two branches have merged.

82. See Gabriel Almond and Sidney Verba, *The Civic Culture* (Princeton, N.J.: Princeton University Press, 1963), p. 247.

83. Freeman, *Women's Liberation,* pp. 52–53.

84. See ibid., pp. 55–56 for a list of officers' backgrounds.

85. Maren Lockwood Carden, *The New Feminist Movement* (New York: Russell Sage Foundation, 1974), p. 52.

86. Freeman, *Women's Liberation,* p. 150.

87. Ibid., pp. 84–85.

88. Ibid., p. 85.

89. *National NOW Times,* October 1982, p. 3.

90. O'Connor, *Women's Organizations',* chap. 5.

91. Speech of Eugene Anderson, "Unchaining the Demons of the Lower World or the Petition of Ninety-nine Percent Against Suffrage," Hotel Dempsey, Macon, Georgia, published under the auspices of the Georgia Association Opposed to Woman Suffrage (n.d.).

92. *The Phyllis Schlafly Report,* July 1975, p. 4.

93. Roger W. Cobb and Charles D. Elder, *Participation in American Politics: The Dynamics of Agenda Building* (Baltimore: The Johns Hopkins University Press, 1972). The authors point out that issue expansion is a commonly utilized tactic of interest groups trying to widen the attraction of their cause.

94. Flexner, *Century of Struggle,* pp. 299–301.

95. Janet K. Boles, *The Politics of the Equal Rights Amendment* (New York: Longman, 1979), pp. 67–72. See also, "Insurance Blamed in Sex Bias," *The New York Times,* June 2, 1982, p. 12.

96. *NARAL Newsletter* (August–September 1978), p. 3 and *NARAL Newsletter* (April 1976), p. 1. See generally, Andrew H. Merton, *Enemies of Choice: The Right to Life Movement and its Threat to Abortion* (Boston: Beacon Press, 1981).

97. Vose, *Constitutional Change,* chap. 3 and Flexner, *Century of Struggle,* chap. 22.

98. See Carrie Chapman Catt and Nettie Rogers Shuler, *Woman Suffrage and Politics* (Seattle: University of Washington Press, 1923), pp. 134–147 for a discussion of the role of the Brewers' Association in spreading the word about the evils of woman suffrage. For an excellent account of antisuffrage movement tactics, see Vose, *Constitutional Change,* pp. 46–66.

99. Catt and Shuler, *Woman Suffrage,* chaps. 25, 30, and 31.

100. Boles, *Politics of Equal Rights,* pp. 80–81. See also, Kent L. Tedin et al., "Social Background and Political Differences Between Pro- and Anti-ERA Activists," *American Politics Quarterly* 5 (July 1977):404.

101. Flexner, *Century of Struggle,* chap. 22.

102. Boles, *Politics of Equal Rights,* pp. 67–69.

103. *Roe v. Wade,* 410 U.S. 113 (1973).

PART I

Political Rights and Realities

Although the U.S. Supreme Court confirmed that women, indeed, were citizens of the United States as early as 1875, the Court also held that citizenship did not include a basic political right—suffrage.[1] In fact, an additional forty-five years of intensive pressure was necessary to bring about ratification of a constitutional amendment guaranteeing the right to vote to women. And, an even more striking example of the limited citizenship rights of women can be seen in their historic inability to serve as jurors. It was not until 1975 that the U.S. Supreme Court ruled that the Sixth Amendment's guarantee of a trial by jury included the right to have a jury drawn from a pool that included women in proportion to their actual presence in the community.[2]

Although few laws any longer bar or impair women's participation in the political arena, vestiges of those barriers persist. Cultural and social attitudes continue to impede women's full exercise of political rights. Existence of these extralegal barriers is particularly evident in the composition of state and national legislative bodies. For example, in the 98th Congress, less than 5 percent (23 of 535) of the lawmakers are women. And, the sexual composition of other legislative and judicial bodies generally is only slightly more representative.

The kinds of rights sought by each women's rights movement and how those rights were perceived by the public have been critical to the respective movements' abilities to secure greater political rights. Additionally, the relative capacity of both the pro and anti movements to gain supporters and ultimately to achieve their goals often have hinged on the public's perception

41

of the "good" sought. Voting, for example, is not a pure public good. Once members of a class secure the right to vote, members of the same class may opt not to exercise the franchise. However, during the suffrage movement, its opponents often characterized the franchise as a pure "public bad" that would negatively affect both men and women. Thus, a critical element in achieving the vote was the suffrage leaders' ability to counter these arguments by stressing the more limited nature of voting rights for women and by emphasizing its potential positive effect on society.

Other efforts for expanded political rights, however, have not given rise to strong anti movements. Often, pro groups have not appeared to pose any significant threat to the political or social order. In the mid-1800s, for example, when few gave the suffrage cause much chance of victory, even though it was characterized as a universal bad, no antisuffrage movement of any significant size developed. Likewise, in the 1970s, radical feminists received only token opposition to one of their goals—replacement of the present political system—largely because of the remote possibility of their success. Clearly, the debate over the nature and implications of the political rights sought, as well as the probable chance of victory by the various women's movements, often have proven to be critical parts of the battle.

The nature of this struggle for rights and the ensuing problems of implementing those victories are the topics of the next two chapters. Chapter 3 discusses the attempts of women to secure legal rights in as well as expanded access to the political arena. Chapter 4 then examines the impact of the attainment of these political rights. There, the questions how, why, and to what extent women have participated in the political process since the early 1900s are addressed. An attempt also is made to explain what barriers still remain to the attainment of a full and equal role for women in civic life.

NOTES

1. *Minor* v. *Happersett*, 88 U.S. (21 Wall.) 162 (1865).
2. *Taylor* v. *Louisiana*, 419 U.S. 522 (1975).

3 The Struggle for Political Rights

The Declaration of Sentiments issued at the Seneca Falls Convention submitted the following as proof of man's "establishment of an absolute tyranny" over women:

> He has never permitted her to exercise her inalienable right to the elective franchise. He has compelled her to submit to laws, in the formation of which she had no voice. He has withheld from her rights which are given to the most ignorant and degraded men—both natives and foreigners. Having deprived her of this first right of a citizen, the elective franchise, thereby leaving her without representation in the halls of legislation, he has oppressed her on all sides.[1]

Given these feelings, it is not surprising that a resolution calling for suffrage was passed at the convention. Votes for women, however, was a radical idea in 1848, and in fact, it was the only resolution not adopted unanimously. Given that convention attendees were more liberal than most, it becomes easier to understand why many long, hard years of organizing, petitioning, and educating the public and government officials were necessary before suffrage was finally attained by constitutional amendment in 1920. In part, this chapter is a story of that effort.

43

THE WOMAN'S RIGHTS MOVEMENT AND THE BALLOT

The women who attended the 1848 covention were primarily concerned with securing greater economic and social rights. In fact, at least initially, the right to vote was only a secondary concern. Lucretia Mott, in particular, feared that a demand for the franchise would make women look "ridiculous" and urged her sisters to "go slowly."[2] In spite of her caution, however, the ballot was demanded on the basis of the belief that women possessed certain natural, inalienable rights of citizenship. Paraphrasing the Declaration of Independence, women at the Seneca Falls convention proclaimed:

> We hold these truths to be self-evident: that all men *and women* are created equal; that they are endowed by their Creator with certain inalienable rights; that among these are life, liberty and the pursuit of happiness.[3] [emphasis added]

Thus, paralleling the Garrisonian branch of the abolitionist movement, Elizabeth Cady Stanton and others vigorously advocated woman suffrage based on their belief that women were first and foremost individuals and citizens equal to men and thus they deserved not only the same political but also the same economic and social rights.[4]

Involvement in the abolition effort led many woman's rights movement leaders to see the two issues as intimately linked. In fact, most believed that once society accepted the concept of individual rights as the rationale for enfranchising blacks, suffrage would logically be extended to women. While their logic might have been correct, their estimation of the public's reaction to woman suffrage was not. Woman's movement leaders failed to realize that their demands for female suffrage, which directly challenged societally determined role divisions between men and women, were far more threatening to the social order, at least in the North, than was suffrage for blacks. In addition, because the demand for female suffrage was coupled with calls for other more controversial changes in women's status, many came to link suffrage with these other reforms. In the pursuit of their radical (by 1850s standards) reforms, the woman's rights activists chose not to form an association to present their views exclusively. Rather, they continued to rely largely on abolitionist associations to spread their ideas, apparently perceiving little need to establish a national association to work for women's rights alone.[5]

Instead, during the pre-Civil War period, Northern and Midwestern organizational activity was limited to little more than yearly conventions held to address women's common problems and to discuss strategy to obtain the vote. Often, announcements of these meetings were carried in abolitionist newspapers as well as in women's magazines.[6] In addition to these conventions, petition campaigns, a strategy regularly employed by abolitionist-based

Female Anti-Slavery Societies, were used to demand suffrage in some states. Petition campaigns, however, while sometimes successful in bringing about legislative change involving property or marital rights, failed to produce any state constitutional suffrage amendments.

With the advent of the Civil War, even these minimal independent efforts were abandoned. Many women who had participated in woman's rights activities directed their energies into the war effort and to the campaign for an antislavery amendment. Fully expecting women's rights to be granted simultaneously with Negro rights, Anthony, and Stanton, for example, helped to form the Woman's National Loyal League to work for the enactment of an amendment to abolish slavery.[7] The belief of woman's rights advocates that ratification of such an amendment would pave the way for women is evident in the following resolution introduced by Angelina Grimké Weld at a League meeting in 1863:

> *Resolved,* There never can be a true peace in this Republic until the civil and political rights of all citizens of African descent and all women are practically established.
>
> I rejoice exceedingly that the resolution should combine us with the Negro. I feel that we have been with him; that the iron has entered into our souls. True, we have not felt that slave-holder's lash; true, we have not had our hands manacled, but our *hearts* have been crushed. Was there a single institution in this country that would throw open its doors to the acknowledgment of women's equality with man [until] twenty years ago?...
>
> But woman is full-grown today, whether man knows it or not, equal to her rights, and equal to the responsibilities of the hour. I want to be identified with the Negro; until he gets his rights, we never shall have ours.[8]

Hopes, however, for simultaneous rights soon were dashed. Republican politicians, fearing that support of woman suffrage would doom the chances for ratification of an amendment enfranchising Negroes and thus the party's opportunity to be "rewarded" with the votes of two million Southern Negro males, opted not to mix the two issues.[9]

Many abolitionist men also turned a deaf ear on the woman's cause. For example, in 1866, the American Anti-Slavery Society rejected appeals to unite the two causes. Therefore, women formed a new abolitionist organization along with men who supported their cause. The resulting organization was the American Equal Rights Association. Its stated purpose was universal suffrage for blacks and women.[10] The older Anti-Slavery Society's reaction to the new group was anything but supportive. In fact, its leaders made every effort to deny proponents of universal suffrage the traditional communication lines used by women in the prewar years—access to the abolitionist press.[11]

Even the American Equal Rights Association, however, soon abandoned woman suffrage when it supported the proposed Fourteenth Amendment to the U.S. Constitution. When a majority of its members agreed that "Now is the Negro's hour," Stanton, Anthony, and a few other women were furious. They were particularly incensed by the group's support of text contained in the Fourteenth Amendment that would introduce the word *male* into the U.S. Constitution for the first time.[12] Not only did the Stanton and Anthony forces argue that women should not be left out of any attempt to secure fuller rights for freed slaves, but they voiced their fears that this clause would necessitate an additional constitutional amendment before women could vote in federal elections. However, although they felt betrayed by the Association's support of the Fourteenth Amendment, these women were not yet ready to sever their ties with the organization they had helped to found.

The event that finally caused Stanton and Anthony to leave the American Equal Rights Association was its support of the proposed Fifteenth Amendment, which, when ratified, would give black males the right to vote. The then-controversial amendment read, "The right of citizens of the United States to vote shall not be denied or abridged by the United States or by any State on account of race, color, or previous condition of servitude." Feverish attempts to have the word "sex" included proved futile as women once again were told that the rights of black men must come first.

Interestingly, until passage of this amendment, woman's movement leaders believed that the question of voter qualifications was a matter for the individual states. With enactment of the Fifteenth Amendment, however, it became clear that an amendment to the U.S. Constitution would in all likelihood be necessary before women could vote in national elections. Thus, faced with the apparent need to alter their strategy, which had sought suffrage legislation on a state-by-state basis, and abandoned by the American Equal Rights Association, which failed to support a proposal to call for a woman suffrage amendment, Stanton and Anthony founded the National Woman Suffrage Association (NWSA) in 1869.[13] NWSA dedicated itself to the joint causes of securing greater rights for women in all spheres of life, including work, marriage, and education *and* a national constitutional amendment to enfranchise women.

Later that year, Lucy Stone, who had remained a member of the American Equal Rights Association, founded the more conservative American Woman Suffrage Association (AWSA), which continued to believe in the feasibility of a state-by-state route to woman suffrage. In AWSA's pursuit of that lone goal, it astutely tried to avoid association with controversial issues that could cloud the suffrage issue. Its voice, *The Woman's Journal,* which regularly echoed its founders' beliefs that other reforms would follow suffrage, was a successful and well-financed paper aimed at the rising number of middle-class women who, in the latter two decades of the nineteenth century, would provide the base for the new women's clubs and eventually the suffrage movement.

Unlike NWSA, whose leaders had few dealings with abolitionists, AWSA leaders continued to expect that abolitionists and Republicans would adopt their cause as soon as the issue of Negro rights was resolved. This hope and the strategies adopted to support it (the state-by-state route, for example, was proposed so as to leave the federal arena open for debate on Negro suffrage) were counter to everything Stanton and Anthony believed. So too was AWSA's organizational structure. Composed of official state delegations and strong local affiliates, AWSA required that new members be sponsored by at least two persons who already belonged to the association.

The far less formal structure of NWSA reflected Stanton and Anthony's more liberal ideology and strategies. Because they believed that a federal amendment was preferable to AWSA's state-by-state approach, initially little effort was made to establish a state or local associational structure. This often resulted in the loss of potential members when state woman's rights associations affiliated with AWSA because their participation appeared more appreciated and their efforts, seemingly, could have greater impact.[14]

Only gradually did Anthony and Stanton realize that unlike the abolitionists who faced few problems in convincing slaves of their oppressed status, they had to convince many women who were unaware of or completely satisfied with their status. Therefore, shortly after ratification of the Fifteenth Amendment, Stanton and Anthony began a concerted effort to organize other women. For example, reaching out beyond the abolitionist movement, they attempted to attract the support of women they had met during the Civil War in sanitary commissions—women who generally were middle class and who previously had not been active in politics or in the abolitionist movement. Stanton and Anthony also sought to gain sympathizers from those women who were members of the short-lived, postwar Working Woman's Association (WWA), an organization founded by Anthony in 1868 to allow her to obtain the requisite credentials to attend a National Labor Conference meeting to press for women's rights.[15] WWA members, as wage earners, and like commission women, had not been previously involved in any women's rights activity. Women from both new groups, however, were considerably more conservative about women's position in society than either Anthony or Stanton. Thus, efforts to attract these women and others eventually led to a considerable toning down of NWSA's radical demands for divorce reform and equal rights and to an increasingly narrow focus on the suffrage issue. However, before this toning down of NWSA's rhetoric, its image as an organization dedicated to radically altering society was widespread.

One of the vehicles by which this reputation was fostered was *The Revolution*, a biweekly paper in which Anthony and Stanton regularly propounded on a wide range of controversial subjects, including divorce reform and prostitution. Even the paper's name was the subject of much debate. Lucy Stone reportedly was aghast when she first heard it. And, because *The Revolution* was heavily financed by radical Democrat George Francis Train, much attention was given to the extremist policies he favored. Thus, Republic abolitionist members of AWSA, who believed suffrage should remain isolated from any other issues, were horrified by *The Revolution's* association with Train as well as its regular discussions of topics such as wife swapping.[16]

Aware of its image problems, NWSA made attempts to "conservatize" the organization and to narrow its goals. For example, in 1869, Francis Minor, a prominent attorney whose wife, Virginia, was the president of the Missouri Woman Suffrage Association (MWSA) and a close friend of Susan B. Anthony, put forth his belief that women, as citizens, were entitled to vote under the existing provisions of the Fourteenth Amendment.[17] In an address before a St. Louis meeting of MWSA with Anthony in attendance, Minor enunciated his legal theory in the "St. Louis Resolutions." Resolution Three stated:

> That, as the Constitution of the United States expressly declares that no state shall make or enforce any laws that shall abridge the privileges or immunities of citizens of the United States, those provisions of the several state constitutions that exclude women from franchise on account of sex, are violative alike of the spirit and letter of the Federal Constitution.[18]

Later, summarizing the thrust of the Resolutions for *The Revolution,* Minor wrote:

> These resolutions place the cause of equal rights far in advance of any position hereintofore taken. Now, for the first time, the views and purposes of our organization [NWSA] assume a fixed and definite end. We no longer beat the air—no longer assume the attitude of petitioners. We claim a right, based upon citizenship.[19]

Thus, Minor believed that should his theory be used as the basis for litigation challenging the disenfranchisement of women, demands for suffrage would be viewed much less frivolously.

Minor's Resolutions were widely publicized by NWSA leaders. Along with an explanatory letter from Minor, they were published in two consecutive issues of *The Revolution.* Soon thereafter, ten thousand extra copies of those editions were printed and distributed throughout the nation and to all members of Congress.[20] Additionally, speeches given by NWSA leaders often included references to Minor's legal theory, but at least initially, NWSA continued to channel most of its energies into the quest for a suffrage amendment.

In fact, the impetus for a concerted effort to test the logic of Minor's argument did not arise until January, 1871, when Victoria Woodhull made a presentation to Congress urging legislators to pass enabling legislation to give women the right to vote under the newly enacted Fourteenth Amendment.[21] Interestingly, her arguments were very similar to those earlier posited by Minor, although he had not called for enabling legislation, but the Resolutions were never credited as a source of her ideas.[22]

Woodhull, a notorious spiritualist, was the first woman to open a brokerage firm on Wall Street. Bankrolled by Cornelius C. Vanderbilt, the "Bewitching Broker" as she was called, began to dabble in politics in 1868. For example, she and her sister, Tennessee Clafin, published *Woodhull and Clafin's Weekly,* a paper that publicized their controversial views. Believing marriage a form of sexual bondage, Woodhull publicly advocated free love— a woman's right to love whom she pleased outside of the bonds of matrimony. In addition, Woodhull regularly used her newspaper to campaign for legalized prostitution, dress reform, and many other controversial causes.

As a consequence, Woodhull was regularly vilified in the press not only for her public pronouncements but also for her personal living arrangements. Although she was divorced from her first husband, Woodhull continued to live not only with him but also with another man. The "Terrible Siren," as she was nicknamed by the press, claimed to be married to her lover, but no record of their marriage was ever found, even though they did obtain a license to wed.[23]

Thus, when she chose to address Congress on the opening day of NWSA's convention, it was not surprising that Woodhull's actions attracted public attention. Many NWSA members, however, chose to ignore her infamous reputation and went to the Capitol to hear her before their meeting commenced. After listening to her proposal, NWSA leaders invited Woodhull to repeat her remarks at their "opening meeting later that day."[24]

The resulting publicity attendant upon Woodhull's appearance had mixed benefits for NWSA. On the negative side, its alliance with Woodhull caused some members of the press to ridicule the organization openly and to link NWSA and suffrage with declining moral standards. In fact, numerous articles and cartoons were printed depicting Woodhull and those in favor of votes for women as "free lovers." This muddying of the issue of suffrage further tarnished NWSA's image and hindered its drive for the vote. In fact, AWSA, trying hard to preserve its own public image, quickly passed the following resolution in an effort to disassociate itself from NWSA and free love:

Resolved ... That the claim of woman to participate in making the laws she is required to obey, and to equality of rights in all directions, has nothing to do with special social theories, and the recent attempts in this city and

elsewhere to associate the woman suffrage cause with the doctrines of free
love, and to hold it responsible for the crimes and follies of individuals, is an
outrage upon common sense and decency, and a slander upon the virtue and
intelligence of the women of America.[25]

More astute than NWSA leaders, AWSA leaders recognized that linkages
between suffrage and more radical issues, particularly those as controversial
as free love, would damn their cause.

On the positive side, the "Woodhull Convention" infused NWSA
members with a new sense of purpose and generated some favorable publicity
along with the bad. The *Washington Republic,* for example, described the
annual meeting as follows:

A good deal was said by the speakers concerning the proposed interpretation of the existing constitutional amendments. It was thus a convention
with a new idea. The reporters could not say that the old, stock, arguments
were used. There was an air of novelty about the proceedings, indicating
healthy life in the movement. The consequence was that the cause of
woman's enfranchisement made a new, sudden, and profound impression in
Washington.[26]

Francis Minor quickly moved to seize upon the enthusiasm that
Woodhull's remarks engendered and to counter any adverse publicity that
Woodhull brought to NWSA. In fact, he urged that test cases quickly be
brought to determine if the courts would obviate the need for additional
legislative action. Because a number of legal scholars and judges had publicly
agreed with Minor's arguments, and more importantly, because the Chief
Justice of the U.S. Supreme Court, Salmon Portland Chase, had offered his
sentiments that it would be wise for women to test the parameters of the
Constitution to determine if they were enfranchised by its provisions, women
greeted this "New Departure" in strategy with great excitement.[27]

It appears, however, that NWSA leaders did not expect a favorable
decision to be forthcoming from the courts. Rather, their goal appears to have
been to use litigation to obtain *a* decision from the Supreme Court. NWSA
leaders clearly anticipated a strong written dissent from the Chief Justice[28]
and believed that his opinion could be used as a means to educate and to
inform the public on the issue of woman suffrage. In essence, litigation was
attempted to convince the public that suffrage was not a public bad. Indeed,
the need for enlightened and favorable discussion of woman suffrage was
particularly acute. The Woodhull affair had tarnished both suffrage and
NWSA's image. A serious, nonemotional discussion of the issue, therefore,
was greatly needed.

Litigation was viewed as a conventional method of public debate that
would focus national attention on suffrage. Only one of the three major test
cases brought by NWSA members, however, was given a full hearing by the

U.S. Supreme Court. Fittingly, it involved Virginia Minor. In *Minor* v. *Happersett,* Virginia Minor, with her husband as coplaintiff (as a married woman she had no right to sue in her own name), sued a St. Louis registrar after he refused to allow her to register to vote. Francis Minor claimed that his wife's rights under the Fourteenth Amendment were violated because she was denied "the privileges and immunities of citizenship, chief among which is the elective franchise."[29] This argument, however, was rejected by the Missouri courts and the Minors appealed their case to the U.S. Supreme Court. In 1875, in upholding the Missouri court's determination, Chief Justice Morrison R. Waite, (Chase had died in 1873) maintained that suffrage was not a right of citizenship. Writing for a *unanimous* Court, Justice Waite noted:

> *If the law is wrong it ought to be changed, but the power for that is not with us.* The arguments addressed to us bearing upon such a view of the subject may perhaps be sufficient to induce those having the power to make the alteration, but they ought not to be permitted to influence our judgement in determining the present rights of the parties now litigating before us.[30] [emphasis added]

After the *Minor* decision, NWSA accepted Waite's advice and again turned to more traditional modes of political activity. Given Minor's decisive defeat, it was clear that a victory would not be forthcoming from the U.S. Supreme Court any time in the near future. Thus, it was believed that further litigation would only destroy any credibility NWSA had established. NWSA, therefore, refocused its efforts on obtaining a constitutional amendment.

Indeed, the organization had never really abandoned this tactic. From 1868 to 1875, its leaders made many attempts to have a female suffrage amendment added to the Constitution. In the 1870s, for example, NWSA members testified before Congress in support of a bill that would have given women in the District of Columbia the right to vote. Their efforts, however, were of no avail even on that limited level.

NWSA also continued to use other avenues to advocate its goals. Many of its efforts, by necessity, were aimed at education. NWSA leaders realized that members of the public as well as elected officials needed to be better informed on the question of suffrage and their fears of societal change assuaged before suffrage could be attained.

This strategy of education and agitation can be traced to several woman's rights leaders' exposure to Garrisonian abolitionism. Garrison had previously argued that to bring about social and legal change one must first change ideas. So, in addition to testifying before congressional committees on the necessity of a woman suffrage amendment, NWSA leaders staged a number of what today would be called "media events." For example, at the July 4,

1876 Centennial celebration in Philadelphia, Anthony led a delegation of women onto the platform where the Emperor of Brazil and assorted dignitaries were assembled. Anthony handed a woman's rights declaration to the chair of the event, U.S. Senator Thomas W. Ferry, and then turned and marched out of the hall with other women who handed out extra copies of the document to the startled audience. Once outside, the women mounted another platform and read the Woman's Declaration to the large crowd assembled in Independence Square. In that declaration they demanded the inclusion of women on juries and the end of taxation without representation, among other things.[31]

In this as well as its other efforts, NWSA never was joined by members of AWSA. Indeed, AWSA continued to take every precaution to distance itself from the more radical group and even chose a different strategy to get the vote. While NWSA pursued its quest for a national suffrage amendment, AWSA persisted in its attempts to change state constitutions. Neither organization, however, made many inroads after 1875. Suffrage had been sufficiently complicated by NWSA's advocacy of other goals to produce considerable antisuffrage reaction, even though no strong opposition group arose.

Arguments against suffrage, however, were numerous. Many citizens believed that the Bible itself counseled the exclusion of women from politics. In fact, antisuffrage forces relied heavily on Genesis and St. Paul and maintained that God created separate spheres for man and woman—man's place was out in the world, which included politics, while woman's proper place was in the home, away from politics.[32] Suffrage opponents further argued that the "natural roles" for women were those of wife and mother. Thus, any change in this natural order would destroy society. Others claimed there was no need for suffrage because a woman's husband would fully protect her rights. They argued that if women got the vote, the only result would be to set wife against husband, which would result in destruction of the family. In fact, in the first U.S. Senate debate on the question of woman suffrage, a speech made by Senator George H. Williams summarized many of these arguments:

It has been said that "the hand that rocked the cradle ruled the world," and there is truth as well as beauty in that expression. Women in this country by their elevated social position, can exercise more influence upon public affairs than they could coerce by the use of the ballot. When God married our first parents in the garden according to that ordinance they were made bone of one bone and flesh of one flesh; and the whole theory of government and society proceeds upon the assumption that their interests are one, that their relationships are so intimate and tender that whatever is for the benefit of one is for the benefit of the other.... The woman who undertakes to put her sex in an adversary position to man, who undertakes by the use of some independent political power to contend and fight against man, displays a spirit which would, if able, convert all the now harmonious elements of society into a state of war, and make every home a hell on earth.[33]

These or similar sentiments probably were shared by most men and women in the 1860s.[34] Public opinion, including that of most women, generally at best was negative, and more often than not hostile, toward expanded political rights for women. These negative attitudes were exacerbated by some movement members' advocacy of controversial pure public goods. In fact, ideas such as divorce reform and free love were viewed by most as public bads. Additionally, the reluctance of the Republican party to support woman suffrage foreclosed the possibility of a quick legislativie victory. Last, NWSA's weak organizational structure, which was limited to a loose national leadership group with few actual members, made impossible any mass uprising to demand the vote. Thus, when these factors were added to the division within the movement that occurred in 1869 and the movement's limited source of potential supporters, the minimal headway made toward suffrage is more easily explained. It was not until reconciliation occurred between NWSA and AWSA and a new source of supporters was available in the late 1800s that significant progress was made.

THE SUFFRAGE MOVEMENT AND THE BATTLE FOR THE VOTE CONTINUED

Clearly, efforts to secure the vote had borne little fruit by 1890. Although Wyoming enacted a woman suffrage law in 1869 while still a territory and was admitted to the Union as the first suffrage state in 1890, numerous suffrage campaigns in other states met with failure for many of the same reasons that plagued the NWSA's efforts at the national level: inadequate organization, too few members, and lack of popular support. In addition, state suffrage campaigns often faced stiff opposition from liquor interests who feared that temperance-minded suffrage workers would vote for prohibition. Thus, although AWSA continued its attempts to remain above reproach, its leaders simply could not overcome the myriad extant problems. Much more than respectability was necessary before women would receive the vote. While the necessary changes ultimately occurred, the result was a radically altered women's rights movement. In fact, the transformation was so great that by 1890 one can begin to talk of a new movement, which we have labeled the suffrage movement. In that year, largely because of the efforts of Alice Stone Blackwell, Lucy Stone's only daughter, the two older, major organizations of the first woman's rights movement, NWSA and AWSA, joined forces to become the National American Woman Suffrage Association (NAWSA).

In ideology, NAWSA more closely resembled the more conservative AWSA, whose philosophy had slowly become dominant over the years, which made merger possible. As a result, while some of the broader goals of the woman's rights movement espoused by NWSA had been achieved (greater educational opportunities for women, for example—see Chapter 5), many others, including significant divorce reform, trade unionism, and the legalization of prostitution, were dropped by NAWSA in favor of a single cause—woman suffrage.

The chances for success of a new movement spearheaded by NAWSA were aided by a variety of factors. First, thousands of previously unorganized, more conservative women were mobilized. This process began in the 1870s with the founding and subsequent phenomenal growth of the Women's Christian Temperance Union (WCTU).[35] Although WCTU's prime goal was abolition of the liquor trade, under the able leadership of Frances Willard, the former Dean of the Women's College of Northwestern University, it became a leading advocate of woman suffrage. Willard convinced WCTU members that woman suffrage was a necessary antecedent to attaining prohibition. Thus, she was able to bring many of WCTU's over 200,000 members, most of whom were traditional, religious women, into the suffrage cause. The WCTU's impact was particularly important in the South, where its goals were very compatible with religious fundamentalism. The influx of WCTU members into the suffrage movement further exacerbated the rightward drift of NAWSA as WCTU leaders began to become powerful forces in the new suffrage movement.

The phenomenal growth of the club movement in the 1880s and 1890s was a second factor assisting the development of the suffrage movement.[36] In 1888, for example, Susan B. Anthony, recognizing the possible political usefulness of these clubs for the suffrage cause, helped create an alliance of these groups, which was called the National Council for Women.[37] An even larger and more powerful umbrella association, the General Federation of Women's Clubs (GFWC), claimed a membership of over two million by 1910.[38] In general, two types of clubs were affiliated with GFWC. The first type consisted of the self-improvement groups, which often had a literary theme. These groups tended to attract educated, married, middle-class women. Confined to the home for most of the day, these women sought female companionship and intellectual stimulation to fill their leisure time. The second, and more important type, however, consisted of the civic and department clubs that sprang from the progressive movement. Most of the civic clubs were organized to improve municipal services and to bring about government reform, while the department clubs promoted specific issues such as abolition of child labor or improved conditions for working women.[39] It was within these progressive-type organizations, in fact, that many women came to recognize their inferior political status and their need for the ballot.

Without it, they saw little chance to enact government reform or legislation to improve the status of working women or children. Thus, like WCTU members, many club women and those allied with the progressive movement, became active in the suffrage cause, even though the GFWC did not formally endorse woman suffrage until 1914.

Like temperance workers, these new supporters of woman suffrage were fairly conservative in their view of women's proper sphere. While as a result of their within-group discussion, many had come to support woman suffrage, most were opposed to any more radical changes in woman's role. They believed that a woman's proper place was in the home. Indeed, they chose to do club work rather than seek paid employment outside of the home because club activities did not divert substantial amounts of time away from their more important domestic duties. They saw progressivism and efforts to secure unadulterated foods, child labor laws, and better government as merely extensions of their traditional role. Even those who joined the National Consumers' League (NCL), a progressive association formed to improve working conditions, were in basic agreement with the idea that a woman's "sphere" should be restricted to home. Although NCL and the National Women's Trade Union League,[40] fought for improved factory conditions, they did so to make certain that poor women would be able to perform their roles as mother and housewife more satisfactorily. Thus, the views of these new suffrage proponents were very different from those postulated earlier by the leaders of the first woman's rights movement. Statements of women such as Elizabeth Cady Stanton, who had written in 1848, "There is no such thing as a sphere for a sex. Every man has a different sphere, and one in which he may shine, and it is the same with every woman; and the same woman may have a different sphere at different times,[41] clearly were not part of the underlying ideology of the second women's rights movement. In fact, NAWSA's narrow issue focus and rationale for seeking the ballot reflected the desires and viewpoints of the new supporters of woman suffrage—WCTU members, club women, and Southerners.

That these women were considerably more conservative than those in the first movement is undeniable, but their conservatism was in many ways merely a reflection of the ideological changes that most members of their social strata had undergone since the Civil War. The postbellum era had been the occasion of several trends and changes that were to alter the native-born, white, middle-class view of democracy and politics. In the South, newly freed slaves and Northern carpetbaggers helped to produce the corruption and turmoil of the Reconstruction. In the North, waves of new immigrants crowded into urban areas where their votes often formed the backbone of powerful political machines. The West also had its fair share of political machines. Thus, in view of this seemingly nationwide corruption, many came to believe that certain segments of society should be kept out of politics, or at least, that only the "better" elements of society should be in positions of political control. The notion that all mankind was endowed with inalienable, natural political rights quickly gave way to the idea of "political capacity," or "educated suffrage," phrases used to describe the philosophy that only those who had the ability to participate should have the right to do so.

In fact, antisuffrage forces began to voice their opinion that adding women to the list of voters only would increase the number of "poor, ignorant and immoral" elements, thus outnumbering the "patrician, intelligent and impeccably proper" voters.[42] According to one commentator writing during this period:

> It is the influx of foreign ignorance *en masse* that threatens our country hourly.... There are millions of men in the world for whom despotism is a necessity, and it is this class who immigrate to us everyday, who are undermining our institutions and shaking the very pillars whereon the house standeth, like their vengeful prototype. If Woman Suffrage is to be allowed, we double not only the numerical force of this threatening majority, but its moral—or immoral—influence.[43]

Aileen Kraditor argues that women in the suffrage movement did not necessarily disagree with the above premise that "undesirables" must be kept in check but only with respect to how this might be done.[44] Suffragists proclaimed that they had the necessary "capacity" to exercise the franchise and defend their ability on two grounds. First, they reasoned that *as women* they had special contributions to make to the more efficient and honest running of government. Second, they argued that their "capacity" rested in their membership in that segment of society best suited to participate—the native-born, white, middle class.

One version of their first line of reasoning was that women were inherently less corruptible and less influenced by partisan loyalties. Thus they argued that they would become an important bloc of voters in passing progressive legislation and in defeating political machines. Suffragists even asserted that the moral nature of women would mean a reduced likelihood that the nation would go to war if women were allowed to vote.[45]

A closely related position was that women had a *duty* to bring their expertise into the legislative process. Thus, their status as housewives and mothers became prime reasons for giving women the ballot. For example, Jane Addams, the founder of Hull House, noted:

> Women who live in the country sweep their own dooryards and may either feed the refuse of the table to a flock of chickens or allow it innocently to decay in the open air and sunshine. In a crowded city quarter, however, if the street is not cleaned by the city authorities no amount of private sweeping will keep the tenement free from grime; if the garbage is not

properly collected and destroyed a tenement house mother may see her children sicken and die of diseases from which she alone is powerless to shield them, although her tenderness and devotion are unbounded. She cannot even secure untainted meat for her household, she cannot provide fresh fruit unless the meat has been inspected by city officials, and the decayed fruit, which is so often placed upon sale in the tenement districts, has been destroyed in the interest of public health. In short, if woman would keep on with her old business of caring for her house and rearing her children she will have to have some conscience in regard to public affairs lying quite outside of her immediate household. The individual conscience and devotion are no longer effective....

...If conscientious women were convinced that it was a civic duty to be informed in regard to these grave industrial affairs, and then to express the conclusion which they had reached by depositing a piece of paper in a ballot-box, one cannot imagine that they would shirk simply because the action ran counter to old traditions.[46]

While motherhood was an important argument for suffrage, the belief of many of its proponents that middle-class, native-born women would be better voters by virtue of their social status often was carried to the extreme. Some maintained, for example, that the votes of native-born, white women could be used to outweigh those of Negroes in the South or immigrants in the North. Others called for the imposition of literacy or educational qualifications to reduce the number of immigrant and Negro voters. In 1893, for example, the following resolution was passed by NAWSA:

Resolved, that without expressing any opinion on the proper qualifications for voting, we call attention to the significant facts that in every State there are more women who can read and write than all negro voters; more white women who can read and write than all negro voters; more American women who can read and write than all foreign voters; so that the enfranchisement of such women would settle the vexed question of rule by illiteracy, whether of homegrown or foreign-born production.[47]

This resolution and others similar to it clearly were designed to add to the base of the suffrage movement by appealing to those who wanted to keep the "foreign born" and Negroes out of politics, or at least dilute their political strength. They were not, however, necessarily the views of all NAWSA leaders but clearly were politically expedient. Even as late as 1919, in denying the membership application of a black women's organization, the New England Federation of Women's Clubs, NAWSA justified its refusal by noting its leaders' beliefs that if NAWSA welcomed black women, Southern Democrats' votes in Congress would be jeopardized.[48]

There is, however, ample evidence that more than simple political expediency often also was present. For example, in 1894 NAWSA president, Carrie Chapman Catt, proclaimed:

This Government is menaced with great danger.... That danger lies in the votes possessed by the males in the slums of the cities, and the ignorant foreign vote which was sought to be brought up by each party, to make political success.... There is but one way to avert the danger—cut off the vote of the slums and give to woman, who is bound to suffer all, and more than man can, of the evils his legislation has brought upon the nation, the power of protecting herself that man has secured for himself—the ballot.[49]

These ideological differences, particularly on the race issue, were not the only distinguishing factor between the first and second movements' struggle for the vote. The strategies of NAWSA also differed radically from those of NWSA. This difference, however, was due at least in part to changing beliefs of the American populace. According to Eleanor Flexner, by 1890, "Woman suffrage was not yet generally accepted, but it was no longer considered the province of eccentrics and crackpots."[50] Additionally, with each succeeding year, the number of converts to the cause—women, men, and politicians— grew. Thus, the political and social climate that suffrage leaders faced was considerably different from that faced by women in 1848 or 1869. And, as Kraditor has noted, this difference sharply affected the strategies adopted by each:

The pioneers of the suffrage movement, living in a time when victory for their cause seemed eons away, did not have to concern themselves too much with tactics. They could afford to state their ideals in ringing declarations on democracy that would admit of no qualifications or exceptions. In fact, they had to do so, for only ideals that could inspire a martyr's dedication could sustain these women through the physical violence and almost unbearable ridicule to which they were subjected. Later, when victories could be won here and there at the cost of small concessions to political expediency, the hard facts of political life and the equivocal position in American society of these middle-class women exerted a pull away from the high ideals and ringing declarations. To win support from needed allies they compromised with those principles perhaps more than the requirements of the alliances dictated. More often than not they voiced the ideals and advocated the compromises at the same time.[51]

The compromises noted by Kraditor and the movement's racist and antiimmigrant sentiments, were not the only strategic differences in the two movements. For example, NAWSA initially attempted to secure the vote on a state-by-state strategy and did not work for a national constitutional amendment. This tactic was adopted, at least in part, so as not to offend Southern women and/or politicians who were wedded to the notion of states' rights. In fact, NAWSA's decision to go the "state route" can be traced to 1893, when its members voted to hold its convention in Washington, D.C.

only every other year. NAWSA president, Susan B. Anthony, recognized that this change in meeting site would reduce the women's chances of pressing Congress for a constitutional amendment. And, although she strongly advocated the need to continue congressional lobbying, the motion was carried. The result of this change in focus was exactly what Anthony had expected. The constitutional amendment became a dead issue in Congress and was not resurrected until 1913.

NAWSA's resultant organizational structure was consistent with its pursuit of the state strategy. Like AWSA, it was composed of state organizations with a loose national leadership, at least until 1915. In fact, to gain greater Southern support, in 1903 it even adopted its own "states' rights" plank allowing each state to set its own membership standards.

These policies virtually guaranteed state organizational autonomy but appeared to do little to facilitate state constitutional changes. Although there were some early suffrage victories in Colorado (1893) and Idaho (1896) and when Wyoming (1890) and Utah (1896) entered the Union as suffrage states, no other states enfranchised women until 1910. Thus, the tremendous effort expended on suffrage campaigns (Flexner cites 480 efforts in 33 states, 17 actual referendum votes, but only two victories from 1870 to 1910) went largely unrewarded.[52] While a few more states added woman's suffrage provisions to their constitutions between 1910 and 1913, this was largely due to successes of the progressive and not the suffrage movement.[53] Thus, it became increasingly clear to NAWSA leaders that they would never win woman suffrage provisions in every state constitution. Even though contrary to critics' predictions, no terrible consequences occurred in the states that allowed women to vote, states along the entire eastern seaboard seemed particularly intractable.

Reasons for suffragists' failure to win victories along the East Coast were numerous. First, NAWSA leadership often was ineffective, providing little direction for their organization or for other supporters of suffrage. The association itself did not even have a real national headquarters. The NAWSA's president's hometown became the temporary base of operations, while the other officers also performed their duties at home.[54] Additionally, a series of weak NAWSA presidents was particularly problematic during such a critical period. State associations, without national direction, floundered. States where suffrage campaigns were launched were chosen in a haphazard fashion that often led to needless expenditures of time and energy in lost causes.

A second problem faced by NAWSA was the increasing sophistication of its well-organized and well-financed opposition. Suffrage victories in Washington and California in 1910 and 1911 and Arizona, Kansas, and Oregon in 1912 convinced opponents that the issue was alive and well and had to be fought. Liquor interests and political machines, sometimes financed by big business, began impressive antisuffrage campaigns that often were combined with voting fraud when necessary. In fact, opposition to suffrage was so widespread in the South that chances for success there seemed particularly unlikely. In 1915, this organized opposition contributed to the defeat of a suffrage referendum in four eastern states in a period of but a few weeks. These defeats and recognition of the growing organization of antisuffrage forces finally led NAWSA leaders to recognize the need for a new strategy. While the election of Carrie Chapman Catt as NAWSA president in late 1915 facilitated change, even before she reorganized NAWSA a new strategy was being tried.

In late 1912, the NAWSA Board appointed Alice Paul, who had worked with English suffragists, to its congressional committee. Paul took over as chair in 1913 and quickly infused new life into a committee that, prior to that time, had done no work for a national suffrage amendment. She immediately began to build up and to tap existing support for a constitutional amendment. A woman of exceptional zeal, within a few months, she was able to organize over 5,000 women to parade through the streets of Washington for suffrage the day before Woodrow Wilson's inauguration. Marchers dressed in white, some even on horseback, slowly made their way down Pennsylvania Avenue where they encountered antagonism from some spectators. Although NAWSA had obtained a parade permit, police offered the marchers no assistance. Thus, many sectors of the public were outraged about the absence of *protection* for the females. This sense of outrage plus the very size of the parade that was staged when all eyes were on the U.S. capital, resulted in a spectacular media event that brought incalculable press attention to the suffrage movement. Capitalizing on this free, favorable publicity, the committee launched a national women's suffrage petition drive and began to send regular delegations to see President Wilson to press for a national solution.

Paul, sensing momentum and believing in a national strategy, formed a new organization in April 1913 to work exclusively for a national amendment. Thus, while she retained her chair of the NAWSA Congressional Committee, a break with the larger organization was inevitable given Paul's flamboyance and the static nature of NAWSA in 1913. At the NAWSA convention held that year, Paul's insistence that a federal amendment be the sole target of suffrage forces was at odds with the beliefs of most NAWSA leaders, who continued to cling to the state-by-state approach, and in fact, were gearing up for the 1914 New York referendum.[55] Thus, not surprisingly, Paul was removed as chair of the congressional committee.

After her fall from grace with NAWSA, Paul focused her full energies on her new group, the Congressional Union. Following the lead of British suffragettes, the Congressional Union began to hold the "party in power" responsible for failure to pass a suffrage bill, a tactic also strongly opposed by

NAWSA. In 1914, Union members actively campaigned against candidates of the Democratic party for Congress. All the while, the Union, later called the National Woman's Party, pressed Congress for a federal amendment. Their effort resulted, at least, in a renewed interest in a suffrage amendment, a proposal that had been nearly dormant for over twenty years.

In turn, many of NAWSA's own members, excited by the Congressional Union's enthusiasm and focus, pressed its leaders to work more actively for a constitutional amendment.[56] Carrie Chapman Catt needed little convincing. After state referenda defeats in 1916, she devised what was termed a "Winning Plan"; its object was to direct all NAWSA's resources and cooperating organizations toward the goal of achieving a woman suffrage amendment to the federal constitution by 1922. A key component of the plan was national coordination whereby all state association activity was to be geared toward this *single* goal. Reversing NAWSA's policy of state autonomy, Catt declared:

> This Convention must not adjourn, should it sit until Christmas, until it creates a logical and sensible policy toward the Federal Amendment.... If it be decided that we *do* want enfranchisement by the Federal route, then at least thirty-six states must sign a compact to go after it with a will....
>
> National Boards must be selected hereafter for one chief qualification—the ability to lead the national fight. There should be a mobilization of at least thirty-six state armies, and these armies should move under the direction of the national officers. They should be disciplined and obedient to the national officers in all matters concerning the national campaign. This great army with its thirty-six, and let us hope, forty-eight divisions, should move on Congress with precision, and a will.... More, those who enter on this task, should go prepared to give their lives and fortunes for success, and any pusillanimous coward among us who dares to call retreat, should be courtmartialled.
>
> Any other policy than this is weak, inefficient, illogical, silly, inane, and ridiculous! Any other policy would fail of success.[57]

Catt's Winning Plan was quite detailed. Associations in suffrage states were to pressure their legislators to request that Congress pass a constitutional amendment. Additionally, national officers handpicked states for new campaigns where passage of a state amendment was feasible. Other state associations were to direct their efforts toward presidential suffrage or voting rights for women in party primaries in states that allowed the legislature to make these changes. Catt believed it was critical "to keep so much 'suffrage noise' going all over the country that neither the enemy nor friends will discover where the real battle is."[58] To keep the battle national in scope, Catt targeted Southern and Northern states for intense activity to break the spirit of opponents. And, to speed up the process even more, Catt planned to have support for the suffrage amendment included in both party platforms by 1920 and ratified by the states by 1922.[59]

While World War I, like the Civil War before it, diverted much of the suffrage leaders' energies, unlike Stanton and Anthony earlier, Catt wisely insisted that suffrage work continue to come first and that NAWSA continue to follow her plan. Slowly it began to produce results. The antisuffrage "Solid South" was cracked in March 1917 when women in Arkansas won the right to vote in state primary elections. In addition, the North Dakota, Rhode Island, Nebraska, and Michigan state legislatures enacted presidential suffrage laws. And in the same year, New York voters approved the addition of a suffrage amendment to their state constitution.[60]

While these events resulted in the enfranchisement of more and more women, strong suffrage opposition in the U.S. Senate prevented proponents from securing the necessary two-thirds majority required for a constitutional amendment. Southern senators held steadfastly against the amendment and were joined by others from New England and some eastern states. Opposition was justified on the rationale of "states' rights,"[61] but many women, particularly those in Southern suffrage associations, rejected the truth of this claim. Southern senators, for example, supported a prohibition amendment and were not upset by the national government's intrusion into this area that could have been left to the individual states. In fact, Southern proponents believed that the true motive of Senate opponents was a combination of resistance to any change in woman's role and fear of what female suffrage might do to the lucrative cotton industry in the South and Northeast. In those sections of the country, manufacturers relied heavily on cheap, female labor, a resource that Senate suffrage opponents believed could be threatened should the amendment be passed and women voters use their ballot strength to secure enactment of equal pay and/or factory inspection laws.

Thus, NAWSA leaders, recognizing that changes had to be made in the composition of the U.S. Senate before passage of the suffrage amendment could become a reality, launched a campaign to defeat their opponents who stood for reelection in 1918. The political clout of the suffragists produced the defeat of two powerful opponents of the amendment, Senators Weeks of Massachusetts and Saulsbury of Delaware. When this show of force was coupled with the addition of several more states into the suffrage column—South Dakota, Michigan, Oklahoma, Iowa, Minnesota, Missouri, Ohio, Wisconsin, and Maine—quick passage of the Nineteenth Amendment in the next legislative session called by President Wilson was virtually assured.[62] Meeting in a special session in the spring of 1919, first the House of Representatives (May 20th) and then the Senate (June 4th) passed the suffrage amendment. Ratification by the necessary thirty-six states was completed in 1920, and the first national election with full woman suffrage occurred in November of that year.

National Woman's Party members along with those in NAWSA celebrated the ratification of the Nineteenth, "Susan B. Anthony," Amendment. The Anthony Amendment, however, did not appease the desire of the Woman's Party for full equality. Its leaders, in fact, quickly turned their energies toward the passage of an amendment to ban all discrimination based on sex. Their view of women's role, however, differed from that held by most women. Even a majority of suffragists wanted no further changes made in women's status. Their one agreed-upon goal had been suffrage. Once it was secured, the base of the movement quickly began to disintegrate.

Without another common issue or set of issues to unite them, the many and varied women's groups that had made possible the passage of the Nineteenth Amendment began to go their separate ways. Some suffrage leaders tried to counter this phenomenon by starting new organizations. Some members of NAWSA established the National League of Women Voters (NLWV) in 1919 to work to educate female voters concerning the election and legislative processes. Others, like Catt, became involved in the growing peace movement that later was to become quite controversial.[63] These efforts aside, many felt powerless to stop fractionalization of the movement. Even while state ratification of the Anthony Amendment was pending, Anna Howard Shaw, a past NAWSA president, lamented, "I am sorry for you young women who have to carry on the work in the next ten years, for suffrage was a symbol, and now you have lost your symbol. There is nothing for women to rally round."[64]

Some suffrage leaders, particularly those active in the newly formed NLWV believed that there was a chance to save the movement. They would begin by identifying issues of concern to women. They sensed that most participants in the suffrage movement were issue oriented and that their continued involvement in the political process could be had if the right kind of an association could be formed. Therefore, NLWV moved to create an umbrella-type organization composed of a variety of women's groups previously active in the suffrage cause. That association, called the Women's Joint Congressional Committee (WJCC), was established in late 1920 to identify and to lobby for the enactment of national legislation of concern to women.[65] With fourteen sponsoring organizations and a total membership of 10 million, the WJCC quickly moved to become a clearinghouse of sorts for women's issues and to avoid duplication of effort among its constituent groups.[66]

The WJCC, itself, did not endorse particular pieces of legislation or even take a stand on issues. Instead, its bylaws set up a process whereby member organizations forwarded their positions on issues to the WJCC. When at least five member groups endorsed a particular piece of legislation, a subcommittee of all member associations that advocated the legislation was set up by the WJCC to lobby for the measure. This subcommittee then elected its own officers and worked independently of the larger organization in its efforts in the legislative arena.

CITIZENSHIP RIGHTS AFTER SUFFRAGE

One of the first causes the WJCC took on was congressional passage of a bill creating independent citizenship for married women. In the United States, prior to the 1920s, a woman's citizenship was determined solely on the basis of her husband's—if a female married someone other than a U.S. citizen, she automatically lost her claim to American citizenship. World War I drove home many of the unfortunate ramifications of this law when American women married aliens in increasing numbers. Loss of citizenship had devastating effects on many women. For example, some states prohibited noncitizens from practicing certain occupations; others forbade aliens from buying property or even inheriting from relatives. The socially prominent Gladys Vanderbilt, for example, had all of her property seized pursuant to the Alien-Property Act when she married an Austrian.[67]

After ratification of the Nineteenth Amendment, NLWV and other women's groups, trying to capitalize on their perceived new political clout, lobbied Congress for a change in these unfair naturalization laws. In 1920 they even convinced both major parties to include such demands in their respective platforms.[68] And a WJCC committee was set up to lobby for passage of such a bill. The first result of the efforts was the Married Women's Independent Citizenship (Cable) Act, which was passed by the U.S. Congress in 1922. It was, however, only a partial victory. Under the new law women (unlike men) who married aliens were to be treated as naturalized citizens only—not as native-born Americans.

The WJCC, at least initially, however, was more successful in other lobbying efforts. As later discussed, it lobbied for a variety of bills, and more importantly, the Sheppard-Towner Maternity Act to fund prenatal clinics to lower the high childbirth mortality rates in the United States. Much of its ability, however, was tempered once women's real political clout was recognized by legislators. When women proved not to be a powerful bloc of voters, the ability of the WJCC to function as a lobby group was severely strained. Before this recognition dawned, however, women's groups were able to secure some additional political rights, particularly in the areas of office holding and jury service.

ELECTED OFFICE

After ratification of the Nineteenth Amendment, suffragists considered themselves to be eligible to run for and to hold elective office. A few states, however, initially tried to make it difficult for prospective women candidates. In Arkansas, female candidates were forced to withdraw from their respective races, and the New Hampshire attorney general issued an opinion stating that women were not made eligible to run for office by the Nineteenth Amendment. This latter opinion, however, was ignored by women candidates in that state and two were victorious at the polls.[69]

Some antisuffrage forces saw the slight uncertainties that surrounded women's legal rights to hold office as their last opportunity to fight the suffragists' gains. In Detroit, Michigan an opponent of woman suffrage sued for the removal of a married female justice of the peace on the grounds that as a married woman she was not a person as a matter of law and therefore unable to hold public office.[70] The judge hearing the case dismissed the anti-suffragist's complaint concluding that the Nineteenth Amendment settled decisively the question of women's eligibility to hold public office. In most states this was true. Indeed, in the first elections after passage of the Nineteenth Amendment, women campaigned for and won public offices in 23 states.[71]

JURY SERVICE

Jury service, although more frequently considered a political duty than a political right, was closely allied with office holding by suffragists. Although state laws involving both often were phrased in similar terms, i.e., using the words male or men to describe those eligible to run for office or to sit on juries, there was far greater hostility to female jurors than to women officeholders or public officials. Often, that hostility was based on the belief that woman jurors would be upset or embarrassed by what they heard in courtrooms.

The decision whether or not to allow women to serve as jurors often turned on judicial interpretation of the term male, i.e., whether it had to be read literally or only in the generic sense. These interpretations were dependent on many factors—precedent, the personal biases of the judges, the conclusions of legal authorities consulted and perhaps most importantly, the judge's or state legislature's view of jury service—was it a privilege *or* duty of citizenship?

This privilege/duty distinction closely parallels the distinction between pure and limited public goods. Unlike voting or office holding, which are purely voluntary, noncompulsory political acts, jury service frequently is not. Consequently, for those who viewed jury service as an onerous burden where the seamier side of life often was revealed, it was logical to stress the compulsory nature of jury *duty* and thus the potential negative impact on family life. Opponents charged that women would be forced to leave their children unattended and then risk insult at the courthouse and shock and embarrassment in the courtroom when bodily parts or certain incidents were discussed during the course of the trial. For example, in Wyoming, where women first were allowed to serve as jurors in 1869, fathers sung to their children, "Don't cry baby, don't be in a fury; 'Cause Momma's gone to sit on the jury."[72]

Opponents of women's service also pointed to the historical evolution of the jury system. As originally described in *Blackstone's Commentaries*, a jury was defined as a body of "twelve good men." In fact, from earliest times, only two instances existed where women could be called on to serve as jurors. Both involved verification of pregnancy. In both circumstances the female jurors had only an examination function. This role, however, soon diminished as physicians became more readily available and assumed these duties.[73]

It was not until the development of the first woman's movement that the question of equal women's participation on juries was even raised. One of the many reforms sought by Anthony and Stanton was a change in the laws prohibiting women from sitting on juries. After the passage of the Fourteenth Amendment, they argued that to allow black men but not any women the right to sit on juries violated the protections afforded citizens under the constitution. This argument, however, was dealt a severe blow in 1880 when the U.S. Supreme Court held that a black defendant's constitutional rights were violated when blacks were excluded from jury service; however, the scope of this decision was limited by the Court when it affirmed the rights of states to "confine the selection of jurors to males."[74] With this decision, the Court in effect laid to rest the issue of jury service for women for many years. Given that there was so much opposition to a noncompulsory good, woman suffrage, it is not surprising that claims for an even more threatening right—jury service—fell on deaf ears.

With the development of the suffrage movement, the jury service question was again raised. It never was, however, a central concern of the suffragists. Votes for women was their prime goal, and most believed the ballot would have to be obtained before jury service could even be broached.

After the passage of the suffrage amendment, however, legal challenges were made to state exclusion of women from jury service. In Michigan, for example, the Nineteenth Amendment was held to make women eligible for jury service even though the state constitutional provision relating to jury service contained the word "men."[75] Other state courts, however, rarely were willing to apply the broad definition embraced by the Michigan courts. Many judges followed the reasoning of a New Jersey court that was called upon to interpret a state statute that referred to electors as "he." In rejecting the petitioners' claim that the Nineteenth Amendment required a liberal interpretation of the statute, the court reasoned:

> The Nineteenth Amendment to the federal constitution...makes no provision whatever with reference to the qualification of jurors. It alone confers the right of suffrage.[76]

Even in some states where jurors were designated by statute as "electors," women were excluded from jury service by judicial interpretation. In Massachusetts, selection of jurors was made from "persons eligible to vote." Therefore, the right of women to serve on juries was demanded soon after ratification of the suffrage amendment. However, in 1921, Justice Oliver Wendell Holmes, then a Massachusetts jurist, spoke for that state's highest court and disallowed women from jury service in the absence of specific legislation.[77]

In those states where women's claims to jury service were rejected, they often faced long, protracted legislative fights.[78] This was due, at least in part, to the demise of the strong women's coalition and growing recognition of women's limited political strength.

Interestingly, many of the arguments used by jury service opponents were similar to, but apparently more effective than, those used by antisuffrage forces. One female Republican member of the Connecticut legislature testified, for example, "Women should be more concerned over the breaking down of homes than over the breaking down of the jury system."[79] Others argued that jury service would unsex a woman, while still others voiced concern about the impropriety of women jurors being sequestered overnight.[80]

In sum, efforts of the suffragists to secure additional political rights, including jury service, faltered in the mid-1920s like the movement itself. Initially, suffrage leaders single-mindedly sought access to the ballot. Their success in 1920 was a function of a unique set of factors that would not come together again for fifty years. For a brief period of time, the necessary prerequisites for a successful social movement were present. A majority of the public agreed that women should have the vote. The arguments and events of the previous seventy years apparently had convinced a majority of Americans that women had the capacity to vote responsibly and that this single change would not bring about the ruin of the family or society. Indeed, for the many who believed the arguments posited by Jane Addams and other progressives, the vote actually was expected to help protect and strengthen the family. Thus, when NAWSA leaders dropped the more radical demands that had been sought by earlier woman's rights movement leaders and altered their logic for the vote, they helped make suffrage almost a conservative cause. Their advocacy of the ballot for "traditional" reasons made the vote appear to be a nonthreatening, nonuniversal public good, which in turn dramatically improved its chances of passage. This change in tactics made it possible for politicians in the major parties to support the amendment and to adopt party platforms urging its passage.

The narrower focus and more conservative ideology also encouraged many women of different persuasions to support and work for the vote. Furthermore, the previous mobilization of middle-class women by the club, progressive, and temperance movements provided the organizational base (a large, diversified membership) necessary to transform tacit female support of suffrage into a powerful political movement. Last, the ability of NAWSA leadership in the person of Carrie Chapman Catt to capitalize on this public support and organization strength made possible the passage of the Anthony amendment in 1920.

However, once Catt and other leaders turned their energies to other issue areas, agreement on goals broke down. In some areas, most notably the passage of the Cable Act, women were successful largely because legislators feared their wrath. Once that anxiety proved unfounded, more controversial kinds of political rights proved difficult to obtain. For example, although most suffragists believed that jury service was important at least symbolically, few found it to be an issue easy to rally support for given that many opposed it as a pure public good. Consequently, given the noncritical nature of the remaining political rights not enjoyed by women, there was little pressure for expanded legislation in the period from 1925 to the 1960s.

Jury Service: Current Women's Movement

Until the rise of the women's movement, little progress was made in respect to securing wider female participation on juries. In 1957, with little pressure from women, Congress enacted legislation that made all women, regardless of state laws, eligible to sit on federal juries. Its constitutionality, however, was challenged immediately,[81] and while a federal judge upheld the right of women to sit on federal juries, he noted his belief that women might be prohibited from serving on state juries. Not surprisingly, many states soon enacted laws to allow women to serve on state juries on either an "exemption allowed" basis or if women actually registered their willingness to serve. In many instances, these devices proved as effective as total exclusion and perhaps more dangerous to women's status because of their subtlety. For example, in 1961, Justice Harlan, writing for the U.S. Supreme Court, upheld Florida's "automatic"[82] exemption statute and noted:

> Despite the enlightened emancipation of women from restrictions and protections of bygone years, and their entry into many parts of the community formerly considered to be reserved to men, woman is still regarded as the center of home and family life.[83]

Thus, until 1975, courts in the United States continued to allow states to exempt or prohibit women from jury service. As discussed in Chapter 2, educational, employment, and reproductive freedom rights have been major goals of the current women's movement. Jury service laws, although important, never were a specific target of protracted women's group activity during this period. In fact, most men and women continued to believe that jury service was not a major issue of sex discrimination. In 1972, however, the National Federation of Business and Professional Women submitted an amicus curiae (friend of the court) brief in a Supreme Court case challenging gender-based discrimination in jury service.[84]

Generally, however, the major challenges to discriminatory jury service laws have come from feminist attorneys in court and not from women's rights groups. Thus, it was not until 1975, in *Taylor* v. *Louisiana*[85] that the U.S. Supreme Court held that the Sixth Amendment required that a jury be selected from a jury pool drawn from a representative cross section of the community. The Court then went on to say that when women were systematically excluded from jury panels, as they were in Louisiana, which allowed women to voluntarily register for service, the representative cross-section requirement was not satisfied. Thus, in prohibiting automatic exemptions based on sex, the Court invalidated the laws of almost twenty states. The Justices, however, did not go so far as to say that all types of exemptions for women were unacceptable. The decision left open the possibility that certain types of exemptions for women would be upheld if they did not operate to "unreasonably" exclude large numbers of women from the jury pool.

In the aftermath of *Taylor*, several states enacted legislation to exempt prospective jurors who have major childrearing responsibilities or "women" with such duties.[86] In 1979, in *Duren* v. *Missouri*, a case sponsored by the Women's Rights Project of the American Civil Liberties Union (ACLU), the Court struck down a section of Missouri's jury service law that granted an automatic exemption to women.[87] This decision, however, did not prohibit the granting of exemptions for those who have child-care responsibilities. Just as members of many professions (physicians, firefighters, ministers, etc.) can be exempted from service, so too can women who cannot make other arrangements for childcare. Allowance of these provisions has also minimized the potential for public furor should women be compelled to serve and leave their children unattended. Thus, these exemptions have made jury service a nonuniversal public good and, therefore, far more palatable to most.

EXPANDED OPPORTUNITIES IN THE POLITICAL SPHERE

The Current Women's Movement

It was not only jury service, however, that concerned women's rights activists. In fact, as previously noted, jury service was not a top priority in women's efforts to gain expanded political rights. Access to elective and appointive office has always received greater attention. As early as June 1963, the President's Commission on the Status of Women reported its belief that "public office should be held according to ability, experience, and effort, without special preferences or discriminations based on sex."[88] Its report, *American Woman,* also recommended increased appointment of women to important political positions. Commission members went so far as to recommend promulgation of an executive order:

1. designating a cabinet officer to implement and make progress reports on whether the commission's recommendations were being followed in the agencies of the federal government;

2. establishing an interdepartmental committee to assure coordination among departments in reaching these goals; and,

3. creating a citizens advisory committee to meet with the designated cabinet officer to further assure compliance as well as to suggest further courses of action.[89]

The commission was not alone in urging fuller political rights for women. For example, in one of NOW's first letters to prospective members, its purpose was explained:

to initiate or support action, nationally or in any part of this nation, by individuals or organizataions, to break through the silken curtain of prejudice and discrimination against women in government...the political parties, the judiciary...and in every field of importance in American society.[90]

Nowhere among NOW's specific goals enunciated at its first national meeting in 1967, however, was a specific call for additional *political* rights. This absence is largely attributable to the fact that the political inequalities experienced by these women's rights activists were quite different from those encountered by leaders of the early woman's rights and suffrage movements. While a variety of laws and practices kept women out of jobs or hampered their abilities for advancement in the 1960s, women enjoyed most basic political rights. Consequently, NOW devoted most of its early efforts to alleviating discrimination in the economic, educational, and social spheres, where the problems were more immediate. Many NOW members believed that once equality came in those spheres, the notion of female governmental officials—appointed or elected—would be more acceptable to the general populace.

Those who participated in the diverse kinds of groups that constituted the younger branch of the movement played an even more minor role in the battle for increased political rights and opportunities for women in the existing political system. Two factors largely account for this lack of participation. First, following the line of reasoning they ascribed to as members of the New

Left, most women in the younger branch either rejected the political system as corrupt and/or believed that the end of women's oppression would not come about through participation in, or through merely altering, the political system.

Numerous rationales were offered by various younger-branch women for not pursuing the goal of increased participation. Politicos, for example, are a collection of groups of men and women who believe that women's oppression is traceable either to racism, capitalism, and/or imperialism. Hence, they believe that women's inferior status would be remedied only when these systems are overthrown and replaced by a new political order. Thus, women in these groups believe that reform of existing structures is undesirable because reform might delay revolution.[91]

A larger and more significant segment of the younger branch, called radical feminists, has identified the patriarchal sex role system as the root of the problem. These radical feminists argue that all social institutions (including political institutions) are built on this system. As a result, radical feminists believe that an end to oppression and discrimination against women in the political arena would come only after sex role stereotypes and their supporting structures (love, the family, etc.) are abolished.[92] A third wing of the younger branch, socialist feminists, maintains that the patriarchal, social, and political systems as well as the capitalist economic system must be overthrown before women will be free.

Most radical feminists and social feminists[93] initially believed, as did politicos, that participation in, or reform of, the present system was pointless. While some of the early women's liberation groups did call for the "full participation [of women] in the decision-making processes and positions of our political, economic and social institutions,"[94] the focus of most of these small groups was largely on the raising of individual women's consciousness as a prelude to social and hence political revolution and/or providing limited help to local women in specific issue areas.[95]

More recently, some women from the younger branch, including socialist feminist Zillah Eisenstein, have argued that the seeds for a revolution to overthrow the patriarchal, social, political, and capitalist systems might be found in some of the political reforms advocated by liberal feminists, including some of those reforms supported by NOW.[96] It should be reiterated, however, that the ultimate goal of most feminists in the younger branch is abolition or overthrow of the present political system. Thus, this goal of revolution, while political in a broad sense, is not political in the narrower context discussed here.

Even had their goals been more conventionally political, the very structure of the younger branch provides a second reason for the absence of political activity by its members. As Freeman has noted, even had these small groups wanted to work effectively within the broader national political

sphere, their loose, fractionalized organizational structure effectively prohibited them from that kind of participation.[97] Efforts to expand both the
political rights and political activity of women in the present political system,
therefore, have had to be left to groups in the older branch, most notably the
National Women's Political Caucus.

The National Women's Political Caucus (NWPC)

The NWPC was established specifically to improve women's political
status and to fill the void that had been left when groups such as NOW and the
Women's Equity Action League (WEAL) initially chose to concentrate their
efforts in areas other than political rights. Shirley Chisholm, one of its
founders, stated its function as "not to be the cutting edge of the women's
liberation movement, but the big umbrella organization which provides the
weight and muscle for those issues which the majority of women in this
country see as concerns."[98] Women from a wide variety of women's
organizations quickly joined the caucus; in fact, many of its founders—
Chisholm, Gloria Steinem, Bella Abzug, and Betty Friedan—had previously
founded NOW and simultaneously held leadership positions in that organization. NWPC goals included increasing support for women candidates,
reforming party structures to assure equitable representation of women,
publicizing women's issues when they were at stake in elections, and
monitoring the selection of women party convention delegates.[99]

As a political organization, NWPC is unique in its multi-partisan base.
To accommodate the needs of its members and to fulfill its commitment to
increased representation in the political parties, however, it maintains special
Democratic and Republican Task Forces. And, since its creation, NWPC has
had a noticeable impact on Democratic party rules and practices but only
limited success in securing feminist reforms within the Republican party. The
different levels of progress in the two parties may be due, in part, to the more
conservative nature of the Republican party and the fact that NWPC is
composed of a sizeable percentage of women who identify themselves as
liberal Democrats.[100].

The first significant NWPC gains occurred just prior to the 1972
Democratic presidential nominating convention. When the McGovern-
Fraser Commission called for party reforms to assure that women comprised
40 percent of convention delegates, NWPC held training sessions across the
country for the women delegates to persuade prospective delegates to adopt a
strong stand on women's issues in the Democratic party platform. During the
convention itself, NWPC members worked with others from NOW to gain
planks favoring the ERA and federal funding of child-care centers. Disregard-
ing conventional political wisdom, NWPC members even introduced a
minority plank calling for a woman's right to abortion. (The U.S. Supreme
Court's decision guaranteeing this right did not come until 1973.) A lengthy

floor fight ensued, and the minority plank went down in defeat but by only a small margin. This near victory sufficiently exhilarated feminists at the convention that they decided to nominate one of their own, Frances "Sissy" Farenthold (later president of Wells College in New York) to run as George McGovern's vice-presidential running mate. Farenthold's vote total fell far short of that received by Thomas Eagleton. This show of strength, however, alerted party leaders that women were a force with which to be reckoned.[101]

By 1976, the NWPC was prepared for large-scale campaign activity at all levels. It questioned presidential candidates concerning their stands on a wide range of issues important to women. In addition, it monitored the candidates' campaign staffs for examples of the nominee's true commitment to women's status—the number of women in important decision-making positions. The NWPC also oversaw the presidential delegate selection process to ensure the success of women. At the Democratic presidential nominating convention itself, NWPC led the move for a written guarantee that women would constitute 50 percent of the delegates at the 1980 convention. While this proposal failed, in order to prevent an embarrassing floor fight, soon-to-be-nominated candidate Jimmy Carter met with feminist leaders to reach a compromise. The resultant "deal" involved Carter's promise to appoint women to high-ranking positions in his administration should he be elected. Other parts of the compromise included provisions in the party rules that mandated that "future conventions shall promote equal division between delegate men and delegate women"[102] and required the Democratic National Committee (DNC) to encourage the state parties to adopt rules to effectuate this goal.[103] In 1978, the DNC did pass a resolution that required that 50 percent of the 1980 convention delegates would be women.

After Carter's election, the NWPC joined with several other women's organizations to form an Ad Hoc Coalition of Women's Groups to make sure that his promises to appoint women would be kept. Lists of qualified women were compiled and delivered to the transition team and the president-elect met with women leaders. The efforts of the NWPC and the coalition were rewarded with the appointment by Carter of the largest number of women ever to high positions in a presidential administration. Older-branch groups including NWPC also were successful in pressuring Carter to appoint women to federal judgeships. Working with the Federation of Women Lawyers Screening Panel and NOW, NWPC worked to identify qualified women and to inform those women about how to apply for judicial positions.[104]

In addition to monitoring this appointment process, NWPC also has continued to attempt to increase the number of women elected to public office. It regularly holds training seminars for women candidates and gives financial and volunteer support to women candidates who support feminist issues. The amount of money made available by the NWPC has risen sharply over the years from zero in 1974 to one-half million dollars in 1982. In this respect, it is quite unlike the League of Women Voters, which simply stresses voter education and does not endorse candidates.

In 1980 the caucus not only held training sessions for candidates, but it also again held orientation meetings for prospective delegates to the Democratic National Convention. During the 1980 Democratic convention itself, NWPC along with other older-branch women clearly had a significant impact, particularly on the party platform, which included several feminist planks opposed by Carter. For example, the party supported federal payments for medicaid abortions and a prohibition against the national party giving financial support to candidates opposed to the ERA.

In contrast, NWPC members made little impact on the Republican party's 1980 presidential platform. In fact, the Republican nominee, Ronald Reagan, was elected in a landslide victory running on a conservative (perhaps even what might be labeled antifeminist) platform, which contained provisions calling for a constitutional amendment to end abortion, an affirmation of the party's belief "in the traditional role and value of the family in our society," and a restatement of "the importance of the support for the mother and housemaker in maintaining the values of this country."[105] The platform also did *not* contain an endorsement of the ERA, which had been supported in several previous platforms.

Despite this resounding defeat for women's rights, many NWPC financially supported candidates won their races—6 of 10 in Florida, 14 of 21 in North Carolina, and 8 of 15 in Oklahoma.[106] In fact, over 100 women won additional seats in the nation's state houses in 1980.[107] More women were also elected to the U.S. Congress than ever before. Some of those elected in 1980 and 1982, however, were not strong supporters of women's rights. In fact, some got significant support from the anti-ERA forces, thus revealing the important political impact of that faction of women and their followers. The NWPC, however, has attempted to work with these new members of Congress through the Congressional Caucus for Women's Issues, formerly called the Congresswomen's Caucus, to which most female members of Congress belong.[108]

With the defeat of the ERA, NWPC, like NOW, has refocused its energies on electing women to political office and to defeating state legislators who worked against the ERA.[109] Its "Win With Women" campaign is directed at getting more women into state as well as the national legislature, and the caucus' recent gains in membership should help to meet its goals. In fact, in 1982, NWPC saw 51 percent of its endorsed candidates for political office elected.

Another group that has taken an active role in facilitating the election of female candidates is the Women's Campaign Fund. Established in 1973, it is the only organization whose sole goal is to help fund the campaigns of progressive, pro-ERA, prochoice women candidates. To facilitate this task, the fund regularly relies on direct-mail campaigns, which have raised hundreds of thousands of dollars for female candidates. While initially most of its monies went to national races, like the NWPC, the fund is increasingly putting a stronger emphasis on state and local campaigns so that women will be able to "pay their dues" at the local or state level and then move up to national office.[110]

CONCLUSION

While direct action to expand women's political participation has been left to members of the older branch of the movement, some of the practices and activities of the younger branch probably have given a few women the strength and self-confidence to seek political office. The kinds of community work engaged in by younger-branch members as well may have provided a springboard into politics for some. There is also some evidence that the questioning of the existing political and economic order by radical feminists has influenced the views of women active in women's rights movements more generally. For example, a 1976 poll of women active in NOW, the Commission on the Status of Women, WEAL, the NWPC, and the Coalition of Labor Women (all organizations from the older movement) found that the women expressed dissatisfaction with the present two-party system and favored third- or fourth-party movements.[111] In fact, many women from both parties took an active part in the minor candidate John Anderson's unsuccessful bid for the presidency in the 1980 election. To summarize, by 1980, as a result of the action of the nineteenth and twentieth century women's movements, most legal barriers to women's full political participation had been overcome. And, in fact, both national political parties had made rule changes either to mandate or to require increased women's participation. As is detailed in the following chapter, it is not so much the rights anymore that need expansion but a change in social attitudes so that women may freely exercise their gains.

NOTES

1. Elizabeth Cady Stanton, Susan B. Anthony, and Matilda Joslyn Gage, eds., *History of Woman Suffrage*, vol. I, 1848–1861 (Rochester, N.Y.: Charles Mann, 1881), p. 70 (hereafter, HWS I).

2. Quoted in Eleanor Flexner, *Century of Struggle* (New York: Atheneum, 1974), p. 76.

3. Quoted in HWS I, p. 70.

4. See Ellen Carol DuBois, *Feminism and Suffrage: The Emergence of an Independent Woman's Movement in America, 1848–1869* (Ithaca, N.Y.: Cornell University Press, 1978), pp. 35–37. See also, Ellen Carol DuBois, ed., *Elizabeth Cady*

Stanton/Susan B. Anthony—Correspondence, Writings, Speeches (New York: Schocken Books, 1981).

5. In fact, during this period most women belonged to the American Anti-Slavery Society. It had a loosely organized central committee but attempts to establish a more permanent organization were rejected as "a burden, a clog, an incumbrance, rather than a help." Letter from Angelina Grimké Weld to the Syracuse National Woman's Rights Convention held in September, 1852. Quoted in HWS I, pp. 540–541.

6. Flexner, *Century of Struggle*, p. 82. For examples of the "calls," see Judith Papachristou, *Women Together: A History of Documents of the Women's Movement in the United States* (New York: Alfred A. Knopf, 1976), pp. 22–29.

7. Flexner refers to this group as the National Woman's Loyal League. *Century of Struggle*, p. 110.

8. Angelina Grimké Weld, "The Rights of Women and Negroes," a speech delivered at the Woman's National Loyal League, Cooper Institute, New York, May 1863; reprinted in Elizabeth Cady Stanton, Susan B. Anthony, and Matilda Joslyn Gage, *History of Woman Suffrage*, vol. II, 1861–1876 (New York: Fowler and Wells, 1882), pp. 54–56 (hereafter, HWS II).

9. Flexner, *Century of Struggle*, pp. 142–143. See also DuBois, *Feminism and Suffrage*, chap. 7, where she notes how the Republican party abandoned the woman suffrage issue in the 1867 Kansas campaign. After this, Anthony and Stanton had nothing to do with the Republicans.

10. DuBois, *Feminism and Suffrage*, pp. 63–66.

11. Ibid., pp. 73–77.

12. The critical section of the amendment reads:

Section 2 ... or in any way abridged, except for participation in rebellion, or other crime, the basis of representation therein shall be reduced in the proportion which the number of such *male* citizens shall bear to the whole number of *male* citizens twenty-one years of age in such State. [emphasis added]

13. DuBois, *Feminism and Suffrage*, pp. 189–193.

14. Karen O'Connor, *Women's Organizations' Use of the Courts* (Lexington, Mass.: Lexington Books), p. 35.

15. DuBois, *Feminism and Suffrage*, chap. 5.

16. For an account of AWSA leaders' opposition to Anthony and Stanton's affiliation with Train, see Papachristou, *Women Together*, pp. 59–60 and Ida Husted Harper, *Life and Work of Susan B. Anthony*, vol. I (Indianapolis: Bowen Merrill Co., 1898), pp. 293–294. Garrison's letter to Anthony reproduced below well illustrates how Train was viewed by many.

Jan. 4, 1868

Dear Miss Anthony:

In all friendliness, and with the highest regard for the woman's rights movement, I cannot refrain from expressing my regret and astonishment that you and Mrs. Stanton should have taken such leave of good sense as to be travelling companions and associate lecturers with that crack-brained harlequin and semi-lunatic, Geo. Francis Train. You may, if you choose, denounce Henry Ward Beecher and Wendell Phillips (the two ablest advocates of woman's rights on this side of the Atlantic), and swap them off for the nondescript Train, but in thus doing, you will only subject yourselves to merited ridicule and condemnation, and turn the movement which you aim to promote into unnecessary contempt.

... He is as destitute of principle as he is of sense, and is fast gravitating toward a lunatic asylum. He may be of use in drawing an audience, but so would be a kangaroo, a gorilla, or a hippopotamus.

Your old outspoken friend,
William Lloyd Garrison

Letter later published in *The Woman's Journal,* March 11, 1899.

17. Rheta Childe Dorr, *Susan B. Anthony: The Woman Who Changed the Mind of a Nation* (New York: Frederick A. Stokes, 1938), p. 226.

18. Reproduced in HWS II, p. 408.

19. Minor letter to *The Revolution* published October 28, 1869, p. 259.

20. HWS II, p. 411.

21. This kind of legislation would have been easier for proponents to secure. While a constitutional amendment would have required a two-thirds majority of the Congress, enabling legislation required only a simple majority.

22. For a discussion of Woodhull's failure to credit Minor, see O'Connor, *Woman's Organizations',* p. 37.

23. Edward T. James, ed., *Notable American Women, 1607–1950, A Biographical Dictionary,* vol. III (Cambridge: The Belknap Press of Harvard University Press, 1971), s.v. "Victoria Woodhull." See also, Johanna Johnston, *Mrs. Satan* (New York: Popular Library, 1967).

24. The full text of her remarks delivered to Congress are contained in Paulina W. Davis, *A History of the National Woman's Rights Movement, for Twenty Years* (New York: Journeymen Printers' Co-operative Association, 1871), p. 95. Woodhull's comments at the NWSA meeting, "A Lecture on Constitutional Equality," also are reprinted in Davis.

25. Quoted in HWS II, pp. 810–811.

26. Reprinted in HWS II, pp. 441–442.

27. O'Connor, *Women's Organizations',* p. 39.

28. Ibid., p. 52.

29. Quoted in HWS II, pp. 728–729.

30. 88 U.S. (21 Wall.) at 162 (1875).

31. For the full text of this Declaration of Rights, see Mari Jo and Paul Buhle, *The Concise History of Women Suffrage* (Urbana: University of Illinois Press, 1978), pp. 297–303.

32. The loss of power by traditional clergymen to the revivalists and radical reformers like William Lloyd Garrison who openly called for equal rights for women probably helped precipitate these religious attacks. Keith E. Melder, "The Beginnings of the Women's Rights Movement In the United States, 1800–1842," (Ph.D. dissertation, Yale University, 1964), pp. 435–436. It also is likely that traditional clergy were particularly reluctant to give up control over women who often played a key role in the education and financial support of the clergy.

33. Congressional Globe, 39 Cong., 2nd sess., part I, p. 56.

34. See Aileen S. Kraditor, *The Ideas of the Woman Suffrage Movement, 1890–1920* (New York: Columbia University Press, 1965, Anchor Books, 1971), chap. 2 for a full discussion of arguments against female suffrage as they had been developed by 1890.

35. A comprehensive history of the WCTU can be found in Mary Earhart, *Frances Willard: From Prayers to Politics* (Chicago: University of Chicago Press, 1944).

36. For a discussion of the component organizations within the club movement, see Margaret Gibbons Wilson, *The American Woman in Transition: The Urban Influence 1870–1920* (Westport, Conn.: Greenwood Press, 1979), chap. 5. See also, Karen J. Blair, *The Clubwoman as Feminist: True Womanhood Defined, 1868–1914* (New York: Holmes & Meier, 1980).

37. DuBois, *Stanton/Anthony*, pp. 175–178.

38. Papachristou, *Women Together*, p. 115.

39. William H. Chafe, *The American Woman: Her Changing Social, Economic, and Political Role, 1920–1970* (New York: Oxford University Press, 1972), p. 16.

40. William L. O'Neill, *The Woman's Movement: Feminism in the United States and England* (Chicago: Quadrangle Books, 1969), p. 48. See chap. 5.

41. "There is no Such Thing as a Sphere for Sex," reproduced in Leslie B. Tanner, ed., *Voices From Women's Liberation* (New York: Mentor Books, 1970), pp. 40–41.

42. Kraditor, *Ideas of Woman Suffrage*, p. 20.

43. Rose Terry Cooke, "Average Woman," *Remonstrance* (1892), p. 1, quoted in Kraditor, *Ideas of Woman Suffrage*, p. 20.

44. Ibid., p. 21.

45. Ibid., p. 50.

46. Jane Addams, "Why Women Should Vote," *Ladies Home Journal* (1909); reprinted in Emily Cooper, ed., *Jane Addams: A Centennial Reader* (New York: MacMillan, 1960), pp. 104–107.

47. Quoted in Kraditor, *Ideas of Woman Suffrage*, p. 110.

48. Ibid., pp. 168–169.

49. *The Woman's Journal*, December 15, 1894.

50. Flexner, *Century of Struggle*, p. 218.

51. Kraditor, *Ideas of Woman Suffrage*, p. 212.

52. Flexner, *Century of Struggle*, p. 222.

53. In 1913, Illinois lawmakers enacted a statute pursuant to state constitutional law giving women the right to vote in presidential elections.

54. Flexner, *Century of Struggle*, p. 248.

55. Not only was there disagreement over a state versus a national amendment, but also over the Congressional Union's militant tactics. See "The Congressional Union," NAWSA Convention, Washington, D.C., December 14–19, 1915, reproduced in Mari Jo and Paul Buhle, *The Concise History of Woman Suffrage*, pp. 424–429.

56. Carrie Chapman Catt and Nettie Rogers Shuler, *Woman Suffrage and Politics* (New York: Charles Scribner's Press, 1973), p. 229.

57. Quoted in Flexner, *Century of Struggle*, p. 280.

58. Ibid., p. 281.

59. Ibid.

60. Ibid., p. 290.

61. This argument closely parallels that made by Southern legislators who opposed ratification of the Equal Rights Amendment.

62. Flexner, *Century of Struggle,* pp. 311–313.

63. Chafe, *The American Woman,* p. 36.

64. See Mary Carroll, "Wanted—A New Feminism: A Interview with Emily Newell Blair," *Independent Woman,* 9 (December 1930):499 for a discussion of Howard's concerns.

65. J. Stanley Lemons, *The Woman Citizen: Social Feminism in the 1920s* (Urbana: University of Illinois Press, 1973), p. 55.

66. Membership in the WJCC varied yearly. Among the organizations that belonged at one time or another were the League of Women Voters, the National Federation of Business and Professional Women, the General Federation of Women's Clubs, the WCTU, the American Association of University Women, the YWCA, the National Women's Trade Union League, and the National Consumers' League.

67. Lemons, *The Woman Citizen,* p. 65.

68. Ibid., p. 66.

69. Ibid., p. 68.

70. Ibid., p. 69.

71. Ibid., p. 68.

72. Quoted in Thomas Woody, *A History of Women's Education in the United States,* vol. II (New York: Octagon Books, 1966), p. 450.

73. Karen O'Connor, "Sex Discrimination in Action: A Focus on Jury Service for Women," paper delivered at the Annual Meeting of the Southern Political Science Association, 1976.

74. *Strauder* v. *West Virginia,* 100 U.S. 303 (1880).

75. "In Michigan Women are People," *Woman Citizen* 5 (January 8, 1921): 8.

76. *State* v. *James,* 114 Atl. 553 (1921).

77. *In re Opinion of the Justices,* 130 N.E. 685 (1921).

78. Lemons, *The Woman Citizen,* p. 70. For example, although bills were introduced that would have allowed jury service in 1923, 1925, 1927, and 1929, women in Illinois did not win the right to sit on juries until 1939.

79. Quoted in Lemons, *The Woman Citizen,* p. 71.

80. Ibid.

81. *U.S.* v. *Wilson,* 233 F.2d 686, cert. denied, 358 U.S. 865 (1968).

82. The Florida law in question allowed women to serve as jurors, but it required them to register first with the local juror commissioner. Men automatically were added to the list of prospective jurors when they registered to vote. As a result, the jury pool consisted of 10 women and 9,900 men.

83. *Hoyt* v. *Florida,* 368 U.S. 57 (1961).

84. *Alexander* v. *Louisiana,,* 405 U.S. 625 (1971).

85. 419 U.S. 522 (1975).

86. For an excellent discussion of these new laws, see Rhonda Copelon, Elizabeth M. Schneider, and Nancy Stearns, "Constitutional Perspectives on Sex Discrimination in Jury Selection," *Women's Rights Law Reporter* 2 (June 1975): 10.

87. 99 S.Ct. 664 (1979).

88. Report of the President's Commission on the Status of Women, *American Woman,* p. 52.

89. Ibid., p. 54.

90. Quoted in Papachristou, *Women Together,* p. 220.

91. For a discussion of some of the activities of the early politicos, most of whom were socialists, see Judith Hole and Ellen Levine, *Rebirth of Feminism* (New York: Quadrangle, 1971), chap. 2 and Jo Freeman, *The Politics of Women's Liberation* (New York: David McKay, 1975), chap. 4. For a summary of Marxist analyses of women's inferior position in society and how a socialist revolution would rectify the situation, see Zillah R. Eisenstein, "Developing a Theory of Capitalist Patriarchy and Socialist Feminism," in Zillah Eisenstein, ed., *Capitalist Patriarchy and the Case for Socialist Feminism* (New York: Monthly Review Press, 1979), pp. 6–16.

92. See Shulamith Firestone, *The Dialectic of Sex: The Case for Feminist Revolution* (New York: Bantam Books, 1970) for an earlier statement of this position.

93. A collection of articles summarizing this position can be found in Eisenstein, ed., *Capitalist Patriarchy.*

94. From pamphlet, "Chicago Women Form Liberation Group," in Papachristou, *Women Together,* p. 229.

95. Note the following quotation from the Redstockings' *Manifesto:*

> Our chief task at present is to develop female class consciousness through sharing experience and publicly exposing the sexist foundation of all our institutions. Consciousness-raising is not "therapy,"... but the only method by which we can ensure that our program for liberation is based on the concrete realities of our lives....The time for individual skirmishes has passed. This time we are going all the way.

Quoted in Tanner, *Voices From Women's Liberation,* pp. 110–111.

96. Zillah R. Eisenstein, *The Radical Future Of Liberal Feminism* (New York: Longman, 1981), pp. 220–248 makes the argument that liberal feminist reforms may help women become more conscious of their double oppression from patriarchical capitalism.

97. Freeman, *Politics of Women's Liberation,* pp. 142–146.

98. Quoted in Barbara Sinclair Deckard, *The Women's Movement: Political, Socioeconomic, and Psychological Issues,* 2nd ed. (New York, Harper and Row, 1979), p. 366.

99. Papachristou, *Women Together,* p. 245.

100. Deckard, *The Women's Movement,* p. 367.

101. In 1972, at the urging of then Rep. Margaret Heckler (R-Massachusetts), the Republican party platform continued the party's support of the ERA and included a call for childcare, although it was far weaker than the provision included in the Democratic party platform.

102. Quoted in Deckard, *The Women's Movement,* p. 371.

103. During the 1976 Republican convention, feminists struggled to simply hold their own. Against a strong challenge, the party continued its commitment to the ERA.

104. *Women's Political Times,* December 1980, p. 10.

105. *Newsweek,* August 25, 1980, pp. 34–35.

106. *Women's Political Times,* December 1980, p. 10.

107. Ibid., p.4.

108. Deborah Churchman, "Congresswoman's Caucus Wields Clout Beyond Its Size," *Christian Science Monitor,* June 11, 1981, p. 17 and Marjorie Hunter,

"Congresswomen Admit 46 Men to Their Caucus," *The New York Times,* Dec. 14, 1981, p. D–10.

109. Demetra Lambros, "Caucus Indicts Twelve Who Roadblocked ERA," *Women's Political Times,* July 1982, p. 1.

110. Ruth B. Mandel, *In the Running: The New Woman Candidate* (New Haven, Conn.: Ticknor & Fields, 1981), p. 265. Other organizations working for the election of women include the National Women's Education Fund, which provides consultants to advise women on how to run successful campaigns.

111. Barry Sussman, "Feminism Has Taken Hold," *The Washington Post,* September 28, 1976, p. A–12.

4

Women's Political Participation[1]

INTRODUCTION

After passage of the Nineteeth Amendment, laws benefitting women and children were enacted by lawmakers who feared an adverse reaction if they failed to pass legislation of concern to women. As noted, at the urging of women's groups, Congress passed the Cable Act to restore rights of U.S. citizenship to women who married non-Americans. However, the expectations of suffrage movement leaders that women would use the ballot to end political corruption and war, as well as to pressure politicians to pass progressive legislation, were quickly dashed. By the mid-1920s, demands of women activists were no longer well received and in fact defeat was more common than victory.[2] Not only did it become clear that women as a group often were divided on the desirability of certain laws and changes but also that many women seemed to be totally unconcerned and uninterested in politics.[3]

Evidence of this limited interest can be seen in the level of electoral turnout in the 1920s. Although the figures are incomplete, they suggest that in contrast with nearly two-thirds of all men, only one-third of all women eligible voted.[4] Turnout may even have been lower for immigrant, black, and Southern women.[5] Additionally, only a handful of women actually ran for office or tried to become involved in campaign activity. Moreover, in the early years after suffrage, the few who actually were elected or appointed to political office came from the ranks of those who ran as stand-ins or replacements for their husbands.[6]

82

Thus, the removal of legal barriers to political participation failed to result in equality between the sexes in the political arena. To examine why women's political activity failed to meet the expectations of the suffrage leaders,[7] we first must recall that the political rights granted to women by the Nineteenth Amendment were not universal public goods. In 1920, it was still possible to exclude certain classes of women, most notably immigrant and black women, from exercising the franchise through a variety of laws. Politicians, political parties, and society in general created hurdles that prevented women from taking a more active role in the political process. As noted in Chapter 3, the right to run for office was not willingly granted. Additionally, individual women could decide if, and how much, they wanted to participate in politics. And because many women lacked the education, money, contacts, and/or training for public office, their activity in that sphere was even more limited.

These conditions alone, however, cannot account for the persistence of inequality in the political arena. It is our contention that the most significant factor that kept women from exercising their political rights and thus fostered their exclusion from certain aspects of politics, in fact, has been the existence of negative cultural attitudes about women's political activity. The legacy of negative views can also be used to explain the continued lack of full political equality for women. Negative cultural attitudes have affected women's participation in several ways. Specifically, they have made possible the imposition of cultural sanctions and overt discrimination against women who may have wanted to, or actually tried to, take an active role in politics. Because politics is often viewed as a "man's job," they also have prevented many women from becoming involved in politics or acquiring the skills or personal attributes necessary for political activity. Thus, cultural restrictions on the political activity of women have resulted in two additional barriers to full political equality for women: the lack of preparation for political activity by women and sex discrimination. In the following sections we describe, in detail, these barriers and how they have limited and continue to limit the political role of women.

CULTURAL ATTITUDES ABOUT THE POLITICAL PARTICIPATION OF WOMEN

Our knowledge of societal attitudes toward women's political participation both before and shortly after 1920 is scant. Opinion polls and surveys were not developed until the 1930s, and systematic monitoring of political attitudes did not start until the 1950s. Additionally, because widespread concern about the political performance of women is a recent phenomenon, few questions have been asked by pollsters consistently since the 1930s, making historical comparisons difficult. Even so, a picture emerges of a public basically ambivalent to an active political role for women.

Some of the earliest evidence about the public's view of women's role in politics comes from Charles Merriam and Harold Gosnell's study of nonvoting in the 1920s. Their interviews indicated that one reason for the low female voter turnout was women's belief that they should not be involved in politics. This attitude was particularly strong among elderly, immigrant women.[8] Given that there was a widespread belief among many women that they should not vote, we might surmise that the public's disposition toward female participation in more active forms of politics was even more antagonistic.

Indeed, the first nationwide opinion polls conducted in the 1930s revealed that public attitudes toward the participation of women in politics were decidedly negative. At a time when only a handful of women held public office, 60 percent of all citizens rejected the idea that "we need more women in politics."[9] This aversion to the involvement of women in politics was particularly strong with respect to elective office. More than half were opposed to women serving as a governor, senator, or cabinet member, and three-quarters objected to a woman being appointed to the U.S. Supreme Court. When asked in 1937 about their willingness to vote for a qualified woman for president, only 27 percent of all men and 40 percent of all women answered affirmatively. Even in the latter half of the 1940s, a near majority still disagreed with the statement that "not enough capable women are holding important jobs in the United States government." And, while men were more likely to object (53 percent rejected the statement), more than 40 percent of the women surveyed also denied the need for more women in politics. The bias against political activity by women continued to be especially strong where political office holding was at issue. For example, an astounding 88 percent of all men and 87 percent of all women polled in 1946 believed that the office of mayor "should nearly always be held by a man." Three-quarters of the men and two-thirds of the women interviewed felt the same about congressional office holding. In 1949, almost half the public continued to report they would not vote for a woman for president even if she was qualified for the office and nominated by the party for which they regularly voted.

As in the 1930s, these strong feelings about the activity of women did not constitute a universal objection to all types of political participation by women. Attitudes toward the activity of women in some areas of community politics were actually quite favorable. Nearly half of all respondents to a 1946 survey thought a woman was to be preferred to a man as Red Cross chapter head or Parent-Teacher Association president. This apparent divergence between the public's view toward women holding elected office and its opinion about women being active in local affairs was in part based on the perception that community activity represented an extension of a woman's primary roles of mother and homemaker. This notion, introduced by progressive and reform women in the late nineteenth century, had fairly wide support by 1940. By then, many saw as only logical the association between women's "taking care of the family" and "taking care of the community."

Subsequent polls conducted in the 1950s and 1960s found only small changes in the overall picture of the public's beliefs. Most people continued to agree that women could or should take part in school affairs, but more than 40 percent of those interviewed in 1955, 1963, and 1969 said that they would not vote for a woman for president.[10]

Impact of the Current Women's Movement

There is evidence that the current women's movement has had some impact on these kinds of cultural stereotypes. Between 1972 and 1980, for instance, there has been a marked increase in the proportion of the public agreeing with the statement that "Women should have an equal role with men in running business, industry and government." In 1972, only one-third of the population strongly supported such equality, but by 1980, 52 percent voiced their support for this proposition. While men were slightly more supportive of equal roles for women than women were, the difference was not uniform across all age and education categories. Among both sexes, attitudes towards women's role were related to education and to a lesser extent, age.[11] Among the least supportive were women over fifty-five with a high school education or less. In general, much lower levels of support for women's rights are found in the South. Even among women in the South with some college education, only 54.4 percent strongly favored equal roles for women in politics and business compared to 70.2 percent of non-Southern women. In the nation as a whole, there is a similar gap between housewives and women employed outside the home. Fifty-six percent of all employed women favored equality while only 41.7 percent of all housewives supported this notion.[12] Race is also related to support for equal roles, with black men and women both being more supportive than whites of either sex.[13]

In addition to the increase in overall support for equal roles for women in politics, there also has been a sharp increase in the willingness of individuals to vote for a woman for president. Evidence presented by E.M. Schreiber suggests that this increase can be attributed to the women's movement and to the publicity it has received. He reports that it was among the educated public—those most exposed to the women's movement by the media—that the greatest changes in attitudes between 1967 and 1975 occurred.[14] For example, among women college graduates, support for a female president rose from 51 percent in 1967 to 88 percent in 1975; the figures for college men were 58 and 91 percent, respectively. By 1980, more than three-quarters of the public (78 percent of all women, 69 percent of men) indicated that they would vote for a woman for president. Only 39 percent, however, believed that a woman would be elected to that position before the year 2000.[15] Willingness to see a woman elected to a lesser political office (mayor, governor, and representative of Congress) has also increased. As early as 1975, more than 80 percent of the public reported they would support a qualified woman elected to these offices.[16] Similarly, in sharp contrast to the public's attitudes toward women judges in the 1930s, Sandra Day O'Connor's appointment to the Supreme Court was approved by 87 percent of all women and 84 percent of all men.[17]

Recently, perhaps in part because of Watergate, there also has been increased support for the idea that the country would be better off if women had greater input into the political process. In 1970, only slightly more than a third of both men and women accepted this view. By 1975, 57 percent of all women but just 39 percent of all men agreed with this proposition.[18]

Continuing Cultural Barriers

Even with this dramatic improvement in cultural beliefs, stereotypes continue to act as barriers to the full participation of women. A rather widespread view still exists, for example, that the roles of wife and mother and active participant in politics do not mix. Fifty-five percent of all women and 62 percent of all men polled by Lou Harris in 1972 agreed with the statement that "To be really active in politics, women have to neglect their husbands and children."[19] Among women with a college degree, more than two out of five expressed accord with this statement. Thus, even among those most supportive of women's political activity, there is still a belief that conflict may occur between participation and traditional roles. While Harris has not repeated this question since 1972, there is some indication that role conflict continues to be seen as a problem. A 1976 survey of primary election voters in one county in Wisconsin, for example, found in answer to a hypothetical choice situation, a marked reluctance among the electorate to vote for a woman for a judgeship if she had small children. Only 45 percent said that children would make no difference in their choice or that they would vote for the woman over a man. When no children were mentioned, however, 78 percent said they would vote for the woman or that the candidate's gender would make no difference.[20] On a related question in 1977, a majority of respondents in a national sample indicated that they saw the impact of a working mother as harmful to children, especially if the children were young.[21] Because political office holding is a job more demanding than most, even larger majorities see it as detracting from a woman's ability to be a good mother. As we shall see below with reference to actual office-holders, the public apparently does not think a father's ability to do his job is similarly affected by office holding.[22] This belief parallels the findings to be discussed in Chapter 8 that in most homes, the "primary parent" is still the mother. Given the persistence of this fact, whether from sex role sterotyping or as a result of economic necessity, we can expect that many mothers will continue to place their parental responsibilities first and forego or restrict (or be pressured to forego or to restrict) their political activity when they have children at home.

Barriers also remain as a result of continuing negative views about the abilities of women to participate as effectively as men in politics. In particular, many doubt the capacity of a woman to be as "hard-nosed" as a man. A Harris poll conducted in 1972, for example, found that both men and women believed that a woman president would have a harder time dealing with riots, criminals, and big business. Nearly half thought she would have trouble "standing up to the Russians." Pluralities of both sexes, apparently accepting the argument that women are the weaker sex, also agreed that the long hours and pressures of the presidency would wear a woman down more quickly than a man.[23] As recently as 1978, 44 percent of the public agreed that "most men are better suited emotionally for politics."[24] While this represents an improvement in the perception of women's abilities since 1972 when almost two-thirds of the public agreed with the statement,[25] it is obvious that a woman who tries to enter politics even today faces a public that doubts her ability to perform the job as well as a man.

Thus, cultural attitudes toward the participation of women in politics, especially electoral politics before 1970, were generally negative. While the public thought it was acceptable and even desirable for a woman to take an active role in community affairs, most objected to a woman holding major elected office or taking an active role in partisan politics. While much of this opposition has lessened since the advent of the current women's movement, there are still large segments of the population, particularly Southerners, the old, and the poorly educated, who believe an active role for women in politics is unacceptable. Even those who are more open to the idea of greater political participation by women harbor doubts about whether women have the ability necessary for such participation and whether politics mixes well with motherhood.

Given these rather widespread negative beliefs, it is not surprising that women have not become as involved in politics as men. While some women probably refrain because they think such behavior is inappropriate, for others the expected reaction of the public to their political activity, no doubt, is a significant barrier.

One by-product of the negative cultural attitudes toward active political involvement by women is that girls traditionally have not been socialized for an active role in politics. Accordingly, women often are unprepared psychologically for political activity. Studies of young children show that early on boys and girls differ in a number of significant ways in their orientation toward politics. Young girls have been found to be less attentive to, less informed about, and less interested in politics. Additionally, some studies have shown that girls have a more positive view of political leaders.[26]

At least some of the socialization process of men and women into separate political roles occurs in adolescence and in adult years.[27] A particularly critical stage appears to be the birth of a woman's first child. For many, this event signals entrance into adulthood and with it the corresponding adoption of appropriate female attitudes and behaviors.[28] At that time many women appear to become more conservative and concerned with devoting most of their energies to caring for their newborn child.

CIVIC ATTITUDES

Before we begin an examination of the civic attitudes of women and men, we should note that almost all of the civic orientations that are conducive to political activity—efficacy, psychological involvement in politics, and obligation to participate—are strongly related to level of education. With the exception of partisan identity, a psychological tie with a political party, the more educated a citizen, the more likely he or she is to have high levels of the above civic attitudes and, therefore, the more likely the individual is to take part in public affairs.[29]

The strong association between education, participation, and civic attitudes has two important implications for any examination of the relative levels of political involvement or preparedness of the two sexes to participate. First, because women have not always been as well educated as men, we must be careful in any comparison between the sexes to look only at men and women with equal levels of education in answering the question whether the sexes are similarly prepared to participate. Second, because political activists are drawn primarily from the most educated citizenry, we will be particularly concerned with the relative readiness of college-trained men and women. If women in this group are as psychologically primed for political activity as similarly educated men, we can expect more nearly equal levels of involvement. If, however, college-trained women are not as well prepared as men, the overall gap in political activity between the sexes will probably be great.

In addition to education, employment, particularly in certain prestige occupations, has also been suggested as a possible mechanism by which individuals, especially women, can develop higher levels of civic orientation. Therefore, we will also examine whether employed women are as ready as employed men for political involvement.

Citizen Duty

The belief that a citizen has an obligation to vote is perhaps the most elementary civic attitude. In fact, it constitutes the single best predictor of whether a person votes.[30] In 1923, interviews with women nonvoters in Chicago indicated that not only did many not feel obliged to vote, but also more than 10 percent believed that they should not.[31] In fact, one female nonvoter's opinions were as follows:

women should not 'stick their noses in politics.'Her husband's vote was sufficient. Only men and widows should vote. Women do not understand politics and so should not 'butt in men's work.' She was very determined woman suffrage was wrong.[32]

Over the years, as voting became a more legitimate activity for women there was a corresponding increase in their civic obligation to vote. In fact, in 1980, women recorded slightly higher levels of citizen duty than men. Overall figures, however, mask some important differences among different classes of citizens. Women with an eighth-grade education or less have considerably lower levels of citizen duty than more educated women or than the corresponding group of men.

Absence of obligatory feelings to perform even the most rudimentary of political activities—voting—on the part of less educated women and Southerners corresponds with our earlier findings that these groups hold the most traditional attitudes toward women's role. With these exceptions, however, almost all other classes of women have come to believe that they *can* and *should* vote. In fact, among men and women with at least some college education, the citizen duty levels of women in both the South and North are significantly higher than those of similar groups of men. This corresponds with data from earlier studies. For example, in the 1920s, it was poor, immigrant women who were most reluctant for women to vote.[33] As early as the 1950s, Campbell et al. found that college-educated women had citizen duty levels equal to those of men.[34] In general, on questions dealing with attitudes toward the political system, men and women report similar beliefs. If anything, females are slightly less cynical and more positive about democracy than males.[35] This may, however, be changing among feminist women whose trust in government is lower.[36] When we turn to other civic attitudes, however, the condition of equality tends to diminish.

Psychological Involvement in Politics

To examine forms of participation other than voting, political scientists have emphasized the critical importance of political interest and attention to public affairs in determining who participates. These orientations have been labeled by Verba and Nie as "psychological involvement" in politics.[37]

As already noted, the evidence indicates that women in the 1920s had much lower levels of such psychological involvement in politics than men. Nearly 33 percent of all women nonvoters interviewed in Chicago in 1923, for instance, reported "no interest in politics" as their reason for not voting as compared to only 15 percent of nonvoting men.[38] Even in the 1960s, women's interest in politics and national affairs at all education levels was lower than that of similarly educated men.[39]

The women's movement and the other changes in the 1970s have not completely eliminated this disparity between the sexes. When asked in 1980 how regularly they followed government and public affairs, only 21.4 percent of all women compared to 32.8 percent of all men reported that they followed what is going on in politics "most of the time." A similar difference in attention to politics also exists among college-educated men and women under age 35—the group often found to be the most similar. Among young college-educated persons, 35.3 percent of the men but only 13.5 percent of the women reported following politics most of the time. Interestingly, while employment outside the home improved the relative position of women vis-a-vis men among the least educated, it does not seem to help the situation of more educated women. In fact, college-educated women who are employed are equally likely as college-educated housewives to report that they follow politics regularly.

These rather surprising results relative to the impact of employment also are repeated below for most of the other civic attitudes. It appears that while employment broadens the role definition of less well-educuated women with respect to their participation in politics, it has no such additional effect on college-educated women. This occurs because the role definition of college-educated women has already been somewhat expanded by their educational experience. The lower levels of attention to politics among working, college-educated women may simply reflect their lack of leisure time. In other words, their dual role gives them little opportunity to devote time to leisure activities like reading or watching the national news.[40]

However, in at least one area of politics—presidential campaigns—women are almost as involved as men. While studies in the 1940s and 1950s found that they were less interested than men in presidential campaigns, in the 1964 election no such difference was found.[41] Additionally, there is some indication that even in those elections since 1952 when women as a group indicated less campaign interest than men, the gap was much smaller or even nonexistent among citizens with at least some college education.[42] In 1980, however, 56.6 percent of all college-educated men but only 43.5 percent of all college-educated women reported high levels of interest in the Reagan-Carter race, perhaps because neither candidate appealed to women.[43]

Interestingly, in one area of psychological involvement, women reported higher scores than men in 1980. Sixty-nine percent of all women, but only 62.8 percent of all men identified with a political party in that year. This tendency, however, may reflect a lag on the part of women if it indicates that they have been slower than men to join the increasing number of independent voters.[44]

The other measures of psychological involvement indicate a mixed picture. For example, women's lower psychological involvement in politics appears to be closely associated with their inferior level of political information. In 1920, Merriam and Gosnell, for example, found a close relationship between lack of information and lack of interest in the voting process.[45]

Similarly, in 1976, only half of all women compared to 75 percent of all men knew which party controlled the U.S. House of Representatives. And, while by 1980 the difference in knowledge continued particularly among the least educated, a significant gap also existed between college-educated men and women. Ninety-three percent of all men, but only 76.3 percent of all college-educated women knew that the Democratic party controlled the House of Representatives.

These lower levels of involvement in and knowledge about national politics parallel our earlier findings about the persistence of a cultural belief that politics is a more "natural" concern for men. As noted, there is evidence from studies of elementary school children that this difference between the sexes begins early in life.[46] There is some suggestion, however, that this situation may be changing, in part, as a result of the women's movement. Specifically, among citizens found to be most receptive to new ideas about political participation—college-educated women under thirty-five—the sexes are more nearly equal. With the exception of overall attention to politics, there is virtually no difference in talking about, or interest in, campaigns. In addition, the gap between the sexes in following campaigns and political information tends to be somewhat less although not eliminated among the younger college-educated citizens.[47]

Political Efficacy

The last attitude of concern is political efficacy: an individual's belief that he or she can influence governmental decisions. Because confidence in one's ability to affect governmental actions is closely related to a willingness to undertake political activity, we are especially interested in the differences between men and women in this area.

In the 1920s, interviews with individual women revealed their lack of self-confidence about political matters. Although nearly equal numbers of nonvoting men and women doubted the effectiveness of their vote, women were more likely to report "timidity" when it came to casting their ballots. To quote one female nonvoter about why she had never voted, "I ain't got the nerve."[48]

Since the first testing of feelings of political efficacy in the 1950s, women regularly have reported lower levels of efficacy in several areas. The first of these involves awareness of and confidence in the use of political participation other than voting. John W. Soule and Wilma E. McGrath report that in every presidential election between 1956 and 1972, women were more likely than men to believe that "voting is the only way to influence government."[49] In 1980, however, there was no significant difference between male and female respondents, as indicated in Table 4–1. Additionally, while in 1964 the differences between college-educated men and women on this question were considerable, by 1980 there were only small disparities between the sexes in all education categories.[50] Although not indicated in Table 4–1 further analysis reveals that regional disparities were significant; the gap between Southern men and women is considerable. Outside of the South, college-educated women are only slightly less likely than men to be able to think of or feel confident about alternatives to voting.[51] This increased awareness of alternative strategies may reflect both the result of the women's movement and the increase in political activity by many women of all classes in the 1970s.[52]

In one other respect, however, the political efficacy of women continued, even in 1980, to lag behind men. Women continue to report much lower confidence in their understanding of politics. Interestingly, this difference in confidence is even greater among the more educated citizenry. In 1980, for example, overall nearly 78.3 percent of women but less than 62.5 percent of men believed that politics sometimes is so complicated that it cannot really be understood. Among the college-educated, however, the difference was wider. Even though women in this group are more confident of their ability to understand than less well-educated men, more than 66.8 percent of all such women but only 45.7 percent of a corresponding group of men report a lack of confidence in their ability to comprehend the political world.

This relative lack of confidence may be traceable to the relatively lower psychological involvement and information levels of women reported earlier. Because women, even more educated women, are not following politics as closely as their male counterparts, and thus are not as well informed, their lower sense of confidence in their political understanding is to be expected.[53]

In contrast, the more nearly equal levels of local political interest and local political information between all men and women result in more similar overall confidence in understanding of local issues and politics by the two sexes. Between college men and women, for example, the difference in understanding local politics was less than half that found with respect to understanding of politics "in general."[54] Among younger cohorts of college and high school educated men and women, the difference was insignificant.[55] Furthermore, Kathleen McCourt's study of participation by women in community-action groups notes that involvement in such activities tends to break down this vicious cycle even for working-class women. The women in her study reported higher confidence levels as a result of their interest in and subsequent action with respect to local problems.[56]

Political Attitudes of Black Women

The position of black women vis-a-vis the political system would lead us to predict that their attitudes toward participation in that system would be very different from those of nonminority women. One might predict, given their "outsider status" and their generally lower educational and economic status, black women would have very low levels of psychological preparedness

TABLE 4-1
Political Efficacy Levels for Men and Women: 1980

	Education							
	Grade School		High School		College		All	
	Men	Women	Men	Women	Men	Women	Men	Women
Voting is the only way people like me can have any say about how the government runs things	21.2	29.1	35.7	34.3	56.5	50.2	41.5	38.7
Sometimes politics and government seem so complicated that a person like me can't understand what's going on	19.5	10.5*	27.6	18.6*	54.3	33.2*	37.5	21.7*

*Statistically significant at the .05 level or greater.

Note: Figures indicate the percent giving efficacious response to (disagreeing with) each statement.

Source of data: Center for Political Studies, 1980 American National Election Study. Figures compiled by the authors.

for political activity. The research to date, however, suggests that this is only partially true. Minority women appear to have lower levels of citizen duty and trust in government than nonminority women. Similarly, political interest is somewhat lower among black women. Both of these sets of attitude differences appear to reflect the perception on the part of black women that the present political leaders, especially at the federal level, are not concerned about and/or willing to do anything about the pressing problems of these women.[57] This sense of alienation among black women is reflected, however, in their growing approval of political protest.[58] Interestingly, among black women, feminist views are strongly related to this growing alienation from the political system. Among white women, degree of feminism is considerably less related to political attitudes.[59]

Summary of the Differences in Political Attitudes Between Men and Women

In conclusion, women as a group are less well prepared, in terms of the relevant political attitudes, for most political activity than are men. In general, the attitudinal differences between men and women seem to closely parallel cultural views. There are, for example, few discrepancies between most men and women with respect to citizen duty and attitudes relevant to community participation. These are, of course, the two areas where we found little public resistance to participation by women. However, women do appear less ready than men to take an active role in demanding forms of political activity, especially those that would require high levels of political involvement, information, and efficacy.

We should add two caveats to this section on preparedness. The first is that we may not need to wait for the slow process of childhood socialization to occur with respect to a whole new generation of women before women "catch up" with men's readiness for political activity. As noted, there is increased evidence that adults (men and women) are able to adopt new views about their political roles when exposed to such new ideas, either as a result of education, employment, media attention, or political activity itself. McCourt's study of the politicizing effect of community involvement on working-class women is important evidence of this last process. Because they were drawn into political actions to improve conditions in their neighborhood and schools, activities often identified as extensions of mother/homemaker roles, these women's interest, knowledge, information about politics, and confidence to change things grew—often extending to partisan national politics in addition to local nonpartisan politics.[60] We might surmise that a similar phenomenon is occurring among women active on both sides of the women's issues battles during the 1970s and into the 1980s. The national and increasingly partisan nature of these issues, as witnessed by the 1980 Republican and Democratic party platforms, may speed this trend even further. Fulenwider's results on the positive impact of feminism on political attitudes suggest this is already occurring for those supportive of the women's movement.

Our second caveat concerns dimensions of preparedness other than attitudes. While we have focused on the latter in this section, there are other reasons why women often are not as ready as men to take an active role in politics. For example, women have received less education than men because in the past women have not been socialized to prepare for a career. As a result, fewer women can be found in that class of citizens (college educated) that are most frequently recruited for high-involvement political activities such as running for elective office.[61] A particularly potent example of this is the relatively low number of women lawyers—the professional group from which a large number of political officeholders is selected? Thus we can continue to expect that ill-preparedness in this "structural sense" as well as the attitudinal will continue to hamper the movement of women into politics. Before examining the specific political acts in detail, however, we must first discuss one other important barrier to political equality—discrimination by male politicians.

SEX DISCRIMINATION: THE HIDDEN BARRIER

Discrimination based on sex has proven to be a powerful deterrent to political activity by women. Unfortunately, it is very difficult to study or document. Few men are willing to admit that they discriminate. Additionally, what many women see as discrimination against them may be viewed otherwise by men who feel they are simply complying with traditional cultural mores or widely accepted patterns of political behavior.

Two factors seem to motivate most sex discrimination: cultural stereotypes about the abilities and appropriate position of women in politics and self-interest on the part of male politicians who are reluctant to share their power with women or any other "out group." It is usually difficult, however, to determine where cultural attitudes end and self-interest begins because the rationale for the separate treatment of women is generally phrased in terms of these sexual stereotypes regardless of its motivation. Politicians in the 1920s and 1930s, for example, could be openly hostile to the active participation of women in politics by using the justification that "politics was no place for a woman."[62] While today, few have adopted this rationale publicly, some have questioned the emotional stability of women to hold public office. For example, Bella Abzug's style came under attack because it clashed with many people's notion of feminine behavior. She notes, "If I were a man, they would have said I was strong, courageous and a leader. Instead, I was called abrasive and aggressive."[63] Sometimes party leaders claim these prejudices are not their own but those of the citizenry. Thus, they argue women cannot be nominated for office because the public will not elect them.

The close association between cultural stereotypes and sex discrimination means that discrimination is generally greatest where public opinion is most hostile. There is, for example, less discrimination against women in community affairs than there is against a woman who tries to run for elective office. While changes in the 1970s in cultural stereotypes about the political position and abilities of women have led to a decrease in the most blatant forms of sex discrimination, subtler versions still persist.

SUMMARY OF CONDITIONS AFFECTING THE POLITICAL PARTICIPATION OF WOMEN AND A TYPOLOGY OF POLITICAL ACTIVITIES

Three interrelated factors condition the political participation of women: cultural stereotypes about the abilities and appropriate position of women in politics, the preparation of women for political activity, and discrimination by political leaders. As we have indicated, the strength of these barriers has varied not only over time but also among classes of women and types of political activities. In general, the power of these barriers to limit the political activity of women has diminished since 1920, although this phenomenon has been greater for some activities and among particular groups.

With respect to any individual political act, however, the differential in the level of political participation between men and women will depend upon the strength of these three barriers to that particular act. Thus, the smallest differences between men and women should be found relative to communal participation, voting, and other "citizen activities" where these three barriers are relatively weak. Conversely, large sex differences should characterize elective office holding where all three restraints are strong. In addition, because not all women hold the same ideas about women's role in society, some women have faced fewer barriers to participation relative to a specific act than other women. In particular, the views toward politics and the greater readiness to participate in political activity of young and college-educated women lead us to expect the narrowest differences between the sexes will be found in these groups. Correspondingly, the persistence of cultural stereotypes among more traditional citizens—the elderly, poorly educated individuals, and Southerners—should result in more significant sex differences in these classes.

THE VOTE

Anticipation of the consequences of the ballot motivated women in the suffrage movement. They wanted the same rights as men to select the leaders who made the laws and ran the government. The vote was then, as it is now, the most basic form of citizen participation. Indeed, because it requires only minimal levels of involvement and effort, it is not only the most common political activity, it is for many individuals their sole contact with the world of politics.

Because it requires so little effort and because cultural attitudes have generally not been too negative toward the participation of women in such simple citizen activities, we predicted this would be one area where the political activity of men and women would be equal. The 1980 vote turnout figures in fact substantiate this hypothesis: according to the Census Bureau, 59.1 percent of all men and 59.4 percent of all women reported that they voted.[64]

But as Table 4–2 indicates, such equality has not always been the case. In fact, our earlier hypotheses provide us with some reasons for this historical discrepancy. When suffrage was won in 1920, discrimination against women who wanted to vote existed in many areas of the country and it was possible to exclude entire classes of women from exercising the franchise. In the South, the adoption of such measures as the poll tax made it virtually impossible for black citizens, male or female, to vote. Elsewhere in the country, literacy tests and more complex registration laws may have helped to dissuade poor and non-English speaking immigrant women (and men) from voting.[65] The abolition of these types of restrictions has had a particularly dramatic impact on the voting behavior of black women. As a result of the civil rights movement and the various voting rights acts, the proportion of black Southern women who had *never* voted declined from 87 percent in 1952 to 28 percent in 1976.[66] However, because of the even greater increase in political activity by black men, black women still vote less frequently than black males. It should be noted, though, that the voting rates of black women nearly equal those of white citizens of both sexes once controls for education, income, occupation, and age are introduced.[67]

Sanctions and costs associated with voting, however, were not limited to black and immigrant women. Societal and family pressures kept many white and native-born women from the polls. For example, in 1923, several female nonvoters in Chicago cited the objections of their husbands as their reason for not voting. As one woman explained, "I am not looking for a divorce." Others were more afraid of rowdiness or taunts by men at the polls.[68]

Practices excluding women were not the sole or even the most significant reason why so few women actually voted in the early decades after the Nineteenth Amendment was adopted. The more important factor was that many women themselves did not choose to exercise their newly acquired right. Reluctance to vote was especially pronounced among classes of women where there were strong cultural stereotypes of appropriate male and female roles. For example, in the South, where attitudes toward women's role were more conservative, John Stucker reports that only a few women bothered to go to the polls.[69] Additionally, Merriam and Gosnell's study of nonvoting in

TABLE 4-2
Sex Differences in Voter Turnout for President

Percent Voting	1920[b]	1948[c]	1952[c]	1956[c]	1960[c]	1964[c,d]	1968[c,d]	1972[c,d]	1976[d,e]	1980[d,e]
Men	75	69	73	80	80	73(71.9)	76(69.8)	76(64.1)	77(59.6)	73(59.1)
Women	46	56	62	69	69	70(67)	73(66)	70(62)	68(58.8)	70(59.4)
Difference[a]	-29	-13	-10	-11	-11	-3(-4.9)	-3(-3.8)	-6(-2.1)	-9(-.8)	-3(+.3)

[a] A negative sign indicates male advantage. Figures are rounded to nearest whole number.
[b] The figures for 1920 are for Chicago, Illinois reported in Walter D. Burnham, *Critical Elections and the Main Springs of American Politics* (New York: W. W. Norton, 1970), p. 77.
[c] The figures for the 1948 through 1972 elections are from Marjorie Lansing, "The American Woman: Voter and Activist," in Jane S. Jaquette, ed., *Women in Politics* (New York: John Wiley, 1974), p. 8.
[d] Figures in parentheses are from the U.S. Census Bureau. The Census Bureau figures are generally more accurate than those from the Michigan Election Studies. See Aage R. Clauson, "Response Validity Vote Report," *Public Opinion Quarterly* 32, #4 (Winter, 1968–69), pp. 594–598.
[e] The figures for 1976 and 1980 are from the Center for Political Studies, 1976 and 1980 American National Elections Studies. Figures compiled by authors.

Source of data: Compiled by the authors.

Chicago indicates that many older, ethnic, and immigrant women in the North as well chose not to go to the polls. According to one elderly Irish woman, "Women have no business voting. They would be better off staying at home and minding their own affairs."[70] In contrast, in the West, where support for woman suffrage had a long heritage, women were apparently voting in the early 1920s at rates nearly equal to those of men. Similarly, in the first decade after suffrage, women living on Chicago's Gold Coast and in the middle-class districts around the University of Chicago were casting their ballots at more nearly equal levels with men than women living in the city's poorer sections.[71]

While cultural constraints restricted the turnout of many women in the 1920s, by the 1950s (and probably earlier for most women), this barrier was largely eliminated. In fact, by 1980, only among older, poorly educated women was there any evidence of the cultural stereotype that voting is for men only. Accordingly, in these groups, voter turnout among women fell approximately 10 percentage points behind men. At the other end of the spectrum, among young (under age thirty-five), college-educated women, the turnout rates of women equaled those of men in 1980. Fulenwider presents some evidence that feminist beliefs may increase turnout even further, especially for minority women.[72]

One other milder form of cultural restriction, role conflict between motherhood and voting, not only hindered the participation of women in the 1920s but continues to be a barrier for some women. Interviews with women in 1923 and into the 1970s have found that many mothers of young children find it difficult to get to the polls. Accordingly, the turnout rates of young mothers are lower than those of young fathers.[73]

Interviews with Chicago women in 1923 revealed yet one additional factor that kept many women from the polls—lack of preparation for voting. One-third of the women, for instance, had no interest in the campaign, while almost one in ten women cited lack of knowledge about the process as her reason for not voting.[74] Women in the suffrage movement saw this lack of information and training as the main barrier to the full and equal participation of women in politics. To correct this problem, they early on established the League of Women Voters to help educate women for political activity. How many women benefited from the League's efforts is difficult to measure, although we know only a small minority of the original suffrage movement members joined the new organization. Moreover, the League's policy of remaining aloof from partisan politics may have diminished the chances that those who became involved would become active in partisan politics.[75]

While the League may have played an important role for some middle-class women, probably a more important factor in mobilizing large numbers of women to take an interest in and get involved in the voting process was the 1930s Depression. There is evidence that this economic crisis, touching as it did every family in the country, politicized large numbers of immigrants, women, and young people who had previously remained outside the political arena. Kristi Andersen reports that many lower-class women first took an interest in politics during this period.[76] Her study indicates that the voters who were drawn to the polls for the first time in their adult life by the economic crisis surrounding the 1932 election also adopted strong ties to the Democratic party—a tie that served to bind them strongly to that party and to the electoral process.[77]

In sum, between 1920 and 1980, the three barriers to voting by women diminished so significantly that the thirty point difference in turnout dropped to almost zero. Today, only a few women are ill prepared to exercise the franchise or continue to cling to the notion that voting is "a man's game." The one factor, however, that may still negatively affect the voting participation of some women is the presence of small children, who appear to pose practical problems and create some cultural conflicts between motherhood and voting.

GENDER AND DIRECTION OF VOTE

A secondary question to be asked about the voting behavior of women is whether they cast their ballots differently from men. The leaders of the suffrage movement clearly expected women would be a bloc of voters distinct in their attitudes and political behavior from men. When we look at the survey data on opinions, however, we find little evidence of significant gender differences across most issues. But there are a few notable exceptions to this rule. First and foremost, almost all questions dealing with war or international involvement find women to be more pacifist and opposed to the use of force than men.[78] Starting with the suffragists, we find women leading men in their opposition to war. With the advent of public opinion polls in the 1930s, this pattern of gender difference became clearer. For example, in 1952, 45 percent of the women compared to only 37 percent of the men interviewed felt we should have stayed out of Korea.[79] Similar differences of opinion were found on the Vietnam conflict.[80] As recently as May 1982, women were significantly more likely than men to believe the U.S. should "try harder to reduce tensions with the Russians" (52% of women versus 43% of men) rather than "get tougher."[81]

There is evidence, moreover, that women in the past have been more supportive of measures to expand civil rights of blacks and to maintain or increase social welfare programs.[82] More recently, women's greater opposition to nuclear power and weapons has begun to show up in surveys.[83] And, in the 1982 elections, division among the sexes concerning economic issues was particularly apparent. For example, according to *The New York Times*/CBS

News poll, the greatest differences between the sexes was revealed in response to the question, "In the long run, do you think Ronald Reagan's economic program will help the country's economy or hurt the country's economy?" Fifty-four percent of the men but only 39 percent of the women believed that the program would "help."[84]

While issues influence how many citizens vote, party identity—whether or not an individual views him or herself as a Republican, Democrat, or something else—generally is believed to be an exceptionally important determinant of the vote.[85] Until recently, however, men and women have shown little difference in their tendency to affiliate with either party, when age and region of the respondents are controlled.[86]

The absence of significant differences in issue positions, party identity, and vote direction between men and women (differences that are even smaller between spouses),[87] has prompted some political scientists to claim that women are influenced by their husbands in these areas. Indeed, studies of women who have changed their party identification seem to suggest that women switch their party affiliation to agree with their husbands'.[88] This trend, however, may reflect the change in socioeconomic status that occurs for women when they "marry-up" to a higher social class. While both women and men reject the view that husbands influence their wives' vote,[89] there is some suggestion that the flow of communication and influence in terms of trying to change spouses' vote is from husbands to wives.[90]

Given the relative absence of party identity or issue distinctiveness between men and women, we should not be surprised to find little evidence of variation in the way men and women vote in presidential elections. However, in those years in which we find a significant difference between the sexes— 1952, 1968, 1972, and 1980—the differential appears to be traceable to the above-noted divergence in issue positions.

In 1972, for example, 37 percent of all women voted for McGovern, while only 30 percent of men cast their ballots for the peace candidate. This divergence in voting behavior in 1972 is directly attributable to a sharp disagreement between the sexes over the issue of Vietnam. As early as 1968, women were more likely to favor withdrawal from Vietnam and by 1972 nearly half of all women but less than a third of men favored this position. This strong aversion to continuing the war resulted in the above McGovern support among women. This support, moreover, would probably have been even greater if doubts about McGovern's ability to end the war had not become a campaign issue.[91]

The 1980 election again produced a division between men and women. *The New York Times*-CBS exit poll found that among men, 54 percent voted for Reagan, 37 percent for Carter, and 7 percent for Anderson. Women split their vote almost evenly between the two major party candidates, 45 percent for Carter and 46 percent for Reagan.[92] In contrast to the reactions in 1972, the negative attitude on the part of women to the Republican candidate Reagan appears to be both longer lasting and broader based. In every poll since 1980, women of all age and education categories have consistently expressed greater disapproval of Ronald Reagan than have similarly situated men. The negative reaction to Reagan covers virtually every issue area ranging from opinions on his economic programs to his ability to keep us out of war and even his life-style in the White House.[93] Kathleen A. Frankovic traces these negative reactions to Reagan, including the greater reluctance of women to vote for him, to more widespread perception on the part of women that Reagan might get the country into war.[94] Controlling for feminist views, economic position of respondent, and marital status reduced the male-female gap somewhat but not as significantly as attitudes on the risk of war under a Reagan presidency.

An important consequence of these negative attitudes toward Reagan may manifest itself in the 1984 national elections should Reagan again head the Republican ticket. In commenting on the "gender gap" that occurred in the 1982 elections, a leading Republican pollster noted, "if [Reagan's] on the ballot in 1984 [the gender gap] will show up in his race and carry over into other races, maybe a lot more than it did this year, unless we get some changes made."[95]

The potential problem is compounded for Republican strategists given the gender gap in party identification that first emerged in the 1980 election. For example, in 1980, women reported far higher identification with the Democratic party. And in fact, according to Kathleen Frankovic, by 1982, women were significantly more likely than men to adopt a Democratic party identity (41 percent of all women compared with 33 percent of all men). Moreover, unlike previous findings on party identity, in 1982, this gap between men and women did not disappear when age and education controls were introduced.[96]

In turn, women voted more heavily Democratic in the 1982 elections than did men and preferred Democratic candidates nationwide by at least 3 percent (56 versus 53 percent).[97] The most decided pro-Democratic identification and voting patterns were found in unmarried women—64 percent voted for Democratic candidates for the House of Representatives. In contrast, the one-point difference between married men and women voters was not statistically significant.[98] The overall vote preference difference between the sexes, however, was sufficient to affect the outcome of several close races, including those of Senator Lowell Weiker of Connecticut[99] and Governors Cuomo (D-New York) and White (D-Texas).[100]

The Reagan administration, recognizing this problem even before the 1982 election, began to make more direct appeals to women and even to alter its policy positions in order to be more compatible with those of women. And, since the election, the administration and the Republican party have been exploring ways to reduce the gender gap. Thus, Reagan's appointment of two feminists, Elizabeth Dole and Margaret Heckler, to the cabinet and the administration's arguing against the legality of sex-biased insurance tables before the U.S. Supreme Court were viewed as major efforts to appease women voters. Regardless of their success, their actions indicate that politicians may finally have recognized that, properly motivated, women can be a potent political force.

COMMUNAL PARTICIPATION

We turn next to an examination of the involvement of women in communal or cooperative work at the local level. Included in this category of participation are efforts to work with others to solve community problems. Examples of such activities include efforts by environmental groups to stop local industries from polluting the environment, efforts by neighborhood improvement associations to upgrade local living standards, and work of PTAs to improve conditions in the schools. As Verba and Nie indicate in *Participation in America,* such involvement often is ignored in discussions of political activity. The influence group activities have on the local decision-making process, however, clearly qualifies these efforts as highly political.[101]

There are several characteristics of this kind of political participation that would lead us to expect fairly equal male/female involvement. First, as Verba and Nie note, it is less likely to involve conflict than more traditional political work such as campaign activity.[102] Thus, it may be more appealing to women, who are more opposed to conflict, than men. Second, community work is an area of activity where there are few cultural barriers, few role conflicts, and where women seem adequately prepared to participate. The one exception to this last condition may be those women identified earlier as having negative views toward the participation of women in all politics. Finally, there appears to be little discrimination against women who want to get involved in such activities. Generally, there are no community leaders to decide who may participate because leadership generally falls by default to whoever is willing to take up the cause. Thus, in some areas, local officials actually assume that women will organize certain community projects.

Given the apparent acceptance of participation by women in this area rather early on, we might suspect that over time women have been quite active at this level. Indeed, women first began to organize reform associations even before the Civil War.[103] They also took a leading role in the progressive and urban reform movements at the turn of the century, undertaking innumerable drives to improve living and working conditions of the poor as well as to clean up politics in our nation's cities. Since then, women have continued to form the backbone of the volunteer network in this country. For example, a 1965

Department of Labor survey indicated that 60 percent of all volunteers in the United States were women.[104] Additionally, a 1982 Gallup Poll found more women (30 percent) than men (27 percent) reported they were involved in some charity or social service activity.[105] While this community work by women was traditionally dominated by middle-class housewives, most recently there has been an upsurge in activity by poor, black, and working-class women. Focusing on the dismal conditions in their communities and schools, many such women have formed associations to tackle some of the most pressing urban problems.[106] Another recent phenomenon has been the proliferation of organizations of women on the local level to deal especially with women's issues and problems.[107]

Data from two national surveys taken approximately ten years apart substantiate our expectations that women continue to be active in this area. The first survey, conducted in 1967, questioned people about a variety of community activites. Generally, as revealed in Table 4–3, women were less active than men. This difference, however, was largely a function of the significant differences between citizens with less than a high school education. Among men and women who had completed high school, women were as likely as men to indicate they had worked on a local problem and actually more likely than men to report they belonged to a local problem-solving group. The only areas where women fell behind men were in forming a problem-solving group and contacting local public officials. Among college-educated citizens, women were more active than men. Thus, even prior to the current women's movement, many women were taking an equal or greater part than men in community affairs. Indeed, the high levels of participation among college-educated women suggest that they were actually playing a leading role in this aspect of the nation's political life.

Table 4–4 reports similar findings from a study undertaken nine years later in 1976. As Table 4–4 indicates, with the exception of citizens with less than an eighth-grade education, women equalled or exceeded the level of participation of men in most community affairs. Among certain groups, the lead by women was striking. Nearly two out of three college-trained women under age thirty-five reported some activity, but only one-half of a corresponding group of men participated even marginally in community affairs. Although the absolute amount of activity is less among citizens with at least some high school education, the advantage of women is similar. Thus, participation in local communal work appears to be one area of political involvement where many women not only equal the levels of activity by men but actually exceed them.

But in a closely related political activity—involvement in cooperative efforts aimed at solving national problems—even college women report somewhat less participation than a comparable group of men. Although on an

TABLE 4-3
Communal Participation Rates for Men and Women: 1967

	Education							
	Less than High School Graduates		High School Graduates		Some College		All	
	Men	Women	Men	Women	Men	Women	Men	Women
Ever worked with others to solve a community problem	26	20*	33	33	40	45*	31	29*
Ever formed a group or organization to solve a community problem	13	10*	15	12*	22	20	16	13*
Written or contacted a local official about a community problem	18	10*	26	19*	31	28	23	17*
Member of an organization involved in working on community problems	24	19*	32	36*	48	55*	32	32

*Statistically significant at the .05 level or greater. All cells are based on at least 500 cases.

Note: Figures represent the percent who report having participated in each of the four listed community activities.

Source of data: Sidney Verba and Norman H. Nie, 1967 study, *Participation in America,* conducted by the National Opinion Research Center at the University of Chicago. Figures compiled by the authors.

TABLE 4-4
Communal Participation Rates for Men and Women: 1976

	Education							
	Grade School		High School		College		All	
	Men	Women	Men	Women	Men	Women	Men	Women
Join with others to deal with a local problem	9	5*	15	18	32	36	21	21
Attend city council/school board meetings	11	2*	14	15	30	29	20	17*
Sign petition regarding community problem	8	4*	17	17	34	35	22	20
Demonstrate about a local problem	0	less than 1	1	2	3	3	2	2
Write a letter to the editor about a local problem	2	0*	3	4	9	8	5	4
Communicate with a local official	8	4	18	14*	31	29	21	17

*Statistically significant at the .05 level. All cells are based on at least 450 cases.

Note: Figures represent the percent who report having participated in each of the six local communal activities.

Source of data: Center for Political Studies, 1976 American National Election Study. Figures compiled by the authors.

overall basis, few citizens become involved in national issues (only 20 percent of all men and 16 percent of all women report any participation in this area), among the most educated citizenry, 32 percent of the men and 28 percent of the women report some activity. Several factors may be important in explaining this disparity. First, there may be cultural barriers to this activity. The public tends to believe women are not as capable of handling national issues (such as defense) as are men. Second, while a woman may believe that local community work is part of her job as a mother, she may not feel the same about other political activity. Thus she may limit her participation to local affairs, especially school affairs, at least during that period when she has little time for political activity, e.g., when she has young children.[108] Another factor may be the isolation from national affairs associated with staying home and raising young children. Women who work outside the home and thus might not be so isolated do tend to be more involved in national affairs than mothers who are housebound.[109] Finally, the lack of energy and the necessity of hiring a baby-sitter or finding someone to care for her children may present a real obstacle. McCourt reports that among working-class women, both the presence of young children and working outside the home (along with a resistant husband) restrict a woman's activity in even local communal politics.[110]

Before concluding this section, a special note should also be made about black women and a particular type of participation—political protest. In the 1960s, at the height of the sit-in period of the civil rights movement, a study of participants found 48 percent of the participants were black *women* college students.[111] Given Fulenwider's findings concerning black women's acceptance of protest activity, one might expect that the level of protest activity of black women would be higher than white women in the 1970s. This, however, was not the case, although black women were almost as active as white women in this regard and more active than white women in interest-group activity.[112]

PARTISAN ACTIVITY: CAMPAIGN AND PARTY WORK

Our discussion of partisan activity is divided into two sections. The first concerns campaign and party work, the second, political office holding. This has been done because the barriers to holding elected office are far more extensive than to campaign work, where some kinds of women's efforts may be welcomed.

There are several reasons to expect that women will not participate as extensively as men in partisan activities. First, such involvement often runs counter to cultural expectations about women's role in public life. Because this kind of participation involves conflict and competition between contending forces as well as "wheeling and dealing," it may be viewed as incompatible with women's supposedly less conflictual and more moralistic nature. For instance, in 1972, more than a third of the public believed that politics was "too dirty" for women.[113] Therefore, unlike community work, which is often viewed as an extension of the mother and wife roles, partisan activity may be seen as a serious threat to a woman's ability to perform her primary duties. Even if a woman is able to ignore and overcome these cultural roadblocks, the heavy and irregular time demands of involvement in party activities, especially political campaigns, might prove too difficult to manage when she has young children.

Second, the potential for discrimination is greater for partisan, as opposed to nonpartisan activities. Party leaders are in positions that allow them to restrict the participation of women, either by preventing their involvement or by limiting the nature of their tasks. Expectation itself of this kind of discrimination may be a powerful stumbling block. Although the public does not believe parties discriminate against women "in general," they do agree that "women are mostly given the detailed dirty work chores in politics, while men hold the real power." This view is particularly strong among college-educated women, the very group that is potentially the most active.[114] Similarly, a majority of the public believes women are discriminated against in obtaining top jobs in government.[115] It would not be surprising, therefore, if many women chose to channel their energies into community or other nonpartisan work where they are more likely to be given positions of authority.

Finally, most women feel an obligation to vote. Their levels of interest in politics, as well as their information about and in particular, confidence in their knowledge of local affairs, especially among better-educated women, prepare them well for community activities. However, these factors may not carry over to national political involvement. The generally lower levels of political interest, involvement, information, and efficacy of women concerning "politics or national affairs" might be a serious obstacle to their participation in extralocal political campaigns and party work. Additionally, the relative absence of women in certain "power" positions, including those of union leaders and corporate executives, may result in their not being asked to become involved in a particular campaign.

Only a relatively few citizens take a very active role in any single political campaign. In 1980, for instance, less than 40 percent of the public reported engaging in the most common form of campaign activity, trying to influence another person's vote. Even smaller numbers took a truly active role in that campaign. In fact, less than 10 percent of the public engaged in each of the following: attending a campaign meeting, contributing money, working for a candidate, or displaying a campaign button or poster. Because national polling did not begin until 1952, our information about the role of women (as well as men) in such activities in the 1920s, 1930s, and 1940s is limited, yet we know that in the years immediately following passage of the Nineteenth Amendment, women tended to avoid all partisan work, including campaign activity. Following the lead of the National League of Women Voters, many viewed partisan politics as immoral. Others were shut out by political party leaders. This changed somewhat in 1932 when Mary "Molly" Dewson became head of the Women's Division of the Democratic party. Under the sponsorship of both Franklin and Eleanor Roosevelt, Dewson, a former NCL leader, actively recruited 15,000 women to spread the word about New Deal programs. In 1936, 60,000 women precinct workers canvassed for the Democratic party. Party efforts to recruit women campaign workers, however, declined after Dewson's retirement.[116]

The decline of political machines, however, in the 1940s and 1950s forced leaders to rely increasingly on volunteers, including women, to run campaigns. Although this factor, when coupled with Dewson's efforts, probably contributed to an increase in women's campaign activity, the first national survey of citizen level campaign activity in 1952 still found that women were considerably less involved in campaigns than men.[117]

Since 1952, however, there has been a gradual decline in the overall gap in campaign activity between the sexes. In 1980, only slightly fewer women than men generally reported engaging in at least one of the following campaign acts: contributing money, attending a political meeting, and influencing another's vote or displaying a button or poster.[118] As Table 4-5 reveals, by using a measure summarizing all these campaign activities, it is found that the gap is greatest among older men and women with less than an eighth-grade education. The difference between the sexes in this category corresponds with the more negative cultural attitudes toward female political participation by women in this group and their low campaign interest, attention, and psychological involvement. Among the college educated, while both sexes were very active compared to less educated men and women, the 7 percent difference separating the sexes in 1976 had declined to 3.7 percent by 1980.[119]

It should be noted, however, that reports from other elections have not always found a negative disparity between college-educated men and women. Marjorie Lansing, for example, found that 60 percent of all college women as compared to 54 percent of all such men participated in one or more political activities in the presidential campaign of 1960.[120] An examination of the individual acts comprising the summary campaign activities measure reveals that the negative disparity between more educated men and women in 1980 was limited to only two areas, influencing another's vote and wearing a campaign button. Overall, in this group, 49 percent of men and 46 percent of women reported influencing another's vote. College women and, indeed, all women with better than an eighth-grade education were actually *more* likely

TABLE 4-5
Percent Reporting At Least One Campaign Act among Men and Women: 1980

	Education							
	Grade School		High School		College		All	
Age	Men	Women	Men	Women	Men	Women	Men	Women
18-34	29.7	22.4	28.1	26.7	54.5	51	42.4	36.1
35-54	34	33	41.7	32.1	54.2	52.3	45.9	39.4
55 and older	31.8	19.6	40.4	37.6	38.5	33.3	35	25.0*
Average	32.0	23.1*	35.3	28.5	51.5	47.8	48.2	33.4*

*Statistically significant at the .05 level.

Note: Figures represent the percent who indicate they did *at least* one of the following in 1980 campaign: attended a rally or campaign meeting, worked for a candidate or party, tried to influence another person's vote decision, displayed a poster or wore a button, gave money to a candidate or party.

Source of data: Center for Political Studies, 1980 American National Election Study. Figures compiled by the authors.

to report having attended a campaign meeting or rally or worked for a candidate than corresponding groups of men.[121] Additionally, other studies of campaign activity reveal the difference between the sexes with respect to influencing another's vote has been the case in every presidential campaign since 1952.[122] Indeed, with the lone exception of influencing another's vote, women have nearly equaled, and college women exceeded, the level of campaign participation by men in many of the presidential election campaigns since 1960.[123]

One possible reason for this difference may be found in the relative preparation of men and women for this kind of participation. As we saw earlier, although campaign interest among at least the well-educated men and women has become more nearly equal over time, there still exists a significant difference in attention to media reports about politics. We speculate that this lack of attention is correlated with and possibly results in women's much lower levels of information about politics as well as their low confidence in their own understanding of it.[124] Thus, it seems that many women's more limited knowledge and confidence may be important factors in explaining why some do not engage in influencing as readily as men. In this respect it is interesting to note that among young, college-educated men and women, where attention to the media, information, and corresponding confidence in one's understanding are more nearly equal, the difference between the sexes in reported attempts to influence others' votes is also similar.[125] Some have even offered as another possible explanation for women's relative reluctance to convince others about how to vote the reluctance of men to give weight to their pronouncements on politics.[126]

Although lack of psychological preparation may explain the difference between men and women with respect to influencing another's vote, a different barrier can also be relevant for some women—conflict between parental and political roles. An examination of the campaign participation of college-educated men and women over the life cycle reveals that young women with no children actually were nearly as active in the 1976 presidential campaign as young men. There is, however, a noticeable decline in activity for women who have preschool children as illustrated in Figure 4–1. This decline results in a large gap in activity between parents of young children.[127]

Additionally, although women's campaign activity continues to lag behind men, both among parents of school-aged children and older citizens, an examination of individual campaign acts reveals that in these groups, the male lead is a function of two previously discussed activities—influencing another's vote and contributing money. Among parents of preschool children, however, mothers fall behind fathers in *all* activities. While it is difficult to explain this phenomenon, the most obvious reason would seem to be the lack of time for campaign participation. While young mothers can participate in community work, the disruptiveness and long hours associated with campaign activity are apparently more difficult to manage.[128]

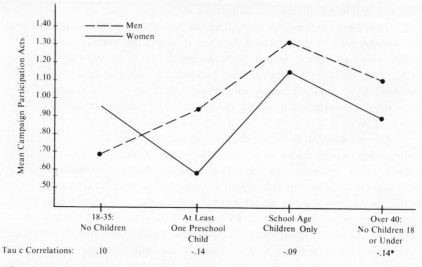

Tau c Correlations: .10   -.14   -.09   -.14*

*Statistically significant at the .05 level.

Note: Mean scores shown based on an N size of at least 60.

Source of data: Center for Political Studies, 1976 American National Election Study. Figures compiled by the authors.

Figure 4-1.   Mean Campaign Participation Acts of College-Trained Men and Women: 1976

We should note, however, that not only participation, but also the difference between the sexes in interest and attention to the campaign appears to be greater among young parents than it is in other life-cycle groups. This suggests a more pervasive role conflict than that which can be attributed to a lack of time. As we shall see in our discussion of women in political office, this delayed start by young mothers in partisan politics has important implications for their ability to compete equally with men in other aspects of electoral politics.

WOMEN AND "DIRTY WORK"

One last point is in order. Studies of campaign and party workers seem to substantiate the widespread belief that women who take an active part in campaign affairs are assigned menial tasks such as stuffing and addressing envelopes and making "get out the vote" telephone calls, although this may be changing.[129] According to Moon Landrieu, a former mayor of New Orleans,

"Women do the lickin' and the stickin' while men plan the strategy."[130] Surveys of women who should know, those who are active in electoral politics, find widespread agreement that male leaders discriminate against women party members. The Center for American Women in Politics (CAWP) interviews of elected officials found that in every category of elected office, nearly three-quarters of the women interviewed agreed that "Many men in party organizations try to keep women out of leadership roles."[131] While a study done by Ellen Boneparth suggests this may be changing, especially in campaigns with women candidates,[132] the Capitol Hill Woman's Political Caucus reported that even in 1976 few women—10 of 69—had held the important jobs on presidential campaign staffs. In commenting on these latter findings, Miriam Dorsey, head of the Caucus, said, "Women definitely play a much more significant role than they ever have in the past, but if women think they hold the real power, they're kidding themselves."[133] With the possible exception of the Anderson campaign, the 1980 presidential campaign staffs also had few women in important decision-making roles.[134] This disparity in the nature of male and female work in campaigns indicates that even though the overall figures in campaign participation are approaching parity, unequal treatment of women by political organizers continues to produce something less than full equality.

Thus, there are several factors preventing women from exercising completely their political rights vis-a-vis campaign activity. First, for some women, generally the less well educated, cultural barriers continue to prevent full participation. Second, for others, such as young college-educated mothers, a more limited kind of cultural constriction—role conflict between motherhood and political activity—at least temporarily causes them to fall behind men in their campaign participation. Third, women more generally seem to be inadequately prepared, relative to similar groups of men, for a particular kind of campaign activity—influencing others' votes, although our data on young women and Fulenwider's on feminists suggest this may be changing.[135] Finally, discrimination by organizers of campaigns often relegates even active women to inferior and menial work. Decision-making posts generally remain in the hands of men. This last point is critical for it helps to explain why the disparity between men and women in important party positions and electoral offices is so much greater than it is on the level of ordinary campaign work.

WOMEN AND THE POLITICAL PARTIES

It is not only in political campaigns that women often play secondary roles. The position of women in the actual organizational structure of the political parties also has been quite restricted. Although at the time of suffrage, both major parties created women's divisions or bureaus and instituted regulations requiring each state to be represented on the national committees by a man and a woman, little real power was granted to women. As Eleanor Roosevelt commented, "Fifty-fifty looks better on paper than it has worked out in practice."[136] Although women achieved some influence during the Roosevelt era, their position soon declined. Today it still appears that women have to work harder and longer (in terms of years) if they want to achieve a position of importance in the party.[137] While these differences between men and women activists may reflect a difference in ambitions and goals (women are less likely than men activists to desire electoral office, especially at high levels—although equally likely to want party office),[138] a more compelling explanation may be the stereotypes and discriminatory practices of male party leaders. According to Millicent Fenwick, former Representative from New Jersey, "When those smoke filled rooms open, there's hardly ever a woman inside."[139]

As noted in Chapter 3, the National Women's Political Caucus (NWPC) was formed in 1971, in part, to combat this discrimination. Since then, the Caucus, working with women in the parties, has had an important impact on the position of women in the organizations. Dramatic improvement has come at the level of the national party conventions, particularly in the Democratic party. Since 1968, with the adoption of Democratic party reforms, women have gone from roughly 14 percent of all Democratic delegates to better than 30 percent in 1972 and 1976 and 50 percent in 1980.[140]

Republican women have had notably less success in achieving parity in numbers, although they played an important role in their party's abandonment of its support for the ERA, its call for a constitutional amendment banning abortions, and the inclusion of a plank prohibiting the appointment of prochoice judges in its 1980 party platform. In fact, it is important to note that many women active in the Republican party, including Phyllis Schlafly, have close ties to or leadership roles in anti groups. It was this increasing move to the "right" by the Republican party that prompted Mary Crisp, the cochair of the Republican National Committee, to resign from that position.

Interestingly, Crisp and other women from both parties found a more receptive welcome for their efforts in the campaign of the independent candidate, John Anderson. Crisp even became the cochair of this effort. Women also had prominent positions in some of the other minor parties' presidential campaigns. For example, activist La Donna Harris was the vice-presidential nominee of the Citizen's Party. Thus, although the barriers to women's participation in the parties are declining as is evidenced by the fact that in 1982 both the executive director of the National Republican Congressional Committee and the political director of the Democratic National Committee were women, the overall position of women within both parties is far from equal at the highest ranks. Additionally, when it comes to obtaining their party's endorsement for elective office, women also have faced difficulties.

WOMEN IN ELECTIVE OFFICE

Women have long been severely underrepresented in elective office. During any single year between 1917 and 1970, women never constituted more than 5 percent (and generally far fewer) of the members of the U.S. Congress or of the state legislatures.[141] Although by 1983, this percentage rose considerably, women generally still held less than 10 percent of the positions of most elective bodies. Thus, by 1983, there were, for example, only twenty-three women in Congress (two in the Senate and twenty-one in the House) and no state governors. In state legislatures, while women have made dramatic gains since 1968 when only 4 percent of all officeholders were women, they still only constituted 13 percent of all members in 1983[142] (see Figure 4-2). Interestingly, It should be noted that a record number of women actually sought elective office in November 1982: 56 for the U.S. Senate and House and 1,666 for the state legislatures.[143]

This progress, in terms of the women's rights movement, however, is tempered by the fact that many of the women elected of late openly oppose many policies advocated by the women's movement. Senator Paula Hawkins (R-Florida), for example, has taken stands against the ERA and abortion. She exemplifies the kind of women the Republican National Committee (RNC) has actively attempted to recruit. In fact, the RNC has funded, trained, and supported many conservative women, especially on the state level. Since most women candidates lack political experience and the ability to raise funds, this assistance can be credited with the phenomenal success of the Republican party in getting women elected. In 1978, 63 of the 66 women elected for the first time to state legislative offices were Republican.[144]

Yet, there is still a wide disparity between the number of men and women in public office compared to the more nearly equal participation of the sexes in the other aspects of political activity. As in our examination of other types of political activity, the obstacles that keep women out of political office seem to fall in roughly three categories: cultural stereotypes, especially role conflict, inadequate preparation, and discrimination. Although most of these barriers have been eliminated or weakened in the other areas of political activity, they continue to be much more powerful vis-a-vis political office.

These barriers act in two ways to keep the numbers of women in elective office low: first, they deter many women from running for office and second, they keep others who run from succeeding. Studies of women who actually seek elective office indicate that the first set of hurdles can be the most formidable. It has been found that when women run against men, the rate of electoral success of men and women is nearly equal. R. Darcy and Sarah Slavin Schramm, for example, found no significant difference in the percentage of the vote received by men and women candidates for Congress when party and incumbency of opponent and candidate were controlled.[145] Similar results were obtained in a comparison of men and women running for

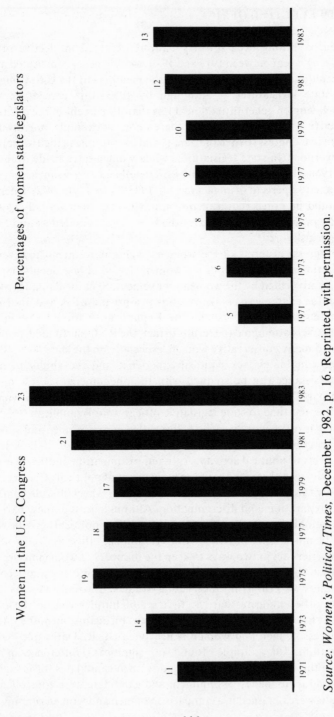

Percentages of women state legislators

Women in the U.S. Congress

Source: Women's Political Times, December 1982, p. 16. Reprinted with permission.

Figure 4-2. Recent Increases in Women Elected Officials: Congress and State Legislatures

other political offices.[146] An important question, therefore, is why have so few women sought elected office in the first place?

Barriers to Running

As the section on public attitudes revealed, many people continue to have considerable reservations about women holding elective office. As late as 1978, almost one-third of the public agreed with the statement, "Women should take care of running their homes and leave running the country up to men."[147] Even among women active in electoral politics, there are many who do "not necessarily" agree that "more women should run for public office in the future."[148]

The notion that women should not hold elected positions no doubt keeps many women from "throwing their hats in the ring." They simply do not believe it is appropriate behavior for a woman. Even those who reject this stereotype may choose to channel their energies elsewhere rather than face potential social sanctions. For instance, majorities or near-majorities of women politicans interviewed by the CAWP at every level of office agreed, "In general, voters are more reluctant to support women candidates."[149] Marcia Manning Lee also found that among women who were active in electoral politics, and thus, might consider running for office, more than three-quarters felt that "most men would prefer women to contribute to politics in ways other than running for elected office" and almost half thought most women would also be of this opinion.[150]

These cultural prohibitions against running and their resultant impact on the number of women contesting office are even more important for women of childbearing age because of the fairly widespread public agreement that a woman would have to neglect her children to be active in politics. Acceptance of this attitude keeps many women from seeking office when their children are young. According to one woman state legislator who had postponed running until her children were older: "To be very frank, I couldn't have done it. I really couldn't have been an effective legislator if my children were little. I'm just not of that temperament. I would have carried too much of a load of guilt."[151] Men, however, do not appear to hold these same reservations.[152]

Even if a woman could reject or overcome the alleged incompatibility of the two roles, she might not run for office for fear of the public's or her own family's negative reaction. Mothers of young children who have contested office tell many stories about the hostile and snide question asked by voters about who was taking care of their children.[153] This has often been a particular problem for women who run for national office, which necessitates a move to Washington, D.C. In several such instances, the women's opponents have sought to picture them as "abandoning their families."[154] Empirical evidence strongly indicates that some or all of these conditions associated with motherhood do act as a strong deterrent in keeping young women out of elected office. For example, half of the women in Jeane Kirkpatrick's study of female state legislators had run for office only after their children were grown and only one had attempted it when she had a child under six.[155] A more recent examination of male and female politicians by the CAWP found that the majority of women in every office have no children under eighteen years of age, and far fewer women than men were parents of young children.[156] There is some suggestion that the limiting influence of children is more pronounced if the public office held involves spending some time away from home. For example, 35 percent of the men but only 16 percent of the female state legislators in the CAWP study had children under twelve. No difference in ages or number of children was found in a sample of men and women school-board members.[157]

Evidence that women delay or fail to contemplate seeking elective office until their children are able to take care of themselves can also be seen in the age profiles of elected officials. Every study to date has found that women are older than men when they first run for elected office.[158] As we saw in the last section, this conflict between parenthood and politics channels many women away from not only elected office but also away from partisan or campaign activity, at least while children are young. As Lee notes, this late start in partisan politics per se has important ramifications on their eventual success in getting elected:

> The discouraging effect of children on women's desire to seek public office also greatly restricts their ability to run for office after the children have left home. Because of children, women may fail to gain the experience in their twenties, thirties, and early forties that their male counterparts are acquiring. When, at last, they are free, they may lack the political know-how and connections to effectively compete against the more experienced men. In short, most men interested in politics get a head start and it is very difficult for women to catch up.[159]

Thus, the conflict between parental roles and partisan politics, especially elective office, partially explains why so few women hold elective office. Not only does the presence of children cause some women not to run, but also, for others, the lag in involvement means that women are often less well prepared to contest office should they decide to run after their children are grown.

One other closely related aspect of role conflict that keeps many women out of politics is spousal preference. Surveys of political office-holders of both sexes find evidence that acceptance of political activity by one's spouse and family is more critical for a woman than it is for a man in deciding to run for political office. Again, this may be especially true for offices that require relocating or considerable time away from home.[160] Commenting on the higher reported support by spouses and families of female legislators, the authors of one study concluded:

It is likely that women whose families disapprove of their political activity fail to seek office in the first place, resulting in a high degree of family support among those who enter office. Men, taking for granted positive sanctions for public activity, perhaps viewing such activity as an important adjunct to their occupations or as their primary career commitment, are less likely to seek family approval before entry into politics.[161]

Similarly, in Kirkpatrick's study of women state legislators, all the married women agreed that the most important requirement for successfully managing a family and a political career was a cooperative husband. According to one woman legislator,

> I don't think a woman should even get into this if her husband isn't a secure person, confident of himself and his accomplishments and his ego and so on. If it is going to be a threat to your husband then you get into it with the risk of your marriage. If your husband is a strong man and self-confident and approves of your activities, it can be great.[162]

It is very likely that one of the reasons why so few women ran for office before the 1970s was that marriages in which a husband would provide the necessary support for a wife who wanted to be active in politics (or in other careers outside the home) were rare. One of the benefits of the women's movement and a factor in the rise in the number of women in office may well be the growth of the idea of shared marriages where both partners have careers and split family and housekeeping responsibilities. However, there are still only a few of these relationships. As Illinois State Representative Susan Catania notes, "It's just a fact of life that political husbands have not developed in as large numbers as political wives."[163]

Socialization of women into occupations that are either incompatible with a political career or are perceived as such by officials who supervise the candidate selection process also limits the potential number of female office seekers. For instance, the most traditional female career, that of homemaker, as the comments above make clear, is often incompatible with politics. The homemaker without young children at home and with a supportive spouse, however, may have an advantage over the employed man or women.[164] Similarly, other traditionally female occupations are less congruent with politics than are the more male-dominated professions. In particular, the difficulty women in the past had in obtaining law degrees has resulted in only a few female attorneys, and law is the career that a large percentage of politicans use as a springboard to public office. In general, occupations chosen by women are often less conducive to office holding than are those opted for by men. Susan Welch presents convincing evidence that the relative paucity of women from the "eligible pool" of potential political candidates is an important reason, although not the only one, for their absence from state legislatures, especially in the "upper" or more prestigious houses.[165] Commenting on this problem, the authors of the CAWP report concluded:

The occupational skills of women may not be perceived and acknowledged as conferring competence for political office *because* they involve tasks executed by women and may be either unfamiliar to or automatically devalued by influential males. Moreover, women's occupations may well be characterized by lower probabilities of exposure to politically active individuals and networks. Therefore, there is some reason to suspect that the occupations of women, *regardless* of their formal prestige or intrinsic skills, are not as likely as those of men to aid recruitment to office and political mobility.[166]

The growing number of women with full-time careers in traditionally male professions, especially the law, may result in more women being elected to office. It is interesting to note that in recent sessions of Congress, an increasing number of the women have been young lawyers who are either unmarried or the mothers of young children. There is some evidence that this type of individual not only has been able to overcome traditional stereotypes about women, motherhood, and politics, but also experiences an easier time with her male colleagues because her background and legal training is similar to theirs.[167]

Cultural dictates also have kept many women from receiving adequate preparation for contesting political office. Because women are socialized to eschew politics or at least to maintain only minimal involvement in it, and because those who do become interested tend to channel their energies into local community nonpartisan work, women often lack the confidence and information necessary to run for office. Lee found that among men and women politically active in New York's Westchester County, only women with a high sense of political confidence ran for office.[168] Kirkpatrick's study presents further evidence of how a lack of confidence can affect the number of female candidates. She found that 60 percent of the female legislators waited to be asked to run.[169] This tendency of women to wait to be asked may contribute to their low numbers in politics. According to Sissy Farenthold, a former gubernatorial candidate in Texas, "For any woman who wants to go into politics, I advise that she run first. If she waits to be drafted, she won't ever make it to the legislature."[170]

For some, the problem may be inadequate political party experience and work rather than a lack of information and confidence. Several authors have found that female candidates are much more likely to receive a party's nomination for office if they have been active in party affairs.[171] This activity seems less necessary for men.[172] Party experience, it appears, often substitutes for the "weaker" occupational or educational background of women.[173] Greater need for party experience, coupled with the fact that women often avoid partisan work, results in a small pool of potential female candidates. Although some evidence shows that women may be able to translate their community work into the experience necessary for political office, problems exist with this tactic. Women active in the League of Women Voters, for instance, must sever all ties with the organaization when they run for office. Former League members are denied even the moral support of that organization because of its policy of not endorsing any candidates. Other women's organizations rarely have the financial ability to support a candidate—at least when compared to male-dominated groups.

Because women, even women active in public affairs, often are insufficiently prepared to run for political office, groups like the NWPC and the National Women's Education Fund, an organization founded to increase the proportion and influence of women in politics through education, have been formed. Both of these organizations have developed programs to train women in the necessary skills to conduct political campaigns and get elected to office. Often the job of these organizations involves convincing women they have the necessary qualifications for running.

Yet another barrier that keeps many women from contesting elected office is discrimination by male party leaders. As we noted, it is often difficult to document the existence and importance of this barrier to political office holding by women. It seems clear that sex discrimination was a more potent problem for women before the 1970s. But even today, the citizenry seems aware that the parties are reluctant to nominate women, and it appears that well-informed individuals are even more likely than the average citizen to know of such discrimination.[174] Mandel notes that there often appears to be a hidden "quota" on the number or percentage of women that male politicians and the public will accept in public office.[175] Interviews with women who run for office are full of comments about how political leaders ignored their request to be placed in nomination or failed to support them against male candidates in the primary or general election.[176] The parties seem particularly reluctant to nominate a woman for prestigious or powerful offices. When women do get party support, it often is to run for positions that men do not want. In states such as New Hampshire, where the legislative bodies are large, provide low pay, and have little power, there are many more women legislators than in states like New York, where the legislature is small, powerful, and well paid. Political party leaders are also apparently quite willing to nominate a woman when the prospects for victory are low.[177] As Bella Abzug once observed, "Most women who do get backing are running in districts that the party feels are impossible to win. If the race begins to look winnable, prominent male politicians move right in."[178]

Another situation where women have enjoyed a kind of relative success has occurred after the death of an office-holding husband. Indeed, most of the women who served in the U.S. Congress prior to World War II were widows of former representatives.[179] Often, however, these women were expected to be caretakers and not seek election in their own right. Of those who later contested election for the position they held, few won. As Diane Kincaid has documented, the vast majority of congressional widows faced primary or general election opponents, and many were defeated in their efforts to run for their husbands' congressional seats.[180] One notable exception to this trend was Rep. Lindy Boggs (D-Louisiana). After the disappearance of her husband in a flight over Alaska, the widow of the House Majority Leader was appointed to his seat and subsequently elected to this position in 1974. In a more traditional vein were the actions of Senators Muriel Humphrey (D-Minnesota) who declined to seek election after serving out the unexpired portion of her husband's senatorial term and Maryon Allen (D-Alabama). In 1978, Allen unsuccessfully sought election to her deceased husband's seat in the U.S. Senate.

Before concluding this section, we should note that there is a growing body of evidence that as more women run for office, some of the above barriers weaken. The success of other women, in particular, seems to provide a role model for still other women, encouraging them to run for office.[181] The public's resistance to women also apparently lessens when elected women perform successfully in office (although it should be pointed out that when one women fails to live up to the public's expectations, it can hurt other women candidates). Susan A. McManus, for example, has found that one-third of the persons sampled in Houston acquired positive, personal attitude changes toward women in politics generally on account of their perception of the excellent performance of the city comptroller, now mayor, Kathy Whitmire. Perhaps her most significant finding was that attitudinal change was unrelated to the socioeconomic or ideological backgrounds of her respondents.[182]

Barriers Preventing Success

Widows who have served out the remainder of their husbands' terms often have not been "qualified" in the traditional sense. Also, at times, some wives have agreed to serve out the remainder of their husbands' terms to spare a governor from making a controversial or politically untimely appointment. Consequently, when they sought office on their own, some became the immediate targets of party regulars. They, and other females as well, face an uphill battle. In commenting on the problems that Jeannette Rankin (D-Missouri), the first woman elected to Congress in 1916 encountered, her campaign manager said to her:

> I am shocked at the prejudice that exists against a woman going to Congress.... The biggest campaign of education that is going to be required is to the effect that a woman can...do the work there and should be sent there, rather than the question of you, individually going. Were it not for "the prejudice" there would be nothing to it. That prejudice, however, is substantial.[183]

Even today women still face much of this same kind of prejudice. During her successful gubernatorial race in 1974, Ella Grasso, for example, confronted an opponent whose slogan proclaimed, "CONNECTICUT CAN'T AFFORD A WOMAN GOVERNOR." Because of these kinds of attitudes, many women try to downplay their sex. It has been reported that one woman candidate, for instance, wore only grey suits during her campaign to force the public and her opponent to deal with her positions on the issues and not her femininity.[184] Others claim it is often difficult to get the media to treat them as serious candidates and not fashion copy or freaks. In contrast, some female candidates feel that their uniqueness benefits them by making the public more aware of who they are. A few think women candidates may profit in the post-Watergate era because as former Rep. Yvonne Braithwaite Burke has noted, "There is a built-in feeling that women are honest."[185]

There is some evidence that the press and the public have begun to ignore the gender of the candidate.[186] But for women with young children, public hostility can still be intense. Some have opted to keep their families out of their campaign; still others have confronted the issue head on. Rep. Patricia Schroeder (D-Colorado) once began her speeches with the following disclaimer about her husband and young children: "Hi there, I'm that radical you've all heard about, who doesn't shave under her armpits and leaps over barricades screaming obscenities. I keep both children in the freezer, and my husband is short, has feathers, and goes 'cluck, cluck.'"[187] Although this tactic worked for Schroeder, it is not an approach that other women are likely to use or one with which they would feel comfortable.

The most important problem for female candidates, however, appears to be the lack of organization support, especially money, rather than the public's reaction to their candidacy. Without party workers and funds, a female candidate often has to build her own organization and seek out contributors. Such efforts obviously reduce the time available for campaigning.

Another problem traditionally encountered by many women who try to put together a campaign organization is their lack of political experience. In commenting on her efforts to become mayor of Syracuse, New York, Karen DeCrow, a former president of NOW, recalled how little knowledge of such matters she had: "I realized that I had been completely unschooled in the kinds of skills that people need to run for public office. These are skills that a lot of men get in business... public speaking, debating skills, the ability to handle the media without quaking in your boots, and the ability to handle a hostile situation."[188] Increasingly, however, women find that other women and women's organizations are willing to work for them because they are women. The efforts of the NWPC and similar groups to school women in the finer points of campaign management are also beginning to pay off. As former Rep. Elizabeth Holtzman (D-New York) noted, "In some ways it's easier for women to run today [1980] than it was when I first ran 10 years ago. There are other women who've done it, and these role models make politics easier to consider. Also, women's groups are better organized and more prepared to help with campaigns."[189] Holtzman's own political career supports her statement. When she first ran for the elective office in 1970, she received no help from the women's movement, but in her 1980 senatorial race, although she failed to win, she received money and organizational support from NOW, the Women's Campaign Fund, and numerous other women's associations.[190]

There appears to be almost universal agreement among women candidates, however, that it is more difficult for women than men to obtain the funds needed to run. The problem seems to stem from the expectation by party leaders and traditional campaign contributors about the seriousness and potential success of female candidates. As *Time* magazine notes, "It becomes a catch-22 situation: women find it hard to attract heavy contributions because they seem less likely to win than male opponents, and women are less likely to win because they cannot raise big money."[191]

The money woes of women at the federal level are exacerbated by the rising cost of campaigns—$500,000 for a House seat and $1 million for a Senate race are not unusual. Campaign finance laws that prohibit candidates from borrowing or receiving more than $5,000 from their spouses, although candidates themselves can use unlimited amounts to fund their own campaigns, also hamper women's races. Because in many marriages the family's assets are in the husband's name, a married man who runs for office has greater access to the family's resources than does a married woman candidate. As Representative Geraldine Ferraro, who had to sell her own property and take out personal loans to raise money for her campaign, laments, "Unfortunately, that's the way women have to do it. Women have got to learn to write checks for other women."[192]

Recent efforts by groups such as NOW, the National Women's Political Caucus, and the Women's Campaign Fund, however, may help to alleviate the financial obstacles faced by women candidates. NOW, for example, collected over 3 million dollars to spend on feminist[193] candidates in the 1982 election.[194] Additionally, in 1982, NOW had eight political action committees (PACs) operating in thirty-nine states to assist NOW-supported candidates. A third of NOW's campaign dollars were targeted on state and local campaigns.

The National Abortion Rights Action League's (NARAL) PAC additionally conducted a million dollar fund-raising drive to assist prochoice candidates.[195] Thus, in the wake of the ERA defeat and attempts to restrict reproductive freedom, NOW and several other groups plan to continue to channel large sums of money to prowomen's rights candidates. The determination of these groups to become more involved in political campaigns, particularly now that monies no longer need be spent on the ERA ratification effort, may signal a major change in electoral politics.

For example, during the last year of the ratification effort, NOW received close to one million dollars a month in contributions. According to Eleanor Smeal, the immediate past president of NOW, those dollars will now be spent on electing feminist candidates.[196] Thus, this kind of support for feminist candidates, particularly if it is targeted on female candidates, could eventually make a major difference in the numbers of women elected each year at all levels of government.

Women as Elected Officials

Election to public office often does not end a woman's problems. Interviews with female public officials indicate that many of the barriers to election also may act to keep women in secondary positions once in office. At least some of the difficulties encountered in achieving positions of authority or power in an elected body are the result of a lack of seniority, often due to the fact that many women delay seeking office until their children are raised. As positions of power in legislatures are often gained according to length of time served, this late start means women are at a disadvantage. Kirkpatrick claims that the high turnover in most state legislatures may mean this is not always a problem at that level, but it is obviously a great barrier for women in Congress. There, seniority is important, and the number of terms served by women has tended to be far fewer than those served by men.[197]

Perhaps a more serious problem women officials experience is discrimination by fellow politicians. Kirkpatrick's study of "effective" female state legislators reports rather widespread agreement among the women that they encountered some problems in office because of their gender. Their difficulties fell into several categories. Fairly common were reports of symbolic "put downs," including being referred to as "the sweetheart of the chamber," and being excluded from some of the after-hours male get-togethers where important decisions are often made. Women also reported that they had to work harder than men to get recognition from their male colleagues, yet women had to be careful not to appear too aggressive as this was perceived as unfeminine. The most serious problem, and one widely recognized by the women, was that the men in control of the legislature often tried to keep women out of the positions of power. The women who broke into leadership positions usually had to fight male prejudice in order to get there.[198]

The problems are not limited to women at the state level. Interviews with women members of the U.S. Congress as recently as 1980 noted many of the same difficulties. Former Rep. Elizabeth Holtzman recalls being asked to make coffee by a male senator. Additionally, Rep. Majorie Holt (R-Maryland) has recounted how one of her colleagues could only comment on the pretty dresses she wore, and another promised to "give [her] a big kiss" if she would support a bill he wanted passed.[199]

Attitudes of men, however, appear to be changing, especially toward the new breed of women legislators who often are drawn from the same mold as the typical male legislators. Rep. Ferraro, for instance, is quoted as saying, "[I have] worked hard to establish [my] credentials as a lawyer and now as a legislator. I've been in a male profession for 20 years as a lawyer and a prosecutor. I'm not having any problems."[200]

For other women officials, however, stereotypes appear to persist and the resultant discrimination by male officials often means elected female officials find that they have to work harder and longer to gain the acceptance of their male colleagues. Comments New York State Senator Linda Winikow, "We women have to work twice as hard to prove that we're worthy."[201]

Most of the women who are elected, however, think they are more than adequately prepared for their jobs. Indeed, there is agreement among the women in both the CAWP and Kirkpatrick studies that they are in *some* ways better public officials than are their male colleagues. On the plus side, majorities of women at all levels of public office agree that "Women in office generally devote more time to the job than do men," and that "Women in office are better at the 'human relations' aspect of the job." These beliefs, moreover, are supported by the actual reports of male and female officials regarding the number of hours a week they spend on their legislative work and the reported emphasis they give to constituents' problems. Both these advantages seem to be linked to role differences between men and women. The greater free time to devote to the office is a function of the fact that more men than women public officials hold down other jobs besides their political one. A comparison of men and women legislators who hold additional nonlegislative jobs, however, found no difference in the hours they devoted to their legislative work.[202] The greater receptivitiy to constituents' needs, also found in Kirkpatrick's study, seems to follow from the different backgrounds and recruitment paths of males and females in public office. The greater experience of women in problem-solving, cooperative-community organizations apparently carries over into the approach of women to their careers as public officials.[203]

The picture is, however, not all positive. One-third of all public officials polled in the CAWP study agreed, "In general, women in office are not as politically astute as men," and one-third of the men and one-fifth of the women were of the opinion that "Women officeholders' qualifications and training usually are not as good as men's." Not surprisingly, given cultural attitudes and socialization, women public officials seem particularly hesitant about their financial and economic judgment.[204]

With respect to women's issues, the data concerning commitment, effectiveness, and power of elected women appear mixed. In the early 1970s, Kirkpatrick found little support for the women's liberation movement or its policy goals among female state legislators, although almost all favored the ERA.[205] Women in Congress, however, formed a Congresswomen's Caucus, in part, to concentrate their efforts on common, women's concerns.[206] A recent study suggests, moreover, that the more liberal women members of the House of Representatives may indeed be voting as a bloc.[207] Commenting on this trend, the author of the study notes, "The emergence of 'liberal' unity among Congressmen can easily be argued to be the result of a feminist coalition—if not truly 'feminist' in orientation, at least a coalition of feminist members of the House."[208] In this same vein, most major pieces of national legislation affecting women in the 1970s were introduced or sponsored by women legislators.

The mere existence of an activist group of women and the Congress-women's Caucus may help to increase the power of women members not only on feminist issues but also as a group in their dealings on other matters with their male colleagues. For example, the woman who led the ERA ratification effort in the Georgia Assembly believes that female legislators have earned the respect of many of their colleagues, even those against the amendment, that works to the advantage of women in getting other important pieces of legislation approved.

Thus, even in elected office, men and women are not yet equal. Women still face barriers to equality and they bring to their job the legacy of a different socialization experience and public service background. Only a few women have been able to overcome the obstacles to participation in this area. Considerable change in the attitudes of the public, party leaders, and women themselves must be forthcoming before women can fully exercise all their political rights. However, it appears that the presence of popular women in elective positions substantially raises the public's perception of other female candidates. Given this finding, it is possible that with the growing number of women officeholders, public perceptions may change quite dramatically in a relatively short period of time.

WOMEN IN APPOINTED POSITIONS

Many of the problems faced by women in elective office also apply to women in appointive governmental positions. Until recently, women have made few inroads in this area. Franklin D. Roosevelt was the first president to appoint a woman to a cabinet level position—Frances Perkins as Secretary of Labor in 1933. Only seven other women have ever held cabinet positions (Oveta Culp Hobby, Health Education and Welfare (HEW), 1953–1955; Carla Hills Housing and Urban Development (HUD), 1975–1977; Juanita Kreps, Commerce, 1977–1979; Patricia Roberts Harris, HUD, 1977–1979, HEW, 1979–1980; Shirley Hufstedler, Education, 1979–1980; Elizabeth Dole, Transportation, 1983–; and Margaret Heckler, Health and Human Services, 1983–) out of the 500 plus individuals who have served as department secretaries. Carter's appointments of Kreps and Harris as original members of his cabinet made him the first president to select more than one woman to fill these important positions. Moreover, he followed up these appointments with the appointment of 52 subcabinet level positions during his first 16 months in office. Ronald Reagan also appointed two women in his cabinet but nominated only forty-one women to subcabinet level positions, although Jeane Kirkpatrick was appointed U.S. representative to the United Nations.[209] Additionally, the National Women's Political Caucus has charged that many of the early Reagan appointments (before Dole and Heckler) "aren't power appointments.... And they're often women's jobs: treasurer of the United States, director of the women's bureau. Carter made substantive appointments."[210]

President Carter also nominated more women to serve on the federal bench than any other president in the nation's history. When Congress passed the Omnibus Judgeship Act in 1977, which authorized the creation of 152 new federal judgeships, the National Woman's Political Caucus and the Coalition for Women's Appointments—an umbrella group composed of fifty women's organizations—began to pressure the Carter administration to appoint women to these new seats on the bench. These efforts and the commitment of the Carter administration to finding and appointing qualified female jurists ultimately led to the appointment of forty new women to the federal bench bringing the total to forty-six.[211]

It should be noted, however, that while President Carter appointed all eleven women who serve on the Court of Appeals, only 14 percent (n = 29) of his 203 district court appointees were female.[212] At the district court level, the custom of senatorial courtesy, which allows senators a potential veto over court appointments made in their states, provides an opportunity for individual senators to discriminate against prospective female nominees. While several women's groups are trying to identify those senators who consistently pass over qualified women and then pressure them to stop this practice, recently they have met with only limited success, particularly given President Reagan's failure to even consider most women. Although Reagan did appoint the first woman, Sandra Day O'Connor, to the Supreme Court, during his first sixteen months in office he appointed only three women to fill the sixty-five lower court vacancies that became available.[213]

The impact of women judges appointed in the 1970s, however, is only beginning to be studied. Thomas G. Walker has found that Carter's female appointees to the federal district court are not as supportive of women's rights issues as their male counterparts.[214] Their very presence on the bench, however, particularly at the Court of Appeals level, could make other jurists more sensitive to problems of sex discrimination.[215] And, it appears clear that during her first term on the United States Supreme Court, Sandra Day O'Connor, although generally voting with the conservative bloc of the Court, adopted positions advocated by women's right's activists in gender-based discrimination cases 66 percent of the time.[216] Perhaps most importantly, the simple fact that large numbers of women have been appointed to the federal bench could prompt more women to run for state court judgeships and/or lead to wider public acceptance of women in these positions, particularly if McManus' findings are not an isolated occurrence. Ultimately, however, the number of women in appointed positions (both judicial and executive) will depend on the president. While Ronald Reagan initially showed little inclination to repeat his predecessor's practice of naming significant numbers of women to important positions, his behavior in 1983 began to indicate an awareness of the need to recognize women if he and the Republicans want to be rewarded with their votes at the polls.

THE FUTURE OF WOMEN IN POLITICS

At the beginning of this chapter, we suggested there were three interrelated barriers that prevented women from fully exercising their political rights when these rights were first obtained: (1) negative cultural stereotypes about the role of women in politics; (2) the lack of preparation on the part of women for political activity; and, (3) discrimination by male political leaders. As the discussion of various political activities has shown, these obstacles have gradually diminished in the last sixty years. Indeed, with respect to certain citizen-level activities, women today face few difficulties in participating on an equal footing with men. As we moved beyond the realm of citizen activity, however, we found the barriers to political activity, while diminished in strength since 1920, were still often formidable. Large segments of the public still do not approve of women, especially mothers, devoting considerable time to politics. There even remains considerable doubt about whether women are capable of handling certain political roles. As an indirect result of these attitudes, women tend not to be as psychologically involved, informed, or efficacious vis-a-vis politics as men. In addition, women continue to face discrimination by male politicans who either continue to believe these older cultural stereotypes themselves or, at least, think the public does. The women's movement has begun to make gains in the last ten years, especially among the college educated and young, in breaking down these remaining barriers. It is not likely, however, that all the remaining obstacles will be totally eliminated in the immediate future.

NOTES

1.   Unless otherwise indicated, the data analyzed in this chapter were made avaialable by the Inter-University Consortium for Political and Social Research. The data for 1967 are from Sidney Verba and Norman H. Nie's study, *Participation in America,* conducted by the National Opinion Research Center of the University of

Chicago. The data for the American National Election Studies in 1972, 1976, and 1980 were originally collected by the Center for Political Studies of the Institute for Social Research, the University of Michigan, under grants from the National Science Foundation. Neither the original collectors of the data nor the Consortium bears any responsibility for the analyses or interpretations presented here.

2. William H. Chafe, *The American Woman: Her Changing Social, Economic, and Political Role; 1920–1970* (New York: Oxford University Press, 1972), pp. 27–29.

3. Ibid., pp. 29–30.

4. Charles Merriam and Harold Gosnell, *Non-Voting: Causes and Methods of Control* (Chicago: University of Chicago Press, 1924), pp. ix and 7.

5. John J. Stucker, "Women as Voters: Their Maturation as Political Persons in American Society," in Marianne Githens and Jewel L. Prestage, eds., *A Portrait of Marginality: The Political Behavior of the American Woman* (New York: David McKay, 1977), pp. 271–273.

6. Emmy E. Werner, "Women in Congress: 1917–1964," *The Western Political Quarterly* 19 (March 1966):20. See also, Diane D. Kincaid, "Over His Dead Body: A Positive Perspective on Widows in the U.S. Congress," *The Western Political Quarterly* 31 (March 1978):96–104.

7. It could be that these educated, affluent women, typical of Olson's leaders, simply failed to gauge the lower interest in politics that most women possessed.

8. Merriam and Gosnell, *Non-Voting*, p. 112.

9. This figure and those that follow in this paragraph on attitudes toward women in politics in the 1930s and 1940s are reported in Hazel Erskine, "The Polls: Women's Role," *Public Opinion Quarterly* 35 (Summer 1971):275–290.

10. James G. March, "Husband-Wife Interaction Over Political Issues," *Public Opinion Quarterly* 17 (Winter 1953–54): 468 and Erskine, "The Polls," p. 275.

11. See also Virginia Sapiro, "News From the Front: Intersex and Intergenerational Conflict Over the Status of Women," *The Western Political Quararterly* 33 (June 1980): 264–265 and Claire Knoche Fulenwider, *Feminism in American Politics: A Study of Ideological Influence* (New York: Praeger Publishers, 1980), p. 62 for similar results.

12. See following Table.

TABLE n4-1
Support for Women's Equal Role—1980 (in percents)

	grade school-educated	high school-educated	college-educated
employed women	37	49	69
housewives	33	37	60

Note: Figures represent the proportion answering 1 or 2 to the following 7 point question: Recently there has been a lot of talk about women's rights. Some people feel that women should have an equal role with men in running

business, industry and government. Others feel women's place is in the home. Where would you place yourself on this scale or haven't you thought about it?
1 = Equal Role
7 = Women's Place is in the home.

Source of data: Center for Political Studies, 1980 American National Election Study. Figures compiled by the authors.

13. See also Fulenwider, *Feminism in American Politics,* p. 64.

14. E.M. Schreiber, "Education and Change in American Opinions on a Woman for President," *Public Opinion Quarterly* 42 (Summer 1978):171–182. See also, Myra Marx Ferree, "A Woman for President? Changing Responses: 1958–1972," *Public Opinion Quarterly* 38 (Fall 1974):390–399.

15. *The 1980 Virginia Slims American Women's Opinion Poll,* conducted by the Roper Organization, p. 10 and 33.

16. Sandra Baxter and Marjorie Lansing, *Women and Politics: The Invisible Majority* (Ann Arbor: The University of Michigan Press, 1980), p. 140.

17. *The Gallup Report,* # 191 (August, 1981), p. 4.

18. Connie DeBoer, "The Polls: Women at Work," *Public Opinion Quarterly* 41 (1977): 274.

19. Louis Harris, *The 1972 Virginia Slims American Women's Opinion Poll,* conducted by Louis Harris and Associates, Inc., 1972, p. 15.

20. Ronald D. Hedlund et al., "The Electability of Women Candidates: The Effects of Sex Role Stereotypes," *Journal of Politics* 41 (May 1979):521. The authors do not report differential response rates for male and female respondents.

21. *General Social Surveys, 1972–1978.* Conducted for the National Data Program for the Social Sciences at the National Opinion Research Center at the University of Chicago, *Cumulative Codebook,* pp. 153–154.

22. We may see a decline in this notion in the 1980s after repeated revelations by national officeholders about their problems with alcohol and drug addiction—problems that all have an adverse impact on family life.

23. Harris, *The 1972 Virginia Slims American Women's Opinion Poll,* pp. 39–40.

24. These data are from the 1978 *General Social Survey.*

25. Harris, *The 1972 Virginia Slims American Women's Opinion Poll,* p. 16.

26. See Fred I. Greenstein, *Children and Politics* (New Haven: Yale University Press, 1965); Herbert Hyman, *Political Socialization* (Glencoe, Illinois: Free Press, 1959); Robert D. Hess and Judith V. Torney, *The Development of Political Attitudes in Children* (Chicago: Aldine, 1967); and Anthony M. Orum et al., "Sex, Socialization, and Politics," in Githens and Prestage, eds., *A Portrait of Marginality,* pp. 17–37.

27. For a discussion of the adult socialization model, see Orum et al., "Sex, Socialization, and Politics," in Githens and Prestage, eds., *A Portrait of Marginality,* pp. 17–37 and Virginia Sapiro, "Socialization to Political Gender Roles Among Women," paper presented at the 1977 Annual Meeting of the Midwest Political Science Association.

28. See Naomi B. Lynn and Cornelia B. Flora, "Motherhood and Political Participation: The Changing Sense of Self," *Journal of Political and Military Sociology* 1 (Spring 1973):91–103; R. Darcy, "Life Cycle Change and American

Politics: The Effects of the First Child on Family Members," paper presented at the Third Annual Conference of the Family Study Center (March 1979); and Nancy E. McGlen, "The Impact of Parenthood on Political Participation," *The Western Political Quarterly* 33 (September 1980):297–313.

29.   For a statement of the basic socioeconomic status model, see Sidney Verba and Norman H. Nie, *Participation in America: Political Democracy and Social Equality* (New York: Harper & Row, 1972), pp. 13–15 and 133–136.

30.   Angus Campbell et al., *The American Voter* (New York: John Wiley and Sons, Inc., 1960), pp. 105–110. Citizen duty is measured by agreement with the following questions:

1.   It isn't so important to vote when you know your party doesn't have any chance to win.

2.   So many other people vote in the national elections that it doesn't matter much to me whether I vote or not.

3.   If a person doesn't care how an election comes out he shouldn't vote in it.

4.   A good many local elections aren't important enough to bother with.

High citizen duty is equal to disagreeing with all four questions.

31.   Merriam and Gosnell, *Non-Voting*, p. 37.

32.   Ibid., p. 113.

33.   Ibid., p. 112.

34.   Campbell et al., *The American Voter*, p. 489.

35.   In 1976, for example, nearly equal proportions of men and women disagreed with the following statements: "I don't think public officials care much what people like me think," and "People like me don't have any say about what the government does." Indeed among the college educated, more women than men disagreed with the first statement.

36.   Fulenwider, *Feminism in American Politics*, p. 92.

37.   Verba and Nie, *Participation in America*, p. 83.

38.   Merriam and Gosnell, *Non-Voting*, p. 161.

39.   Judy Bertelsen, "Political Interest, Influence, and Efficacy: Differences Between the Sexes and Among Marital Status Groups," *American Politics Quarterly* 2 (October 1974):415.

40.   Elise Boulding, "Familial Constraints on Women's Work Roles," in Martha Blaxall and Barbara Reagan, eds., *Women and the Workplace: The Implications of Occupational Segregation* (Chicago: University of Chicago Press, 1976), p. 113. She reports that because of the additional household burdens on working women, they report spending less time reading newspapers or watching television news than males.

41.   In 1940, only 23 percent of all women but 33 percent of all men in Erie County, Ohio, expressed an interest in that year's presidential campaign. Paul Lazarsfeld, Bernard Berelson, and Hazel Gaudet, *The People's Choice*, 3rd ed.(New York: Columbia University Press, 1968), p. 45. See also, Campbell et al., *The American Voter*, p. 489 and Susan Welch, "Women as Political Animals? A Test of Some Explanations for Male-Female Political Participation Differences," *American Journal of Political Science* 21 (November 1977):723.

42.   Welch, "Women as Political Animals?" p. 723.

43.   Interestingly, in 1976, campaign interest in the South was more nearly equal for men and women than in the non-Southern regions of the country. Indeed, among

the most-educated Southern citizens, interest in the campaign in which a "native son," Jimmy Carter, was running, was actually greater among women. Fifty-seven percent of white, college-educated women reported high levels of interest in the campaign as compared to only 50 percent of similar men in the South.

44. See Norman H. Nie, Sidney Verba, and John R. Petrocick, *The Changing American Voter* (Cambridge: Harvard University Press, 1976), pp. 47–73.

45. Merriam and Gosnell, *Non-Voting,* p. 183.

46. Orum et al., "Sex, Socialization and Politics," in Githens and Prestage, eds., *A Portrait of Marginality,* pp. 19, 27–28.

47. For example, in 1976, 30 percent of the women versus 44 percent of the college-educated men under 35 report following the campaign in all four media.

48. Quoted in Merriam and Gosnell, *Non-Voting,* pp. 37 and 187–188.

49. John W. Soule and Wilma E. McGrath, "A Comparative Study of Male-Female Political Attitudes at Citizen and Elite Levels," in Githens and Prestage, eds., *A Portrait of Marginality,* p. 183. Two questions that traditionally are included in the efficacy scale, "I don't think public officials care much what people like me think," and "People like me have no say about what government does," probably measure more accurately trust in government or citizen duty than the question relied on by Soule and McGrath. See George I. Balch, "Multiple Indicators in Survey Research: The Case of Political Efficacy," *Political Methodology* I (Spring 1974):1–43. Moreover, with respect to these two questions, there have been few differences in these areas since the 1950s.

50. Note that Soule and McGrath compare male and female college *graduates,* p. 184.

51. In the South in 1980, 54.2 percent of all college men but only 44.4 percent of all women could think of an alternative to the vote. Outside of the South, the figures for college men and women were 57.7 and 53 percent, respectively.

52. For example, see Kathleen McCourt, *Working-Class Women and Grass-Roots Politics* (Bloomington: Indiana Press, 1977), pp. 174–184. She notes that working-class women who take an active role in community politics in Chicago had much higher levels of political information and awareness as a result of their activities.

53. This association between lack of confidence and lack of information was also characteristic of nonvoters in the 1920s. See Merriam and Gosnell, *Non-Voting,* pp. 187–188.

54. In 1976, for example, 69 percent of college-educated women and 77 percent of college-educated men indicated that they did not think "local" politics were too complicated. The figures for politics "in general" were 34 and 53 percent, respectively.

55. A study in 1967 by Verba and Nie contained similarly narrow differences between the sexes on local issues. Overall, 68 percent of all men and 57 percent of all women reported high levels of local understanding in 1967. The percents for each education category for men and women, respectively, were grade school (64,49), high school (69,61), college (74,68). Similarly, questions dealing with an individual's influence in local politics or power in local politics find fewer differences between the sexes than those focusing on national politics. Figures were compiled by the authors.

56. McCourt, *Working-Class Women and Grass-Roots Politics,* pp. 174–184 and 226.

57. Fulenwider, *Feminism in American Politics,* pp. 86–97. See also, Baxter and Lansing, *Women and Politics,* pp. 93–94 and Inez Smith Reid, "Traditional Political

Animals? A Loud No," in Githens and Prestage, eds., *A Portrait of Marginality*, pp. 366–378.

58. In *Feminism in American Politics*, p. 88, Fulenwider reports that political efficacy among black women remained almost unchanged between 1972 and 1976. During the same period, there was a marked increase in the reported efficacy of white women. It must be noted, however, that Fulenwider's measure of efficacy combines four separate indicators. Thus, we do not know if all four are similarly negatively related.

59. Ibid., pp. 90–97.

60. McCourt, *Working-Class Women and Grass-Roots Politics*, pp. 174–184 and 226.

61. For an excellent discussion and a test of the influence of barriers women face, see Susan Welch, "Recruitment of Women to Public Office: A Discriminant Analysis," in *The Western Political Quarterly* 31 (September 1978):372–380. Welch reports that a significant part of the explanation for the few women in elected office may be traceable to such structural factors.

62. See Hope Chamberlin, *A Minority of Members: Women in the U.S. Congress* (New York: New American Library, 1973), p. 55.

63. Quoted in "Is a Woman's Place in the House?" *Time*, November 6, 1978, p. 37.

64. United States Bureau of the Census, *Voting and Registration in the Election of November, 1980*. Bulletin P–20 #370., p. 3. Slightly more women (67.1 percent) than men (66.6 percent) were registered to vote.

65. Merriam and Gosnell, *Non-Voting*, p. 187.

66. Baxter and Lansing, *Women and Politics*, pp. 76–79.

67. See Susan Welch and Philip Secret, "Sex, Race and Political Participation," *The Western Political Quarterly* 34 (March 1981):11–13. For suggestive evidence to the contrary, see Baxter and Lansing, *Women and Politics*, pp. 79–90.

68. Merriam and Gosnell, *Non-Voting*, pp. 100–101 and 116–122.

69. Stucker, "Women as Voters," in Githens and Prestage, eds., *A Portrait of Marginality*, p. 273.

70. Quoted in Merriam and Gosnell, *Non-Voting*, pp. 111 and 113.

71. Stucker, "Women as Voters," in Githens and Prestage, eds., *A Portrait of Marginality*, pp. 273–274 and Merriam and Gosnell, *Non-Voting*, pp. 212–216.

72. Fulenwider, *Feminism in American Politics*, pp.106–107.

73. Campbell et al., *The American Voter*, p. 488 and Gerald Pomper, *Voter's Choice: Varieties of American Electoral Behavior* (New York: Dodd, Mead, 1975), pp. 72–73. In 1976, 69 percent of all mothers with children under eighteen, as compared to 78 percent of all fathers, voted. The greater frequency with which young women cite family emergency or illness as a reason for not voting is also suggestive. Bureau of the Census, *Voting and Registration*, pp. 82–83. Other studies find no such evidence. See, for example, Welch, "Women as Political Animals?" p. 724.

74. Merriam and Gosnell, *Non-Voting*, pp. 37 and 183–194.

75. Chafe, *The American Woman*, pp. 35–37.

76. Kristi Andersen, "Generation, Partisan Shift, and Realignment: A Glance Back to the New Deal" in Nie, Verba, and Petrocick, *The Changing American Voter*, pp. 74–95.

77. Ibid., p. 90.

78. Louis Harris, *The Anguish of Change* (New York: W.W. Norton, 1973), pp. 90–93; Baxter and Lansing, *Women and Politics*, pp. 57–59; Harry Holloway, "Gender and Opinion: An Exploration of Differences," paper presented at the 1980 Annual Meeting of the Southern Political Science Association, pp. 14 and 20–21; and Pomper, *Voter's Choice*, pp. 81–84.

79. Baxter and Lansing, *Women and Politics*, p. 58.

80. Ibid., pp. 58–59; Harris, *The Anguish of Change*, p. 92; and Pomper, *Voter's Choice*, pp. 78–81.

Kathleen A. Frankovic, "Sex and Politics—New Alignments, Old Issues," *P.S.* 15 (Summer 1982):445.

82. Baxter and Lansing, *Women and Politics*, pp. 59–60; Harris, *The Anguish of Change*, pp. 93–94; and Halloway, "Gender and Opinion," pp. 5 and 17.

81. Kathleen A. Frankovic, "Sex and Politics—New Alignments, Old Issues," *PS* 15 (Summer 1982):445.

82. Baxter and Lansing, *Women and Politics*, pp. 59–60, Harris, *The Anguish of Change*, pp. 93–94, and Halloway, "Gender and Opinion," pp. 5 and 17.

83. Frankovic, "Sex and Politics," pp. 444–445.

84. Adam Clymer, "Doubts on Effects of Reagan Policies Spurred Many Voters, Survey Shows," *The New York Times*, November 8, 1982, p. 12.

85. Nie, Verba, and Petrocick, *The Changing American Voter*, p. 304.

86. Naomi Lynn, "Women in American Politics: An Overview," in Jo Freeman, ed., *Women: A Feminist Perspective* (Palo Alto: Mayfield Publishing Co., 1975), pp. 367–368.

87. Richard G. Niemi, Roman Hedges, and M. Kent Jennings, "The Similarity of Husbands' and Wives' Political Views," *American Politics Quarterly* 5 (April 1977):136.

88. Paul Beck and M. Kent Jennings, "Parents as Middle-Persons in Political Socialization," *Journal of Politics* 37 (February 1975):87–93 and Terry S. Weiner, "Homogeneity of Political Party Preferences Between Spouses," *Journal of Politics* 40 (February 1978):208–212.

89. Harris, *The 1972 Virginia Slims American Women's Opinion Poll*, p. 16.

90. Although probably now dated, a 1968 study found that while equal proportions of men and women reported they tried to influence their spouses' vote, 68 percent of all men but only 32 percent of all women reported their spouses did *not* try to influence their vote. Thus, women seem to be talking but men are not listening. Data in Bertelsen, "Political Interest, Influence and Efficacy," p. 416.

91. Pomper, *Voter's Choice*, pp. 78–79.

92. Gerald M. Pomper, "The Presidential Election," in Gerald M. Pomper, ed., *The Election of 1980: Reports and Interpretations* (Chatham, N.J.: Chatham House Publishers, 1980), p. 71. Data from the 1980 Michigan Survey Research Center, however, reveal higher discrepancies between the sexes.

93. Frankovic, "Sex and Politics," pp. 440–442.

94. Ibid., pp. 443–446.

95. Adam Clymer, "G.O.P. Is Disturbed by Women's Role in Election," *The New York Times*, November 18, 1982, p. 16.

96. Frankovic, "Sex and Politics," pp. 446–447.

97.　The ABC pole found a six-point gender gap. Only the one group of men hardest hit by unemployment—the 18- to 29-year-olds—voted more Democratic than women. Clymer, "Surveys Show," p. 12.

98.　Clymer, "G.O.P. Disturbed," p. 16. The Reagan administration's cutbacks in programs affecting single women and its apparent lack of concern with problems of women may be a reason for these facts. See Adam Clymer, "Polls Show a Married-Single Gap in Last Election," *The New York Times,* January 6, 1983, p. 10.

99.　Adam Clymer, "Male-Female Split on Politics Found Decisive in Some Polls," *The New York Times,* October 27, 1982, p. 1 (cont. on p. 12) and Clymer, "G.O.P. Disturbed," p. 16.

100.　Adam Clymer, "Contradictory Lessons of '82 Election," *The New York Times,* November 4, 1982, p. A-18.

101.　Verba and Nie, *Participation in America,* p. 53.

102.　Ibid.

103.　Marilyn Gittell and Teresa Shtob, "Changing Women's Roles in Political Volunteerism and Reform of the City," *Signs* 5 (Spring Supplement 1980): S67–S78.

104.　Reported in Doris B. Gold, "Women and Voluntarism," in Vivian Gornick and Barbara K. Moran, eds., *Women in Sexist Society* (New York: Basic Books 1971), pp. 384–400.

105.　*The Gallup Report,* #197 (February, 1982), p. 25.

106.　Gittell and Shtob, "Changing Women's Roles," pp. S73–S76. See also, McCourt, *Working-Class Women and Grass-Roots Politics;* Norman and Susan Fainstein, *Urban Political Movements* (Englewood Cliffs, N.J.: Prentice-Hall, 1974); and Marilyn Gittell, *Citizen Organization: Participation in Educational Decision-making* (Boston: Institute for Responsive Education, 1979).

107.　Debra W. Stewart, "Institutionalization of Female Participation at the Local Level: Commissions on the Status of Women and Agenda-Building," *Women & Politics* 1 (Spring 1980):37–63.

108.　See McGlen, "Impact of Parenthood." For another analysis of the effect of school-aged children on their parents' political activity, especially their mothers', see M. Kent Jennings, "Another Look at the Life Cycle and Political Participation," *American Journal of Political Science* 23 (November 1979):764–767.

109.　Lynn and Flora, "Motherhood and Political Participation," pp. 97–98.

110.　McCourt, *Working-Class Women and Grass-Roots Politics,* pp. 107–109 and 121–128.

111.　Donald R. Matthews and James W. Prothro, *Negroes and the New Southern Politics* (New York: Harcourt, Brace & World, 1966), pp. 416–417.

112.　Fulenwider, *Feminism in American Politics,* pp. 106–107.

113.　Harris, *The 1972 Virginia Slims American Women's Opinion Poll,* p. 16.

114.　Ibid. Fifth percent of all women (62 percent of college women) and 46 percent of all men agreed with this statement.

115.　*The 1980 Virginia Slims American Women's Opinion Poll,* p. 11.

116.　Chafe, *The American Woman,* pp. 40–41 and 45.

117.　Kristi Andersen, "Working Women and Political Participation, 1952–1972," *American Journal of Political Science* 19 (August 1975):442. The average number of campaign acts for women was .47, for men .71, out of a possible 6.

118.　See following Table.

TABLE n4-2

Male versus Female Involvement in Political Activity—1980 (in percents)

Type of Activity	Males	Females
contribute money to a candidate	6.7	5.3
contribute money to a political party	4.1	3.3
attend a political meeting	8.0	7.2
work for a candidate	3.0	4.0
influence another's vote	39.9	33.2
display button or poster	6.9	6.6

Note: Figures represent the percent that responded affirmatively when asked if they had done any of these campaign acts.

Source of data: Center for Political Studies, 1980 American National Election Study. Figures compiled by the authors.

119.   Race also affects campaign activity. Black women participate less than men of either race or white women. Feminist beliefs, however, sharply increase the political activity of black women. Fulenwider, *Feminism in American Politics,* p. 107.

120.   Marjorie Lansing, "The American Woman: Voter and Activist" in Jane S. Jaquette, ed., *Women in Politics* (New York: John Wiley, 1974), p. 17. Kristi Andersen also found few differences between employed women and all men in 1960, 1964, and 1972: "Working Women and Political Participation," p. 443. Professionally employed women actually participated more than all men from 1956 through 1972 with the exception of 1968. In 1976, looking only at working men and women, we found a narrowing gap among the less educated, from a 19 percent difference overall to a 7 percent difference among workers but no change in the gap between college men and women. For an examination of the role of achieved versus derived status as it affects the campaign activity of women, see Eileen L. McDonagh, "To Work or Not to Work: The Differential Impact of Achieved and Derived Status upon the Political Participation of Women, 1956–1976," *American Journal of Political Science* 26 (May 1982): 280–297.

121.   The following are the percentages of college men and women, respectively, who engaged in each of the following activities in 1980: attended a campaign meeting (11.1,11.3), worked for a candidate (2.6,6.6), wore a button or displayed a poster (8.9,8.4), gave money to a candidate (10.7,12.1), and tried to influence another's vote (49,46).

122.   Welch, "Women as Political Animals?" p. 722; Soule and McGrath, "A Comparative Study of Male-Female Political Attitudes," in Githens and Prestage, eds., *A Portrait of Marginality,* p. 181; and Lazarsfeld et al., *The People's Choice,* p. 50. Controlling for education, age, region, income, employment, marriage, and children, women continued to report less influencing than men in 1952, 1964, and 1972. Even in

1960, when college women were more active than men, they were less likely to try to influence others. See also, Baxter and Lansing, *Women and Politics*, p. 114.

123.   Welch, "Women as Political Animals?" p. 722.

124.   For a similar line of reasoning, see Lazarsfeld, *The People's Choice*, pp. 49–51 and Ronald B. Rapoport, "The Sex Gap in Political Persuading: Where the 'Structuring Principle' Works," *American Journal of Political Science* 25 (February 1981):35–36.

125.   See also, Ronald B. Rapoport, 'Sex Differences in Attitude Expression: A Generational Explanation," *Public Opinion Quarterly* 46 (Spring 1982):86–96.

126.   Bertelsen, "Political Interest, Influence, and Efficacy," p. 417.

127.   The same phenomena do not occur among citizens with less than a college education probably because of the low overall level of activity by both sexes. See McGlen, "Impact of Parenthood," p. 302.

128.   In her study of campaign activists, Ellen Boneparth suggests that children are no barrier to participation because of the relative shortness of most political campaigns. "Women in Campaigns: From Lickin' and Stickin' to Strategy," *American Politics Quarterly* 5 (July 1977):291.

129.   For evidence of difference in activity, see M. Kent Jennings and Norman Thomas, "Men and Women in Party Elites: Social Roles and Political Resources," *Midwest Journal of Political Science* 12 (November 1968):480. See also, Edmond Constantini and Kenneth H. Clark, "Women as Politicians: The Social Background, Personality and Political Careers of Female Party Leaders," *Journal of Social Issues* 28 (1972):217–236. Jeane J. Kirkpatrick, in *Political Woman* (New York: Basic Books, 1974), p. 66, reports that four-fifths of the female legislators interviewed agreed women do the dirty work and men wield the power in most campaigns. Some current research substantiates these results. See Diane L. Fowlkes, Jerry Perkins, and Sue Tolleson Rinehart, "Gender Roles and Party Roles," *American Political Science Review* 73 (September 1979): 777–778, although other data on party activists suggest more Democratic women are managing campaigns. See M. Kent Jennings and Barbara G. Farah, "Social Roles and Political Resources: An Over-time Study of Men and Women in Party Elites," *American Journal of Politics* 25 (August 1981):470.

130.   Quoted in Susan and Martin Tolchin, *Clout: Womenpower and Politics* (New York: Coward, McCann & Geoghegan, 1974), p. 13.

131.   Marilyn Johnson et al., *Profile of Women Holding Office*, II (New Brunswick, N.J.: Center for the American Woman and Politics (CAWP) (1978), p. 39A.

132.   Boneparth, "Women in Campaigns," pp. 293–294.

133.   Quoted in *The New York Times*, April 13, 1976, p. 24.

134.   Leslie Bennett, "Women's Role in the Campaign is Discussed by Female Aides," *The New York Times*, March 20, 1980, C-1.

135.   Fulenwider, *Feminism in American Politics*, pp. 107–109.

136.   Quoted in Martin Gruberg, *Women in American Politics* (Osh Kosh, Wisc.: Academia Press, 1968), p. 62.

137.   Harold D. Clarke and Allan Kornberg, "Moving Up the Political Escalator: Women Party Officials in the United States and Canada," *Journal of Politics* 41 (May 1979):468.

138.   Virginia Sapiro and Barbara G. Farah, "New Pride and Old Prejudice:

Political Ambitions and Role Orientations Among Female Partisan Elites," *Women & Politics* 1 (Spring 1980):20 and Jennings and Farah, "Social Roles and Political Resources: An Over Time Study of Men and Women in Party Elites," pp. 479–481.

139.   Quoted in "Is a Woman's Place in the House?" *Time,* November, 1978, p. 34.

140.   Naomi Lynn and Cornelia Butler Flora, "Societal Punishment and Aspects of Female Political Participation: 1972 National Convention Delegates," in Githens and Prestage, eds., *A Portrait of Marginality,* p. 141; Bill Peterson and David S. Broder, "Women to Occupy Half the Seats at Convention in 1980," *The Washington Post,* December 8, 1978, p. A2; and Gruberg, *Women in American Politics,* pp. 59–60.

141.   Sarah Slavin Schramm, "Women and Representation: Self Government and Role Change," *The Western Political Quarterly* 34 (March 1981):52.

142.   Not surprisingly, the largest number of women officeholders can be found on local school boards. Figures for state legislative races are from the National Women's Political Caucus headquarters. In 1982, women captured 3 new lieutenant governor offices, 11 new Secretary of State offices, and 9 new state treasurer positions.

143.   Nancy Broff and Demetra Lambros, "Steadily Women Continue Political Climb," *Women's Political Times,* December, 1982, p. 1.

144.   A.O. Sulzberger, Jr., "Women Grow as Political Contenders," *Buffalo Courier-Express,* September 7, 1980, C-1.

145.   R. Darcy and Sarah Slavin Schramm, "When Women Run Against Men," *Public Opinion Quarterly* 41 (Spring 1977):1-12. See also, Raisa B. Deber, "'The Fault, Dear Brutus': Women as Congressional Candidates in Pennsylvania," *Journal of Politics* 44 (May 1982):463–479.

146.   Albert K. Karnig and B. Oliver Walter, "Election of Women to City Councils," *Social Science Quarterly* 56 (March 1976):605–613.

147.   NORC, *General Social Survey,* 1978.

148.   Marcia Manning Lee, "Why Few Women Hold Public Office: Democracy and Sexual Roles," *Political Science Quarterly,* 91 (Summer 1976):307. Additionally, among male or female public officials, there seems to be little support for the idea of nominating or voting for women simply because more women need to be elected. Jerry Perkins and Diane L. Fowlkes, "Opinion Representation versus Social Representation; or, Why Women Can't Run as Women and Win," *American Political Science Review* 74 (March 1980):96–102 and Susan Gluck Mezey, "Women and Representation: The Case of Hawaii," *Journal of Politics* 40 (1978):369–385.

149.   Johnson et al., *Profile,* p. 39A. No such difference in perception with respect to voting behavior of the public was found among men and women politicians in Hawaii. See Susan Gluck Mezey, "Does Sex Make a Difference? A Case Study of Women in Politics," *The Western Political Quarterly* 31 (December 1978):496–501. However, women thought that public chauvinism was a campaign liability. See also, Laurie E. Ekstrand and William A. Eckert, "The Impact of a Candidate's Sex on Voter Choice," *The Western Political Quarterly* 34 (March 1981):78–87.

150.   Lee, "Why Few Women Hold Public Office," p. 307.

151.   Quoted in Kirkpatrick, *Political Woman,* p. 235.

152.   Virginia Sapiro, "Private Costs of Public Commitments or Public Costs of Private Commitments? Family Roles versus Political Ambition," *American Journal of Political Science* 26 (May 1982):265–279.

153.   Anita Shreve and John Clemans, "The New Wave of Women Politicians,"

New York Times Magazine, October 19, 1980, p. 109. See also, Ruth B. Mandel, *In the Running: The New Woman Candidate* (New Haven, Conn.: Ticknor and Fields, 1981), pp. 86–96.

154. Mandel, *In the Running,* p. 90.

155. Kirkpatrick, *Political Woman,* pp. 234–235.

156. Beth S. Shapiro and Eleanor C. Main also note a similar effect of children on women running for state legislative positions, "The Recruitment of State Legislators: A Comparison of Male and Female Life Experiences," paper delivered at the 1979 Annual Meeting of the Southern Political Science Association.

157. Johnson et al., *Profile,* pp. 13A and 18A.

158. For example, see ibid., p. 16A; Emily Stoper, "Wife and Politician: Role Strain Among Women in Public Office," in Githens and Prestage, eds., *A Portrait of Marginality,* p. 324; and Paula J. Dubeck, "Women and Access to Political Office: Comparison of Female and Male State Legislators," *The Sociological Quarterly* 17 (Winter 1976):46–48.

159. Lee, "Why Few Women Hold Public Office," p. 306.

160. Johnson et al., *Profile,* p. 19A; Stoper, "Wife and Politician," p. 335; and Mandel, *In the Running,* pp. 70–75.

161. Johnson et. al., *Profile,* p. 19A.

162. Quoted in Kirkpatrick, *Political Woman,* p. 231.

163. Quoted in "Is a Woman's Place in the House?" p. 35.

164. Mandel, *In the Running,* pp. 163–164.

165. Susan Welch, "Recruitment of Women to Public Office," pp. 377–378.

166. Johnson et. al., *Profile,* p. 17A.

167. Kirkpatrick, *Political Woman,* pp. 82–83.

168. Lee, "Why Few Women Hold Public Office," pp. 307–308.

169. Kirkpatrick, *Political Woman,* pp. 71–82.

170. Quoted in Tolchin and Tolchin, *Clout,* p. 78.

171. Johnson et al., *Profile,* p. 28A; Dubeck, "Women and Access to Public Office," p. 49; and Charles S. Bullock and Patricia Lee Findley Heys, "Recruitment of Women for Congress: A Research Note," *The Western Political Quarterly* 25 (September 1972):420.

172. Johnson et al., *Profile,* p. 28A.

173. Clark and Kornberg, "Moving Up the Political Ladder," p. 468.

174. Harris, *The 1972 Virginia Slims American Women's Opinion Poll,* p. 28.

175. Mandel, *In the Running,* pp. 110–114. She reports that one survey of voters found 15 percent objected to having two women serving in statewide office.

176. See examples in Tolchin and Tolchin, *Clout,* chap. 2 and Kirkpatrick, *Political Woman,* chap. 4. One study of Southern state legislators, however, found no difference in the percent of female versus male legislators who reported that they had been recruited to run for office by party officials. Sixty-two percent of the women but only 26 percent of the men, however, believed that it was important to be asked to run by the party. Eleanor C. Main and Beth S. Shapiro, "Different Paths to the State Legislature? A Comparison of Male and Female Apprenticeships," paper delivered at the 1981 Annual Meeting of the Midwest Political Science Association, p. 29.

177. Jennings and Thomas, "Men and Women in Party Elites," pp. 482–483 and Wilma L.B. Rule, "Why Women Don't Run: The Critical Contextual Factors in

Women's Legislative Recruitment," *The Western Political Quarterly* 34 (March 1981):60–77.

178.　Quoted in "Is a Woman's Place in the House?" pp. 34–35.

179.　Werner, "Women in Congress," p. 20.

180.　Kincaid, "Over His Dead Body," pp. 99–100.

181.　Mandel, *In the Running*, pp. 22–26.

182.　Ibid., p. 120 and Susan A. McManus, "A City's First Female Officeholder: 'Coattails' for Future Female Officeholders?" *The Western Political Quarterly* 34 (March 1981):88–99.

183.　Quoted in Chamberlin, *A Minority of Members*, p. 5.

184.　Tolchin and Tolchin, *Clout*, p. 96.

185.　Quoted in "The Year of the Woman," *Newsweek*, November 4, 1974, p. 20. However, Darcy and Schramm find little evidence that being a female candidate increases recognition very much, "When Women Run Against Men," pp. 5–6.

186.　Ekstrand and Eckert, "The Impact of Candidate's Sex on Voter's Choice," pp. 78–87.

187.　Quoted in Tolchin and Tolchin, *Clout*, p. 87. See also, Stoper, "Politician and Wife," pp. 333–334 and Mandel, *In the Running*, pp. 86–96.

188.　Quoted in Tolchin and Tolchin, *Clout*, p. 198.

189.　Quoted in Shreve and Clemans, "The New Wave of Women Politicians," p. 31.

190.　Ibid.

191.　"Is A Woman's Place in the House?" p. 34; see also, Mandel, *In the Running*, pp. 180–200.

192.　Quoted in Shreve and Clemans, "The New Wave of Women Politicians," p. 31.

193.　It should be noted that this money was for either male or female candidates who supported feminist positions. And, while NOW generally supported female over male candidates, it did not support former Rep. Millicent Fenwick (R-New Jersey) in her attempt to represent New Jersey in the U.S. Senate, citing Fenwick's support of the Reagan economic plan, which according to NOW leaders, "has done enormous damage to women." Nadine Brozan, "NOW Elects New Officers and Plots Its Future," *The New York Times*, October 11, 1982, p. 22.

194.　Nadine Brozan, "NOW Convenes to Pick Leaders," *The New York Times*, October 9, 1982, p. 18 and Nadine Brozan, "NOW Elects New Officers." NOW PAC was formed to distribute money to candidates in federal elections and NOW Equality PAC to assist in state and local elections.

195.　Marian Lief Palley, "Beyond the Deadline," *PS* 15 (Fall 1982):590.

196.　John Herbers, "Women Turn View to Public Office," *The New York Times*, June 28, 1982, p. 1 (cont. on p. 11).

197.　Kirkpatrick, *Political Woman*, p. 126.

198.　Ibid., chap. 6.

199.　Kenneth B. Dalecki, "Evolution at the Polls Puts Strain on Male Grip," *Buffalo Courier-Express*, March 20, 1980, p. C-4.

200.　Quoted in ibid., p. C-4. For an analysis of Ferraro's effectiveness as a legislator, see Frank Lynn, "Women's Issues Given Strong Support by Democrats in Philadelphia," *The New York Times*, June 28, 1981, p. 11.

201. Quoted in Shreve and Clemans, "The New Wave of Women Politicians," p. 105.

202. Johnson, et. al., *Profile,* pp. 29A, 42A, and 44A. Interestingly, their male colleagues do not seem to be as aware or at least are not willing to grant that women are better in these areas.

203. Ibid., p. 52A.

204. Ibid., pp. 31A and 44A.

205. Kirkpatrick, *Political Woman,* pp. 164–176. There is continuing evidence, at least at the state level, that women candidates who do not discuss women's issues fare better than those who do. See Susan Carroll, "Women Candidates and Support for Women's Issues: Closet Feminists," paper delivered at the 1979 Annual Meeting of the Midwest Political Science Association and Perkins and Fowlkes, "Opinion Representation versus Social Representation, Or, Why Women Can't Run as Women and Win," pp. 92–103.

206. The Caucus includes male representatives but not all women in the Congress. Its Women's Research and Education Institute conducts useful studies on the impact of proposed legislation dealing with women's concerns. Copies of these analyses are available from the Institute at 204 4th Street, S.E., Washington, D.C. 20003 for a nominal charge.

207. Kathleen A. Frankovic, "Sex and Voting in the U.S. House of Representatives, 1961–75," *American Politics Quarterly* 5 (July 1977):315–329.

208. Ibid., p. 329. For interesting discussions of the issue of representation of women, see Virginia Sapiro, "Research Frontier Essay: When Are Interests Interesting? The Problem of Political Representation of Women," *American Political Science Review* 75 (September 1981):701–716 and Irene Diamond and Nancy Hartsock, "Beyond Interest in Politics: A Comment on Virginia Sapiro's 'When Are Interests Interesting? The problem of Political Representation of Women,'" *American Political Science Review* 75 (September 1981):717–721.

209. Reagan's Record on Naming Women Refuted," *The Atlanta Journal and Constitution,* August 1, 1982, p. 17-B.

210. Ibid. According to the NWPC, Reagan made 682 appointments requiring Senate confirmation by August 1, 1982; only 55 or 8.1 percent went to women.

211. Elliot Slotnick, "Affirmative Action and Judicial Selection During the Carter Administration," paper delivered at the 1982 Annual Meeting of the American Political Science Association and Elaine Martin, "Women on the Federal Bench: A Comparative Profile," *Judicature* 65 (December-January 1982):306–313.

212. Thomas G. Walker, "Affirmative Action in Federal Judicial Selection: Policy and Process Ramifications," paper presented at the 1982 Annual Meeting of the Southern Political Science Association.

213. "Reagan's Record," p. 17-B.

214. Walker, "Affirmative Action." For another study that has noted a difference in how male and female judges handle their cases, see John Gruhl, Cassia Spohn, and Susan Welch, "Women as Policymakers: The Case of Trial Judges," *American Journal of Political Science* 25 (May 1981):308–322.

215. A study of trial court judges conducted in 1978 by Beverly Blair Cook, for example, found that men and women jurists had significantly different attitudes. Twice

as many men believed that women are happiest as housewives, one-third of the men believed that mothers of small children should not work outside of the home, and almost half opposed a woman's retention of her maiden name. Beverly Blair Cook, "Women Judges: The End of Tokenism," in Winifred L. Hepperle and Laura Crites, eds., *Women in the Courts* (National Center for State Courts, 1978). These kinds of attitudinal differences make it particularly important to increase the number of women judges if equality is to be achieved in the courtroom. For studies of differential treatment of male and female defendants, see Elizabeth Moulds, "Chivalry and Paternalism: Disparities of Treatment in the Criminal Justice System," *The Western Political Quarterly* 31 (September 1978):420–429 and Freda Solomon, "Gender Justice: Differential Treatment of Male and Female Felony Defendants," paper presented at the 1981 Annual Meeting of the Western Political Science Association. See also, Herbert M. Kritzer and Thomas M. Uhlman, "Sisterhood in the Courtroom: Sex of Judge and Defendant in Criminal Case Disposition," *Social Science Quarterly* 14 (April 1977):77–88.

216. Karen O'Connor and Lee Epstein, "Sex and the Supreme Court: An Analysis of Judicial Support for Gender-Based Discrimination Claims," *Social Science Quarterly*, in press.

PART TWO

Employment and Educational Rights

Like the battle for political rights, women's struggle to gain access to equal educational and employment opportunities has been a long one. Even before the first woman's rights movement, feminist writers such as Mary Wollstonecraft argued:

> Mankind should all be educated after the same model, or the intercourse of the sexes will never deserve the name of fellowship, nor will women ever fulfill the peculiar duties of their sex, till they become enlightened citizens, till they become free by being enabled to earn their own subsistence, independent of men.[1]

Resolutions calling for equal educational, professional, and employment opportunities were regularly passed at woman's rights conventions in the nineteenth century. Yet, even today, women still constitute less than one-third of all students receiving professional degrees, and the women who work full time outside of the home can expect to earn only about 60 cents for every dollar made by a man.

The efforts of women to rectify these inequalities and the reasons for their incomplete success are the topics of the next two chapters. Chapter 5 will focus on the activities of the various women's movements to expand the employment and educational rights and opportunities of women, while Chapter 6 will examine the progress women have made in these areas and the barriers that remain.

145

In many respects, women's struggle for equal rights in the work force is similar to that faced in the voting arena. Like votes for women, employment and educational rights, including equal pay for equal work and the removal of legal roadblocks to women's practice of some professions, all are "rights" that affect only a limited number of women.

In essence, many laws that equalize employment and educational opportunities are nonthreatening. Women can choose whether or not they wish to work and, if they choose to seek employment outside of the home or get a college degree, whether or not they wish to take full advantage of antidiscrimination legislation. In the educational area the picture is similar. Once barriers to admission are broken, only a small percentage of the female population will opt for certain training. Owing to the nonuniversal and, therefore, nonlife-style endangering nature of rights in these areas, *strong* anti groups have not emerged to lobby actively against or challenge in court the constitutionality of any of the recent employment and educational rights laws.

With only a few exceptions, conservative women's groups have not mobilized to challenge specific laws designed to improve the employment or educational status of women. Conservative women's groups, in fact, have viewed some pieces of antidiscrimination legislation, most notably the Pregnancy Discrimination Act, as fostering motherhood roles, and thus, as nonthreatening public goods.

Furthermore, the younger branch of the current movement has not been a major factor in the attainment of additional legal, economic, and educational rights. This is largely because the ideology and goals of "Women's Liberation" groups, with respect to employment and educational rights for women, parallel their views of political rights. Politicos (especially Marxists) maintain that the end of economic oppression (as well as all other oppression) of women will only come with the overthrow of the present economic system.[2] Socialist feminists, too, expanding on Marxist theory, claim that the capitalist system and the patriarchial class system are both key sources of women's inequality—a situation that will be rectified only with the overthrow of both. Thus, members of both groups tend to adopt the position that reform of the economic system by the establishment of equal opportunity legislation would only delay the revolution and, therefore, should generally be avoided and condemned.[3]

Radical feminists who reject the Marxian analysis as incomplete and argue that the source of women's economic oppression goes deeper and is to be found in the sex role system also often agree with Socialist feminists on the need for a major alteration in the economic system in addition to a sexual revolution to guarantee women equal economic opportunity. However, most radical feminists view the key issue as the abolition of the sex role system, including the family, as prerequisite to economic and educational equality for women.[4] Thus, their strategy for solving economic inequality generally has focused on changing the sex role systems and related institutions and is described in Chapters 7 and 8, although as later discussed, some radical and socialist feminists, frustrated by the inability of their own small groups to mount sustained national action, have participated in reform activities.[5]

Thus, controversy among women concerning the questions of educational and employment rights has been limited. As a result, anti efforts by conservative women and action by younger-branch women are not central to our discussion in Chapter 5 of women's movements' activity. Where organizations have differed about tactics and objectives, those disagreements and their ramifications will be discussed. In the main, however, most objections to expanded rights or implementation of those already won in these two areas have come from men. This can best be seen in our discussion of employer/employee attitudes about women workers in Chapter 6. While opposition from women has proven to be only a minimal deterrent to the expansion of rights in this area, the resistance of men has not been so benign. Indeed, the hostility of men to equal educational and employment opportunities for women was and continues to be a real stumbling block to full equality.

NOTES

1. Quoted in Alice S. Rossi, ed., *The Feminist Papers: From Adams to de Beauvoir* (New York: Columbia University Press, 1973), p. 76.

2. For a discussion of politicos, see Judith Hole and Ellen Levine, *Rebirth of Feminism* (New York: Quardrangle Books, 1971), pp. 108–166 and Gayle Graham Yates, *What Women Want: The Ideas of the Movement* (Cambridge: Harvard University Press, 1975), pp. 88–91. Yates calls this wing of the younger branch, "feminist radicals."

3. For a discussion of socialist feminists, see Zillah R. Eisenstein, ed., *Capitalist Patriarchy and the Case for Socialist Feminism* (New York: Monthly Review Press, 1979) and *The Radical Future of Liberal Feminism* (New York: Longman, 1981) in which she argues that some liberal feminist reforms might facilitate revolutionary change.

4. See, for example, Shulamith Firestone, *The Dialectic of Sex: The Case for Feminist Revolution* (New York: Bantam Books, 1970).

5. See Charlotte Bunch, "The Reform Tool Kit," in *Building Feminist Theory: Essays from QUEST* (New York: Longman, 1981), pp. 189–201 for a discussion of when reform might be acceptable to feminists.

5 The Struggle for Employment and Educational Rights

INTRODUCTION

Distinct eras of women's gains in employment and educational rights and opportunities can be observed that closely parallel, but are not identical to, the periods of women's movement activity delineated in Chapter 2. From 1840 to 1900, young, primarily single, women left their homes in increasing numbers to seek employment in the growing textile industry. Other women, closely allied with the woman's rights movement, sought entrance into higher-prestige occupations, particularly medicine and the law. Many of them were forced to break legal and social barriers to gain admission to professional schools and again later to find even minimal acceptance in their chosen fields. During this period, and even earlier, a large number of women's colleges were founded and some formerly "male only" universities opened their doors to female students.

A second period of change—from 1900 to 1930—is also observable. In those years, the composition of the female labor force was altered dramatically both by the influx of immigrant women into the labor force and by the growth of white-collar jobs for single, middle-class women. These changes were accompanied by an alteration in the ideology of middle-class women active in the drive for suffrage. Increasingly they were less concerned with eliminating all legal, social, and economic barriers for working women and more with protecting working women from unsavory conditions at their place of employment. Employment legislation passed by the urging of those active in the suffrage and progressive movements tended to be based on the same logic as their arguments for the vote—namely, the view that a woman's proper role in life was that of devoted wife and mother. The dominant ideology of the time also was evident in the preparation given to women in American colleges and in the life-style of female professionals.

World War II and the period of the 1950s and 1960s saw yet another radical alteration in the kinds and number of women working outside the home, but substantial legal changes designed to improve women's economic status did not occur until the early 1960s with the passage of the Equal Pay Act of 1963. The period since then has been marked by the activity of women's groups and by the enactment of sweeping antidiscrimination legislation designed to improve women's employment status and educational opportunities. Many of these new laws, however, suffer from uneven enforcement. Thus, efforts to force compliance and to eliminate other barriers to economic and educational opportunity still occupy a good deal of the energies of those in the current women's movement.

THE WOMAN'S MOVEMENT

In colonial times, few individuals—male or female—sought employment outside of the home. While men did much of the heavy work, their wives toiled beside them in the fields. Women also kept house, tended vegetable gardens, and raised poultry to sell for "cash money," which then could be used to purchase goods. Marriage was viewed as a necessity during this period, and men and women often were considered partners. The contributions of both spouses were recognized because the work of each was geared toward the survival of the household as an economic unit. Cooking, baking, gardening, and looming, although perhaps women's work, were recognized as critical to the survival of the family. The coming of the Industrial Revolution, however, altered this delicate balance. As the number of Americans living in cities increased, men entered nonagricultural occupations, while most women stayed at home and continued to provide essential but nonremunerative services: cooking, cleaning, and childrearing. The "business world," was perceived as a "dog-eat-dog" existence from which a dutiful husband was expected to protect his wife. Thus, from the colonial times to the time of the first woman's movement, a woman's proper role did not include obtaining "unnecessary" education[1] or accepting any type of employment unless it was essential for her survival.

Some women, including widows, unmarried and black women, and a few women whose husbands could not earn enough to support the family, however, found it necessary to seek employment outside of the home. Many used their "womanly" skills and became domestics. Others, particularly in the

Northeast, found work in the fledgling textile industry, which relied heavily on cheap (i.e., female) labor. By 1831, women held 80 percent of the positions in New England's textile mills, and in fact, by 1850, over 225,000 American women were employed in that industry.[2] In addition, a growing number of women, primarily young and single, taught in the public schools briefly before marriage.[3] Because of cultural views about women's proper role, however, few women worked after marriage, except the very poor who often were black or immigrants. Thus, although women were able to obtain work, those opportunities generally were limited to but a few types of positions.

This restriction of women's opportunities at the very time of expansion of opportunities for men was the setting in which the woman's rights movement was born. In fact, the Declaration of Sentiments expressed that:

> He has monopolized nearly all the profitable employments, and from those she is permitted to follow, she receives scanty remuneration. He closes against her all the avenues to wealth and distinction which he considers most honorable to himself. As a teacher of theology, medicine, or law, she is not known. He has denied her the facilities for obtaining a thorough education, all colleges being closed against her.[4]

Paralleling their call for suffrage, women based their demands for equal educational and employment opportunities on the principle "that the equality of human rights results necessarily from the fact of the identity of the race in capabilities and responsibilities."[5]

Although deeply concerned about the economic and education plight of women, the early woman's rights movement and its leaders did little to solve those problems. Rather, as noted in Chapters 2 and 3, the women in the movement increasingly channeled their energies into the suffrage struggle. Thus, most of the improvements with respect to working women, women in the professions, and women's educational opportunities in the nineteenth century were accomplished by individual women, working alone, with only limited help from the movement. As a result, the gains tended to fall short of what was needed in the way of full rights and opportunities for all women.

Efforts on Behalf of Working Women

The conditions present in most jobs open to women in factories and in the textile industry prompted protest by women at Seneca Falls. These kinds of jobs required long hours of work at low pay in substandard conditions. Eleven- or twelve-hour workdays were not uncommon.[6]

Hours aside, universally females were paid less than their male counterparts. Depressed wages were the product of a variety of factors. Many men believed that women were inherently inferior and consequently the fruits of their labor were worth less. The relative paucity of women's jobs also contributed to low wages. Rigid societal values limited the number of jobs suitable for women, which resulted in the increasing number of women seeking work in only a few fields. This created a buyer's market where employers could find someone to fill a position even when low wages were offered. The availability of women willing to work at low wages, particularly in the textile industry, contributed to employer willingness to hire women. Although some women recognized the problem this situation created,[7] many employed in the textile industry were not troubled by these inequities. They did not view their jobs as long term, and instead, saw factory employment as an escape route from the farm until a suitable mate was found.[8]

While women at Seneca Falls recognized the problems faced by women workers, efforts to organize them generally met with little success. Men's fledgling skilled craft unions excluded women because they viewed female employees as a threat to men's own job security.[9] Additionally, independent efforts to unionize women were hampered by the absence of skilled female organizers; there were few women leaders with the necessary skills and experience to lead a successful working woman's movement. Development was further hampered in many areas of women's work because women in industry did not view their jobs as permanent. Women working in non-industrial jobs were also difficult to organize. Domestics, for example, often worked alone or with only a few others, which further diminished the chances of collective action.

Some woman's rights movement leaders, however, attempted to address issues important to women workers. In *The Revolution,* for example, they included a large number of articles of concern to working women. Susan B. Anthony, in fact, used *The Revolution* to call a meeting for the purpose of organizing working women. That meeting, presided over by Anthony and a *Revolution* typesetter, Augusta Lewis Troup, who later was to become a prominent union organizer, resulted in the creation of the New York Working Women's Association in 1868.[10]

Although both Anthony and Elizabeth Cady Stanton were deeply committed to the improvement of women's status in all spheres, including employment, they had an additional motive for attempting to organize women workers at this time. As discussed in Chapters 2 and 3, the woman's rights movement was reaching its peak in the late 1860s because many of its goals were too radical to attract Southern or conservative women. Consequently, leaders of the movement sought to create a new source of potential supporters—working women—who thus far had shown little interest in suffrage. Because of their weakening ties with the abolition movement and their need for new allies, Stanton and Anthony were hopeful that they could link the woman's cause with the new labor movement.[11]

The association between working women and the suffrage cause, however, was short lived because Troup quickly came to believe that an association with women's rights could only hurt the cause of working women. She believed that the Working Women's Association had to guard against involvement with "short hair, bloomers and other vagaries."[12] Thus, shortly after organization of the Working Women's Association, Troup founded the Women's Typographical Association (WTA), which was wholly committed to unionization. In contrast, Anthony believed that it was more important to place women in jobs. Therefore, she publicly advocated that employers fill positions of striking men with women.[13] The inability of Anthony and Troup to form an alliance between the suffrage and labor movements had significant consequences for both fledgling movements. Efforts to unionize women were crippled,[14] and attempts to expand the organizational base of the woman's rights movement proved futile.

Increasingly, leaders of the woman's rights movement believed that improvement in working women's condition could only come as a result of suffrage and reform from above.[15] Thus, Stanton, in particular, became more concerned with gaining the support of the new middle-class working woman—writers, teachers, and the few other professionals—than with working-class women.[16] Consequently, the composition of the Working Women's Association gradually changed to include more professionals than laborers. According to Ellen Carol DuBois, by 1869, its active membership was entirely middle class.[17]

While most women who worked during this period were employed in factories, a limited number held "prestige" occupations. It was from this limited pool of professionals that the woman's movement most frequently sought to draw support. From the time of the Seneca Falls convention, in fact, the movement was not only largely dependent upon these educated women to serve as leaders but also to form the core of their strong supporters.

Initially, the movement's ability to recruit "professional" women was limited to but a few occupations because during the 1800s, several roadblocks were erected that affected women's abilities to enter most professions. One noteworthy barrier came in the form of "professionalization"; i.e., a college education or advanced training were required before one could attempt to be licensed to practice certain professions. Since women were routinely denied admission to most colleges and medical and law schools, professionalization completely cut off their access to certain occupations. Additionally, state licensing of "prestige" professions, most notably law and medicine, was another means of inhibiting women's employment opportunities.

One profession especially affected by these new licensing requirements was midwifery.[18] Since colonial times, female midwives had played an important role in society, and in fact, were deemed the only "proper" form of medical assistance for a "respectable" woman. Once educational and licensing requirements for doctors were established, however, midwifery often was made illegal, and ironically, many women died in childbirth rather than seek the assistance of a male physician. After this health care profession was closed to women, a new one, nursing, became an acceptable career alternative for women in the Civil War era.

Because of the increasing number of public schools, another profession open to women in this period was teaching. Many believed that women were naturally suited to teaching given "the greater intensity of the parental instinct in the female sex, their natural love of children, and the superior gentleness and forebearance of their dispositions."[19] It was also argued that the more moral and religious nature of women made them better teachers of young minds than men.[20] The curricula of the schools that these teachers attended also reflected this notion. All placed heavy emphasis on moral training because of the widespread view that a woman's moral character and ability to conceive children would be damaged by too rigorous an education or her brains were too small to absorb such information.[21]

Financial considerations, however, constituted the most important factor for allowing women to teach. As the nation committed itself to universal public education, thousands of new teachers were needed. Men could not be counted on to fill this need because of the numerous, often more profitable opportunities open to them.[22] Young, single, unmarried women, however, were ideal for teaching as well as available in large numbers.[23] In fact, according to Theodore Beecher, a prominent suffrage supporter, "Woman [is] the best, as well as cheapest guardian and teacher of childhood, in the school as well as the nursery."[24] Indeed, because women were expected to teach only until they got married and not to support a family, the salaries of women teachers were often only one-half to one-third of those paid to young men.[25] When economics were combined with the rising number of young women who wanted to work, the result was the massive influx of women into the teaching profession. Thus, by 1880, women constituted 57.2 percent of all elementary school teachers.[26]

Except for nursing and elementary school teaching in which the "natural" abilities of women could be used to provide cheap health care and educational services, the professions were generally closed to women.[27] And, although many involved in the woman's rights movement protested this lack of opportunities and, in fact, verbally supported the right of women to enter the professions, this issue was not pursued by women's organizations during the woman's rights movement. Individually, though, women active in the movement tried to gain access to prestige occupations. Their efforts, even when successful, however, generally resulted in an undersupply of the public good involved—access to a particular profession.

This is perhaps best illustrated by the circumstances surrounding Elizabeth Blackwell's admission to medical school and her subsequent practice of medicine.[28] Blackwell applied to several medical schools and was duly rejected by all. Eventually, she was admitted to Geneva College of

Medicine in 1847 following a unanimous positive vote of the student body. The students believed her attendance would provide them with a target for all kinds of practical jokes and generally enliven their classes.[29] Once Blackwell was admitted, she had to fight for the right to attend anatomy classes. She also had to endure the reactions of faculty and townspeople who "made no effort to conceal their hostility to such a monstrosity as a would-be woman doctor."[30] Despite these problems, Blackwell graduated at the top of her class in 1849. However, she never enjoyed the fruits of that academic distinction. Securing private patients proved extremely difficult. She eventually established her own hospital, the New York Infirmary for Women and Children.[31]

Entry of women into the legal profession provides another example of the kind of struggle for educational and employment equality women faced. Because English common law (the basis for U.S. law) maintained that women lost their legal identity upon marriage, most states refused to allow married women to practice law because they could not be legally recognized in court. This legal disability was further exacerbated by the fact that women, married or not, could not argue that the practice of law was a "natural" extension of their role in life.[32] Indeed, as we noted earlier in Chapter 3, the field of public affairs of which politics and law were prime examples, were considered the "natural" spheres of men. Faced with these problems plus the fears of male lawyers and judges that the admission of women into the profession would diminish it, and without organizational support, the progress of women in this area was very slow.

Given these circumstances, the ease with which the first woman to become a lawyer, Belle Mansfield, entered the law is surprising.[33] Along with her husband, Mansfield had studied for the Iowa bar examination while they were on the faculty at Iowa Wesleyan University. In 1860, a liberal state court judge appointed two prosuffrage bar examiners to quiz Mansfield, and she passed her exam with "High Honors." The same judge then interpreted an Iowa statute that allowed the admission of "white male persons" to the bar as not being an "implied denial to the right of females" to practice law. This broad interpretation paved the way for Mansfield's admission to the state bar and additionally established favorable precedent for other sympathetic judges to cite when faced with similar requests from other women.[34]

Not all state courts, however, were so obliging in their interpretations of state laws similar to Iowa's. Although the Union Law College in Chicago, Illinois conferred its first law degree upon a woman in 1870, the Illinois state court was not nearly so progressive. In August of 1870, Myra Bradwell passed the bar examination but was denied admission to the practice of law based solely on her sex by the state Supreme Court. She appealed this decision to the U.S. Supreme Court. There, the Justices concluded that Illinois possessed the sole right to set standards for admission to practice in its state courts independent of federal supervision. Expanding on the majority's opinion,

Justice Bradley went so far as to remark that "proper timidity and delicacy evidently unfits [women] from many of the occupations of civil life."[35]

Bradwell's and other individual women's attempts to pursue "male" careers during the 1800s represent a classic example of the undersupply of a public goods situation that develops when there is no organized effort to work in common for a particular right.[36] The few women willing to tackle the social and legal barriers to their practice of law or medicine generally had to work unceasingly by *themselves* to overcome these obstacles. Their efforts had little "spillover" effect on the rights of other women. Once these few individuals secured entry to a school or admission to the practice of a profession, their efforts generally ceased or at least slowed.

Thus, the progress of women in the professions and in higher education during the nineteenth century was restricted by the absence of a unified women's movement to push hard for advancement. In fact, across the professions, the gains made were typical of what happens when a few privileged individuals undertake to acquire a public good—only a very limited supply was made available by their efforts.

THE SUFFRAGE MOVEMENT

While educational and employment rights received only isolated support from the woman's rights movement, at least they received the moral and ideological backing of movement leaders and members.[37] During the suffrage movement, however, women's educational and economic rights failed to garner this kind of support. Because of the movement's narrow focus and more conservative ideology, only a few of the groups and associations affiliated with the suffrage cause, most notably the National Woman's Party, continued to believe in and work for equal rights for women in every facet of life. Thus, real progress in these areas during this period—indeed until the 1960s and the rise of the newest women's rights movement—was accomplished either by individual women or those acting in small groups. And, as in the previous period, this tended to result in a severe undersupply of educational and employment opportunities for all women. Additionally, at least some of the "progress" during the suffrage era was actually in some ways regressive as conservative views of women's role in life resulted in legislation and court cases that often limited the opportunities available to women.

While the narrow focus of the suffrage movement and its more traditional view explain much of the difference between the woman's rights and the suffrage movements, another important difference between the two movements was their attitude toward industrial and other blue-collar workers. While women in the first movement had attempted to organize these women to expand their organizational base, most suffragists wanted to have little to do with the immigrant and poor women who worked in factories at the turn of the century. Some suffragists, associating the plight of working women with the rights of foreign-born, uneducated factory workers, appeared originally even to abandon or write off the whole class of women factory workers in their new emphasis on educated suffrage as discussed in Chapter 3.

As the twentieth century approached, however, some women, particularly those allied with the growing progressive movement and not necessarily the National American Woman Suffrage Association (NAWSA) itself, saw the need to address the problems of women who worked.[38] Increasingly during the last decade of the nineteenth century, middle-class women connected with this reform movement began to recognize that most employed women were not working for "pin money" but rather to help support themselves and their families. Given the necessity of work for these women, reformers realized that if these women were going to be able to fulfill their paramount roles of mothers and homemakers, the terrible conditions under which they toiled would have to change.[39]

Eventually, several strategies were adopted to improve the conditions of working women. One, represented by the actions of the National Women's Trade Union League (NWTUL) was aimed at organizing women into units through which they would be able to bargain for shorter hours and better wages.[40] The NWTUL (originally called the Women's National Trade Union League) was formed in 1903 by individuals from both the working-class trade-union movement, especially those in the American Federation of Labor, and middle-class women from the settlement-house movement. The organization was open both to nonunion (allies) and union members—although union women had to form a majority of the Executive Board.[41] At its first national convention in 1907 it adopted a six point platform: "equal pay for equal work; full citizenship for women; the organization of all workers into trade unions; the eight-hour day; a minimum wage scale; and all the principles embodied in the economic program of the American Federation of Labor."[42]

Thus, from the very beginning, it was dedictated to the cause of suffrage for women along with its other goals; however, because of the antiworking-class attitude of the suffrage movement, the WTUL did not play an active role in that cause until after 1912 when working-class women's potential usefulness to the suffrage battle finally was recognized by NAWSA leaders.[43] Although the NWTUL had some early successes in organizing women workers, after 1909 it increasingly devoted its efforts to securing protective legislation for women workers.[44]

This second strategy—protective legislation—also became the dominant goal of another middle-class reform group dedicated to helping working-class women, the National Consumers' League (NCL). The NCL was formed in 1899 by the merger of several city leagues dedicated to the improvement of working conditions in retail shops and factories.[45] Much of the ideology of the NCL was based on the notion that a woman's proper role in life was to be a good wife and mother. Thus, the goals it sought were those its members believed would make it possible or easier for a woman to perform her domestic duties. For instance, progressives in the National Consumers' League believed that the long hours for shop women and those in factories were detrimental to women because they contributed to family instability, negatively affected women's health, and in some instances forced women into less honorable professions.[46] Therefore, the NCL adopted as its major concern the eradication of substandard conditions in U.S. factories and retail establishments. To this end, it sought to educate the consuming public about the conditions that many shop girls faced. NCL members believed that this kind of tactic could effectively prompt consumers to alter their habits and could pressure employers to improve working conditions.[47]

It was, however, on the legislative front that the NCL initially scored its greatest gains. Its efforts resulted in the passage of maximum hour legislation for women in several states, but these victories soon came under constitutional attack by employers.[48] For example, in 1907, an Oregon employer was convicted for violating an NCL-sponsored state law that prohibited women from working more than eight hours a day. Because there was no favorable precedent to support the legislation, NCL General Counsel Louis Brandeis submitted a lengthy brief to the court that contained statistics indicating the negative impact of long hours of work on a woman's health and her reproductive capabilities. In essence, Brandeis' arguments echoed the ideology of the suffrage movement. He argued that women had unique characteristics and therefore were in need of special protective labor legislation.

Although Brandeis' approach was novel for the times, the Supreme Court was receptive to his arguments. In upholding the constitutionality of the Oregon statute in *Muller* v. *Oregon* (1908), Justice Brewer wrote:

That woman's physical structure and the performance of maternal functions place her at a disadvantage in the struggle for subsistence is obvious. This is especially true when the burdens of motherhood are upon her. Even when they are not, by abundant testimony of the medical fraternity continuance for a long time on her feet at work, repeating this from day to day, tends to injurious effects upon the body, and, as healthy mothers are essential to vigorous offspring, the physical well-being of woman becomes an object of public interest and care in order to preserve the strength and vigor of the race....

...Even though all restrictions on political, personal, and contractual rights were taken away, and she stood, so far as statutes are concerned, upon an absolutely equal plane with him [man], it would still be true that she is so constituted that she will rest upon and look to him for protection: that her physical structure and a proper discharge of her maternal functions—having in view not merely her own health, but the well-being of the race—justify legislation to protect her from the greed as well as the passion of men.[49]

Thus, *Muller* established the principle that women workers could *legally* be treated differently from their male counterparts. Although NCL leaders saw this decision as helping women by remedying at least one evil—long hours—in actuality many employers used this decision to justify *not* hiring women or treating their women workers differently. In New York City, for example, hundreds of women typesetters lost their jobs at several local newspapers in the aftermath of *Muller* because their employers claimed that they would be in violation of the law if they forced the women to work long hours on the night shift. The irony of this action was that these were high-paying positions that most of the women desperately wanted to keep. Other available "female" jobs paid far less.

Wages were another concern of the NCL and other progressive organizations during this period. They feared that low wages forced some women into prostitution. Therefore, to protect a woman's virtue, they believed that it was absolutely necessary to secure state minimum wage laws. Again, little thought was given to the possibility that employers would or could hire men at wages lower than the statutory minimum for women, thereby making it a matter of business sense for employers to replace their female workers with cheaper males.

Once the NCL successfully lobbied several state legislatures for the adoption of minimum wage laws, these laws, like the maximum hour provisions before them, soon encountered challenge in the courts. However, the NCL faced several problems in its attempt to defend these new laws: Brandeis, now on the Supreme Court, was unable to handle the litigation,[50] the lawyers challenging the legislation were highly skilled, and perhaps most important, women in the suffrage movement were now openly divided on the issue of protective legislation.

These factors clearly contributed to the NCL's stunning defeat in 1923 in *Adkins* v. *Children's Hospital*. At issue in *Adkins* was a D.C. statute that created a wage board empowered to set minimum wages geared toward "the necessary cost of living" so as to allow women workers to "maintain their good health and [to] protect their morals." During oral arguments before the Supreme Court, lawyers representing the hospital pointed out that the NCL did not represent all women, and, in fact, that women in general were divided on the issues of protective legislation.[51] Based on this and other arguments, but without overruling *Muller* v. *Oregon*, the Court struck down the D.C. law. In handing the NCL and other progressive reformers a severe blow, Justice Sutherland wrote:

The ancient inequality of the sexes, otherwise than physical, as suggested in the Muller Case has continued "with diminishing intensity." In view of the great—not to say revolutionary—changes which have taken place since that utterance, in the contractual, political and civil status of women, culminating in the Nineteenth Amendment, it is not unreasonable to say that these differences have come almost, if not quite, to the vanishing point. In this aspect of the matter, while the physical differences must be recognized in appropriate cases, and legislation fixing hours or conditions of work may properly take them into account, we cannot accept the doctrine that women of mature age, *sui juris,* require or may be subjected to restrictions upon their liberty of contract which could not lawfully be imposed in the case of men under similar circumstances.[52]

The Court also rejected the NCL's contention that low wages necessarily lead to immorality. In dismissing this argument Sutherland claimed:

The relation between earnings and morals is not capable of standarization. It cannot be shown that well paid women safeguard their morals more carefully than those who are poorly paid. Morality rests upon other considerations than wages; and there is, certainly, no such prevalent connection between the two as to justify a broad attempt to adjust the latter with reference to the former. As a means of safeguarding morals the attempted classification, in our opinion, is without reasonable basis. No distinction can be made between women who work for others and those who do not; nor is there ground for distinction between women and men, for, certainly, if women require a minimum wage to preserve their morals, men require it to preserve their honesty.[53]

While the Court dealt a major loss to the NCL, a significant repercussion of the *Muller* case was the increasingly public division among women over the issue of protective legislation. In fact, during and after the *Adkins* litigation, the National Woman's Party's objections to all forms of protective legislation as being incompatible with equal rights for women were highly publicized.[54]

This break in the ranks of women who had urged ratification of the suffrage amendment, coupled with the amendment's passage, undoubtably contributed to the Court's decision. And, *Adkins* probably accelerated the disintegration of the suffrage movement coalition by presenting a major issue that component groups could not agree upon.

After *Adkins,* the NCL kept a low profile, recognizing that public opinion in the U.S. was not particularly receptive to the idea of protective legislation. Even more important, NCL leaders realized that judicial opinion was set against protective legislation. Since *Muller* (maximum hours) was not overruled by *Adkins,* the NCL chose not to jeopardize that victory *(Muller)* and for several years concentrated on educating the public about the importance of protective legislation while at the same time consciously avoiding litigation that could undo *Muller*.[55] In fact, the NCL actively discouraged the enactment of new protective legislation, fearing that additional challenges from powerful, well-financed employers would be forthcoming, giving the Court an opportunity to overrule its 1908 decision.

During this period, although women's working conditions in the United States largely remained the same, the kinds of work women obtained changed considerably. By 1930, 30 percent of the employed women in the United States were engaged in nonmanual occupations—often as clerical workers. In fact, a particularly significant phenomenon occurred during this period—the colonization by women of the new white-collar clerical and sales jobs. From 1890–1920, the percentage of all working women who were employed in this field rose from 5.3 to 25.6.[56] This change in composition of the female work force had an impact on the NCL's fight for improved labor conditions. As the proportion of women working in factories and other occupations that were notorious for their hazardous conditions declined, it became much more difficult to rally for improved conditions. The kinds of occupations that women secured also were the kinds of jobs that have been notoriously difficult to organize. Clericals, for example, are a group that even strong unions have not, at least until recently, even attempted to unionize. Additionally, the large numbers of immigrant women that were employed in factories were often happy to have any job and resisted attempts at organization. This lack of organization and the occupational segregation of women resulted in low wages for women when compared to men both overall and within occupational categories.

The Depression also contributed to this problem. Most people believed that men, rather than married women, should obtain the few jobs available. Some employers even had specific policies that prohibited the hiring of married women or that called for immediate discharge upon marriage. In fact, during the Depression, twenty-six states had laws specifically barring the employment of married women in some occupations.[57] For example, 77 percent of the public school systems surveyed in 1930–1931 had policies against hiring married women, and a majority fired women upon their marriage. Similar laws were adopted in many states and municipalities. Even the national government passed legislation that prohibited the employment of more than one family member from one household—a practice that had a far greater adverse impact on women than men.

Faced with this grim picture and spurred on by FDR's New Deal and its call for all kinds of economic legislation, in 1933 NCL leaders plotted with New York legislators to see new minimum wage laws enacted. While the NCL worked in New York, the state of Washington enacted legislation creating a Minimum Wage Board to determine the adequacy of wages for women to ensure "the decent maintenance of women," and to protect their "health and morals." Alleging a violation of that law, a woman sued her employer for back pay, charging that she did not receive the legal minimum wage of $14.50 for her forty-eight hour week as required by law. The U.S. Supreme Court upheld the constitutionality of the Washington law. In overruling *Adkins,* Justice Hughes wrote:

> What can be closer to the public interest than the health of women and their protection from unscrupulous and overreaching employers? And if the protection of women is a legitimate end of the exercise of state power, how can it be said that the requirement of the payment of a minimum wage fairly fixed in order to meet the very necessities of existence is not an admissible means to that end? The Legislature of the state was clearly entitled to consider the situation of women in employment, the fact that they are in the class receiving the least pay, that their bargaining power is relatively weak, and that they are the ready victims of those who would take advantage of their necessitous circumstances.[58]

Thus, while the NCL began its lobbying activities in the early 1900s, it took almost forty years for it to convince the Court of the constitutionality of its goals. Its inability to meet its objectives more quickly can be attributed to several factors. First, protective legislation was perceived by some as a public bad. Employers repeatedly challenged or threatened to fight the constitutionality of maximum hours or minimum wage laws. Second, there was division among women over its effect on full rights for women—a question that also divided the movement. Although the line of reasoning used by the NCL to justify protective legislation was the same used to justify women suffrage,[59] the single-minded movement never wholeheartedly supported NCL goals. Finally, although this ideology justified the efforts of the NCL and other reformers to help those women who had to work, the larger questions of discrimination were ignored.

One group, in particular, that vociferously opposed the NCL's activities was the National Woman's Party. The NWP believed that protective legislation was a pure public bad that would forestall full sexual equality. Its objections, however, ultimately were overruled when its leaders failed to expand their organizational base. Women directly affected by protective legislation, for example, often were too busy working and tending their families to have the time or energy to devote to fighting its passage. Also, the passage of these laws came slowly on a state-by-state, issue-by-issue approach (first maximum hours and then minimum wage laws), thereby not presenting the necessary catalyst to move working women to action on a nationwide basis. Moreover, most working women were not organized. Only a few belonged to unions. In addition, the large number of established, well-connected women who advocated protective legislation as well as the Supreme Court's definitive decision in *Muller* must have made any attempts at limiting the scope of this legislation look quite difficult.

Thus, even though the NCL was successful in the long run, its actions were attacked from both sides. Moreover, its "victories" eventually provided significant legal roadblocks to full equality.

The NCL, however, at least provided a support organization for working women in industry. In contrast, women attempting either to obtain full educational opportunities or to enter the professions lacked a similar support group during this period. Furthermore, although the percentage of women with college education and advanced degrees rose dramatically, this progress was in many ways deceptive.[60] The expansion of coeducation to include most state colleges and many private schools was met with resistance by many college administrators and faculty. Admission of women often was motivated by economic need and not by acceptance of the idea that women could and should receive a college education. At the turn of the century, many colleges were threatened by the exodus of male students to professional schools that often did not require a college degree as a prerequisite. To counter these declining enrollments, many institutions of higher learning were forced to accept female students. However, in keeping with the prevailing stereotypes about women's mental abilities and "natural" propensities, women, or coeds as they were called, were channeled into liberal arts and other "female" majors. Entire curricula were developed for the near-exclusive study by women. Most notable of these were social work, education, library studies, and home economics. The latter grew out of the child-study movement and a new emphasis in education on preparing students for their future careers. And it followed, because a girl's ultimate "career" was to be that of wife and mother, she should take college courses concerned with the proper running of a home (sewing, cooking, and childcare). This philosophy was, of course, entirely in keeping with the dominant suffrage view that a women should devote her full energies and abilities to being the best possible mother and wife.[61]

Additionally, coeducational institutions began to adopt restrictive admission standards limiting the number of female students. This practice was formalized in 1925 when medical schools adopted a 5 percent quota for female students (a standard that was to remain in effect until 1945). To this problem was added the fact that few—40 out of 482—hospitals in the United States accepted women as interns.[62] The result was a noticeable decline in the number of women doctors, which had reached a high point of 6 percent in 1910. And although at least some earlier progress had occurred in the medical profession, the position of women in law was and remained abysmal. Although by 1916, all states in the Union allowed women to practice law, many law schools denied admission to women as did many professional legal associations.[63] Moreover, in the case of both law and medicine, the few women who entered these professions were relegated to doing what their colleagues viewed as low status "women's work." Female attorneys generally practiced in the areas of matrimonial law or wills and estates, while women doctors became obstetricians or pediatricians, not surgeons.

The progress of women in other traditionally male professions was little better. For instance, a 1921 report by the American Association of University Professors (AAUP) found that in 104 coeducational colleges, even though women made up 31 percent of the students, females constituted only 4 percent of the full professors (but 23.5 percent of the instructors). In 47 percent of these institutions, there were no women at any professorial rank.[64] The depth of the prejudice against hiring women professors was often blatant even among the more "liberal" academicians. In replying to a survey, one dean commented, "When we discover a woman who can handle some subject in our course of study *better than a man* could handle it, we shall not hesitate to urge the appointment of the woman."[65] [emphasis added]

While the situation of women in "male" professions improved only marginally, the crowding of women into their "natural" professions continued unabated. Indeed, virtually all of the "progress" women made in the professions during the suffrage era (the percentage of women working as professionals in 1920 was close to 12 percent) can be attributed to the opening up of several new "learned" occupations for women.[66] The most notable of these were librarian,[67] home economist, and social worker.[68] In fact, many of the women graduating from these programs formed the leadership base of the movement.

Thus, while large numbers of women went to college, their training gave them a perspective largely incompatible with the principle of equal rights. Accordingly, the major legal advances won during this period concerned the legalization of protective legislation—judicial recognition of the fact that women workers needed protection—and were not grounded in notions of equality.

WORLD WAR II

The onset of World War II and the activation of men into the military reversed the economic climate of the 1930s. Women workers were needed to produce armaments and to run other factories. Thus, to meet this need, the U.S. government undertook a massive campaign to recruit women into the paid labor force. This campaign brought about the abolition of many of the employment restrictions affecting women in the 1930s, and consequently women moved into the labor force in large numbers. Between 1940 and 1945, the percentage of employed women rose from 26 to 36 percent. Perhaps the most important aspect of this increase was the rise in the number of married women who joined the labor force during this period. While a relatively high percentage of unmarried women always had worked, few married women except black, immigrant, or those women from very poor families had been employed previously. During the war years, however, 75 percent of the new women workers were married. Between 1940 and 1945, the percentage of married women working rose from 15 to 24 percent.[69]

The average age of these new workers also diverged from previous trends. For the first time, significant numbers of women over 35, who comprised 60 percent of the new workers, entered the labor force. This dramatic alteration in the age distribution of working women challenged many traditional assumptions. For example, many of these women had children at home, although few mothers of preschoolers worked. And, many of these new workers were middle-class women. Drawn into the labor force by the new opportunities open to them, these women often worked not of necessity but out of patriotism or other noneconomic reasons.[70]

As most prewar discriminatory hiring policies were abandoned, they and other women gained employment in a variety of situations formerly closed to them. They became welders, airplane pilots, and Wall Street analysts, for example.[71] Women were particularly welcome in the burgeoning defense industries. In fact, they accounted for 40 percent of the workers in aircraft plants.[72]

Additionally, liberalization of federal government employment practices resulted in the hiring of thousands of women as attorneys and in other professions vacated by men. The number of female doctors grew as the shortage of physicians and male students forced the national government, medical schools, and hospitals to relax their previous restrictive practices. In 1943, the U.S. government finally commissioned women as physicians in the armed services.[73] And, one million women were hired as clericals by the U.S. government to handle the new bureaucracy brought about by the War.[74] Additionally, the national government furthered this progress by endorsing *in principle* the idea of equal pay for equal work.

Unions, too, began to treat women workers more fairly. After congressional passage of the National Industrial Recovery Act in 1933, which recognized labor's right to organize, some unions began to concentrate their energies on mass production industries.[75] In the late 1930s, the Congress of Industrial Organizations began to organize nonskilled workers and thus often had to appeal to women in the factories where unionization attempts were being made. Thus, according to Barbara Deckard, by the end of the war, the number of union women grew from 800,000 in 1939 to more than three million.[76] Unionization and employer need for women workers resulted in a tremendous improvement in women's earnings.

Thus, the war and the employment conditions it created brought about an expansion of economic opportunity that women, acting alone or in small groups, had previously been unable to accomplish. These new rights, however, were limited by the fact that the conditions that necessitated them were temporary. The kinds of permanent legal changes required to produce real equal opportunity were not undertaken. For example, the U.S. government failed to adopt a *law* requiring equal pay for equal work; it simply endorsed the idea. Indeed, the National War Labor Board, which was charged with implementing the equal pay regulation, not only exempted jobs that "historically" were women's or in which all the employees were presently women, but it often refused to hear complaints of sex discrimination in pay.[77] In fact, many employers also ignored the equal pay provision or circumvented it by reclassifying jobs performed by women workers. Similarly, it continued to be legal for employers to refuse to hire older or married women. And, there were no national legal prohibitions against flat refusals to employ women at all. Thus, many job classifications remained male or were only temporarily staffed by women until a more "appropriate" person—a man—could be hired. Union protection of female members also often lagged behind that afforded to men. Separate seniority lists for each sex, for example, were not illegal or uncommon.

Perhaps more important, however, was that the wider range of social and legal changes necessary to allow women workers to compete equally was not even temporarily adopted. Notable among the changes not made were arrangements for adequate childcare for the phenomenal influx of mothers into the labor force. Although other nations at war offered a variety of special programs to assist married women with children, the U.S. government failed to adopt any kind of national child-care system.[78] In 1945, although 100,000 children attended federally funded day-care centers, they were only 10 percent of those in need of such arrangements.[79]

Given concerns about adequate childcare, it surprised many employers as well as the U.S. government that the women who went to work during the war years wanted to stay on the job. Many women, however, had to relinquish their positions to returning veterans who, *by law,* were given preference. Within two months after the end of World War II, almost 800,000 women lost their jobs in the aircraft industry alone.[80] Barbara J. Harris dramatically has stated what happened to women:

> Within a year after the end of the war, women doctors were being removed from hospital and staff positions to make room for returning veterans.... In some industries the number of women laid off was staggering: the Hoover Company, 84 percent; American Brake and Block, 90 percent; American Leather Products, Asbestos Manufacturing Company and Baker Rowland Company, all 100 percent.[81]

Additionally, many corporations reestablished prewar prohibitions against the employment of married women in part because of fears of a postwar recession. And, much of the protective legislation concerning the hours, conditions, and kinds of work women could do were reinstituted. These actions clearly reflected a concerted effort to encourage women to return to their homes, husbands, and children. Within a few short years after the veterans' return, however, large numbers of women reentered the work force but did so by taking traditional jobs at far lower pay than they enjoyed during the war.[82]

This reentrance was a particularly interesting phenomenon given the "return to the home ethos" that characterized the postwar period. Although popular magazines proclaimed the benefits and rewards of suburban living and the homemaker role as a full-time, fulfilling occupation, many married women abandoned this "ideal" for the working world. While according to Betty Friedan, the editors of the *Ladies Home Journal, McCall's,* and *Redbook* created a "feminine mystique," by depicting women as "young, frivolous, almost childlike; fluffy and feminine; passive, gaily content in a world of bedroom and kitchen, sex, babies, and home,"[83] millions of these "contented" housewives sought employment outside of the home—many out of financial necessity. In 1950, for example, for the first time in American history, married women constituted more than 50 percent of all women workers. Nearly 25 percent of them had school-aged children—a dramatic change from the prewar period. These trends continued unabated into the early 1960s.[84]

The post-World War II alteration in the labor force pattern of women workers can be traced to at least two factors. First, contrary to immediate postwar expectations, there was a heavy demand in the 1950s and 1960s for women workers. Traditional "women's jobs," heavily concentrated in the service sector, proved one of the fastest growing areas of the economy. However, at the very time there were additional jobs for women, there was a decline in the available number of women considered acceptable workers by traditional standards. More specifically, as a result of the Depression in the 1930s, which witnessed a marked decline in the birthrate, there were fewer persons (men or women) reaching adulthood in the 1950s and 1960s. When this factor was combined with the trend toward earlier marriage, the result was that there were simply too few single women to fill the demand for women workers.[85] The massive influx of older, married women into the labor market was simply insufficient to meet the demand for women workers. Second, coupled with the demand for women to fill these new positions was an increased need for additional income by many families. This was a result of an expansion in the definition of what constituted economic "necessities" and the spiralling inflation rate. The result was the employment of increasing numbers of working mothers during the 1950s and 1960s.

Changes in the number and kind of working women, however, were not accompanied by any improvement in the economic conditions or rights of women. For the most part, women still were clustered into female jobs. Few held prestigious occupations while the "professions" open to women— nursing and teaching—continued to be almost totally dominated by females.

Additionally, as larger numbers of women sought work outside of the home during this period, the concentration of women in certain fields tended to drive wages downward—at least in relation to those of men. From 1940 to 1960, this wage gap increased steadily, largely due to this ghettoization of female employees in low-paying fields and the nonexistence of national equal pay legislation, resulting in male-female wage differentials in the "typically male" professions.

Just as returning veterans took women's jobs, they also had an effect on the proportion of women in colleges and universities. From 1940 to 1950, the percentage of baccalaureate degrees awarded to women declined by 18 percent. Part of this dramatic change was a direct result of government policy. Large numbers of returning veterans were able to attend college solely on account of the G.I. bill. Before 1940, most men and women alike who enrolled in postsecondary education were from middle-class or well-to-do families. After the war, because of the tuition and living assistance grants available to returning veterans, many men who formerly would have been unable to afford a college education could now do so. Without similar benefits for women, even though they had supported the war effort in the only way they were allowed to (by statute women could not be drafted), a large number of women were priced out of a college education.[86] And, the women who could afford to attend a college or university often met a "veterans first" policy or the stringent kinds of quotas that had been utilized to exclude women before the war.

Even those women who attended college continued to face discrimination. Following previous patterns, women who attended college tended to major in "women's" fields, especially teaching, where the demand for workers was high. Few went on for professional or higher academic degrees, and those who tried to often were denied admission to schools because of their sex.[87] Additionally, continued curricular emphasis on the rewards of motherhood and marriage led large numbers of women to drop out of school to marry. Even those who graduated almost invariably married soon after and never sought employment.

Thus, by the early 1960s, even when women had equipped themselves with the tools necessary for a career, ghettoization and the continuing myths about why most women worked resulted in their wages remaining far below those of men—even when they did the same work. For example, as late as 1960, it was estimated that a woman with a college degree could expect to earn the same wages as a man who had completed the eighth grade.

This kind of discrimination, even though women's abilities had been clearly revealed during World War II, was keenly evident throughout this whole period. For example, in 1948, the U.S. Supreme Court handed down a decision that did little to dispel sexual stereotypes of that era and the atmosphere of acceptance of gender-based discrimination that blossomed after World War II. In *Goesaert* v. *Cleary* (1948), the Court upheld the constitutionality of a state law that prohibited women from working in taverns unless they were the wife or daughter of the owner. Writing for the Court, Justice Felix Frankfurter claimed:

> The fact that women may now have achieved the virtues that men have long claimed as their prerogatives and now indulge in vices that men have long practiced, does not preclude the States from drawing a sharp line between the sexes.[88]

This decision not only justified the action of state legislators who wished to restrict or prohibit women's entry into some professions but also echoed prevailing public sentiment concerning working women.

THE CURRENT WOMEN'S RIGHTS MOVEMENT

As the 1960s approached, some women recognized that gender-based discrimination existed in all spheres. Many of them, in fact, campaigned for John Kennedy, who they believed would support legislation to expand women's rights. Thus, when his first appointees were announced and only two out of 240 were women, many of his female supporters were outraged.[89] To appease these supporters, and, some believe, to get the "administration off the hook on the equal rights amendment question" (Baker et al. suggest that Kennedy hoped the commission would find facts to be used against passage of an ERA),[90] Kennedy signed an executive order on December 14, 1961, creating the President's Commission on the Status of Women. Its mandate was to analyze and recommend changes to end the "prejudices and outmoded customs that act as a barrier to full realization of women's basic rights."[91] When the report of that commission was made public in 1963, perhaps its most concrete recommendations concerned employment and labor standards.[92]

In terms of employment rights and the creation of a women's rights movement, the commission's importance cannot be overstated. Chaired by Eleanor Roosevelt, who had extremely close ties to women active in the progressive movement, the commission brought women together for the first time since the 1930s.[93] Its members were drawn largely from the ranks of business and professional women's clubs with limited representation from organized labor. These women soon formed the leadership nuclei of what we have termed the women's rights movement.[94]

In addition to providing the leadership of the new movement, the federal commission gave women an agenda and publicized that agenda, which resulted in some governmental action. Examples of responses to commission recommendations include several executive orders and the Equal Pay Act. And, only one year after the commission issued its recommendations, the Civil Rights Act of 1964 also was enacted.[95]

The Equal Pay Act

Prior to congressional passage of the Equal Pay Act of 1963 (see Appendix B), several efforts were made to secure such a law. During World War II, the Women's Bureau, a division within the Department of Labor devoted to the improvement of the state of working women, had called for women to be paid equal pay for comparable work. Later, in 1945, legislation calling for equal pay actually was introduced in the House of Representatives but never came to a vote. Although similar legislation was introduced during every subsequent session of Congress until 1963, without presidential backing, equal pay supporters were unsuccessful. Once Kennedy threw his support behind the proposed equal pay amendment to the Fair Labor Standards Act of 1938, it passed quickly.

The Equal Pay Act, however, did not pass in the form advocated by its staunchest supporters. It exempted several classes of workers and, instead of guaranteeing "equal pay for comparable work," it required, in its final form, only that equal pay be had for *equal work*. Supporters, remembering the ingenious reclassification schemes used by employers during World War II, feared that this stricter standard would make it easier for employers to avoid the purpose of the act. Although its provisions clearly did not go far enough to win the enthusiastic support of the radical women in the National Woman's Party, *no* women's groups spoke in opposition to its enactment. According to Irene Murphy, "It was a single issue which bridged the gap between militant feminists supporting the ERA and those in the social welfare movement who opposed it."[96]

Informal opposition, however, came from manufacturers and large companies, especially those who employed large numbers of women.[97] Yet, because their female employees generally held different job classifications than males, the final language of the act made it more palatable to them. When this acquiescence was coupled with public support for the measure,[98] the act's provisions became far less threatening as a nonuniversal public good.

Initially, the Equal Pay Act's greatest impact was on working-class women. In fact, it was not amended to cover administrative, executive, or professional employees until 1972. The Wage Standards Division of the Deparatment of Labor (DOL) was empowered to bring suits on behalf of women who alleged violations of the law. In general, DOL was very successful in terms of attempting to bring about compliance. Since the act allows a woman to file a complaint anonymously, and, therefore, not fear employer retaliation, many complaints were filed and then thoroughly investigated by DOL. In the first ten years of the act's existence, over 100 million dollars in back pay awards were secured by the agency for aggrieved employees, most of them women.[99] In fact, from 1963 to 1979, when DOL was divested of its enforcement powers, although the Equal Pay Act's language is written in terms of *equal* pay for *equal* work, DOL was able to convince the courts to interpret this provision to require that work done must be only "substantially equal."[100] Thus, according to Norma Raffel, in 1977 alone, DOL "found that 19,382 workers (virtually all of them women) were owed $15,512,141 under the Equal Pay Act."[101]

Although DOL was empowered to bring suit against recalcitrant employers, over 95 percent of all complaints were resolved through voluntary compliance.[102] Because DOL investigators conducted periodic on-site investigations of employers to monitor compliance, many employers voluntarily restructured their pay scales, fearing costly back pay settlements knowing the agency's impressive track record.[103]

On July 1, 1979, however, over the protest of many women's groups, enforcement of the Equal Pay Act was transferred to the Equal Employment Opportunity Commission (EEOC), which now is authorized to review equal pay violations along with Civil Rights Act complaints. This was done as part of President Carter's reorganization plan to streamline government. At this writing, the EEOC's effectiveness in enforcing the Equal Pay violations is difficult to gauge.

Even though DOL earlier was successful in bringing about wage parity in individual cases, women's wages on an aggregate level have continued to decline when compared to those earned by men. As discussed in Chapter 6, women have continued to earn far less than men. Some of this difference is directly attributable to the ghettoization of women workers and the resultant underevaluation of the kinds of work generally done by women. However, even when men and women have the same or similar jobs, especially in the professions, women's salaries continue to fall far below those earned by men.[104]

A major move toward pay equality, however, occurred in late 1979. In October, several organizations including BPW, NOW, the Women's Legal Defense Fund, Women Employed, and the Coalition of Labor Union Women, held the first National Conference on Pay Equity.[105] Those in attendance at the conference decided that the following issues were key problems that needed to be addressed so that a coordinated strategy to challenge the pay equity problem could be devised:

1. *Developing Public Understanding and Acceptance of the Issue.*
2. *Developing Legal and Administrative Underpinnings to Support Pay Equity.*
3. *Overcoming Employer Arguments Against Pay Equity such as:*
   Raising salaries to comparable levels might be inflationary.

There are no available funds with which to pay comparable wages.
The free marketplace should determine the level of wages.

4. *Developing a Bias Free Job Evaluation System That will be
    Accepted by Labor, Management and Government.*

5. *Dealing with the Problems Faced by Unions including:*
    Conflicting interests of different occupational groups within their
    memberships.
    Attempts by employers to place the burden of dividing limited
    funds for salaries on unions.
    Potential legal liability for past and current participation in
    discriminatory employment practices, if pay equity is determined
    to be covered by Title VII of the Civil Rights Act.[106]

This strategy was given a tremendous boost in June 1981. In *Gunther* v.
County of Washington, where several women's rights groups argued for pay
equity, the U.S. Supreme Court ruled that gender-based claims of employment
discrimination can be brought even though no member of the opposite sex
holds an equal- or higher-paid job.[107] In *Gunther,* a matron at a county jail
contended that she was denied equal pay for work that was substantially equal
to that performed by prison guards and that even if the work was not
substantially equal, the significant salary discrepancy was due to sex
discrimination. The highest female salary, 668 dollars a month, was lower
than the lowest male salary, 736 dollars a month.

Although the Court's decision was worded very narrowly, it was a
tremendous victory for women's rights groups. Just three years before, when
Denver nurses challenged a wage system that paid them less than tree
trimmers, sign painters, and tire servicemen, a federal district court judge, in
ruling against them, proclaimed the case "pregnant with the possibility of
disrupting the entire economic system of the United States of America."[108]
Thus, although *Gunther* involved more similarly situated employees, the
Court's ruling gave women hope that their efforts may continue to have
impact on salary scales. And, women across the country already appear to be
relying on the Court's decision, even though the comparable work issue was
not addressed head on. In July 1981, 2,000 city employees in San Jose,
California, which has a female mayor and woman-dominated city council,
went on strike to get equal pay for comparable jobs.[109] In 1978, a study
commissioned by the mayor found that male-dominated jobs had higher
salaries than those dominated by women. Examples found of unequal salaries
included the mayor's secretary who made 47 percent less than that made by a
senior air conditioning mechanic and nurses who earned $9,210 a year less
than assistant fire master mechanics.[110]

Thus, while women's salaries generally continue to lag far behind those of
men, recent efforts of women's rights groups on the comparable work issue

and apparent judicial support for that notion may lessen wage gaps in the future.[111] In the wake of the ERA defeat, NOW in particular has targeted this problem,[112] but given the tremendous change this proposal would require in the business sector, substantial opposition is likely to occur. The concept of equal pay for comparable work could so adversely affect many employers, particularly those who thus far have avoided Equal Pay Act problems through ghettoization, that they can be expected to mobilize against this proposal, which to them is a pure public bad.[113]

Executive Orders

In addition to these long-term efforts for equal pay, women's groups also pressured early on for an executive order to prohibit sex discrimination by holders of federal contracts and to remedy sex discrimination within the federal government.[114] In fact, to persuade President Johnson to sign these orders, NOW sent letters to the President, as did the BPW and the General Federation of Women's Clubs. Esther Peterson, who had been instrumental in pressuring President Kennedy to create the Commission on the Status of Women, then as an assistant Secretary of Labor, even persuaded the Secretary of Labor to support the order, thus lending further impetus to the campaign for presidential action.[115]

Although executive orders now prohibit discrimination against female government employees, their major emphasis, and that most heavily lobbied for by women's groups, concerned prohibition against private sector sex discrimination. Executive Order (EO) 11375 (see Appendix B) prohibits those with federal contracts from discriminating against female employees and also requires employers to take affirmative action to redress past discriminatory practices. The Office of Federal Contract Compliance is responsible for general enforcement of the orders, but individual agencies that grant contracts do specialized enforcement. Sections of the order dealing with educational institutions with government contracts are enforced by the Office for Civil Rights within HEW. Potential sanctions for employers who do not adhere to the mandates of either order are great and include cancellation of all federal contracts.[116]

Although EO 11375 became effective in October, 1968, DOL failed to promulgate regulations until June 1970, when they were announced at a conference celebrating the 50th anniversary of the Women's Bureau.[117] The regulations disappointed the many women's groups that had urged the Secretary of Labor to act because just prior to issuance of these guidelines, the agency had issued an order setting out employer affirmative action requirements concerning race. To the women's groups that had urged the issuance of regulations prohibiting gender discrimination since 1967, the call for employers to make "an analysis of the *racial* composition of the work force" was very disappointing.[118] And, although this order led women to step up their lobbying efforts and thus, probably sped up the issuance of the sex-discrimination guidelines, the 1970 guidelines were not nearly so stringent as those that applied to minorities. They only suggested recruiter trips to women's colleges, and one exception did not require employers to provide reasons for not hiring women. Thus, according to NOW, "they create[d] a huge loophole by allowing employers to refuse to hire women if they don't have space to build new restrooms."[119] And, no specific goals or timetables were required in terms of *sex* discrimination.

Even though the regulations were weak, NOW and WEAL both decided to take action to press the executive branch. In June of 1970, NOW filed a blanket complaint against 1,300 corporations and companies that received federal contracts. WEAL filed a complaint against the University of Maryland. At the same time, it requested that an investigation be made of all American colleges and universities and alleged a pattern and practice of discrimination.[120] WEAL and WEAL members also filed complaints against several other universities, while NOW filed complaints against Harvard and the entire State University of New York system. Noting the real absence of women faculty at the nation's law and medical schools, WEAL filed a complaint against every medical school in late 1970s; the Professional Women's caucus did the same against all law schools.[121] During this campaign, complaints also were filed by hundreds of local groups, and even some radical feminists found themselves filing complaints or writing letters to HEW or to their congressional representatives, urging that timely investigations of sex discrimination be made.

The EO inclusion of affirmative action guidelines created a very real backlash in academia, however. Even though all that is required of universities is a showing that they make an effort to find women faculty and not that they actually hire them, white male professors and several Jewish organizations immediately took up the charge of reverse discrimination. Several males, in fact, filed charges of reverse discrimination with HEW's Office for Civil Rights, now a part of the Department of Education.

By 1972, largely on account of WEAL's efforts, HEW had received over 350 sex discrimination complaints. Because of staffing problems, HEW sent all individual sex complaints to the EEOC and proceeded to handle only class actions. However, after six Jewish organization representatives contacted Secretary Elliot Richardson about their distress over the affirmative action aspects of EO 11375, the reverse discrimination complaints of individual male professors were given priority—at the same time women's complaints were being sent to another agency.[122]

HEW's insensitivity to executive order compliance and its failure to investigate sex-based claims under the order led WEAL to file suit against the agency in 1974. WEAL sued both HEW and the DOL on behalf of NOW, the

Federation of Organizations for Professional Women, and the Association of Women in Science.[123] Agency enforcement of the order was critical because the order does not provide a private right of action such as exists under Title VII, which has allowed women's groups to bring their claims before the federal courts.

During the course of *WEAL et al.* v. *Califano,* HEW and DOL admitted that they had failed to enforce the bars against sex discrimination adequately. Thus, in late 1977, a consent order was entered that required both agencies to formulate standards and time frames for handling sex-discrimination complaints, hire additional personnel to comply with the terms of the order, provide WEAL's lawyers with detailed accounts of their enforcement activities, and pay WEAL's attorney fees and costs incurred during the course of litigation.[124] This was a continuing order, and the named enforcement agencies continue to send periodic enforcement reports to WEAL.[125]

Although WEAL and several other organizations continue to watch the civil rights enforcement agencies closely, discrimination in academia continues. For example, although women received 19.3 percent of all Ph.D.s in Political Science granted between 1977–1980, in 1980, they were only 3.4 percent of the full professors in Ph.D.-granting institutions.[126] Thus, while discrimination by federal contractors and against women in academia is barred by executive orders issued at the urging of women's rights groups, these orders have failed to have a major impact. Enforcement by federal agencies, even after those agencies have been sued by women's groups, has been lax, and few employers (businesses or universities) have been barred from doing business with the federal government or have had their contract funds terminated. Women's rights groups, therefore, have sought other avenues to remedy discrimination.

The Civil Rights Act of 1964

While Commission on the Status of Women members recognized that employment discrimination was rampant, no specific call was made by the commission for an antidiscrimination provision. However, one was enacted soon after the committee report was made public. Title VII of the Civil Rights Act of 1964 prohibits discrimination based on sex in all terms, conditions, or privileges of employment (see Appendix B). To enforce its provisions, the Equal Employment Opportunity Commission (EEOC) was created.

The inclusion of the "sex" prohibition in the Civil Rights Act, a provision largely geared to alleviating racial discrimination, originally was tacked on to the bill by a Southern member of Congress to make a joke of the bill, divide supporters, and thereby lead to its defeat.[127] According to Jo Freeman, Martha Griffiths (D-Michigan) intended to sponsor the addition but upon hearing of a Southern representative's decision to include sex in the bill, she deferred, believing that his sponsorship would bring 100 additional votes.[128] Griffiths calculated correctly and the bill, in its entirety, was passed.

The enactment of this major piece of anti-sex discrimination is interesting because *no* organized women's group spoke in its behalf, although Griffiths and other female representatives lined up solidly behind its passage. Unlike the large number of women's groups that had testified in favor of the Equal Pay Act, that action was missing here. Writing in 1971, Caruthers Berger posited that the solid support for the Equal Pay Act just one year earlier and lobbying by the National Women's Party led to the addition of the sex discrimination prohibition.[129] Jo Freeman, however, questioned his conclusions, noting Berger's long association with the NWP and statements to the contrary from Rep. Griffiths.[130] Ironically, it was not the actions of existing women's groups, but instead the EEOC's nonenforcement of this act that proved the catalyst for the formation of the rights branch of the current women's movement. From the beginning, EEOC officials refused to take the sex-discrimination provision seriously, noting its lack of legislative history and the mirth that it inspired when it reached the floor.[131] Repeatedly, the agency failed to investigate complaints of sex discrimination, which prompted Griffiths to attack the agency's inaction from the floor of the House of Representatives. As noted in Chapter 2, Griffiths was not the only person concerned with EEOC negligence. Many women, frustrated by the EEOC's incompetence and the Commission on the Status of Women's inability to act, met in October 1966 and formed the National Organization for Women. One of NOW's first goals was the eradication of sex discrimination, but without EEOC support they could do little.

Thus, unlike the Equal Pay Act that was vigorously enforced by DOL, enforcement of the sex-discrimination provision of the Civil Rights Act by the EEOC was totally inadequate. To alleviate this problem, NOW and several other women's rights groups took a number of actions that occurred almost simultaneously. First, all during 1966 pressure was put on the EEOC to hold hearings so that it could issue regulations to implement the sex-discrimination prohibition of Title VII of the act that prohibits employment discrimination.[132] These hearings were finally held in May 1967.[133]

Second, while the EEOC was considering possible regulations, women kept up pressure on employers and the EEOC. New York City NOW members, for example, picketed *The New York Times'* offices to protest its maintenance of sex-segregated help wanted advertisements, and later in December 1967, NOW held what Freeman calls "perhaps the first contemporary feminist demonstration."[134] Its members, along with many from other women's rights groups, picketed EEOC offices around the country to draw attention to EEOC inaction. It also filed suit against the EEOC for failing to enforce Title VII and, in Pittsburgh, in response to a complaint filed by NOW, the Commission on Human Relations brought suit against Pittsburgh Press claiming it violated Title VII by the paper's publication of sex-segregated advertisements.[135] Third, in addition to pressuring the EEOC, NOW and other women's rights groups also began to lobby Congress for passage of the Equal Employment Opportunity Act. They believed that the EEOC needed powers to bring suit if discrimination was found after an investigation—prior to this, all the EEOC could do was seek voluntary compliance. The Act, as ultimately passed in 1972, also widened the coverage of the Civil Rights Act to include employers and unions of eight or more workers, employees of both state and the national government, and employees of educational institutions.

Finally, women's rights groups recognized that they would need to litigate to obtain employment rights. Although the EEOC has been empowered to bring lawsuits against private employers since 1972, most observers give the EEOC very low marks for enforcement. Agency backlogs are tremendous. In 1977, approximately 130,000 complaints had not yet been investigated. It is not uncommon for an aggrieved party to wait as long as three years before the EEOC even attempts to resolve her suit.[136] This has caused many women to retain their own lawyers after filing with the EEOC in an effort to expedite resolution of their claims.

Because Title VII litigation often involves complex issues of fact and the introduction of statistical information, particularly where a pattern and practice of discrimination is alleged, most aggrieved women have not had the resources necessary to retain attorneys to handle their claims. Thus, many women's rights groups have been extensively involved in both counseling and representing women who claim employment discrimination.

Additionally, NOW's recognition that political pressure alone might not be sufficient to change the EEOC's inaction concerning sex-discrimination complaints led it to begin discussions concerning the formation of a legal arm to litigate violations of both the Civil Rights and Equal Pay Acts.[137] While several other women's rights organizations concerned with employment and educational discrimination were formed shortly after NOW's creation by those unhappy with some of NOW's policies on more controversial kinds of issues,[138] all agreed that it was imperative to force the EEOC to treat sex-discrimination complaints seriously. Thus, other groups also took steps to form legal funds to litigate sex-discrimination complaints.[139]

This strategy was entirely in keeping with the ideology of the emerging rights branch of the movement. Women sought changes in discriminatory practices, some of which would allow them better to pursue motherhood and a career. At this early stage of the movement, however, NOW upset many more conservative organizations by calling for an end to:

all policies and practices...which in the guise of protectiveness, not only deny opportunities but also foster in women self-denigration, dependence, and evasion of responsibility.[140]

In keeping with this philosophy, women began to use political and legal pressure to expand employment rights under Title VII by attacking several types of discriminatory practices.

BFOQs

One of the first actions taken by NOW was an effort to limit the scope of the bona fide occupational qualification (bfoq) exception of Title VII of the Civil Rights Act of 1964 (see Appendix B). Although the Civil Rights Act prohibits sex discrimination, it allows an employer to take sex into account when it is a bfoq for a particular position. Examples of legal bfoqs include hiring only females as wet nurses or hiring only male actors to play Batman. Interpretation of the provision, however, led to some controversy among women's groups because an expansive interpretation of the bfoq provision would allow most protective legislation to remain on the law books, while a narrow one would have invalidated most of these laws.

Thus, according to Babcock et al., as soon as the potential ramifications of a narrow interpretation of the bfoq were realized, several reform women's and labor groups wrote to the director of the EEOC urging him to construe Title VII to allow "differential legislation" for females, noting that it had beneficial effects on their health and well-being.[141] Among these groups were the Young Women's Christian Association (YWCA), the American Association of University Women (AAUW), the NCL, the ACLU and the International Union of Electrical, Radio and Machinists Union (IUE), a union later to play an important role in pregnancy discrimination litigation.

In contrast, representatives from the National Woman's Party and BPW and Rep. Griffiths all spoke in favor of a narrow construction of the bfoq, which would necessitate an end to protective legislation. Additionally, Marguerite Rawalt, legal counsel for NOW, testified that NOW opposed state maximum hour laws and laws setting weight lifting maximums or limiting night work. According to Rawalt, "Such laws prevent women from being hired, promoted, transferred, and recalled to work after layoff."[142] Noting NOW's participation in an employment discrimination case then pending in California, Rawalt stressed the fact that many state laws operated to deprive women of jobs they desperately needed to support their families. NOW's position was that women did not work for pin money; they worked instead out of necessity and that protective legislation often only protected women from obtaining or retaining higher paid jobs. These sentiments were in sharp contrast to those of the NCL. Its representative testified, "While men may also require protection from over-time hours, as a group their need is less than that of women, who usually spend more time on family and home responsibilities."[143]

Although there was conflicting testimony from women's groups concerning the desirability of protective legislation, the EEOC took two actions signalling its support for women's rights groups. First, in 1968, the General

Counsel of the EEOC submitted a friend of the court brief in a case originally sponsored by NOW stating that Title VII invalidated California's laws that prohibited women from lifting weights or working overtime. The federal district court adopted the EEOC's position and in *Rosenfeld* v. *Southern Pacific Co.,*[144] ruled that the California law, cited by the railway as its reason for not hiring women as agent-telegraphers, was a violation of Title VII of the Civil Rights Act.[145]

After *Rosenfeld,* some employers tried to justify discriminatory employment practices by equating business necessity allowed under the bfoq with what many termed "customer preference." For example, in spite of contrary urgings from women's groups, airline companies had long refused to hire men as flight attendants, citing customer preference.[146] They argued that traditionally women were viewed as the more nurturing and comforting of the sexes and should an emergency arise in the cabin, male passengers would reject handholding-type overtures from male attendants. Although the U.S. Supreme Court denied certiorari in *Diaz* v. *Pan American Airlines,* it let stand a finding by the Fifth Circuit Court of Appeals that the bfoq exception allowed for only business *necessity* and not convenience exceptions. Thus, Pan American's refusal to hire male attendants was found to be illegal.[147]

Second, the EEOC enacted guidelines that interpreted the bfoq very narrowly. Ironically, these regulations, fought for by many women's rights organizations, invalidated most protective legislation—laws that earlier were upheld only after long court battles by the NCL during the suffragist period. Those social reformers, many of them suffragists, were content with women's role as the center of the family and only wanted legislation to assure that women who worked were met with the fewest possible job-related hindrances to the carrying on of their primary roles, those of wife and mother. While those on the President's Commission also appeared to accept this view, by the late 1960s, most women in the rights movement saw protective legislation as a real impediment to job equality.

Thus, women's rights groups continued to challenge any kind of "protective" legislation and the courts, in particular, have been very receptive to their activities. In fact, on only one occasion has the U.S. Supreme Court relied on the bfoq to justify an employer's refusal to hire women. In *Dothard* v. *Rawlinson* (1977),[148] the Court upheld Alabama's refusal to hire women as prison guards in the state's correctional facilities. There, the Court, however, narrowly construed the bfoq. In essence, the Court took notice that conditions in Alabama's dormitory-style prisons were so bad that really no one should work in them, but since someone had to, it was reasonable for the state to hire only males.[149]

"Sex Plus"

A second area of early concern to women's rights groups was employer discrimination against women with children, or what has been termed, a "sex plus" provision. For example, in *Phillips* v. *Martin Marietta Co.* (1971), some women's groups attacked a company employment policy that permitted the hiring of men—but not women—with school-aged children. The case was sponsored by the NAACP Legal Defense Fund and Human Rights for Women, and the ACLU filed an amicus curiae brief apprising the Justices of women's interest in the case and its potential ramifications on equal employment opportunity. Their arguments led the Supreme Court to rule that "persons of like qualifications be given employment opportunities regardless of their sex,"[150] discounting notions that women with young children would miss more work than their male counterparts because of women's child-care responsibilities.

Pregnancy Discrimination

During the 1970s and 1980s, many forms of pregnancy discrimination, including forced leave, loss of seniority, lack of medical coverage, and outright dismissal, were challenged by women's rights groups. NOW included paid maternity leaves, laws to allow women to return to their jobs with no loss of seniority, as well as child-care centers in demands made at its first conference. When it first decided to target pregnancy discrimination in employment, however, some conservative women, including many in WEAL, voiced their concerns that the movement should focus its energies on less-controversial issues.

The first real schism in the area occurred when the Women's Law Fund was founded by some WEAL leaders who disagreed over WEAL's involvement in *Cleveland Board of Education* v. *LaFleur* (1974),[151] a case challenging the automatic dismissal of pregnant schoolteachers in their fourth month. Nevertheless, both NOW and the Women's Rights Project of the ACLU as well as the IUE filed friend of the court briefs to support the arguments made by the Women's Law Fund, which ultimately sponsored the case. In *Cleveland,* the U.S. Supreme Court eventually ruled that the school board's policy that required a pregnant woman to take unpaid leave five months before her due date and prohibited her from returning to the classroom until the semester after her child was three months old violated the due process clause of the Fourteenth Amendment.[152] In rejecting the school board's arguments that "the first cutoff dates are necessary to maintain continuity of classroom instruction," and that "some teachers become physically incapable of adequately performing certain of their duties during the latter part of pregnancy," the Court concluded that the mandatory cutoff dates bore "no rational relationship to the state's interest in preserving the continuity of instruction." The majority also found there was no reason to require *all* women to leave work because only some women may be physically incapable of work in the last months of pregnancy.

While *Cleveland* constituted a victory for women's rights groups, the Court did not address whether employers should treat pregnancy like other medical conditions and not one unique to women. The former was the interpretation supported by numerous women's rights groups.[153] In fact, based on recommendations of the Citizens Advisory Council on the Status of Women and women's rights groups, in 1972 the EEOC had adopted regulations that specifically rejected the "pregnancy is unique" argument.[154] The Court, however, did not adopt this view. Two years later, in *Geduldig* v. *Aiello* (1974), a case challenging California's refusal to pay pregnancy disability benefits to women workers, the Justices upheld the constitutionality of a plan that excluded any coverage for pregnancy including the normal hospital stay. The Justices found the plan was reasonable because all risks were not covered, and there was "no evidence in the record that the selection of the risks insured by the program worked to discriminate against any identifiable group or class in terms of the aggregate risk protection."[155] Although *Geduldig* was a major loss for the women's rights groups involved, most commentators believed that this decision was grounded not in constitutional theory but in economic realities—the California plan simply had not been set up to handle these additional claims. Prior to *Geduldig*, in two major cases, *Reed* v. *Reed* (1971)[156] and *Frontiero* v. *Richardson* (1973),[157] the Court struck down laws that treated women differently from men, holding that certain kinds of sex discrimination were prohibited by the Fourteenth Amendment. Because only women get pregnant, the Justices found no sex discrimination in *Geduldig*.

Successes of women's rights organizations in litigating *Reed, Frontiero,* and *Cleveland* had lulled attorneys into believing that the Court was willing to expand the protections of the Fourteenth Amendment to prohibit a wide variety of gender-based discriminatory practices. As *Geduldig* proved, however, this was not to be the case. Thus, given the Court's opinion in *Geduldig*, feminist lawyers turned to Title VII for possible relief against on-the-job pregnancy discrimination.

The first test of this strategy came in an IUE sponsored case, *General Electric (GE) Co.* v. *Gilbert* (1976).[158] Unlike the situation in *Geduldig*, in which a judicial finding of discrimination might have bankrupted the state disability system, *Gilbert* involved a *private* employer's plan that contained a maternity exclusion clause that was very similar to California's. Because *Gilbert* was styled as a Title VII class action lawsuit and involved only one, albeit large, company, many court observors believed that the Justices would find in favor of the pregnancy discrimination claim. However, in rejecting the arguments put forth by IUE lawyers that a penalty on the birth process was inherently discriminatory, the Court disregarded EEOC guidelines that interpreted such programs as discriminatory. It also found no Title VII violation because there was no showing of employer discrimination. Writing for the Court, Justice Rehnquist adopted the reasoning of the lower court, which had concluded that pregnancy "is not a disease at all and is often a voluntarily undertaken and desired condition."[159]

Immediately after this decision, outraged women's rights groups lobbied Congress for legislation that would explicitly prohibit discrimination against pregnant women.[160] Their efforts resulted in passage of the Pregnancy Discrimination Act (see Appendix B), which was enacted in 1978. Given the nonthreatening nature of this legislation and, in fact, its promotherhood stance, it is not surprising that no opposition was heard from conservative groups.[161] Although the proposed legislation was not popular with employers, most women agreed that pregnant women should receive the same kind of health and disability coverage as their male counterparts. In fact, many conservatives believed that the absence of this kind of legislation encouraged abortion; prochoice women believed that the absence of such protection denied many women the right to chose whether or not to have a child.

Absence of strong opposition to the Pregnancy Discrimination Act, when viewed in the context of a public good, is not surprising—there was nothing compulsory about the law in terms of its impact on *employees*. Employers, however, who must adhere to its provisions lobbied vigorously against its passage. Under the terms of the law as enacted, a woman who opts for the more traditional role and leaves her job to rear her children loses nothing and may gain payment for her doctor and hospital expenses depending on when she leaves her job. There is nothing in the law that *requires* women to stay on the job. It only allows those who wish to do so, for whatever reason, to work while they are able free from adverse employer action. Also, it prohibits an employer from penalizing a woman who becomes pregnant or has a child. For example, the statute outlaws the formerly common employer practice of disallowing all of a woman's seniority when she returned to work after childbirth. This kind of practice clearly penalized motherhood, something both pro- and anti-ERA supporters found objectionable.

Retirement Benefits

Another area of concern to women's rights groups was and continues to be discrimination in retirement benefits, including those paid under the Social Security Insurance (SSI) program and benefits paid out under private employment plans. Although only those plans carried by private employers involve Title VII, both are considered here.

Long before the rise of the current women's movement, the National Federation of Business and Professional Women had attempted to secure passage of legislation to remedy inequities in the Social Security system. Not surprisingly, one of the conclusions of the 1963 report of the President's Commission on the Status of Women, noted the pervasive discrimination against women in the system. The SSI program, as it is set up, reflects the ethos that in the traditional family, the husband is the sole salaried wage earner, while the wife is assumed to stay at home and rear her children. This unpaid housework is not recognized under the Social Security system. Thus, women's groups have attacked the program on three fronts: (1) its assumption of traditional roles; (2) its lack of recognition of the unsalaried women's contribution to the economic unit; and (3) the lower benefits for working, married women.[162]

The SSI program's assumption of traditional roles was attacked head on by the ACLU's Women's Rights Project in *Weinberger* v. *Wiesenfeld* in 1975.[163] Upon the death of his wife, Stephen Wiesenfeld applied for Social Security benefits because he had been dependent on his wife for his and their child's support—Ms. Wiesenfeld has been employed as a teacher, while her husband had stayed home to care for their young daughter. When the Social Security Administration denied his claim for survivor's benefits, a local newspaper reported the event. A WEAL leader, knowing of the WRP interest in benefits discrimination, contacted Wiesenfeld and urged him to contact the WRP, which later agreed to represent him. The case eventually was heard by the U.S. Supreme Court, which found that the purpose of the benefits law was to "provide children deprived of one parent with the opportunity for personal attention of the other." Thus, the Court found that the "gender-based discrimination [of the Act] was entirely irrational," and therefore, unconstitutional.

In *Wiesenfeld,* the Court recognized that Congress had enacted the challenged provision based "on the presumption that women as a group would choose to forego work to care for children." These stereotypes often find their way into the law and have yet to be done away with completely. Given the biases of many male legislators and the economic costs involved in many of these changes, it is easy to see why substantial legislative changes in this area have not occurred.

Questions involving government pension plans and their treatment of unsalaried married women also have been the target of lawsuits. For example, in *McCarty* v. *McCarty* (1981),[164] which involved a divorced woman's claim to part of her husband's military pension, the Supreme Court ruled that upon dissolution of the McCarty's marriage, federal law precluded a state court from dividing military nondisability retirement pay pursuant to state community property laws. This decision was greeted with shock and criticism from women's rights groups.

The decision was particularly difficult for women's groups to understand given that during the same term the Court had upheld provisions of the Selective Service Act excluding women from compulsory registration. In that case, the Justices had built their opinion on traditional views of women and their abilities;[165] in *McCarty,* the Court ignored that view refusing to recognize that a career was next to impossible for a woman married to a serviceman or to recognize the economic contributions made by women in these circumstances to the overall family unit.

Thus, shortly after the adverse decision, women's rights groups again went to the Congress as they did after *Geduldig* in an attempt to obtain legislation to invalidate the Court's decision. These efforts led to passage of legislation in 1982 that overturned the Court's decision and provided recognition of the economic contributions of the wives of military personnel. This amendment to the 1983 defense appropriation bill requires that military retirement pay must be given the same status as any other pension when state divorce courts consider how marriage assets are to be divided.[166] Thus, according to Reps. Patricia Schroeder (D-Colorado) and William Whitehurst (R-Virginia), cosponsors of the amendment, the extended coverage concerns "an issue which strikes at the very heart of the traditional family concept, offering recognition and protection to those women willing to make the required sacrifices in support of a husband's military career."[167]

Recognition of the limits to which the Supreme Court could be pushed on some aspects of the pension discrimination issue, as illustrated in *McCarty,* has led women's rights groups to lobby Congress extensively for pension reform. One of the most ambitious pieces of legislation thus far proposed was the Fraser-Keyes bill, the Equity in Social Security for Individuals and Families Act.[168] The bill initially was drafted by Arvonne Frazer, a former WEAL president (and wife of one of the cosponsors) and Jane Chapman of the Center for Women Policy Studies, and organization that regularly is called on to testify in Congress about proposed laws concerning women. A revised version was resubmitted in 1979. At the core of both versions is recognition of a housewife's contribution wherein a homemaker would not be treated as a dependent but instead would get credit for a portion of the salary earned by her spouse. The proposed 50 percent credit would also benefit many working women who earn far less than their husbands. The homemaker's credit would in turn guarantee to nonworking women some form of retirement insurance, as well as disability insurance coverage.

Because calls for change may alter stereotypical roles or at least legislative institutionalization of these roles, some women have ridiculed proposed changes. For example, after Sylvia Porter discussed the potential Social Security liability for husbands if their wives' unsalaried work was "assigned financial values," Phyllis Schlafly and other anti-ERA supporters distributed copies of the article to those in attendance at the National Women's Conference in Houston where a very popular button was "Wages for Housework."[169] Although Schlafly used arguments like Porter's to defeat the ERA, she did not make a real effort to mobilize her followers against proposed changes in retirement insurance, largely because her efforts at that time were directed against the passage of the ERA.

It is not only within the Social Security System that women have experienced sex discrimination. Working women have historically fared poorly in private retirement plans as well. Generally, these plans either require women to pay more into a plan to get a pension equal to their men coworkers, or the plans pay women less if they paid in equally. In *Los Angeles* v. *Manhart*[170] (1977), women's rights groups submitted amicus curiae briefs urging the U.S. Supreme Court to find that a pension plan that deducted a larger monthly amount from the paychecks of female employees so that upon retirement they could receive the same monthly benefits as men was a violation of Title VII. Los Angeles' lawyers had justified these provisions by noting that women as a class live longer than men. Therefore, they reasoned that since women would receive pension benefits for a longer period of time, it was necessary as well as equitable for women to pay in more money so that they eventually could get the same monthly benefits as men. In *Manhart,* both parties accepted the veracity of actuarial tables that establish that women, as a class, live longer than men. Women's groups, however, argued that under Title VII, women must be treated as individuals. Therefore, they argued that women employees' larger contribution to the pension plan equaled employer discrimination in terms of wages and compensation. The Supreme Court agreed with their arguments.

In the wake of this decision, women around the country began to challenge the legality of their pension plans. For example, in October 1982, the United States Supreme Court heard arguments in a pension discrimination case which involved a challenge to an Arizona plan that paid higher monthly retirement benefits to men. The Justices were told by the insurance industry that banning of actuarial tables in retirement plans could bankrupt several pension plans and cost as much as 20 billion dollars.[171] Later, in January 1983, the Court heard arguments in a suit filed by a Long Island University female faculty member who alleged that her university's pension plan (which covered 85 percent of all private and 40 percent of all public college and university professors[172]) violated Title VII because it used sex-based mortality tables to calculate benefits. A three-judge Court of Appeals had ruled that the plan was discriminatory because the tables resulted in 11.3 percent lower monthly benefits for female retirees who contributed sums equal to those paid by their male colleagues. Thus, the Court of Appeals ordered the Teacher's Insurance and Annuity Association to use "unisex" mortality tables to calculate benefits to be paid to those who retired after May 1, 1980. Interestingly, when the case was argued before the United States Supreme Court, the United States Solicitor General, on behalf of the Reagan administration, filed an amicus curiae brief on behalf of the university professor urging the Court to uphold the decision of the lower court. In fact, quite possibly in a move to appease female voters, the government abandoned its normal position that proof of discriminatory intent be shown and noted, "It is clear that proof of invidious intent is unnecessary, where, as here, the employees are explicitly differentiated on the basis of sex."[173]

Although NOW and several other women's groups participated in one or both cases, having learned from the *Geduldig* and *Gilbert* decisions, these groups also are lobbying Congress to pass legislation that would prohibit the use of gender in establishing insurance rates or payout levels.[174] NOW,

NWPC, the Women's Legal Defense Fund, WEAL, BPW, and the American Association of University Women have directed much of their efforts toward passage of a sweeping package of provisions included in what is called the Women's Economic Equity Act, sponsored in the House of Representatives by Rep. Patricia Schroeder.[175] While some of the act's proposals, including child-care tax credits and Individualized Retirement Account (IRA) provisions, were enacted as part of the Reagan tax cut bill,[176] those dealing with nondiscrimination insurance and private pension reform were not passed in 1982.[177] Pension reform, both in terms of equalizing benefits and expanded coverage[178] for women workers, thus remains an important goal of the women's rights movement in its struggle to alleviate all forms of employment discrimination.

Sexual Harassment

Sexual harassment, like other forms of employment discrimination, is another issue of increasing concern to those in the women's movement. It is estimated that 88 percent of all women workers experience some kind of sexual harassment at their places of employment.[179] In some instances, sexual requirements have been placed on women workers as conditions for job retention, advancement, or salary raises. Other less flagrant forms include verbal abuse, sexist remarks, offensive touching, or patting and leering. This kind of treatment makes working conditions difficult for women and often leads victims to seek other positions, thereby causing them to lose seniority and other accrued benefits.[180] Problems of sexual harassment have not been confined to the labor sector. In fact, the NOW Legal Defense and Education Fund has established a special Sexual Harassment in Education Project to provide legal assistance for students and faculty members who find themselves victims of harassment.[181]

Public awareness of sexual harassment has evolved only during the last few years. In fact, it was not until 1977, that a federal Court of Appeals found that sexual harassment was sex discrimination prohibited by Title VII.[182] Later, in 1979, another U.S. Court of Appeals concluded that an employer could be held liable under Title VII for a supervisor's harassment of female employees.[183] Then, in November 1980, the EEOC, at the urging of several women's rights groups, adopted regulations making sexual harassment an impermissible form of sex discrimination prohibited by Title VII (see Appendix B).

When additional hearings were held on these guidelines in spring 1981, Phyllis Schlafly testified in opposition. Basing her testimony on her belief that harassment "is not a problem" and that only those who "ask for it" actually find themselves victims, she asked the Commission members to strike the regulations as inconsistent with Title VII.

Schlafly's comments surprised and angered many. Clearly, stringent regulations could be threatening to some men who harass women, but women have little to lose from the regulations. In fact, for conservative women, they guarantee that women have recourse against ungentlemanly conduct; for women's rights supporters, they provide legal recourse for discriminatory conduct that has a pervasive impact on the employment status of many women.

Thus, a variety of discriminatory employment practices have been challenged by women's rights groups under executive orders and the Equal Pay and Civil Rights Acts. At first, their efforts were directed toward blatant types of discrimination—help-wanted ads, protective legislation, and refusal to hire women with children. But, by the 1980s, attention turned to more sophisticated issues of discrimination including pension plans and sexual harassment. However, some women, particularly those in select professions, generally are not protected by the provisions of these laws. For example, while Title VII prohibits law firms from discriminating against women in their initial decision to hire, according to at least one federal court, it does not cover partnership arrangements. In early 1983, though, the U.S. Supreme Court agreed to review that decision. In a situation somewhat analogous to the tenure situation at universities, lawyers generally work as associates in a firm (which is a partnership arrangement) for five to eight years. Then, based on evaluations of a person's performance and other criteria, an individual is asked to become a member of the firm (a partner) or to leave (somewhat similar to a denial of tenure). In 1981, in a case where a woman lawyer alleged that she was not made a partner at the law firm of former U.S. Attorney General Griffin Bell, the Court found a First Amendment right to freedom of association allowed a firm to decide, free from government scrutiny, whom to hire. And, most male firms continue to prefer men as co-workers. In a study of Harvard Law School graduates conducted several years after their graduation, 25 percent of the males but only 1 percent of the females in private practice had been made partners.[184] Although times have changed from the 1950s, when U.S. Supreme Court Justice Sandra O'Connor, ranked close to the top of her class at Stanford Law School, could not get a job (other than that of a legal secretary) in a private firm, women still are far from reaching equality in the legal profession even though they now comprise 14 percent of all lawyers.[185] For example, a study conducted of the nation's largest 50 law firms in 1980 "found only 85 women among the 3,987 partners at those firms."[186]

Similar kinds of problems exist in the medical profession. Although medical schools and hospitals, as employers, can no longer discriminate against women, most physicians work alone or in small practices not covered by provisions of any equal opportunity legislation. Salary differentials in the legal and medical professions also continue unabated even though the Equal Pay Act prohibits this practice. For example, in 1981, women attorneys' salaries were only 70.7 percent of those paid to men; female physicians earned only 80.9 percent of what their male counterparts earned.[187]

While these areas have proven particularly problematic for women's rights advocates, women have continued to target discrimination in education, believing that their actions could eliminate sex role stereotypes that contribute to these practices as well as increase the number of women prepared for certain occupations.

Education

Unlike women in the other two women's movements, women, particularly in the rights branch of the current movement, immediately recognized inequalities in the educational system, its resultant impact on employment opportunities, and the need for concerted action to improve conditions. While many younger-branch women were instrumental in founding women's studies programs, rights branch women pushed for laws to end discrimination. And, even before the rise of the rights branch, the National Federation of Business and Professional Women long urged abolition of quotas for women in schools (they were used to limit women's access) and actively encouraged women to go back to school. Reflecting this kind of concern with respect to older women, President Kennedy's Commission on the Status of Women, urged government support of continuing education for homemakers.[188] But while Commission members recommended "imaginative counseling which [could] lift aspirations beyond stubbornly persistent assumptions about 'women's roles' and 'women's interest,'"[189] their comments about education clearly reflected the view that a woman's primary role was motherhood. For example, instead of criticizing the emphasis many colleges placed on home economics, the Commission bemoaned the fact that "even women's colleges have given remarkably little serious thought to the better preparation of their students for the homemaking most of them will do."[190]

With the formation of NOW and later WEAL, however, the focus soon turned toward educational equality for women. Noting that the near absence of women in high paying, prestige professions and in leadership positions was a function of limited educational opportunities for women, in 1967 NOW called for passage of federal and state legislation to ensure that women "be educated to their full potential."[191] WEAL, reflecting its narrower focus, declared:

> Our primary thrust should take the direction of counseling girls toward higher career aspirations, facilitating upward employment for all married women, and supporting the liberation and fulfillment of women in accordance with their own aspirations and abilities.[192]

This concern for a woman's right to achieve her full educational potential was a key element in women's rights organizations' support of Title IX of the Educational Amendments Act of 1972.[193] Title IX prohibits sex discrimination in any elementary, secondary, and postsecondary schools if the institution is the recipient of any federal monies. The law itself is fairly simple; most of the controversy over it has occurred in the drafting of regulations and enforcement stages (see Appendix B).

Prior to introduction of this legislation, with the full support of a wide variety of women's groups, Rep. Edith Green held hearings in 1970 that revealed extensive discrimination against women in the nation's schools. Two years later, when Green consequently introduced Title IX, she asked women's groups *not* to testify for the bill, believing that the chances of passage would be greatly enhanced if less attention were given to its provisions. Thus, given that little negative publicity was given to the amendment, no women's groups rushed to testify against its passage, and it was voted into law.

Actual implementation of Title IX, however, has become a battleground for conservative versus liberal women's groups. In 1974, the Education Amendments gave Congress forty-five days in which to disapprove of any administrative regulations concerning implementation of any laws regarding education. The regulations, as finally adopted and approved, prohibit sex bias in three major areas: (1) admissions; (2) treatment of students; and (3) hiring personnel practices.

Admissions. Title IX regulations do not outlaw single-sex schools. Historically, this is an area that has produced division even among women who advocate full educational equality. According to a 1973 Carnegie Commission report, "various studies have shown that women who attend women's colleges have academic records superior to those of their co-educational sisters, on the basis of such measures as persistence, proportion going on to graduate education, and proportion receiving Ph.D.s."[194] Findings of this sort have led many women to support sex-segregated colleges, while many men cling dearly to the concept of male-only institutions. Thus, it is not difficult to see why this kind of an exemption was incorporated in the Title IX admissions regulations.

In spite of these regulations, however, some women have felt that they were being denied equal educational opportunities and equal protection of the laws as guaranteed by the U.S. Constitution by state maintenance of sex-segregated schools, particularly where school systems maintain superior "boys-only" schools. Thus, it was the Philadelphia Board of Education's refusal to allow Sharon Vorchheimer to attend an all-male school noted for the strength of its science and mathematics curriculum that led her to pursue her rejection all the way to the U.S. Supreme Court. In *Vorchheimer* v. *School Board of Philadelphia*, with both NOW and the WRP participating, the U.S. Supreme Court in a 4 to 4 vote, upheld the ruling of the Court of Appeals, wherein it had found the school board's action not unconstitutional (a violation of Title IX was not alleged because of the exemption in the regulations), "at least as applied to special academic high schools with admission based on application."[195]

In June 1982, however, in a case similar to *Vorchheimer,* the Supreme Court ruled that Alabama's maintenance of a nursing school that admitted women only was unconstitutional. Writing for the Court, Justice O'Connor noted:

> Although the test for determining the validity of a gender-based classifica-
> tion is straightforward, it must be applied free of fixed notions concerning
> the roles and abilities of males and females. Care must be taken in
> ascertaining whether the statutory objective itself reflects archaic and
> stereotypic notions. Thus, if the statutory objective is to exclude or
> "protect" members of one gender because they are presumed to suffer from
> an inherent handicap or to be innately inferior, the objective itself is
> illegitimate.[196]

Thus, although the Court relied on the Fourteenth Amendment and not Title IX, it is now clear that some types of single-sex schools can no longer be maintained.[197]

Student Treatment. Although there is philosophical disagreement on sex-segregated schools, the major area of Title IX controversy has been over those policies concerning treatment of students. Among the things covered by this provision are educational programs and activities, comparable facilities, counseling, and athletics.

While HEW was in the process of drafting regulations to enforce equity in these areas, an amendment to the Education Amendments of 1974 was introduced that would have exempted revenue-producing intercollegiate sports from coverage. While women were able to prevent this amendment from becoming part of the House-Senate version of the bill, they soon had to fight other attempts to undermine Title IX's integrity. Although latest regulations require only that "athletic benefits, opportunities and treatment must be 'equivalent' in availability, equality and need," the male sports establishment, particularly the powerful National Collegiate Athletic Association (NCAA) has denounced them and continues to work to weaken provisions of Title IX and its accompanying regulations.[198] When this "good," a multimillion dollar a year business, was threatened, it is easy to see why the male sports establishment rose up in protest. They were threatened and they acted. Although no schools have had federal funds cut off in response to charges of sex discrimination or unequal treatment of female athletes, few universities devote equal or even near-equal sums to the sexes. However, the close monitoring done by women's groups has led many schools to make major changes in their physical education and sports scholarship programs. For example, a study conducted by the NCAA found that 664 new sports programs were added for women at 693 colleges and universities since 1979.[199]

Areas of equal treatment of students that have resulted in dissension among *women* almost universally include situations where sex role stereotyping of female students are challenged. In 1975, shortly after the first set of Title IX guidelines were announced and signed by President Ford, a tremendous outcry was raised when HEW officials ruled that father/son breakfasts were prohibited by Title IX. ERA opponents charged that this was a first step toward destruction of the family and unwarranted governmental action.[200] Although this incorrect interpretation of Title IX resulted in angry letters to HEW from conservative women and extensive media coverage, conservative women's groups were even more upset about moves being made in the schools and by publishers to remove sex-role stereotyping from textbooks.

In 1974, even before issuance of the Title IX guidelines, Congress enacted the Women's Equity Educational Act (WEEA) at the urging of women's rights groups. It created a program of grants and contract programs "for the development of models and tools with which to overcome sex bias, stereotyping and discrimination in education."[201] Administered by HEW, it provided millions of dollars to educational institutions to meet Title IX mandates as well as to eliminate sex role stereotyping in educational materials and programs. The Education Amendments of 1978 further expanded the potential effectiveness of WEEA by allocating an additional 80 million dollars to "provide educational equity for women in the United States." Monies also were allocated for improved Title IX enforcement.

Although the government is charged with enforcement of Title IX, as supplemented by WEEA, to monitor Department of Education enforcement and to end sex role stereotyping in schools, many women's organizations have established committees or separate funds devoted solely to this purpose. The largest part of the NOW Legal Defense and Education Fund is called PEER, Project on Equal Education Rights. Although it and several other groups monitor sexism in the schools, elimination of many forms of gender bias is far from complete.

Women's group efforts in this area also are beginning to face organized opposition from right-wing groups that oppose the inclusion of feminist or even nonsexist ideology in school textbooks. Here again, we see the public goods notion give rise to the creation of opposition group tactics. In fact, in 1979, Republican leaders sought the support of Phyllis Schlafly and her supporters for the "Family Protection Act" (FPA), which if ultimately passed, will deny "federal funds for purchase of textbooks that 'belittle women's traditional role in society.'"[202] Others who support the FPA bills want not only to combat the inclusion of feminist thought in textbooks but also discussion of ecology, evolution, and race. These persons correctly view textbooks as shapers of a child's view of the world, a fact that has been recognized by women's rights groups who saw the need to replace stereotypical women by showing students that women had many options in today's society. Should the conservatives triumph, as they have in California and Texas, two of the largest textbook markets in the United States, book publishers will be likely to conform to their demands.[203] Here again, conservatives see the depiction (and not necessarily advocacy) of women in certain, nontraditional roles as threatening to the status quo. If a particular text is adopted, all children will be exposed to it and probably assimilate some of its values. Consequently, school board purchase of nonsexist books can be viewed as a public good posing a sufficient life-style threat to create an effective anti group.[204]

It is interesting to note that it is in the area of nonsexist books—where the opposition has arisen—that members of the younger branch of the movement have been most involved. Many have started feminist bookstores, for example, which often serve as a gathering place for supporters.

Younger-branch members also often were instrumental in the founding and continued vitality of women's studies programs around the country. By 1982, these programs, in fact, had grown to over 300, and there now are more than 30,000 women's studies courses offered in colleges and universities around the country.[205] Although the women's studies programs are not directly affected by Title IX, those in women's studies programs frequently serve as monitors for campus compliance.

Hiring and Personnel Practices. Title IX is now construed to prohibit employment discrimination in all educational institutions receiving federal assistance, and it is under this provision that most complaints have been brought.[206] Although there has been a growing number of women obtaining Ph.D.s, this growth has not been reflected in the faculties of the nation's universities, particularly research-oriented institutions. Although women make up slightly over 25 percent of the nation's college faculty members, in the main these women are clustered at women's, small Catholic, or community colleges.

Even if a women secures an academic position, she may face a variety of forms of discrimination ranging from blatant to the most subtle. Although both Title VII and Title IX prohibit discrimination, the kinds practiced in academia have proven very difficult to establish owing in large part to the deference most judges give to the judgment of a woman's peers as to the quality of her teaching and research.

Late in 1978, a U.S. Supreme Court ruling did nothing to help the problem. In deciding *Keene State College* v. *Sweeney,*[207] the Court found that an employer charged with discriminating under Title VII need only "articulate" *but not prove* some legitimate, nondiscriminatory reason for not promoting a woman—a decision that did not bode well for future suits. It would take a university only a little imagination to come up with some kind of reason not to promote anyone—whether female or male.

Recently, however, the Supreme Court gave new life to those who charge sex discrimination in academic employment suits. In *North Haven Board of Education* v. *Bell* (1982),[208] the Court ruled that the legislative history of Title IX supported arguments that it was to prevent discrimination in employment even though the statute is silent on that point. Thus, while the implications of this decision are yet to be fully realized, Title IX may provide another tool by which women's groups can combat sex discrimination.

It may be, however, that as in other areas of Title IX implementation, women's groups will be forced to go to court instead of relying on DOE to enforce its provisions. In fact DOE's record for enforcement probably has been worse than that of the EEOC in the employment discrimination area. For example, while many schools, in response to public pressure have changed several of their practices, according to PEER, 99 percent of Michigan's school districts violated at least one of Title IX's procedural requirements.[209] Other studies have found that DOE investigates few complaints, and, in fact, resolved only 179 over a four-year period.[210] Even when school-board officials have notified DOE that they would be unable to comply with provisions of Title IX, DOE has not stopped payment of funds or initiated complaints.

The U.S. Commisision on Civil Rights, in assessing enforcement of Title IX from 1977 to May 1980, found agency action "unduly slow." The Commission also found compliance reviews were far behind schedule and that the agency had failed to collect adequate data to determine if violations of the law existed.[211]

Comments concerning Reagan administration enforcement are even more negative. In fact, according to Judith Lichtman, executive director of the Women's Legal Defense Fund, "The [Reagan] administration is doing no enforcement under Title IX."[212] Widespread recognition of this problem has even led the Women's Law Center to sue DOE in an effort to get the courts to order the agency to enforce its own regulations.[213]

Women's rights groups, however, have not relied exclusively on the courts to protect educational equity. In fact, they have repeatedly found themselves fighting off efforts of the Reagan administration in this area. For example, in 1982, Vice President Bush's Task Force on Regulatory Reform announced that it was reviewing guidelines on intercollegiate athletics as was DOE.[214] Additionally, the feminist director of the WEEA Program was dismissed in April 1982 and replaced by a woman from the New Right who had advocated elimination of WEEA just two years before.[215] She in turn replaced all the project proposed reviewers with members of Phyllis Schlafly's Eagle Forum.[216]

Educational equity programs have not only faced opposition within the executive branch. In 1982, Sen. Orrin Hatch (R-Utah) introduced a bill that would have made Title IX applicable only to programs that actually received federal funds.[217] The U.S. Commission of Civil Rights immediately announced its belief that the Hatch proposal "would roll back much of the protection against sex discrimination."[218] Although this bill was strongly supported by the New Right, the Congresswomen's Caucus immediately responded. In fact, Rep. Claudine Schneider introduced a resolution expressing the sense of the House "on the need to maintain Title IX guidelines to insure equal educational rights and opportunities."[219] Although Hatch then withdrew his bill, it is expected to be reintroduced. At this time, WEAL and NWPC in particular are continuing to pressure Congress and the Reagan administration to avoid further cuts in these programs and to ensure full compliance with existing laws.

Thus, while Title IX has had a major impact on educational equity,[220] conservatives continue to target its regulations for change, while funding for all of the educational equity programs including enforcement has been adversely affected by Reagan budget cuts. Conservatives view many of Title IX's mandates as theatening and in fact have charged that WEEA programs are a "money machine for a network of openly radical groups"[221] that seek to abolish traditional sex roles. Thus, given the perceived quality of many of these efforts to bring about educational equity, it is not surprising that resistance has occurred.

CONCLUSION

Prior to the 1960s, most of the progress made in employment and education came about as a result of individual efforts or employer demand. Neither women's movement attempted to attack head on the problems in either sphere although they supported notions of increased opportunity.

During the 1960s, however, many of the groups involved in the current women's movement made expanded employment and education rights a major priority. Through legislation and executive branch lobbying and litigation, employment and educational opportunities have been expanded tremendously, although women's wages and numbers in certain occupations continue to lag far below those of men.

Gains in this area have been fostered by two factors. First, even most conservative women viewed most of the legislation as a public good. Not only do some of the laws protect motherhood—the Pregnancy Discrimination Act is one example—but according to some, the protections found in many of those laws negated the need for the ERA. Phyllis Schlafly, for example, has noted that both the Equal Employment Opportunity Act of 1972 and the Education Amendments of 1972 have given women full equal rights in education and employment.

Second, there was little organized business opposition to most of these proposals. However, when more theatening, costly changes including affirmative action and pregnancy disability payments, for example, began to appear in regulations implementing laws or executive orders, a strong backlash arose.

Employers and white males in particular, threatened by a loss of jobs or lessened chances of promotion immediately began to lobby, litigate, and/or simply ignore equal opportunity as well as affirmative action guidelines. They viewed quotas or goals as true public bads that could only hurt their ability to pursue their education or careers.

Additionally, weak enforcement of these more controversial changes continues to impede progress toward full equality. And, Reagan administration policy changes may prove particularly problematic. For example, budget cuts for EEOC enforcement, the funding of several programs authorized under Title IX, and college financial aid in general, all will have an adverse impact on the status of women. Proposed changes in equal opportunity policy including reducing the number of firms required to file affirmative action plans and a lax Civil Rights Division within the Justice Department also place progress in severe jeopardy.[222] Inadequate enforcement by the Executive branch, however, is not the only roadblock to full equality in the economic arena. As we will see in the next chapter, other nonlegal barriers also persist in preventing women from assuming a place of complete equality with men in the market place.

NOTES

1. For example, when M. Carey Thomas, who later became president of Bryn Mawr College, first went to Germany in 1879 to study for a Ph.D., her family and friends refused to mention her name because of their embarrassment over her "unladylike" conduct. M. Carey Thomas, "Present Tendencies in Women's Education," *Publications of the Association of Collegiate Alumni,* series III, no. 17 (February 1908):47.

2. Judith Papachristou, *Women Together: A History in Documents of the Women's Movement in the United States* (New York: Alfred A. Knopf, 1976), p. 126.

3. Sklar has estimated that at least 20 percent of all native-born white women in Massachusetts taught in the public schools during at least some period in their lives. Kathryn Kish Sklar, "The Founding of Mount Holyoke College," in Carol Ruth Berkin and Mary Beth Norton, eds., *Women of America, A History* (Boston: Houghton Mifflin, 1979), p. 181.

4. Reproduced in Elizabeth Cady Stanton, Susan B. Anthony, and Matilda Joslyn Gage, eds., *History of Woman Suffrage,* vol. I, 1848–1861 (Rochester, N.Y.: Charles Mann, 1887), p. 71 (hereafter HWS I).

5. Ibid., p. 72.

6. These conditions prompted some women to strike as early as 1824 to protest a wage reduction that was coupled with an increase in the length of the workday. During the 1830s, there were several other such incidents. See generally, Judith O'Sullivan and Rosemary Gallick, *Workers and Allies: Female Participation in the American Trade Union Movement, 1824–1976* (Washington, D.C.: Smithsonian Institution Press, 1975). See also, Philip S. Foner, *Women and the American Labor Movement: From Colonial Times to the Eve of World War I* (New York: Free Press, 1979), chaps. 3–6.

7. For example, at the 1850 National Woman's Rights Convention it was

Resolved, That women must seek out a new order of employments, to secure for herself virtue and independence; marriage and the needle, heretofore, her only resources, are crushing to both.

Proceedings of the Women's Rights Convention, held at Worchester, Massachusetts, 1851 (New York: Fowler & Wells, 1852), p. 18.

8. W. Elliot Brownlee and Mary M. Brownlee, *Women in the American Economy, A Documentary History, 1675 to 1929* (New Haven: Yale University Press, 1976), pp. 15–16.

9. Ibid., p. 16.

10. According to *The Revolution,* the association was to "act for its members, in the same manner as the associations of working men now regulate the wages, etc., of those belonging to them," September 24, 1868, p. 181.

11. Ellen Carol DuBois, *Feminism and Suffrage: The Emergence of an Independent Women's Movement in America, 1848–1869* (Ithaca: Cornell University Press, 1978), chap. 4.

12. Quoted in Eleanor Flexner, *Century of Struggle* (New York: Atheneum, 1974), p. 134.

13. Edward T. James, ed., *Notable American Women, 1607–1950, A Biographical Dictionary,* vol. II (Cambridge: The Belknap Press of Harvard University Press, 1971), s.v. "Augusta Lewis Troup." When Troup, as president of the WTA, protested the low wages Anthony paid typesetters at *The Revolution,* she was fired. Troup then retaliated by leading the successful fight to prevent the seating of both Anthony and Stanton as delegates from the Working Women's Association at the 1869 National Labor Union convention. This repudiation of Anthony and Stanton essentially triggered the end of the short and fragile liaison between the woman's rights movement and working women and the labor movement. See also, Israel Kugler, "The Trade Union Career of Susan B. Anthony," *Labor History* 2 (Winter 1961):90–100.

14. This schism between the woman's rights and labor movements, however, did not end efforts to organize women workers. The year 1869 saw the establishment of the Knights of Labor, which numbered among its goals "equal pay for equal work," even though the organization had far more male than female members. In addition to the Women's Typographical Union, several other exclusively female unions were begun. In 1869, for example, the Daughters of St. Krispin, modeled after the all-male shoemakers' union, the Kings of St. Krispin, was founded. Often, however, women's unions like the Daughters experienced hostility from men similarly employed and generally were unable to attract enough members to pose any kind of credible threat to employers. As a consequence, when the 1873 panic and the resultant six-year depression occurred in the United States, women's labor unions could not withstand the shock, and most slowly faded away. See generally, O'Sullivan and Gallick, *Workers and Allies,* pp. 11–12; Flexner, *Century of Struggle,* p. 141; and James J. Kenneally, *Women and American Trade Unions* (St. Albans, Vermont: Eden Press, 1978), pp. 1–10.

15. DuBois, *Feminism and Suffrage,* p. 151.

16. Ibid., p. 147.

17. Ibid., p. 151.

18. For a general discussion of the professionalization of medicine and its effects

on midwifery, see Gerda Lerner, *The Majority Finds its Past: Placing Women in History* (New York: Oxford University Press, 1979), pp. 20–23.

19. Horace Mann as quoted in Thomas Woody, *A History of Women's Education in the United States,* vol. I (New York: The Science Press, 1929), p. 463.

20. Sklar, "Mount Holyoke College," in Berkin and Norton, eds., *Women of America,* p. 185.

21. These views persisted until well after the Civil War even though the graduates of some schools, particularly Mt. Holyoke, which as early as 1837 forced its students to take courses that paralleled those taught in male institutions, proved them wrong. While a few "colleges" opened their doors to women in the pre-Civil War era (Oberlin in 1837; Antioch in 1853), often the training received by women students was inferior to that of the male students. For example, Oberlin channeled most female students into its "Ladies Department," whose curriculum in addition to literary and morals courses included sewing and washing for the male students. Even though the first all-female colleges, Vassar (established in 1861), Wellesley (1870), and Smith (1871), instituted curricula identical to those of Harvard and Yale, the poor presecondary education training of most women meant many female students had to take an extensive preparatory course before they could enter the advanced curriculum. For more extensive treatments of the history of female education, see Woody, *History of Women's Education,* I, especially chaps. VII, VIII, and IX; Nancy Green, "Female Education and School Competition: 1820–1850," in Mary Kelley, ed., *Woman's Being: Women's Place: Female Identity and Vocation in American History* (Boston: G.K. Hall, 1979), pp. 127–141; Ann D. Gordon, "The Young Ladies Academy of Philadelphia," in Berkin and Norton, eds., *Women in America,* pp. 74–75; Barbara J. Harris, *Beyond Her Sphere: Women and The Professions in American History* (Westport, Conn.: Greenwood Press, 1978); and Louise Schutz Boas, *Women's Education Begins: The Rise of Women's Colleges* (Norton, Mass.: Wheaton College Press, 1935).

22. The westward migration of men and the tremendous loss of lives that occurred during the Civil War also contributed to the paucity of men available to teach.

23. The number of marriage-aged women considerably exceeded that of men, particularly in the East. New York, for example, had 38,783 more women than men in this age bracket, while in Massachusetts the figure was 27,001. Woody claims this imbalance gave rise to the cry, "What shall we do with our superfluous women?' Thomas Woody, *History of Women's Education,* II (New York: The Science Press 1929), p. 1.

24. Quoted in Woody, *History of Women's Education,* I, p. 462.

25. Woody reports the following as representative monthly salary figures f male and female teachers in the 1840s:

	Men	Women
	(in dollars)	
Maine	15.40	4.80
N.H.	13.50	5.65
Vermont	12.00	4.75
Conn.	15.00	6.50
N.Y.	14.96	6.69

History of Women's Education, I, p. 492.

26. Ibid., p. 499.

27. Indeed, during the 1800s, nursing was hardly considered a "profession" by most. Instead, until a small number of women, including Clara Barton and Dorthea Dix, proved indispensable to the Civil War effort as nurses, nursing was not considered a proper occupation for ladies. For analyses of efforts to professionalize nursing, see Mary M. Roberts, *American Nursing: History and Interpretation* (New York: MacMillan, 1954).

28. Edward T. James, ed., *Notable American Women, 1607–1950, A Biographical Dictionary* vol. I (Cambridge: The Belknap Press of Harvard University Press, 1971), s.v. Elizabeth Blackwell.

29. Flexner, *Century of Struggle,* p. 116.

30. Ibid. This attitude should not be surprising. In fact, during the early 1800s, females were praised for their modesty if they refused to allow a physician to treat them. This kind of thinking made most shudder at the "unladylike" prospect of a female physician.

31. Harris, *Beyond Her Sphere,* p. 89. While the woman's rights movement generally was concerned with other matters, the efforts of individuals like Blackwell and some small groups did much to improve, at least initially, access to a medical education. In fact, in 1852, women in Philadelphia founded an organization:

> 1st. To co-operate with the efforts now being made...to qualify women to become physicians for their own sex and for children.
>
> 2nd. To give kindly encouragement to those females who are engaged in medical studies.

Quoted in Woody, *History of Women's Education,* II, p. 343. The rationale for this support of female doctors, however, was not based on notions of equality. According to Godey's *Lady's Book* (a leading women's magazine), for example,

> Woman has her own sphere in which to act.... She is better calculated for some duties than for others, and we maintain there are none, within the role range of these duties, for which she could have been better designed, or more in the sphere of usefulness, than in this of medicine.

Quoted in ibid., p. 344. This kind of support led to the incorporation of the first institution for the training of female physicians in 1850. The creation of others around the country quickly followed. These institutions accounted for the vast majority of women physicians in the United States as no major medical school accepted women until the 1890s.

This state of affairs had both positive and negative results. On the negative side, the education and quality of female physicians tended to be inferior to that of men (although by today's standards that for both sexes was woefully inadequate). On the plus side, the isolation of women in their own schools plus the support of some women's groups produced a significant number of female doctors. However, when the women's medical colleges and the associations that supported them declined in the 1890s, so too did the number of women doctors, thereby removing many women's access to health care. See generally, Woody, *History of Women's Education* I and II; Harris, *Beyond Her Sphere;* Mary Roth Walsh, *Doctors Wanted: No Women Need*

Apply: Sexual Barriers in the Medical Profession, 1835-1975 (New Haven, Conn.: Yale University Press, 1977); and Elizabeth Blackwell, *Pioneer Work in Opening the Medical Profession to Women* (1895; reprint ed., New York: Source Book, 1970).

32. Harris, *Beyond Her Sphere,* p. 11.

33. See Aleta Wallack, "Arabella Babb Mansfield (1846-1911)," *Women's Rights Law Reporter,* 2 (April 1974):3-5.

34. Thus, women also became lawyers in other states where the state laws were written in sex-neutral fashion. For example, Phoebe Cousins, an active member of NWSA and a close friend of both Susan B. Anthony and Virginia Minor, was admitted to practice in Missouri in 1870 under a statute that said "any person" could be licensed if they possessed the requisite qualifications. In fact, Cousins' law school accomplishments often were praised in NWSA publications as a model for other women to follow. This praise, however, never included strong organizational efforts to assist women to become admitted to the bar. See D. Kelley Weisberg, "Barred From the Bar: Women and Legal Education in the United States, 1870-1890," *Journal of Legal Education* 28 (1977):485-507.

35. *Bradwell* v. *Illinois,* 16 Wall. 130 (1873).

36. Early efforts to expand educational rights during this period also are illustrative of the undersupply problem. The expansion of higher education for women was accomplished almost entirely as a result of the individual efforts of dedicated women like Emma Willard, who founded the Troy Female Seminary in 1821, and Mary Lyon. The latter spoke and traveled extensively through the East to raise money for the founding of Mt. Holyoke. Similarly, the founding of most of the private, eastern women's colleges and seminaries were made possible by grants from wealthy patrons, male and female. In the western state college systems, as well, the efforts of individual women often made possible the eventual integration of these institutions, although financial need was also a motivation. See generally, n. 21.

37. While educational and employment rights received ideological support, some believed that they were a woman's right, while others viewed access to education and the professions as dependent upon whether or not they were part of, or in furtherance of, a woman's traditional role.

38. There was, however, a considerable amount of overlap between the progressive movement and NAWSA. Several influential members of the former, including Jane Addams of Hull House and Florence Kelley of the National Consumers' League, held leadership positions in NAWSA. And, these women's concern for others is not surprising. In fact, Barbara Harris argues this transition from college to settlement house was a natural one for women educated at Vassar, Smith, and Wellesley. In these institutions (as well as many others) the goal was "to produce educated *women,* who combined intellectual achievement with feminine virtue." Many of their alumnae consequently found social work an appealing profession. It drew on their educational training, satisfied their desire for social service, and conformed to their continued belief in the nurturant, self-sacrificing female temperament. *Beyond Her Sphere,* p. 118.

39. Foner, *Women and the American Labor Movement,* p. 291. See also, Jill Conway, "Women Reformers and American Culture, 1870-1930," *Journal of Social History* 5 (Winter 1971-72):164-177.

40. Kenneally, *Women and American Trade Unions,* chaps. 5 and 6.

41. Foner, *Women and the American Labor Movement,* pp. 299–300.

42. Ibid., p. 304.

43. Ibid., pp. 481–486. The union between suffrage forces and the NWTUL was an uneasy one and born from expediency on the part of both. The NWTUL started working hard for suffrage after its poor treatment at the hands of male unionists and after its change of policy favoring protective legislation. In order to get laws passed, NWTUL leaders believed it was necessary for working women to have the vote.

44. Ibid., p. 479.

45. See generally, Maude Nathan, *The Story of An Epoch-Making Movement* (Garden City, New Jersey: Doubleday, 1926) and Clement E. Vose, "The National Consumers' League and the Brandeis Brief," *Midwest Journal of Political Science* 1 (November 1957):267–290.

46. See generally, Josephine Goldmark, *Impatient Crusader: Florence Kelley's Life Story* (Urbana: University of Illinois Press, 1953).

47. In furtherance of this strategy, the NCL initiated the Christmas "Shop Early" movement. In the early 1900s, it was the custom in most retail establishments to stay open until the last customer left for the day. Thus, many women were forced to work twelve-hour days during the holiday season with no extra remuneration. Its "Shop Early" campaign was designed to get patrons to do their Christmas shopping not only before the end of the season rush but early in the day as well, thereby allowing shop clerks the opportunity to enjoy this time of year with their families. The NCL also tried, in the spirit of the shop early effort, to inform the public about unsafe factory conditions. For example, it issued a series of consumer information pamphlets called the White List—a regularly published roster of all companies that voluntarily complied with the NCL's suggested factory standards. See generally, Nathan, *Epoch-Making Movement* and Karen O'Connor, *Women's Organizations' Use of the Courts* (Lexington, Mass.: Lexington Books, 1980), chap. 4.

48. Clement E. Vose, *Constitutional Change* (Lexington, Mass.: Lexington Books, 1972), chap. 7 and Vose, "The National Consumers' League." For a discussion of the legal arguments made in these cases, see Judith Baer, *The Chains of Protection: The Judicial Response to Women's Labor Legislation* (Westport, Conn.: Greenwood Press, 1978).

49. 208 U.S. at 421 (1908).

50. Felix Frankfurter then replaced Brandeis as the chief counsel for the NCL. For an account of Brandeis' continuing interest in NCL litigation and his behind-the-scenes support of Frankfurter, see Bruce Murphy, *The Brandeis/Frankfurter Connection* (New York: Oxford University Press, 1982).

51. In fact, they specifically noted that the National Woman's Party supported total equality of the sexes and viewed "protective legislation" as inherently unequal treatment of women. Noted in Barbara Allen Babcock et al., *Sex Discrimination and the Law* (Boston: Little Brown, 1975), pp. 48–49, n.76.

52. *Adkins* v. *Children's Hospital,* 261 U.S. 525 (1923).

53. Ibid.

54. For a more detailed account of this split, see Vose, *Constitutional Change,* chap. 7.

55. Ibid.

56. Lois Scharf, *To Work and To Wed: Female Employment, Feminism and the*

Great Depression (Westport, Conn.: Greenwood Press, 1980), p. 10. Also reflecting the changing job opportunities for women was the growth of professional business and commercial schools. Institutions like Katherine Gibbs schools mushroomed in response to the demand of business for trained young women to staff the expanding number of clerical and secretarial openings.

57.   Carol Hymowitz and Michaele Weissman, *A History of Women in America* (New York: Bantam Books, 1978), p. 306. While the National Federation of Business and Professional Women's Clubs lobbied against state laws prohibiting the employment of married women and the League of Women Voters attempted to prevent congressional passage of federal laws outlawing federal employment of more than two persons from one household, their actions generally had but limited impact possibly because women also disagreed on this issue. Florence Kelley, of the NCL, for example, opposed any effort or legislation to further employment opportunities of married women. Scharf, *To Work and To Wed,* p. 17.

58.   *West Coast Hotel* v. *Parrish,* 300 U.S. 379 (1937).

59.   Both argued, for example, that (1) women were not equal to men; (2) women needed protection; (3) a woman's place was in the home; and (4) woman's primary role was motherhood.

60.   For example, the percentage of the total college and first professional degrees awarded to women between 1900 and 1920 rose from 19 to 34 percent, masters degrees 19 to 30 percent, and Ph.D.s 6 to 15 percent. United States Department of Labor, Bureau of Labor Statistics, *Women's Bureau 1969 Handbook.*

61.   The General Federation of Women's Clubs and its affiliates even promoted this philosophy in the lower grades. It, in fact, was instrumental in getting home economics adopted in high schools around the country.

62.   Barbara Sinclair Deckard, *The Women's Movement,* 2nd ed. (New York: Harper and Row, 1979), p. 317. Thus, it is not surprising to note that women constituted between only 4 and 6 percent of the nation's physicians from 1910 to 1940.

63.   For example, the New York City Bar Association refused to accept female members until 1937. This kind of discrimination plus social mores that militated against women seeking careers in the law resulted in women making up 2 or less percent of all attorneys through 1940.

64.   Woody, *History of Women's Education,* II, p. 329.

65.   Quoted in ibid.

66.   Nurses and teachers, however, constituted 75 percent of all professionals. Harris, *Beyond Her Sphere,* pp. 104–105. In fact, "three out of four new career women in the 1920s and 1930s went into teaching or nursing." William H. Chafe, "The Paradox of Progress," in Jean E. Friedman and William G. Shade, eds., *Our American Sisters,* 2nd ed. (Boston: Allyn and Bacon, 1976), p. 386.

67.   Women were considered naturally suited to be librarians because dusting and taking care of books were akin to housework.

68.   Rosalind Rosenberg, "The Academic Prism: The New View of American Women," in Berkin and Norton, eds., *Women of America,* pp. 322–323. Indeed, by 1910, the U.S. Census reported there were 16,000 social workers, of which 56 percent were women. By 1920, that percentage rose to 66.

It should also be noted that the fairly common practice of many woman professionals to remain single or to give up their career altogether when they married echoed the prevailing sentiment of the day. In fact, although during the decades of the suffrage movement more married women than ever before worked, the greatest number was concentrated among poor and black women. Scharf, *To Work and To Wed*, p. 16. At the highest professional levels, few women attempted to combine work and marriage. Only 12 percent of all professional women were married, and 75 percent of women with Ph.D.s remained single. William H. Chafe, *The American Woman: Her Changing Social, Economic and Political Role, 1920–1970* (New York: Oxford University Press, 1972), p. 100.

Lois Scharf has noted commentary that suggests that Vassar's addition of domestic science and home economics courses to its curriculum in the 1920s was part of a larger effort to try to assist its students find a way to integrate a career and marriage. Administrators hoped these courses would "help break down the barriers between work and home...and improve performance in both areas for women who had two vocations—successively, if not simultaneously." *To Work and To Wed*, chap. 2. Other colleges also attempted to assist women to manage a home and career. For example, the Institute to Coordinate Women's Interests at Smith College tried several different options—cooperative nurseries, communal laundries, and central kitchens—in an effort to assist college-educated wives to combine a family with a career outside of the home. But with hardly any organizational support, little came of these limited efforts.

69. Chafe, *American Woman*, pp. 144–145.

70. Ibid.

71. Harris, *Beyond Her Sphere*, p. 144.

72. Hymowitz and Weissman, *History of Women*, p. 312.

73. Additionally, the 5 percent quota on female medical students was dropped in 1945. Harris, *Beyond Her Sphere*, pp. 144–145.

74. Hymowitz and Weissman, *A History of Women*, p. 312.

75. Lois Banner, *Women in Modern America* (New York: Harcourt Brace Jovanovich, Inc., 1974), pp. 190–191.

76. Deckard, *The Women's Movement*, p. 319.

77. Harris, *Beyond Her Sphere*, p. 153.

78. This stood in stark contrast to the actions of other countries. Great Britain, for example, although one-third the size of the United States, cared for three times as many children in government-funded centers. Working mothers were given time off to shop, and central kitchens were established wherein women could pick up meals, at cost, on their way home from work. Hymowitz and Weissman, *History of Women*, p. 313.

79. Chafe, *American Woman*, p. 170 and Banner, *Women in Modern America*, p. 205.

80. Hymowitz and Weissman, *History of Women*, p. 314.

81. Harris, *Beyond Her Sphere*, pp. 154–155.

82. Ibid., p. 155.

83. Betty Friedan, *The Feminine Mystique* (New York: Dell, 1963), p. 30.

84. Additionally, by 1965, 35 percent of all married women with husbands present worked. In fact, 42.7 percent of mothers with school-aged children worked as did 23.3 percent of those with preschool-aged children. United States Department of Labor, Bureau of Labor Statistics, *Perspectives on Working Women: A Databook* (Bulletin #2080) (October, 1980), p. 27.

85.   Valerie Kincade Oppenheimer, *The Female Labor Force in the United States* (Berkeley: Institute of International Studies, 1970), pp. 171–189.

86.   *Women's Bureau, 1969 Handbook.* Women also suffered greater economic problems because of societal expectations concerning how "coeds" should dress—expensively. Thus, women not only failed to receive governmental tuition assistance but also had to spend large sums on clothes.

87.   Harris, *Beyond Her Sphere,* p. 165. See also, Jessie Bernard, *Academic Women* (New York: New American Library, 1966), chaps. 1–4.

88.   335 U.S. at 466 (1948).

89.   Banner, *Women in Modern America,* p. 231.

90.   Mary Anne Baker et al., *Women Today: A Multidisciplinary Approach to Women's Studies* (Monterey, Calif.: Brooks/Cole Publishing Co., 1980), p. 24.

91.   Executive Order 10980 (December 14, 1961).

92.   Judith Hole and Ellen Levine, *Rebirth of Feminism* (New York: Quadrangle, 1971), p. 21.

93.   The establishment of the Commission with Roosevelt as its chair also was done to keep campaign promises to the former first lady, who initially had opposed Kennedy as the Democratic nominee.

94.   As noted in Chapter 2, this leadership source was expanded when most state governors followed Kennedy's initiative and created their own state commissions.

95.   Another example of governmental reaction to the Commission report was President Kennedy's issuance of a directive reinterpreting an 1870 law that had long been used to bar women from high levels of the federal government. Hole and Levine, *Rebirth of Feminism,* p. 21.

96.   Irene Murphy, *Public Policy on the Status of Women* (Lexington, Mass.: Lexington Books, 1973), pp. 25–26.

97.   Ibid.

98.   For example, even as early as the 1940s and 1950s (in 1954 it was 87 percent), large majorities responded affirmatively to the following question posed by pollster George Gallup: Do you approve or disapprove of paying women the same salaries as men, if they are doing the same work?"

99.   Norma K. Raffel, "Federal Laws and Regulations Prohibiting Sex Discrimination," in Eloise C. Snyder, ed., *The Study of Women: Enlarging Perspectives of Social Reality* (New York: Harper and Row, 1979), p. 106.

100.   *Shultz* v. *Wheaton Glass Co.,* 421 F. 2d 259 (3rd Cir.), cert. denied, 398 U.S. 905 (1970).

101.   Raffel, "Federal Laws," in Snyder, ed., *The Study of Women,* p. 106.

102.   Ibid.

103.   See Babcock et al., *Sex Discrimination,* pp. 440–508.

104.   For example, 1981 figures continue to reveal significant differences in salaries received by women professionals. In fact, a study done of Harvard graduates found that among graduates of the School of Public Health, the average female salary was $21,300 as compared to $37,800 for males. Major discrepancies also were revealed among School of Education graduates where women's average salaries were $18,700; men's $26,150. Project on the Status of Women, *On Campus with Women* 30 (Spring 1981):1.

105.   Nancy D. Perlman and Bruce J. Ennis, *Preliminary Memorandum on Pay Equity: Achieving Equal Pay for Work of Comparable Value* (Center for Women in

Government mimeo, April 1980), p. 1.

106.   Ibid., pp. 4–5.

107.   49 U.S.L.W. 4623 (June 8, 1981). While many corporations challenged the use of the Civil Rights Act for salary inequity where women were not doing the same jobs as men, the Court said that coverage of the 1964 Act allowed such claims because otherwise large classes of women would never be able to challenge discriminatory salary schedules. Thus, in effect, although this was not an Equal Pay Act lawsuit per se, the Court in essence expanded the concept of equal pay.

108.   Perlman and Ennis, *Pay Equity,* p. 6.

109.   "2,000 Go on Strike Over Unequal Pay," *The Atlanta Constitution,* July 6, 1981, p. 6–A.

110.   Ibid.

111.   For a discussion of the role of unions in the pay equity issue, particularly their use of the concept as an organizing tool, see Wendy Kahn and Joy Ann Grune, "Pay Equity: Beyond Equal Pay for Equal Work," in Ellen Boneparth, ed., *Women Power and Policy* (Elmsford, N.Y.: Pergamon, 1982), pp. 75–89.

112.   Nadine Brozan, "NOW Convenes to Pick Leaders," *The New York Times,* October 9, 1982, p. 18.

113.   Concerning conservative efforts to narrow the scope of employment discrimination protections through litigation, see Karen O'Connor and Lee Epstein, "The Importance of Interest Group Involvement in Employment Discrimination" *Howard Law Journal,* 25 (November, 1982), p. 301.

114.   Jo Freeman, *The Politics of Women's Liberation,* (New York: David McKay, 1975), p. 75.

115.   Ibid., p. 193.

116.   For an excellent discussion of the scope of executive orders, see Babcock et al., *Sex Discrimination,* pp. 509–599.

117.   Hole and Levine, *Rebirth of Feminism,* p. 46.

118.   Ibid., p. 45.

119.   Quoted in ibid., p. 46.

120.   Ibid., pp. 46 and 96.

121.   Ibid., p. 97.

122.   Freeman, *Women's Liberation,* pp. 200–201.

123.   Current Activities of the Center for Law and Social Policy, September 1979, p. 22.

124.   Ibid.

125.   In November 1980, President Carter signed Executive Order 12250 to give the Justice Department power to "coordinate" enforcement efforts of civil rights laws affecting education. "The impact of the new order hasn't been measured at all yet," according to a top civil rights official. Quoted in *PEER Perspective* 7 (February 1981):5.

126.   Figures compiled by the American Political Science Association.

127.   Caroline Bird, *Born Female: The High Cost of Keeping Women Down* (New York: David McKay, 1968), chap. 1.

128.   Freeman, *Women's Liberation,* p. 53.

129.   Caruthers Gholson Berger, "Equal Protection, Equal Employment Oppor-

tunity and Equal Enforcement of the Law for Women," *Valparaiso Law Review* 5 (Spring 1971):326–373. For a contrary conclusion, see Babcock et. at., *Sex Discrimination*, p. 161.

130.　Freeman, *Women's Liberation*, p. 54 n. 24.

131.　The first director of the EEOC even went so far as to say that the law was "'conceived out of wedlock' and that men were entitled to female secretaries." Quoted in Jo Freeman, "Women and Public Policy: An Overview," in Boneparth, ed., *Women Power and Public Policy*, p. 53.

132.　Women's rights groups were particularly concerned with the impact of two discriminatory practices—sex-segregated help-wanted advertisements and the effects of protective legislation. For example, early in 1966, the Washington, D.C. chapter of BPW passed a resolution calling for the EEOC to issue regulations to end male and female help-wanted ads. The Citizens Advisory Council on the Status of Women, which was established by executive order at the suggestion of the Commission on the Status of Women, then sent copies of that resolution to the several State Commissions on the Status of Women, just prior to the National Conference meeting. Later, at the founding meeting of NOW, those present sent telegrams to the EEOC Commission urging it to outlaw those advertisements. Hole and Levine, *Rebirth of Feminism*, p. 84.

133.　During those proceedings, a NOW representative testified that "merely the repetition of Help-Wanted Male, Help-Wanted Female, plays a role conditioning part in continuing myths that rely on false assumptions about sex in relation to work." Quoted in Hole and Levine, *Rebirth of Feminism*, p. 42.

134.　Freeman, *Women's Liberation*, p. 77.

135.　*Pittsburgh Press Co.* v. *Pittsburgh Commission on Human Relations*, 413 U.S. 376 (1973). NOW became party to the suit at the Supreme Court level and was supported with amicus curiae briefs from members of WEAL, the Women's Law Fund, and the Women's Rights Project of the ACLU. Although the EEOC had succumbed to feminist pressures and announced regulations prohibiting male and female help-wanted ads, the Supreme Court upheld the agencies' construction of Title VII by only a one vote majority.

136.　Raffel, "Federal Laws and Regulations Prohibiting Sex Discrimination," in Snyder, ed., *The Study of Women*, p. 107.

137.　O'Connor, *Women's Organizations'*, chap. 5.

138.　Ibid., pp. 102–108.

139.　The American Civil Liberties Union also created a Women's Rights Project to handle sex-discrimination complaints in a systematized manner. Ibid., chap. 5.

140.　Quoted in Freeman, *Women's Liberation*, p. 74.

141.　Babcock et al., *Sex Discrimination*, p. 262. This book contains an excellent summary of the protective legislation controversy that actually began in the 1920s. See pp. 229–282.

142.　Statement of Marguerite Rawalt to the Equal Employment Opportunity Commission at Public Hearings held May 2, 1967, p. 1, reported in Babcock et al., *Sex Discrimination*, p. 266, n. 60.

143.　Statement by Katherine P. Elickson of the NCL before the Equal Employment Opportunity Commission, May 2, 1967, p. 5, reported in ibid., n. 59.

144.　444 F. 2d 1219 (9th Cir. 1971).

145. In *Rosenfeld*, the court's decision invalidated a California law limiting the number of hours (10) that women could work each day and the weights that they could be required to lift on the job.

146. Freeman, "Women and Public Policy," in Boneparth, ed., *Women, Power and Public Policy*, p. 53.

147. 442 F. 2d 385 (5th Cir. 1971), cert. denied, 404 U.S. 950 (1971).

148. 433 U.S. 321 (1977).

149. In *Dothard*, both the Women's Rights Project and the Women's Legal Defense Fund submitted amicus curiae briefs urging the Court to interpret the bfoq provision very narrowly if the Justices were to find that Alabama's refusal to hire women guards was not a violation of Title VII. O'Connor, *Women's Organizations*, pp. 97 and 113–114. See also, Note, "Sex as a Bona Fide Occupational Qualification: Title VII's Evolving Enigma, Related Litigation Problems, and the Judicial Vision of Womanhood after *Dothard* v. *Rawlinson*," *Women's Rights Law Reporter* 5 (Winter–Spring 1979):107–164.

150. 400 U.S. 542 (1971).

151. 414 U.S. 632 (1974).

152. The case was not litigated under Title VII, however, because the act's coverage was not expanded to include schoolteachers until 1972, after the case was initiated.

153. Babcock et al., *Sex Discrimination*, p. 314.

154. Ibid., p. 315. Again, as in *Cleveland*, Title VII did not apply because a state policy was at issue.

155. 417 U.S. 484 (1974). *Geduldig* was sponsored by Equal Rights Advocates, a California-based, feminist, public interest law firm. The firm received substantial amicus support from the WRP, NOW, IUE, and even WEAL, whose leaders by 1974 realized the pervasive consequences of pregnancy-based discrimination.

156. 404 U.S. 71 (1971).

157. 411 U.S. 677 (1973).

158. 429 U.S. 125 (1976).

159. For a thorough discussion of pregnancy discrimination litigation, see Nancy S. Erickson, "Pregnancy Discrimination: An Analytic Approach," *Women's Rights Law Reporter* 5 (Winter–Spring 1979):83–106 and update of same, *Women's Rights Law Reporter* 7 (Fall 1981):11–16.

160. For an excellent discussion of these activities, see Carol Schiro Greenwald, "Women's Rights, Courts and Congress: Conflict Over Pregnancy Disability Compensation Politics," paper given at the 1978 Annual Meeting of the American Political Science Association. See also, Joyce Gelb and Marian Lief Palley, "Women and Interest Group Politics: A Comparative Analysis of Federal Decision-Making," *Journal of Politics* 41 (May 1979):362–392.

161. See Patricia Huckle, "The Womb Factor: Pregnancy Policies and Employment of Women," *The Western Political Quarterly* 34 (March, 1981), 114–126. She notes that the National Conference of Catholic Bishops Committee for Pro-Life Activities and the American Citizens Concerned for Life, Inc., both antiabortion groups, did speak in favor of the bill but with reservations concerning its possible interpretation that would allow for abortion funding. The final wording of the bill reflects a compromise of their views and those of prochoice groups. There is no

requirement that abortion costs be covered nor any prohibition against their being covered.

162.   For excellent discussions of the inequities in the Social Security system see, Grace Ganz Blumberg, "Federal Income Tax and Social Security Law," in Anne Foote Cahn, ed., *Women in the U.S. Labor Force* (New York: Praeger Publishers, 1979), pp. 237–248.

163.   420 U.S. 636 (1975).

164.   453 U.S. 210 (1981).

165.   *Rostker* v. *Goldberg,* 453 U.S. 57 (1981).

166.   "Divorcees Voted Military Pension Rights," *The Atlanta Constitution,* July 29, 1982, p. 2–A.

167.   Amy Shannon, "Relief Slated for Military Ex-spouses," *Women's Political Times,* September 1982, p. 1.

168.   Rae André, *Homemakers: The Forgotten Workers* (Chicago: University of Chicago Press, 1981), pp. 213–214.

169.   André, *Homemakers,* p. 216.

170.   *City of Los Angeles* v. *Manhart,* 435 U.S. 702 (1977).

171.   Timothy Adams, "Battle of Equal Pension for Men, Women Goes to High Court," *The Atlanta Journal and Constitution,* November 7, 1982, p. 30A.

172.   "Text of Court Decision Equalizing TIAA Benefits for Men, Women," *The Chronicle of Higher Education,* October 13, 1982, p. 26.

173.   "Pensions Varied on Sex Basis Under Attack by U.S. in Court," *The New York Times,* January 12, 1983, p. 10.

174.   NOW in particular is pressing hard for laws to affect the insurance industry, which it views as a major opponent in the ERA struggle.

175.   H.R. 3117 and S. 888.

176.   Patricia Marks, "Legislative Update," *Women's Political Times,* September 1982, p. 11. The IRA provisions allowed unemployed housewives to set up their own pension funds with resulting tax advantages. For an analysis of the IRA and other sections of the act (adopted or pending), see Women's Research and Education Institute (WREI), *Pro/Con Analysis of the WOMEN'S ECONOMIC EQUITY ACT* (Washington, D.C.: n.d.).

177.   For more information about pension reform, see Pension Rights Center, *Women & Pensions,* paper prepared by The Center at 1346 Connecticut Avenue, N.W., Washington, D.C. 20036.

178.   Only 32 percent of women workers were even covered by pension plans in 1979. WREI, *Pro/Con Analysis,* p. 1.

179.   Project on the Status and Education of Women, "Sexual Harassment: A Hidden Issue" (June 1978):1. For other discussions of the problems of sexual harassment, see Note, "Legal Remedies for Employment-Related Sexual Harassment," *University of Minnesota Law Review* 64 (1979):151 and Symposium, "Sexual Harassment," *Capital University Law Review* 10 (1981):445–708.

180.   For an excellent analysis of the problem, see Catherine A. MacKinnon, *Sexual Harassment of Working Women* (New Haven: Yale University Press, 1979).

181.   Phyllis L. Crocker, "Annotated Bibliography on Sexual Harassment in Education," *Women's Rights Law Reporter* 7 (Winter 1982):91.

182.   *Bundy* v. *Jackson,* 561 F. 2d 983 (D.C. Cir. 1977). Also, in 1977, the Court of

Appeals in the 3rd Circuit held that sexual harassment is actionable under Title VII if sexual compliance is made a condition of employment or requirement for advancement. *Tomkins* v. *Public Service Electric and Gas Co.,* 568 F. 2d 1004 (3rd Cir. 1977).

183.   *Miller* v. *Bank of America,* 600 F. 2d 211 (9th Cir. 1979).

184.   *On Campus with Women* 30 (Spring 1981), p. 1.

185.   Frank J. Prial, "More Women Work at Traditional Male Jobs," *The New York Times,* November 15, 1982, p. 1.

186.   David M. Margolick, "Wall Street's Sexist Wall," *The National Law Journal,* August 4, 1980, p. 1.

187.   United States Department of Labor, Bureau of Labor Statistics, *News* (March 7, 1982), Table 3.

188.   Commission on the Status of Women, *American Women,* pp. 11–13.

189.   Ibid., p. 13.

190.   Ibid., p. 17.

191.   "NOW Demands," quoted in Papachristou, *Women Together,* p. 222.

192.   Quoted in ibid.

193.   For an excellent account of the lobbying activities that led to passage of Title IX, see Marian Lief Palley and Joyce Gelb, *Women and Public Policies* (Princeton: Princeton University Press, 1982).

194.   Quoted in Babcock et al., *Sex Discrimination,* pp. 1014–1015.

195.   430 U.S. 703 (1977).

196.   102 S. Ct. 3331, 3336 (1982).

197.   For an analysis of O'Connor's voting record during her first term on the Court, see Karen O'Connor and Lee Epstein, "Sex and the Supreme Court: An Analysis of Judicial Support for Gender-based Claims," *Social Science Quarterly,* in press.

198.   Lyle Denniston, "Sex bias in sports not gone," *The Atlanta Journal and Constitution,"* October 24, 1982, p. 1–C (con't. on p. 14–C).

199.   *On Campus with Women* 29 (Winter 1981):12. Other evidence of the effectiveness of Title IX includes the fact that "in 1972, only 7 percent of all high school varsity athletes were girls," but by 1981, that percentage was 35 percent. Additionally, before passage of Title IX, no colleges offered athletic scholarships to women. By 1982, over 10,000 such scholarships were awarded to women. Denniston, "Sex bias," p. 14–C.

200.   Joseph A. Califano, Jr., *Governing America* (New York: Simon & Schuster, 1981), pp. 223–224.

201.   *On Campus with Women* 22 (Winter 1979):6.

202.   Carol Felsenthal, *Phyllis Schlafly: The Sweetheart of the Silent Majority* (Garden City, N.Y.: Doubleday, 1981), p. 319. See also, Janet K. Boles, "Social Movements as Policy Entrepreneurs: The Family Protection Act and Family Impact Analysis," paper delivered at the 1982 Annual Meeting of the American Political Science Association.

203.   "Groups Fighting Sexist, Racist Texts Called 'Censors,'" *PEER Perspective* 6 (March 1980):2.

204.   In 1976, for example, the *Washington Post* noted that "the chief compromises today [in textbook adoption] are in response to conservative forces." Quoted in "Censors," p. 2.

205.   Marilyn J. Boxer, "For and About Women: The Theory and Practice of Women's Studies in the United States," *Signs* 7 (Spring 1982):661–695.

206.   PEER, *Stalled at the Start* (n.d.), p. 19. Title IX currently necessitates that all federal funds to an institution be terminated if there is sex discrimination in any program.

207.   444 U.S. 1048 (1978).

208.   72 L.Ed. 2d 299 (1982).

209.   PEER, *Stalled at the Start,* p. 24.

210.   Ibid., p. 29.

211.   Given agency inaction, most changes have come about as a result of lobbying by national or campus women's or parents' groups that are determined to see sexist policies ended. WEAL, for example, has sued HEW to enforce Title IX as well as other anti-sex discrimination laws, and it continues to monitor the agency's actions in this area.

212.   Quoted in "Women and Education: Will They Have the Same Rights as Men," *Glamour,* March 1982, p. 93.

213.   David Margolick, "Undaunted by Loss on Equal Rights, Women Look to Courts to Curb Bias," *The New York Times,* June 29, 1982, p. 11.

214.   "Women in Education," p. 93.

215.   Patricia Marks, "Educational Equity Stung by Right-Wing," *Women's Political Times,* July 1982, p. 3 (con't. on p. 19). See also, "New Congress, Administration May Threaten Title IX, WEEA," *PEER Perspective* 7 (February 1981):1.

216.   Ibid.

217.   S. 1361, withdrawn.

218.   "Women and Education," p. 93.

219.   Marks, "Legislative Update," p. 11.

220.   National Advisory Council on Women's Educational Programs, Title IX: *The Half-Full, Half-Empty Glass* (Washington, D.C.: Government Printing Office, 1981).

221.   Marks, "Educational Equity," p. 3.

222.   See Sara E. Rix and Anne J. Stone, *Impact on Women of the Administration's Proposed Budget* (Washington, D.C.: The Women's Research and Education Institute for the Congressional Caucus for Women's Issues, April 1982), pp. 17–23.

6 Women's Marketplace Activity[1]

INTRODUCTION

As detailed in Chapter 5, the expansion of educational and employment rights for women that occurred during the early woman's rights and suffrage movements failed to produce full and equal participation. In fact, by 1965, although larger numbers of women were attending college or working outside of the home, the words, of the first woman's rights leaders had continuing validity: men still "monopolize[d] all profitable employments, and from those a woman [was] permitted to follow, she receive[d] scanty remuneration."[2]

This slow progress was partly due to the absence of laws guaranteeing equal employment or educational rights for women during the two early women's movements. In fact, the "protective" laws that were passed at the urging of most women's groups during the suffrage era actually reduced women's employment opportunities in many areas.[3]

In the 1960s and 1970s, renewed efforts by women, particularly those in the rights movement, began to break down legal barriers to employment. After the enactment of the Equal Pay Act of 1963 and the Civil Rights Act of 1964, women actively lobbied all three branches of government for enforcement of the provisions in those acts. These efforts, however, failed to produce parity between men and women in both the employment and educational spheres. For example, although by 1981, women constituted over 40 percent of all persons who worked (58 percent of all women actually worked at least some of the year outside of the home), the median weekly salary of females employed in full-time, year-round jobs was but 59 percent of what male workers earned, as revealed in Table 6-1.

210

TABLE 6-1
Women's Median Annual Earnings as a Percent of Men's

Year	Women's Earnings as a Percent of Men's
1955	63.9
1960	60.8
1965	60.0
1970	59.4
1975	58.8
1980	59.9
1981	59.2

Note: Figures are for individuals employed full time, year-round, who are 14 or older.

Source of data: United States Department of Labor, Bureau of Labor Statistics.

In the educational area as well, the progress of women in the last fifteen years, while impressive, has not yet closed the gap between the sexes, particularly in science and mathematically-oriented educational programs. Although Title IX specifically prohibits discrimination in school admission, women still fail to pursue certain majors, even though they comprise more than 50 percent of all college students.[4]

Paralleling our findings in the political area, our findings in the economic area show that legal change is a necessary but an insufficient condition for equality. Because the employment rights gained during the 1960s and 1970s were like the political rights of the 1920s and thus not pure public goods, it is not surprising that all women have not been affected equally. Individual women could and did choose the extent to which they wanted to partake of new education and employment rights. Yet some women continue to be prevented (directly or indirectly) from exercising these rights. While part of the solution to the continued inequality of women lies in the need for additional legal guarantees and the active enforcement of existing laws, these changes alone will not result in full equality. Rather, as in the realm of politics, additional barriers besides legal ones continue to limit the progress of women in the marketplace. More specifically, the advancement of women in the educational and employment spheres has been hampered by the same three roadblocks that also limited the equality of women in politics, namely: (1) cultural stereotypes about the roles and abilities of women, which in turn, contributes to (2) a lack of preparation or needed resources on the part of women for full-time commitment to any and all occupations and professions, and (3) discrimination by employers and fellow employees. The last of course, is only partially dependent on cultural stereotypes. As in the field of politics, much of the discrimination by employers as well as fellow employees against women stems from self-interest or the inability of some men to accept a female co-worker as an equal.

In the sections to follow, we will explore how these barriers, both in the past and present, have hindererd the ability of women to utilize the new opportunities that have been opened up to them. We will also look at how the barriers have changed over time, especially in the last two decades. Finally, we will try to identify what changes must yet occur before the women of tomorrow can be truly equal.

FACTORS CONDITIONING ATTITUDES
TOWARD WORKING WOMEN

Attitudes toward working women have fluctuated over time far more than have attitudes concerning women's political participation. This difference may be attributed to the fact that the most common form of political activity engaged in by women—voting—has very little (if any) disruptive effect on the family or social structure. A woman's participation in the paid labor force, however, has far greater impact on the family and on the marketplace. While the trend since the Industrial Revolution has been toward a growing acceptance of working women, there have been several periods in the last two centuries when relatively positive attitudes about the employment of women have been followed by periods of more negative and restrictive views. The cause for these reversals in opinion is not always easy to pinpoint. While financial considerations sometimes appear to be quite important (the 1930s Depression, for example), often no pressing economic reason for heightened conservatism is apparent. For example, during World War II, most Americans heartily approved of the employment of married women. In the decade after the war, however, even though there continued to be a relatively heavy demand for women workers, the public's attitude toward the employment of married women became less supportive. This divergence in the 1950s between what women actually were doing (entering the marketplace in ever-increasing numbers), and what the public *thought* women should be doing (staying home and raising a family) has been commented upon by numerous scholars. In fact, this paradox has been identified by at least one historian as a key factor in the rise of the women's movement in the 1960s.[5] The role of the women's movements in changing public attitudes also is a matter of debate. As in the political arena, here, too, there is a suggestion that for certain cultural stereotypes the movements may have played a critical role. Other attitudinal changes, however, seem only weakly influenced by them. As we shall see, another possible catalyst of attitude change is the experience of the workplace on the women who actually find themselves, for whatever reason, employed outside the home.

Employers, too, have played an important role in attitudinal development. Marxists and others maintain that business executives who benefit from a readily available reserve of cheap labor, encourage the cultural stereotypes that women's work is only secondary.[6] As economist Valerie Kincade Oppenheimer has observed, employers often appear willing to drop certain stereotypes and encourage others to do so if demand for women workers is high and the supply is artificially constrained by these cultural views. For example, she reports that during the 1940s and 1950s employers were willing to hire married women in the absence of available single women even though they had previously condemned this practice.[7]

Economic self-interest of male employees also may be a key factor in conditioning attitudes toward women workers. It has been argued that men will be more likely to oppose women workers when they see their own jobs or wages as vulnerable. Opposition on the part of male-dominated labor unions to many affirmative action programs seems traceable in part to this fear. Similarly, some male workers may encourage occupational stereotyping to dissuade women from applying for "men's" jobs, thus keeping the supply of workers for such jobs artifically low and the wages in some "male" occupations high. Male attitudes may be of particular importance in the 1980s if the economic downturn and decline in the number of available jobs continue.

In sum, several factors appear to influence cultural attitudes about women working. Many are inextricably bound with equal employment opportunity laws and their enforcement. While it is beyond the scope of this work to assess the relative influence of each of these factors, we will try to point out their possible roles in structuring public sentiment in this area at various times.

In the sections to follow, our focus will be on two aspects of cultural attitudes that have been and continue to be the main stumbling blocks to full economic equality of women. Our first concern will be with attitudes toward the employment of women per se. We will be particularly concerned with attitudes toward work-force activity by married women, especially mothers. If these attitudes are negative, many women may refrain from seeking salaried positions, fearing adverse comment from their friends or family. Additionally, many economists hypothesize that negative attitudes may indirectly foster and maintain the lower status of women in the workplace.[8] Some of these scholars, for example, view negative attitudes toward working women as responsible for the deficiencies in preparation for full-time, good-paying work suffered by many women (our second barrier).[9] Other theorists trace the persistence of the third barrier, discrimination by employers, both in the hiring and treatment of female employees, to the influence of these stereotypes.

They identify these attitudes as contributing to the real or assumed lack of commitment to work on the part of women. This lower commitment, in turn, serves as the basis or excuse for some hiring practices that place women in dead-end, low status, low-paying positions.[10]

Our second concern will be with attitudes concerning women's qualifications to perform certain kinds of work. Public perceptions of the abilities of women also have both direct and indirect influences on the status of women as workers. Indirect influences, which contribute to the training and hiring of women in crowded "women's occupations," are particularly critical.[11] With respect to both sets of attitudes, we will be concerned not only with what the general public thinks about these questions, but also with what women, employers, and male employees believe.

ATTITUDES TOWARD MARKETPLACE ACTIVITY BY WOMEN

The few women who worked outside the home during the colonial period encountered little public resistance, largely due to recognition of the heavy demand for female labor. Because of the shortage of men to perform many critical jobs—those requiring physicians, innkeepers, and shopkeepers, for example—the public was hesitant to condemn women who provided these services.[12] Even in the early industrial period when factories were established, the employment of young, single women was viewed positively by many.

As industrialization proceeded, however, the division of roles between the sexes became more pronounced. Increasingly, men went "out" to work and women stayed home. The symbol of the new middle class became the wife of leisure, although there was little real "leisure" associated with running a home in the mid-1800s. Many of the poor, black, and immigrant families could ill afford the luxury of a nonworking wife, yet the common practice even in these classes was for women to work only before marriage. Additionally, public sentiment toward single working women was not overly or consistently favorable. Especially in periods of economic crisis, there were loud protests against the employment of *any* women who had other means of support.[13] Moreover, many members of the middle class viewed all work, but especially factory work, as a corrupter of young women—sure to destroy their femininity and their subsequent ability to be good mothers and wives. As was discussed in Chapter 5, the middle-class women in the National Consumers' League lobbied for legislation to improve factory conditions, but still looked unfavorably on married women working, unless employment was an absolute necessity.

With the development of many new white-collar jobs at the beginning of the twentieth century, it became increasingly acceptable for young, middle-class women to work outside the home. The era of the 1920s and the "new woman" may have been a particularly favorable time for young working women.[14] Attitudes toward the employment of married women,[15] however, remained decidedly negative as revealed in some of the first public opinion polls taken in the 1930s.[16] Perhaps in part because of the Depression, in 1936 only 15 percent of the public gave an unqualified favorable response to a question concerning the advisability of married women working. The reasons given most frequently by those who objected were: (1) women take men's jobs (36%); (2) a woman's place is in the home (35%); and (3) one is guaranteed a happier homelife or healthier children if women do not work (21%).[17] In 1937 and 1938 when the question was rephrased to include the possibility of a married woman working "if she had a husband capable of supporting her," less than a quarter of the public (25% of the women but only 19% of all men) approved of a woman working. There was also widespread support for the practice of refusing to hire or actually firing women who could depend on their husbands for support. Over half of all respondents, for example, declared they would favor a law prohibiting married women from working for their state or local government if their husbands earned $1000 a year.[18]

World War II radically reversed this picture. Suddenly, there was a tremendous need for workers, and women generally were often the only workers available. Mindful of the public sentiment, the propaganda campaign used by the U.S. government to "pry" women out of their homes did not challenge stereotypical views about women's nature or proper social roles. Rather, the arguments employed to get women to join the war effort temporarily were based on patriotic appeals, references to the "glamour" of working, or claims that the duties of mother and wife included work in the war industries so soldier sons and husbands could come home from the battles abroad sooner.[19] One recruitment poster, for example, proclaimed, "Longing won't bring him back sooner...GET A WAR JOB!"[20] Women were also assured that factory work would not destroy their femininity—indeed the similarity of housework and factory work was a common theme.[21] In response to this propaganda, public support for married working women rose dramatically. When questioned, 60 percent of the public said married women should take jobs in the war industries. The percentage climbed to more than 70 percent when the qualification "without children" was added.[22] Interestingly, the polls revealed that more women than men favored married women's employment.[23] In addition to this new acceptance of married women workers, large majorities (between 66 and 78 percent, depending on how the question was phrased) also favored the concept of equal pay for equal work.[24]

The favorable sentiments, however, were prevalent only during the war. At its end, fueled in part by the fears of public officials and male workers about a shortage of jobs,[25] the nation embarked upon a "return to the home ethos." Popular magazines proclaimed the benefits and rewards of suburban living and caring for the home as a full-time, fulfilling occupation. This change in public sentiment was quickly registered in public opinion polls. In the immediate postwar years, only 18 percent gave unqualified approval to a married woman working if her husband was capable of supporting her.[26] When questions raised the specter of a "limited number of jobs," 86 percent disapproved of "a married woman holding a job in business or industry when her husband was capable of supporting her," a percentage that was higher than many of those found in the midst of the Depression.[27] Even when the specter of a limited number of jobs was not raised, and the question asked only about "married women with no children under 16," only 34 percent of all men surveyed in 1946 gave unqualified approval to a woman working if her husband could support her. In contrast, 42 percent of all women viewed this in a positive light.[28]

As noted in Chapter 5, married women continued to join the labor force in increasing rates despite public opinion. Interviews with working women suggest that one of the ways they resolved the apparent divergence between cultural standards (married women should not work) and their own behavior (working) was by citing economic necessity as their reason for working outside of the home. This reason appears to have been particularly common among mothers with young or preschool children.[29] By claiming that they were working for the needs of their family, they could justify their employment as an extension of the motherhood/wife role.[30]

While the motives articulated by women workers in the 1940s and 1950s may have been socially acceptable, once in the marketplace, many found they liked their work and wanted to stay.[31] Even in the 1950s, when the dominant cultural ethos maintained that women could only find happiness and fulfillment by staying in the home and raising a family, 75 percent of all married working women, when interviewed, were satisfied with their job. Even more significantly, only 22 percent preferred full-time housework to continued employment.[32] This enjoyment of and satisfaction with their work are important parts of the explanation why the women who went to work continued to stay on the job. It also explains why others joined them even in the face of less-than-overwhelming social support for their actions. Furthermore, the sense of self-worth and pleasure these working women found and the economic rewards their work brought to their families seem to have had a more important permanent influence on public attitudes toward women working than did World War II.

Employers played a catalytic role in this attitudinal change. Their demand for women workers made possible the increased employment of women from the 1940s into the 1960s. Because this demand occurred at the very time when there were fewer single women to fill it, employers were willing to discard many of their own prejudices and biases against married women.[33] Once on the job, the changing attitudes of the women themselves toward work outside the home further disarmed public resistance. Thus, by 1969, 55 percent of all respondents approved of a married woman earning money in business or industry, an increase of 37 percent since 1945.[34] Interestingly, this rather impressive change in popular sentiment occurred just prior to the women's movement's capture of the public's attention.

ATTITUDES TOWARD WORKING WOMEN: THE IMPACT OF THE WOMEN'S RIGHTS MOVEMENT

The popularity of the women's movement in the 1970s and its focus on a woman's right to work, have facilitated the positive attitude on behalf of the public toward married working women. By the end of the 1970s, the vast majority of the public had come to accept paid employment of married women. For example, in 1978, large majorities of those interviewed who had a high school or a college education approved of a married woman working even if her husband was able to support her—there was a gain of 18 percent in only nine years. Among certain categories of respondents, notably working women, the college educated, and the young, support for married working women was overwhelming. Eighty-four percent of all employed women approved compared to only 66 percent of all housewives. Among college-educated working women under thirty, 98 percent endorsed this practice. Only among the elderly or those less-educated was approval for women workers considerably lower. These figures seem to indicate that the public was largely supportive of the employment of married women.[35]

Acceptance of the idea that participation in the labor force is not exclusively a man's right, however, is tempered by the view that a salaried position is of primary importance for men but only secondary for women. For example, it appears that most people still believe that a married woman should accept a job outside of the home *only* if she is not taking a job away from a man. As recently as 1977 when asked, "If there are a limited number of jobs, do you approve or disapprove of a married woman holding a job in business or industry when her husband is able to support her?" levels of support in all segments of the population for married working women plummeted. Overall, 64 percent disapproved (62% of all men, 66% of all women), while, as expected, working, college-educated women, and young women were much more supportive of the employment of married women even if jobs were limited. Yet, the highest approval rate even among these groups was only 60 percent. When these figures are compared to 1946 responses to the same question, we find only a 20 percentage point improvement in 30 years.[36] Furthermore, 38 percent of respondents questioned in 1976 favored laying-off married women first if a company was forced to cut back.[37] Thus, given high unemployment rates in the 1980s, there is a strong likelihood of a reversal in public support for the employment of married women.

Not only do significant segments of the population still expect women to give up their jobs in times of shortage, many also cling to the view that employment of a married woman is acceptable so long as it does not infringe upon her husband's career. For example, in 1977 when queried about whether "it was more important for a wife to help her husband's career than to have one herself," 57 percent of all respondents agreed. Interestingly, more women than men (60 versus 53 percent) thought that a man's career should come first.[38] The view of many that a woman's career is secondary is also revealed by the widely held view that "it is much better for everyone involved if the man is the achiever outside of the home and the woman takes care of the home and family." In fact, only 31 percent of the male and 37 percent of the female respondents disagreed with this statement. Likewise, in 1979, 77 percent of all women and 68 percent of all men were in accord with the view that a woman should give up her career if her husband has to relocate.[39] And, in another poll, two-thirds of the sample responded that they believed that a woman should reject a job promotion if it meant she and her husband would have to relocate.[40]

There is, however, some evidence that this view may be changing. For instance, in 1964 among some groups of college-educated women, more than 80 percent believed that is was more important to help their husband's career than to have one themselves; however, by 1977, more than 50 percent of all working women with a high school education or better rejected the view that it was better for the man to be the achiever as did majorities of young (under 30) high school and (under 50) college-educated women.[41] Additionally, another recent study found that a growing number of young women today think that it is acceptable for a woman to work even if her husband objects.[42] The husband's job, however, is not the only factor that historically has been considered more important than a woman's career. Since the early days of the Industrial Revolution, taking care of one's children always has been assumed to be a woman's primary role in life. Thus, paralleling our findings with respect to political participation, our findings in this area show that the public always has held reservations about working women with child-care responsibilities.

ATTITUDES TOWARD WORKING MOTHERS

Early in the Industrial Revolution, in England and in some parts of the United States, whole families often were hired for factory work, apparently with public approval. By the mid-1800s, however, public sentiment was anything but favorable toward working mothers. As already discussed, the evils of factory life and the toll it took on working women and their families were an important rationale for much of the progressive legislation enacted in the early 1900s. Although most married women who worked left their jobs upon the birth of their first child, the National Consumers' League and others tried to limit the hours of women's work to assure that those who had to work would be able to spend some time with their families.

The almost universal practice of women leaving their jobs after the birth of their first child was in keeping with the educated public's view that the roles of mother and employee were incompatible. Even in the 1920s, an era of relatively high support for working women, the majority of professional women saw their choice as either marriage and a family *or* work. During this period, only 19.3 percent of all professional women were married, and most viewed a family and a profession as mutually exclusive.[43]

In the 1930s and 1940s, one of the most frequently voiced objections to married women working was that the practice posed potential harm to children. Even in the 1960s, when more than 30 percent of all mothers with children under sixteen were employed outside the home, a sample of married men cited child neglect as their main objection to the growing practice of a woman with children working.[44]

As we have already noted, the mothers who were employed outside the home in the 1950s, especially those with young children, tended to cite economic need as their motivation for working. While most of these women wanted to stay on the job, many apparently suffered guilt about neglecting their parental role. Overall, working mothers were no more likely than nonworking mothers to report *ever* having had feelings of inadequacy as a parent, but they did report experiencing these feelings more frequently. Working mothers also were more likely to report that they did not spend enough time with their children.[45] It appears that the role conflict between working and motherhood was most unsettling for mothers of preschool children. In fact, working women with younger children were more likely to report negative or ambivalent self-perceptions.[46]

Although the 1960s and 1970s saw a massive increase in the number of mothers working, as revealed in Table 6-2, altering public sentiment toward the employment of young mothers has been a more gradual process. Leading forces in this process include working women themselves and perhaps, the women's movement. Karen O. Mason et al., report that between 1964 and 1970, the proportions of women in certain subgroups of the population who thought a working mother could establish just as warm and secure a relationship with her children as a mother who did not work rose significantly with the change being sharpest for educated women.[47] By 1977, almost half of a national sample agreed with this view, as revealed in Table 6-3. Although not indicated in Table 6-3, among women who worked, there was particularly

TABLE 6-2

Labor Force Participation Rates of Married Women, Husband Present, by Presence and Age of Own Children: Selected Years, 1950–1982

| | | | | With children under age 18 | |
| | | | *Participation rate (percent of population in labor force)* | | |
Year*	Total	With no children under age 18	Total	6 to 17, none younger	Under 6
1950 ...	23.8	30.3	18.4	28.3	11.9
1955 ...	27.7	32.7	24.0	34.7	16.2
1960 ...	30.5	34.7	27.6	39.0	18.6
1965 ...	34.7	38.3	32.2	42.7	23.3
1970 ...	40.8	42.2	39.7	49.2	30.3
1971 ...	40.8	42.1	39.7	49.4	29.6
1972 ...	41.5	42.7	40.5	50.2	30.1
1973 ...	42.2	42.8	41.7	50.1	32.7
1974 ...	43.0	43.0	43.1	51.2	34.4
1975 ...	44.4	43.9	44.9	52.3	36.6
1976 ...	45.0	43.8	46.1	53.7	37.4
1977 ...	46.6	44.9	48.2	55.6	39.3
1978 ...	47.6	44.7	50.2	57.2	41.6
1979 ...	49.4	46.7	51.9	59.1	43.2
1980 ...	50.1	46.0	54.1	61.7	45.0
1981 ...	51.0	46.3	55.7	62.5	47.8
1982 ...	51.0	46.2	56.3	63.2	48.7

*Data were collected in April of 1951–1955 and March of all other years.

Note: Children are defined as "own" children of the women and include never-married sons and daughters, stepchildren, and adopted children. Excluded are other related children such as grandchildren, nieces, nephews, and cousins, and unrelated children.

Source of data: U.S. Department of Labor, Bureau of Labor Statistics, *Perspectives on Working Women* (June, 1980), p. 4 and Howard V. Hayghe, Office of Current Employment Analysis, Bureau of Labor Statistics, Oral Report.

strong sentiment that such a warm relationship between children and a working mother was possible. Indeed, among college-educated working women, more than 88 percent agreed with the statement. Similarly, working mothers of the 1970s, seemed to experience less guilt about the influence of their work on their ability to be parents. They still were more likely than full-time homemakers, however, to report that they did not spend enough time with their children.[48] Yet, another survey found many working mothers (43%) felt that they made up for this deficiency by improving the quality of the time they spent with their children.[49]

The relative influence of a woman's own work experience and the women's movement in shaping this attitudinal change is difficult to gauge. The importance of labor force experience is evident from the figures showing that working women at all education levels are more likely than men or nonworking women to report a belief that working mothers can be adequate parents. Yet, the fact that this view is so much stronger among all college-educated women suggests the ideology of the women's movement may be having additional, independent impact on the attitudes of these women. Interestingly, men in all segments of the population are much less likely to agree that a working mother can have relations with her children as good as those enjoyed by nonworking mothers. The differences between the sexes are

TABLE 6-3
Attitudes toward Working Mothers: 1977

	Education					
	Less than High School		*High School*		*Some College*	
Age	*Men*	*Women*	*Men*	*Women*	*Men*	*Women*
Under 30	53	64*	57	64	63	79*
31-40	58	57	44	69*	59	91*
41-50	33	37	24	56*	64	82*
51 or Older	27	32	33	52*	29	60*
Overall	35	40	42	60*	53	78*

*Statistically significant at .05 level or greater.

Note: Figures represent the percent agreeing (strongly &/or just agree) with the following statement. "A Working mother can establish just as warm and secure a relationship with her children as a mother who does not work."

Source of data: The National Opinion Research Center, General Social Survey, 1977. Figures compiled by the authors.

perhaps most telling among the college educated and the young. In the former category, 78 percent of the women but only 53 percent of the men in 1977 believed such a situation was possible. Among people aged 30 to 40, many of whom no doubt have children, the gap was an astounding 34 percentage points. A remarkable 70 percent of the women but only 36 percent of the men believed that working would have no impact on a working mother's relations with her children. These disparities between the sexes on both questions about working mothers suggest the strong possibility of conflict between parents over the issue of mothers working.

A related question about the impact of a working mother on preschool children produces a similar pattern of responses, but there is much greater agreement by all segments of the population that this situation would have negative consequences for the child, as revealed in Table 6–4. More than two-thirds of those interviewed in 1977 (73% of all men and 62% of all women) felt a preschool child suffered if his or her mother worked. Among educated young adults, there was a considerable difference of opinion between the sexes about the impact of employment on small children, even though most sociological research supports the notion that little harm and perhaps some good comes to small children when mothers work.[50] In fact, in 1978, only 23 percent of the public *disagreed* with a statement that women with young children should *not* work outside of the home unless it is financially necessary.[51] Thus, as in the realm of politics, we can predict that many women will forego, if economically possible, seeking positions outside of the home while they have young children to care for rather than act counter to the sentiments of their husbands, society, or their own beliefs regarding the impact of their employment on their ability to be a good mother.

This review of the public's attitudes toward the relative importance and place of women's work outside the home helps us to understand the lower commitment of women, especially in the past, to salaried employment. Quite simply, prior to 1940, employment was looked upon only as something to do before they took up their *real* life's work—being wives and mothers.[52] Even after 1940, when the prospect of two stages of work-force participation seemed more likely and resistance on the part of the public to married women working diminished, the place of work in most women's lives was no doubt less important than their parental and spousal roles. Even today, many women and an increasing number of men consider their own marketplace activity as secondary to a family and marriage.[53] However, there is evidence that women, especially young women, are increasingly rejecting these cultural views about the place of work in women's lives. Many are preparing for and committing themselves to a lifetime of paid employment.[54] A 1979 Virginia Slims public opinion poll reports that nearly half—46 percent—of all women preferred an outside job to homemaking (an increase from 35% in 1974).[55] This desire to work apparently is not limited to women who already are working. Among nonworking women, 73 percent of those under thirty and 62

TABLE 6-4

Attitudes toward Working Mothers of Preschool Children: 1977

	Education					
	Less than High School		High School		Some College	
Age	Men	Women	Men	Women	Men	Women
Under 30	57	47*	37	45	31	63*
31-40	32	46	36	46	34	71*
41-50	19	24	18	42*	36	41
51 or Older	10	19*	22	30	24	43
Overall	22	27	29	40*	31	56*

*Statistically significant at .05 level or greater.

Note: Figures represent the percent disagreeing with the following statement: A preschool child is likely to suffer if his or her mother works.

Source of data: The National Opinion Research Center, General Social Survey, 1977. Figures compiled by the authors.

percent of those in their thirties plan to work in the future. Even among mothers under thirty, 44 percent report they would probably look for a job if day-care facilities were available.[56]

Among certain classes and age groups, the proportion of respondents favoring work over traditional roles is striking. In 1976, for example, 3 percent of working women desired to be full-time housewives. In 1957, this figure was 20 percent.[57] Similarly, when female high school seniors were asked about families in which there were no children, only 24 percent viewed an arrangement in which the husband would work and the wife would stay home as either desirable (5 percent) or acceptable (19 percent). Forty percent viewed this option as unacceptable. Interestingly, more male seniors clung to traditional role divisions as the desirable or acceptable options. Only 15 percent of them found the family in which the wife was a full-time housewife unacceptable; twelve percent actually rated it desirable.[58]

Paralleling the attitudes of the general public were the attitudes of these same high school seniors who were more likely to find the traditional division of labor more desirable or acceptable when the presence of preschool children was introduced into the scenario. Even then, however, 87 percent rated the option of part-time work by wife and full-time work by husband as at least somewhat acceptable.[59] Increasing acceptance of women's employment though has not necessarily been accompanied by a change in attitudes about men and work. Among the high school seniors who reported support for female workers, few found it even somewhat acceptable for a husband not to work or to work part time even if his wife was employed.[60]

Although stereotypical attitudes continue to exist, many women see themselves as long-term members of the labor force. This increased commitment to full, life-time work activity, moreover, does not seem solely a function of financial need. While majorities of women give economic reasons for going to work, polls of employed wives in the mid-1970s found that 82 percent would continue to work even if they did not have to earn a living. Just nineteen years earlier, only 58 percent of a similar group of women reported this kind of commitment.[61]

Women not only want to work but they increasingly want a good job and a career. A national study of women workers done in the early 1970s found that women were as likely as men to want jobs that were interesting, challenging, and intellectually demanding.[62] Similarly, the 1980 Virginia Slims poll reported that 36 percent of employed women and 45 percent of employed men were concerned about achieving success in their careers. The poll also found an increase from 39 percent in 1970 to 45 percent in 1979 in the proportion of women who planned to make their jobs full-time careers.[63] This increased commitment and interest may well produce some improvement in women's position in the marketplace. We can speculate that as more young women reject the notions that they will work only briefly and that their work is secondary to their roles of mother and wife, the likelihood will be greater that these women will also reject their second-class status in the labor market.

Attitudes toward the employment and place of employment for women, however, are not the only attitudinal barriers to the equality of women in the marketplace. One other set of very restrictive cultural views concerns the ability of women to perform certain jobs or to undertake certain training or education.

CULTURAL STEREOTYPES ABOUT THE ABILITIES OF WOMEN

As we saw in Chapter 4, negative stereotypes about the mental and physical abilities of women have prevented their progress in politics. Many of these same stereotypes also hinder the progress of women in the economic realm.

In the nineteenth century many persons believed that women simply lacked the mental, physical, and emotional aptitudes necessary for any work outside the home. Not only were women viewed as incapable of most work but it was feared that if they worked, the results would prove disastrous. For instance, in the 1870s, a major medical text claimed:

> During the epoch of development, that is from the age of fourteen to eighteen or twenty...the system...is peculiarly susceptible, and distur-

bances of the delicate mechanism [the menstrual function] we are considering, induced... by constrained positions, muscular effort, brain work, and all forms of mental and physical excitement, germinate a host of ills. Sometimes these causes, which pervade... our... schools... produce an excessive performance of the... function, and this is equivalent to a periodical hemorrhage.[64]

This kind of medical "knowledge" not only kept middle-class women out of the workplace, it also was used as the rationale for preventing them from acquiring an education or any skills other than domestic ones.

With the growth of women's colleges and the entrance of a few women into certain male professions these stereotypes were weakened but far from eliminated. As late as 1891, some women in the suffrage movement still believed:

Women cannot maintain the same intellectual standards as men. The claim of ability to learn, to follow, to apply knowledge... does not imply a claim to be able to originate, or to maintain... the robust, massive intellectual enterprises which... are now carried on by masculine strength and energy.[65]

Even as late as the early 1900s, this line of reasoning was the cornerstone of legal arguments for protective legislation.

Surveys taken in the 1940s show that the intervening years did not completely dispel this view. Forty percent of the public continued to believe that men were more intelligent than women. Additionally, a majority felt men were more creative than women, and pluralities of men (and many women) also accepted the view that men were more likely to possess a large range of job-related emotional and mental traits including the ability to make decisions, handle people, accept new ideas, be even tempered, and maintain a level head. They also believed that men possessed more common sense than women. While far fewer women accepted these evaluations, pluralities agreed that men were more creative, even-tempered, and level-headed.[66]

These attitudes were not restricted to the average citizen. William Chafe notes that in 1946, the dean of the all-women Barnard College, Margaret Pickel, wrote in a *New York Times* article that females, when compared to males, had less physical strength, a lower fatigue point, and a less-stable nervous system. She concluded by noting that "By middle age, when men are at their best, a devoted woman worker is apt to degenerate into fussiness or worse."[67]

Even today, many stereotypes about innate mental abilities persist. Perhaps one of the most damaging is the view that women possess lesser mathematical and related "numbers" abilities than men.[68] As a result, many high school and college counselors, for example, persist in tracking women students toward the social sciences and away from the hard sciences.[69]

Other stereotypes about sex-based deficiencies provide the backbone for the view that women will not be as productive or as successful as men in many or most jobs. Fifty-two percent of women and 62 percent of men questioned in 1972, for example, thought women did not have the physical stamina of men.[70] Logic and emotion are other areas in which the public perceives deficiencies in women. In 1970, 58 percent of all women and 68 percent of all men saw women as more emotional and less logical.[71]

Negative views about the abilities of women have been attacked by feminists, and there is evidence that their arguments are beginning to have some effect. For example, by 1975 only 39 percent of all women still believed that women were more emotional and less logical than men.[72] This is not the only stereotype that shows some signs of demise. In 1972, a plurality of the public agreed with the statement that one of the reasons why men have been more successful in business, politics, and leadership positions is that "Men are born with more drive and ambition;" by 1976, however, in response to a slightly different statement, only 39 percent of the public agreed that "men have more top jobs because they are born with more drive and ambition to be successful."[73] Slightly more women (63%) than men (58%) rejected this stereotype.[74]

Another area where traditionally women have been viewed as inferior is in their ability to direct the work of others. This perception often translates into an unwillingness to work *for* a woman. In 1953, 75 percent of all men and 57 percent of all women in a national sample indicated that if given a choice, they preferred to work for a man. Only 21 percent of the men and 29 percent of the women responded that the gender of their boss made no difference.[75] By 1979, however, two-thirds of the male and female respondents said that gender made no difference.[76]

Progress with respect to other stereotypes, however, has been slow. Dramatic evidence of deep-rooted prejudices about women's abilities to undertake certain jobs can be found in the responses to a set of questions posed to a national sample in 1979. When respondents were asked if they would have more confidence in a man or a woman in various occupations, more than half said they would prefer a male police officer, and half preferred a man as a commercial pilot. Similarly, more than a quarter had more confidence in a male lawyer or doctor. These responses, however, reflect a marked improvement since 1976 when men were preferred for a much larger number of occupations.[77]

While some studies of young children done in the 1970s found a decrease in occupational stereotyping, others found little evidence of change.[78] Children regularly exposed to television where the portrayal of women is very stereotyped are particularly likely to think that women can hold only a limited number of jobs.[79] Among women college students as well, there is evidence that the perceptions of what women should do and can do effectively restrict career choice.[80]

TABLE 6-5

Women as a Percentage of All Persons Employed in Selected
Occupations

Occupation	Percent Women
Librarians	84.6
Registered Nurses	95.8
Teachers, (except College & University)	67.1
Elementary School Teachers	82.2
Clerical and Kindred	78.4
Bank Tellers	94.0
Bookkeepers	90.6
Cashiers	85.1
Receptionists	98.0
Secretaries	99.0
Telephone Operators	92.3
Engineers	4.7
Lawyers & Judges	20.7
Physicians, Dentists, & related practitioners	23.2
Airline Pilots	Less than 1
Managers & Administrators	28.4
Craft and Kindred Workers	5.6
Mechanics & Repairers	2.1
Protective Service Workers (Police, Fire Fighters, etc.)	7.6

Note: The figures are based on a survey of one-quarter of the households in the Current Population Survey. Because of the nature of the Survey and sampling error, these figures may vary from those found in other sources.

Source of data: United States Department of Labor, Bureau of Labor Statistics, "1981 Weekly Earnings of Men and Women Compared in 100 Occupations" (March 7, 1982).

The implications of these rigid occupational stereotypes is obvious. They restrict choice for both sexes and foreclose many fields to all but the most determined women. The resultant "crowding," revealed in Table 6-5, additionally marks some jobs as "women's work," a fact that has historically depressed wages and prestige in those fields. (Note that the traditional "men's work" jobs—those with less than 30 percent women—include some of the most high-paying and prestigious occupations.) These factors, in turn, have influenced the attitudes and performance of women workers, promoting a vicious circle from which there appears to be little escape for most women.

This attitudinal overview helps us to develop a better understanding of the factors that historically have contributed to the relatively poor economic position of women. Specifically, these attitudes appear to be at the heart of the lack of preparation of women for work as well as the discrimination faced by many women on the job.

PREPARATION OF WOMEN FOR EMPLOYMENT OUTSIDE THE HOME

One of the most immediate effects of the historical attitudes toward the place of paid work in women's lives has been the lack of preparation of women for full, life-time careers outside the home. In the nineteenth and for much of the twentieth century, because social mores maintained that a woman's primary roles were those of mother and wife, girls were socialized and trained for those jobs and not for paid work. They were encouraged to develop both "feminine" psychological traits and occupational skills appropriate and necessary for getting and keeping a husband, for raising a family, and for maintaining a home. Neither these feminine psychological traits nor the domestic skills were ones in demand by most employers.[81]

As already discussed in Chapter 5, young women were not encouraged and at times were even prevented from acquiring the education necessary to enter well-paying occupations and professions. The gradual expansion of academic opportunities for women did little to change this situation. Most women in high school and even many in college took courses in home economics or domestic science under the assumption that these programs were the best preparation for their future occupations as wives and mothers. Even those who majored in other areas chose or were channeled into fields like teaching, nursing, and later, clerical or business-type courses and social work. All of these were considered compatible with a woman's personality and inherent abilities. Nursing and teaching in particular drew on "female" traits and could be practiced temporarily before marriage or later in life if widowed.

During the post-World War II era when increasing numbers of women worked and did so for longer periods of their adult lives, cultural attitudes and the absence of laws preventing discrimination in educational programs meant that the preparation of women for full, life-time employment continued to lag seriously behind men. Because most young women did not plan on having a permanent, lifelong career, both their educational aspirations and achievements were lower than young men's. Few women undertook the lengthy, rigorous educational programs that would have been necessary to enter prestige professions. Occupational stereotypes about what women should and/or could do also discouraged young women from considering careers in these fields.[82] For both these reasons, even those women who undertook training to prepare themselves for a job tended to concentrate their course work in traditional female fields—nursing, teaching, and liberal arts at the college level and clerical business courses and home economics in high school vocational programs.

In other ways, as well, young women in the 1960s were often unprepared for the competitive world of work. Matina Horner's studies of college women in the late 1960s revealed what she labeled a "fear-of-success"—an anxiety on the part of women to achieve in male-dominated fields.[83] Replications of Horner's work have suggested that what she may have found was instead fear of sex-atypical behavior and/or a fear of rejection by men.[84] Examination of childrearing practices traced this lack of motivation to achieve to the encouragement by parents of femininity in young girls.[85] These same parental practices resulted in the girls seeking to "please" rather than desiring to achieve.[86]

As noted in Chapter 5, the women's rights activists in the 1960s and 1970s began to mount serious challenges to both the legal and attitudinal barriers surrounding the preparation of women for work. Their efforts were partially rewarded in the legal arena in 1972 with the passage of Title IX. This law as well as the increase in confidence of young women in their own abilities and commitment to full, life-time work have begun to have some noticeable impact on women's education, although a gap between the sexes still exists in several areas of study.

Future improvement in the distribution of women students in all majors is hampered not only by the lack of adequate enforcement of Title IX but also by the persistence of remaining cultural views. Surveys and studies of young women in the 1970s continue to show the strong influence of gender stereotypes. More specifically, females are still more likely to estimate they will fail at a new task—especially if that task is one traditionally labeled as "masculine." Even female achievers tend to underestimate their abilities more so than successful males. Women often attribute their success to luck, while men trace their achievements to their intelligence or to other abilities.[87] Women's underestimation of their own abilities and worth may directly contribute to their lower life-time earnings expectations as well as to the salaries they ask for and get when they interview for a job.[88]

In general, the more traditional a girl or woman's view of sex roles, the more likely she is to "fear success" in any area, especially in "male" jobs. Young women who cling to stereotypes have lower educational aspirations and achievements. Even if they obtain a higher education, they are more likely to prepare for careers in "female fields."[89] Lower levels of educational and psychological preparation, moreover, are not limited to only the traditionally minded female. The persistence of the view that it is a woman's duty alone to care for young children, tends to hinder preparation for a full, life-time career even among those who consider themselves "liberated."

There are, however, several positive signs on the horizon. Many of the conditions most conducive to greater independence, higher achievement motivations, and sex-atypical careers for women are becoming more common. Among the more important of these factors are working mothers who enjoy their jobs,[90] and supportive males who have abandoned traditional sex roles and are willing to accept, date, and marry successful, career-oriented women.[91] These conditions alone, however, will not be sufficient to produce equality of career readiness among men and women as long as outmoded views about gender roles continue to influence the information and advice girls and women receive about career possibilities.

The portrayal of women in the media and in school textbooks have an especially restrictive or limiting influence on career goals of young girls. Surveys of television shows, for example, reveal that few women are shown in career situations. Similarly, until recently, elementary school textbooks regularly portrayed women in only mother or traditional employment roles.[92] While Title IX was enacted to do away with some of the blatant and obnoxious discriminatory practices encountered by female students, actual enforcement of the act has been spotty. However, the mere threat of potential loss of federal funds appears to have made some school districts adopt less biased textbooks. For example, it is estimated that since 1974, the number of pages devoted to women's accomplishments in schoolbooks has risen from one to fourteen pages.[93]

Textbooks and television, however, are not the only sources of stereotypes about career options. Many high school, college, and even career advisors regularly, however unintentionally, track women toward "feminine" occupations. For example, many high school guidance counselors neglect to point out to young women that they probably will work most of their lives. Some direct students to take clerical courses or those that will be compatible with motherhood and marriage, even though pay in these fields is low and demand for workers in these areas not expected to increase in the decades ahead.[94]

As noted, this misguided "guidance" is not limited to high school students. Older women, too, often are directed into sex-traditional training and other postsecondary educational programs. Often this "channeling" occurs simply as a result of failure of traditionally-male (e.g. welding, drafting) adult programs to advertise in places where women might see or hear about them.[95] Even when women decide to pursue adult vocational education, the majority end up in courses like "business office" or health or cosmetology programs, which often lead to low-paying jobs.[96]

Another more subtle way the message of career or occupational opportunities "appropriate" for women is conveyed is by the absence òf women in certain jobs or educational programs. Studies of both vocational and college programs show that young girls tend to shy away from disciplines where there are few women either in teaching or administrative positions.[97] No women or only a few in a particular area convey to other women that women either are not welcomed or that several roadblocks stand in their way. Particularly with younger women, their knowledge of the potential for discrimination often creates a vicious circle: many young girls and/or women, facing the prospect of jobs with little challenge or future, either decide they do not want to work and/or undertake less training, assuming they will be hired for only "women's jobs" anyway.[98] The training and vocational sex-equity programs adopted in the 1970s may eventually break this cycle if Reagan budget cuts are not too severe.

Even if women are able to overcome traditional attitudes and become prepared to take an equal role with men, their equality is not assured. Two important groups can be expected to resist further change: employers who gain economically from the low wages paid for "women's jobs" and male workers who feel threatened by the prospect of competition for traditionally male jobs.

DISCRIMINATION BY EMPLOYERS

Discrimination by employers against women workers stems from two sources, cultural attitudes and economic self-interest. There is, however, considerable reason to believe economic self-interest is more important. Prior to 1940, for example, as long as there was a sufficient number of men or unmarried women to fill their needs, employers were willing to abide by cultural stereotypes and not hire married women. Only in a few industries, most notably the textile industry where large numbers of cheap, skilled laborers were required, were employers willing to hire married women.[99] Beginning with World War II, however, when the demand for female labor outpaced the supply of available unmarried women, many employers dropped their restrictions against hiring married women.[100] This reversal of previous practice contributed, at least indirectly, to changing cultural attitudes about the appropriateness of women working outside of the home.

Although today, most employers readily employ married women, they are still influenced by and, in turn, influence cultural stereotypes about the work commitment and abilities of women. A study of corporate executives regarding women in management, for example, discovered:

> Eight in ten felt "women have less motivation than men," one-third felt that "women are not as capable in managerial positions as men," one-third said

that "absenteeism among women is higher than men," and just under
three-quarters felt that "women are not as totally committed to management
as men." Most believed women wanted jobs, not careers.[101]

These kinds of attitudes form the basis for hiring practices that keep women
out of management and decision-making positions. Furthermore, the supposed inability of women to handle certain tasks means many employers still
routinely fail to hire women for these jobs even though Title VII prohibits use
of these presumptions.[102]

The preferences and prejudices of male employees also may be used as the
basis for not hiring women for certain supervisor positions.[103] Francine D.
Blau, for example, has documented that in some industries, stereotypes about
what women can do may persist even when other industries are successfully
using women workers in comparable job categories.[104] While recent legislation
and court cases have outlawed the most blatant of these practices, they
continue to persist because of the failure of the government or women who are
discriminated against to take matters to court. Only if women are able to force
compliance with the law, change stereotypes, and demand equal pay for
comparable work can employers be expected to change their otherwise
profitable practices regarding women workers.

In this light, the current effort of women in the clerical trades to organize
and demand better pay and working conditions is an interesting development.
While many women professionals formed their own pressure groups in the
1960s, clerical workers have long been considered difficult to organize.
Recently, however, in many cities around the nation, secretaries and other
women in the "steno pool" have begun to form groups including Women
Office Workers and 9 to 5 to put pressure on their bosses to treat them more
fairly and with greater dignity.[105] The partial success of these groups to win
concessions from their employers bodes well for this kind of group activity.
However, for women in the secretarial trades and other occupations as well,
the discrimination often comes not from employers but fellow employees.

DISCRIMINATION BY MALE EMPLOYEES

The role of male workers in influencing the job and wage opportunities of
women cannot be ignored. Fear that women would take their jobs was the
second most commonly cited reason for men's opposition to women working
in polls conducted in the 1930s, 1940s, and 1960s.[106] Even as late as 1975,
interviews with male high school students found that 25 percent agreed that
"working women take jobs away from men."[107]

Male unionists, in particular, have traditionally viewed women workers
as a threat. The history of the interaction of women workers and unions is
replete with examples of discrimination against women, ranging from refusal

to allow women to form or join unions to separate seniority lists and differential wage scales for union men and women. Such practices were common until recent court rulings made them illegal.[108] Even in unions that are predominantly female, women have faced discrimination in attaining positions of authority. As late as 1972, the International Ladies' Garment Workers Union, whose membership is 80 percent female, had but only one woman official.[109] Similarly, although 30 percent of the American Federation of Labor-Congress of Industrial Organizations' (AFL-CIO) 13.6 million members are women, the first woman was not elected to its executive council until 1980.[110]

The historic problem of women being ignored by unions' organizing ·efforts has even more negative consequences than the absence of women in positions of authority in unions. Traditionally, union leaders, perhaps wishing to keep women out of certain job categories, have argued that women were difficult to organize. Thus, in 1980, only 17 percent of all women workers were union members.[111] This absence of union protection is an important part of the reason why the working conditions and pay scales of women have lagged behind those of men.

New interest by union leaders in creating unions for those engaged in the clerical trades and other women's jobs, however, may open up a whole new era in the relationship of women workers with the union movement. Additionally, given the general decreasing appeal of unions to many workers, several unions have stepped up their recruitment of women. If these organizational efforts are successful, the wages and working conditions of women should improve.

Women trying to break into the skilled trades, however, still face a particularly difficult time. Unions and union apprentice systems often are closed to them because of stereotypes about the seriousness and abilities of women to undertake hard, dirty work. Employers and unions have intentionally failed to notify women of openings, used questionable screening tests and age requirements, and required sponsoring agents, all in efforts to keep women out.[112] Thus, it is not surprising that in 1976 women constituted only slightly better than 1 percent of all registered apprentices, and most of these were in the poorer-paying occupations.[113]

For those women who enter crafts, the hostility of male co-workers often makes success difficult.[114] One woman apprentice, for example, reported having to wait until the laughter died down before she got an answer to a job-related question. Another told about being subjected to a daylong barrage of sexual innuendos and jeers that left her feeling "battered." A third woman apprentice recalled being continuously watched by fellow workers who were sure she would falter any moment.[115] While much of this discrimination by male unionists is a function of stereotypes about the abilities and seriousness of women workers about their jobs, at least some is traceable to a simple unwillingness to share power or good wages with women.[116] These sentiments, however, are beginning to change as women union members have begun to work together and to press the union hierarchy to listen to and act on their demands.

Union and other blue-collar men are not alone in viewing women workers as a threat and treating them accordingly. Women who work in other traditionally male professions encounter many of the same problems as those trying to enter the skilled trades. Men already on the job tend to shut women out of the informal workers' networks, thus denying them access to information and peer support often critical to success and/or advancement.[117] Whether this is based on economics or simply feeling more comfortable with members of one's own sex, the results can have important career advancement consequences. For example, in the legal profession, advancement and prestige come only after an individual is made a partner. This normally occurs after a person has served a period as a salaried associate in the firm. Because women often find themselves out of informal workers' networks, many feel that the men who vote on partnerships do not know them as well and, therefore, do not vote to offer them partnerships.

Female academicians also face similar problems. Prior to the 1970s, women regularly were shut out of what was termed the "old boy" network. This often made it difficult to find out about new research or job openings. In turn, this made it more difficult for women to do up-to-date research and have their findings published. Another sector of this vicious circle also made it almost impossible for women to be hired at prestigious universities or to achieve high academic rank and tenure.[118] In response to these problems, women in most academic disciplines have established women's caucuses or professional groups, in part, to function as "old girl" networks and to facilitate women's entry into and advancement in the profession.

SEXUAL HARASSMENT

Another form of "on-the-job" discrimination currently gaining public recognition is sexual harassment of women workers by male employers and employees.[119] For women on the job, this problem is perceived as a serious one. Interestingly, most male executives think the whole issue has been "greatly exaggerated."[120] Men seem particularly unaware of the negative effects of subtle forms of harassment including off-color jokes and suggestive comments. But for women on the job, it is often these kinds of behavior that make them "feel like an inconsequential show piece rather than an intelligent business person."[121] Even though the EEOC has issued guidelines making sexual harassment unlawful, few companies have taken any action to stop such behavior. Moreover, many women doubt that the government action will be able to prevent this subtle discrimination.[122]

The realistic appraisals by male executives of how a typical company president would handle evidence of sexual harassment suggest eradication of the problem may indeed be difficult: more than half thought the typical president would do nothing if confronted with what looked like harassment.[123] For the woman who has to endure this behavior, the choice may be to quit, learn to say no gracefully, or give in to sexual advances to keep her job.[124] Heightened awareness of the problem, however, may lead some women to assert their rights and file complaints, particularly when more than one employee finds herself the object of harassment. Public reinforcement of the notion that many women are targets of harassment out of no fault of their own may remove the stigma some women may feel is attached to those making charges and tend to facilitate greater awareness of the problem. An additional factor that may expedite this process is the growing recognition of the monetary cost of sexual harassment. According to a U.S. Merit Systems Protection Board report, sexual harassment of federal employees alone costs 95 million dollars a year in terms of decreased worker productivity, increased medical bills and sick leave usage, and the replacement of workers who leave their jobs because of harassment.[125] To remedy this problem, the board has recommended strong enforcement of existing rules prohibiting harassment. If other employers also begin to think of the problem in dollar amounts, we may see a quicker end to the problem faced by substantial segments of the female work force.[126]

IMPACT OF CULTURAL ATTITUDES, LACK OF PREPARATION, AND DISCRIMINATION ON THE POSITION OF WOMEN IN THE MARKETPLACE

The discussion above makes it clear that just as is the case in politics, the barriers to equality for women in the marketplace go beyond legal ones. Thus we should not expect that simply removing legal barriers will result in women assuming a comparable position with men in the educational and economic arenas. The persistence of attitudinal stereotypes about the abilities of women and the place of work in women's lives as well as the lack of preparation on the part of women for certain types of economic activity and discrimination all combine to restrict the progress of women in the marketplace just as they did and still do in politics.

Attempts to identify how each of these three additional barriers continues to limit women in the educational and economic areas and how they might continue to do so in the future are complicated. Interrelationships among the three factors coupled with the fact that among certain classes or groups of women, different ones or combinations of these three barriers prove to be stumbling blocks makes exacting analysis difficult. For instance, at one extreme, some women totally oppose the idea of women working outside of the home. If these women, who are primarily older and less well educated, can afford not to work, the other barriers (lack of preparation and discrimination) are not real problems because they never try to enter the marketplace in the first place. At the other extreme are many younger women who, rejecting stereotypes about the abilities and roles of women, have prepared themselves psychologically and educationally to compete with men in nontraditional occupations. For these women, it is probably discrimination by employers and fellow employees that presents the greatest stumbling block. The majority of women in the United States in the early 1980s probably fall somewhere in between these two extremes. They have rejected some of the stereotypes about women and work but may still believe that their motherhood and wife responsibilities come before their jobs. Professional advancement of these women may be hampered by feelings of guilt and role conflict brought on by these views. The problem, however, may be exacerbated by inadequate educational training given that most women in the work force today were schooled in an era before Title IX.

Keeping in mind these caveats about different groups and classes of women, we will try in the sections to follow to outline how the three extralegal barriers, singly or in combination, have prevented and can be expected to continue to bar the progress of women in various aspects of employment and education.

EMPLOYMENT LEVELS OF WOMEN

In the past, negative attitudes toward the employment of women, (especially married women), the resultant lack of preparation by women for work, and discrimination by employers largely explained the absence of most married women from the marketplace. As we have seen, since the 1950s the belief that married women should not work has been gradually replaced by a general acceptance of this practice. This change in attitude, coupled with the economic realities of the 1970s and 1980s, which forced many women to seek jobs to support their families or themselves, produced a dramatic rise in the percentage of women working—from 38 percent in 1960 to over 52 percent in 1982.[127] Because this rise was accompanied by a declining percentage in the labor force participation of men (75.9 percent), as can be seen in Figure 6–1, the overall labor participation rates of men and women are fast approaching parity. Thus, although not indicated in Figure 6–1, by spring 1982, women constituted 43.3 percent of all workers in the labor force. In light of these figures, the phrase "the working man" seems increasingly inaccurate and inappropriate.

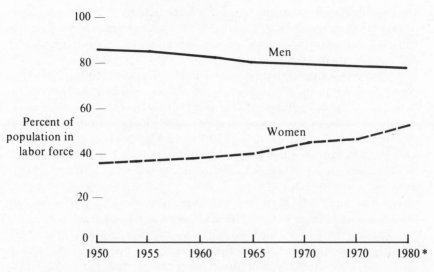

*January–June 1980.

Source: Perspectives on Working Women: A Databook, U.S. Dept. of Labor, October 1980, p. 2.

Figure 6-1. Labor Force Participation Rates of Women and Men, Annual Averages, 1950–1980

This increase in the proportion of women workers is in part attributable to the increasing number of never-married women in the labor force. Between 1960 and 1982, their number as a percentage of all women workers rose from less than 20 to nearly 25 percent.[128] Some of this increase is a function of the larger relative size of the baby boom generation compared to that of their older cohorts.

An even more important factor, however, may be the changing attitude of young women toward the place of work in a woman's life. These changing attitudes are reflected in several ways. First, an increasing number of these single women are choosing to postpone marriage—either to devote time to getting a better education and/or to establishing their careers. This practice results in a growing proportion of young, never-married women in the population. Second, while single women traditionally have worked outside the home in large numbers in this century, between 1970 and 1982 the percentage of never-married women who entered the labor force rose to a new high—from 53 to over 62 percent. Indeed, three-fourths of women between the ages of twenty and fifty-four are in the marketplace.[129] Finally, studies have found that both delayed marriage and work-force activity related to attitudes toward sex roles and work. The more likely the young woman is to believe that work is appropriate for married women, the more likely she is to prepare for and join the labor force.

Changing attitudes toward women's roles, however, are not limited to young, single women. Married women in this age group and older women have grown increasingly open to the idea that married women might work. Accordingly, the proportion of married women living with their husbands who joined the labor force rose from 30.5 percent in 1960 to over 51 percent in 1982.[130] In fact, among the young, the working wife is becoming the norm. While some of this increase is a function of the impact of inflation and the resultant economic need of many families to rely on two wage earners to maintain a decent standard of living, there is also evidence of increasing tolerance of the idea among middle- and upper–middle-income couples.

The attitudes of married women toward a working mother are particularly important predictors of their marketplace behavior.[131] Given this association, we should not be surprised that the proportion of working mothers has increased dramatically since the rise of the women's movement. Unlike in previous generations, in the current one a majority of women with children at home now are gainfully employed. Additionally, during the 1960s and 1970s, even mothers with very young children joined the work force. Indeed, by 1982, the labor force participation rates of women with children under age six was 50 percent. In fact, almost half of all mothers whose youngest child was under three were looking for work.[132]

In addition to more progressive attitudes and the economic need of couples to work, another social change—the rapidly rising divorce rate—also has forced many women including mothers into the marketplace. The decade of the 1970s became the decade of the "displaced homemaker" and the female head of household. In 1982, for example, one out of six families was headed by a woman. This represented a notable increase in this type of family structure since 1970 when only 11 percent of all families were headed by women. And, more than two-thirds of these women with children work.[133] As discussed in Chapter 8, divorced women, both older women whose families are grown and younger women with children still at home, often find the most immediate result of divorce is that they become the sole supporter of themselves and their dependents. The resultant influx of these women into the labor force has meant the number of divorced women workers more than doubled—from 1.9 to over 4 million—between 1970 and March 1982. Additionally, divorced women have the highest labor-force participation rates. In 1982, 75 percent of all such women worked—most have children to support and most of them do so by taking a job.[134] Better than 80 percent of divorced mothers with children over six work as do two-thirds of those with children under six. These women, along with widowed, never-married, or separated mothers who are the heads of their families accounted for one-fifth of all working mothers in 1980 and for a substantial proportion of all families living below the poverty barrier as well.[135] These dramatic changes in the importance of work in women's lives have produced some tremendous dislocations in the life-styles of Americans—especially women.

These changes in the employment patterns of women, moreover, appear to support our finding that at least one of the barriers to women working—negative attitudes toward the employment of married women—is breaking down. As our discussion of barriers suggested with respect to the place of work in women's lives, however, women continue to accord it a lesser place than men, and in fact rank it as less important than their roles of wife or mother.

Continuity of Labor-Force Experience

Before 1940, women, responding to publicly approved practices, quit working permanently when they got married or had children. Beginning with World War II, this pattern changed when older women reentered the labor force. Between 1950 and 1980, the increased commitment of women to their jobs and the growing acceptance of first married women, then women with older children, and then last women with younger children working, have created a new pattern of work-force participation. Increasingly, more women are "dropping-out" of the labor force for only short periods of time when they have young children. This new practice is particularly common among black women and well-paid women of both races.[136] A recent study by the Urban Institute predicted that by 1990 only 25 percent of all American wives will stay at home with their children on a full-time basis.[137]

Dropping-out, of course, is not solely a function of the mother role. The priority of the husband's career also produces temporary dislocations in a woman's work-force participation. Because a woman's salary generally is less than her husband's, if he is offered a better job in another city, it is not uncommon for his wife to make the move with him and start her career anew. This practice gives fuel to the arguments of some employers who prefer not to hire women out of fear that they will not make a career of their job.

Only recently have we seen the phenomenon of married couples' attempting to pursue careers in different locales. The cost, even where a female is paid a salary on par with her male co-workers, is high. Maintenance of two homes, weekend travel, and other additional costs—the highest of which may be emotional—tend to limit this as an option for most married couples, particularly where children are involved.[138]

For whatever reason, in 1978 44 percent of all women married at least ten years reported working seven of the last ten years (a rough measure of "permanent attachment to the labor force"). Reflecting the demands of motherhood, the number of permanents (employed 7 of 10 years) was lowest in the youngest categories of wives—although the younger the woman the more likely she was to have worked at least one year of the last ten.[139] This last practice may reflect the growing expectation and desire of young women to work and probably indicates they will rejoin the labor force at some future date.

Not surprising, and also reflecting the increased commitment of women to work, is the high permanence rate of unmarried women and female heads of household.[140] The great economic need of the latter group no doubt accounts in large part for the phenomenon. Many might like to drop out when their children are home but simply cannot afford to do so.

Part-time Work

A related practice and one that perhaps may be replacing the total stoppage of work, is the assumption of part-time or less than year-round work by women, especially mothers. In 1979, 32.5 percent of all married women who worked were employed part time—a figure that has remained virtually unchanged from 1960.[141] Among mothers, while only one-quarter with children over fourteen worked part time, almost 35 percent of those with children under three were employed on less than a full-time basis.[142]

Another common practice is less than year-round employment. Among the married women who worked in 1979, only half were employed at full-time, year-round jobs. Another 16 percent worked year round in part-time positions.[143] These practices appear to reflect a compromise between the public's acceptance of married women working and their belief that parental and spousal responsibilities should come before a woman's career, especially when children are very young. The most commonly mentioned reason by women for part-year work is "family responsibilities," cited by 44.7 percent in 1979, a decline from 55.2 percent in 1960. Perhaps reflecting the changing attitudes toward such compromising, the percentage of married women who have children and work full time, year-round has risen since 1960. For example, among women with children aged 6–17, year-round full-time workers increased so rapidly that by 1980 they outnumbered part-time or less than year-round workers. Only among mothers with children under three has the major increase in working mothers been among those working less than full time.[144]

While the practice of less than full-time, year-round work or temporarily dropping out of the labor force may be declining for some as a method of combining wife, mother, and worker roles, this does not mean the roles have become totally compatible. For the women who work either part time or full time, compromises are still often necessary. Recognizing this dilemma, some have chosen to remain single or to delay marriage until their careers are well established. Others have chosen not to have children or have postponed childbirth until their late thirties or early forties. Population experts estimate that if present trends continue, perhaps 25 to 30 percent of women currently in childbearing years will never have children. One expert traces this trend in part to the pursuit by young women of their own educational and career goals.[145] However, for married women with children the only solution may be simply to add on the worker role to those of wife and mother. This often is necessary because while men seem increasingly supportive of their wives working, especially if their wages significantly contribute to the family income, many show little willingness to take on additional tasks,[146] as discussed in Chapter 8. The result is that most working women have two or three jobs—employee, housewife, and mother—while most men at best, have one-and-a-half. As one woman interviewed by the National Commission on Working Women stated, "Work has become increasingly a place you go that takes the entire day and have to leave each evening to go to Job 2—Chef, Maid, Housekeeper and Nanny."[147] Working women apparently are increasingly unhappy with this situation. Between 1970 and 1974 among married women living in the North, the percentage agreeing with the view that "men should share the work around the house with women doing dishes, cleaning and so forth," rose from 56 to 80 percent.[148] Unfortunately, translating this view into practice in individual families appears easier said than done. The *responsibilities* of childrearing, housekeeping, and cooking still largely fall on women's shoulders with some of the more obvious results being that women take more time off from their jobs to stay home with sick children, are less willing to take on-the-job training courses, and in general have less time and energy than men to devote to their jobs.[149]

The situation, of course, is even worse for the ever-increasing number of women who head families. They cannot count on help at home except from their children. It is not surprising that these women are concentrated in part-time, temporary, and low-paying jobs that allow them some time for their at-home responsibilities. The end result of all these accommodations by women to prevailing attitudes (as well as necessities) is that the progress of women in their jobs (their salaries and their positions) is limited—especially when we look at prestigious, high-paying jobs or positions of responsibility and authority.

This pattern is directly reminiscent of what we encountered with respect to women and politics. Because of family and home responsibilities, women, unlike men, must at least temporarily (or permanently) forego the single-minded pursuit of their careers. The result, moreover, is exactly like that in politics. Women never are fully able to catch up to the early lead of men. According to one expert,

> The decade between 25 and 35 is when men either succeed or fail. It is the decade when lawyers become partners in good firms, when business managers make it onto the "fast track," when academics get tenure at good universities, and when blue collar workers find job opportunities that will lead to training opportunities and the skills that will generate higher earnings.

If there is any one decade when it pays to work hard and to be *consistently* [emphasis added] in the labor force it is the decade between 25 and 35....

But the decade between 25 and 35 is precisely the decade when women are most apt to leave the labor force or become part-time workers to have children. When they do, the current system of promotion and skill acquisition will extract an *enormous lifetime price.*[150] [emphasis added]

The "enormous lifetime price" is evidenced in the relative wages of men and women. One study, for example, found that in the mid-1970s, approximately 42 percent of the difference between the wages of white male and female workers was attributable to the following factors: women are more likely to work part time, women drop out of the work force for several years at a time, they start full-time work later than men, and they undertake less on-the-job training and education than men.[151] Dropping-out for more than three years has particularly disastrous results and part-time work appears to be no panacea.[152] Thus, one of the direct results of the attitudinal barriers we discussed above is reflected in the lower salaries of women relative to men.

Wages of Women

Contrary to what one might expect given the increased number of women workers and the passage of the Equal Pay Act of 1963, the wages of women, relative to men, have not risen, as revealed earlier in Table 6–1. Even among full-time workers, women still earn only 59 cents for every dollar made by a man. This figure has remained virtually unchanged and if anything declined since the 1950s. These wage discrepancies continue even when we look within broad occupational categories. As revealed in Table 6–6, in 1981 for example, the weekly wage of women in professional and technical jobs who worked full time was just 71.8 percent of what men in these occupations earned. We should note, however, that the wage gap between employed young men and women is less than the gap for older groups. In 1982, for example, women sixteen to twenty-four earned 82 percent as much as men compared with 79 percent in 1979. Women twenty-five and older earned 64 percent of men in 1982, up from 62 percent in 1979. These changes may be partially a function of the economy of the 1980s, which has hurt men more than women, yet, they may in fact reflect the legal and attitudinal impact of the women's movement.[153]

Part of the reason for these differences is, of course, traceable to factors discussed in earlier sections. Women must find compromises between their work and their traditional roles—and often it is their jobs that suffer. Women regularly drop out of their career paths temporarily, start later, work part time for a while, or are forced to change jobs or career paths during their lifetime. Even if a woman continues to work full time, it often is her career that suffers from being a "second-job" to that of homemaker and parent.

TABLE 6-6

Median Weekly Earnings of Workers Employed Full Time in Selected Occupations: 1981 Annual Averages

Occupation	Percent Female Workers in Occupation	Women's Earnings as a Percent of Men's
Professional, technical	42.8	71.8
Managerial-administrative except farm	28.4	60.8
Sales	33.0	52.0
Clerical	78.4	67.0
Craft	5.6	66.5
Operatives except transport	38.8	62.9
Transport Equipment Operators	4.9	77.2
Nonfarm Laborers	10.4	79.3
Service except private household	50.3	71.3

Note: These figures are based on *weekly* wages. Because women are more likely to work less than year-round, the yearly wage gap is greater.

Source of data: United States Department of Labor, Bureau of Labor Statistics, "1981 Weekly Earnings of Men and Women Compared in 100 Occupations" (March 7, 1982). Selected figures.

The earnings of women upon whom this "compromising" has the severest impact are often those who head families. In 1982, the average weekly earnings of women in this situation was $214—compared with $373 for men who headed families, $393 for husbands in one wage earner families and $587 for married couples in two earner families. In 1981, this translated into a median family yearly income of $10,802 for families maintained by women, $19,771 for families maintained by men, $21,707 for families where only the husband worked, and $30,119 for families where both spouses were employed.[154] These figures represent the best possible picture of the situation. When they are coupled with the high unemployment rate among female heads of households (11.1 percent in spring 1982) and these women's high concentration in part-time work (both of these factors are especially true for women with children), the result is a rapidly declining standard of living for these women and their children. Diane Pearce and Harriette McAdoo report that in 1978 (before the recession of the early 1980s), 31.4 percent of female-headed families—50.6 percent of black and 23.5 percent of white female-headed families—lived below poverty level.[155] The rate of growth of this segment of the population has led some to claim that if present trends continue, by the year 2000 all those below the poverty level will be women heads of households and the children in these families.[156] The sources of the problem—marketplace inequalities, rising divorce, out-of-wedlock births, and the growing number of elderly women[157]—show no sign of diminishing. Indeed, the policies of the Reagan administration seem very likely to exacerbate the situation.[158] Thus, the impact of these differences on the life-styles of many women is a growing problem.

The negative influence of discrimination and cultural attitudes about the relative position of work in a woman's life, however, is not limited to wages. The view that a woman's job is only temporary, supplementary, or secondary to her family roles, when combined with the lack of preparation on the part of women for all types of occupations and employer discrimination, also contributes to the over concentration of women in a few low-paying, low-status professions. Indeed, an important part of the lack of progress with respect to wages for full-time employment by women is traceable to the continued concentration of women in low-status, low-paying, high-turnover jobs.

Occupations of Women Workers

A new and increasingly accepted theory offered to explain the economic position of women is the "crowding" thesis. Its proponents argue that the source of women's inferior position in the marketplace can be found in the fact that women are "crowded" into only a few industries or occupations, while men have a considerably wider range of opportunities.[159] The concentration of women in a few occupations, as revealed earlier in Table 6–5, often results in too many women seeking too few jobs. The simple process of supply and demand thus results in lower wages for women. A variant of this approach maintains that crowding goes one step further because women are isolated into a very few low-paying industries. Even if they have high-status jobs in those industries, their incomes are lower than men with similar jobs in well-paying industries.[160] The influence of this segregation on the position of women in the marketplace is significant. With respect to wages, for example, one study found that among married, white college graduates, occupational segregation accounted for nearly 70 percent of the wage differential.[161] Others trace women's lower work commitment to the limited occupational opportunities open to them. These scholars maintain that given the bleak economic picture that women face, women cannot be expected to be as productive as male workers.[162] Indeed, there is evidence that employed women respond to the conditions they find and that knowledge of their dismal on-the-job prospects causes them to lower their aspirations.[163]

The source of occupational "crowding" can be found in the barriers discussed above including the absence of legal protection from many subtle forms of discrimination. Historically, the cultural view that women should not work if at all possible resulted in women having inadequate training for salaried work as well as discrimination by employers. When women entered the labor market in the nineteenth and early twentieth centuries to support or add to the maintenance of their families, generally they were ready only for the most menial of jobs. For example, large numbers of women took positions as domestics and textile workers where they could use their homemaking skills. This crowding of women into a few industrial jobs was paralleled in white-collar occupations and the professions where women soon constituted overwhelming majorities of the work force in the areas they were trained for—clerical work, teaching, and nursing.[164] This concentration of women workers plus the high-turnover of workers in these fields—a direct result of the fact that most working women viewed employment as a temporary condition—often translated into poor work conditions and low pay in these few "women's" fields.[165]

The underpinnings of these cultural stereotypes about women's abilities and roles plus the lack of preparation of women and legal and illegal discrimination by employers and employed men, remained almost un-challenged by women's rights leaders in the nineteenth and early twentieth centuries. Although Anthony and Stanton and later members of the National Woman's Party identified and tried to change laws and stereotypes, their efforts generally were unsuccessful. The post 1940 demand for women workers, based largely on the expansion of opportunities in women's fields and the massive increase in the proportion of women workers who were working for longer periods of their adult life, actually exacerbated the situation of women workers. Even after the passage of antidiscrimination legislation, the majority are still concentrated in a few "women's" jobs. While in certain prestige positions the gains made by women since the 1970s have more than doubled that of the previous twenty years, the picture is still grim. For example, in 1982 women still constituted less than 25 percent of all lawyers, judges, engineers, and physicians. Indeed, in certain women's jobs, notably clerical positions, the ghettoization even increased. Moreover, women still continue to be prepared and are hired for jobs compatible with their domestic roles and/or those in traditional areas.

The work conditions and wages in these "women's" jobs, moreover, continue to be considerably lower than those in "men's" jobs. Studies of pay scales in jobs requiring similar training, skills, experience, and responsibility continue to find that those in jobs in which women are concentrated are considerably lower than those in jobs in which men are found. In the state of

Washington, for example, when jobs with the same number of evaluation points (based on job requirements) were compared, it was discovered that the pay scales for jobs in which women were concentrated averaged 80 percent of those in which men dominated.[166]

Some leaders of various women's groups recently have begun to urge the adoption of legislation or regulations that would require equal pay for jobs of comparable worth or value.[167] The passage of such legislation, however, seems unlikely given the recommendation of President Reagan's transition team on civil rights, which proposed that the whole issue of comparable pay be dropped.[168] While the Supreme Court's *Gunther* decision was a positive step, even if such legislation were passed and antidiscrimination legislation presently on the books were more actively enforced (another prospect that is exceedingly unlikely during the Reagan years), as long as the other barriers (attitudinal, lack of preparation, and hidden or legal discrimination) continue, the result will be the persistent concentration of women in a few low-paying, low-status occupations. Quite simply, if (1) women continue to choose and prepare for jobs that are compatible with their domestic roles or parental abilities, or (2) parents, guidance counselors, educators, and the media continue to channel women into such fields, or (3) employers continue to hire women for such jobs under the assumption that women's family responsibilities will take precedence over their careers, or (4) women lack the ability to perform in other areas, then we can expect to find women continuing to cluster in a few jobs. Additionally, if as some suspect, the growth in "women's" jobs declines in the future, then the economic future of women workers may be grim.[169]

Yet, the future is not all bleak. Among younger women who have rejected older notions about the abilities and proper roles for women and who expect to pursue full-time, life-time careers equal to or more important than their domestic roles, many are training for and entering traditionally male fields. Whether or not these young women actually succeed in these occupations, however, will depend on more than their abilities and training. For many, the pressures of homelife or unequal or unfair treatment on the job may well limit their progress.

Another problem according to Michael and Susan Boslego Carter is that the women in these formerly "male jobs" may have arrived too late. They argue, for example, that these formerly prestigious positions are quickly becoming two-tiered professions. One tier consists of prestige jobs with autonomy, opportunities for promotion, and good pay while the other tier consists of routinized, dead-end, lower-paying jobs. The Carters argue that women, primarily but not exclusively because they are the late arrivals in these professions, are found overwhelmingly in the lower tier.[170] For example, they note that while the number of women in academia is increasing, most have entered at a time when the position of university professor is becoming less well paid and has reduced autonomy. Moreover, the women in academia tend to be concentrated in schools in which these two conditions are most pronounced: junior colleges and undergraduate teaching institutions.[171]

The Carters make a similar argument for the position of women in law and medicine. They note the recent increase in the number of graduates from both types of professional schools to the point where there is rapidly becoming an oversupply of both lawyers and physicians.[172] Thus, recent female graduates have to confront the problem of stiff competition from men for the dwindling number of good jobs. The result is new women lawyers and doctors can be found in the most underpaid, routinized, nonautonomous sectors of both professions (legal clinics and hospital-based practices).[173]

PROSPECTS FOR THE FUTURE

In this review of the status of women in education and in the marketplace, we have tried to indicate that several barriers remain that make the prospect of full equality in the immediate future unlikely. Faced with the persistence of attitudinal barriers and their related implications for the status of women in the work force, leaders of the women's movement have offered several proposals and strategies designed to overcome these barriers. These strategies and proposals fall loosely into two categories. On the one hand, an effort has been made to change the public's views with respect to women and work. Campaigns have been undertaken to make the public aware of discriminatory practices and cultural stereotypes. Special efforts, of late, have been focused on husbands and fathers to make them aware of the need to share parental roles and to provide career support for their wives when needed. The immediate goal of such reeducation efforts is the hope that if individuals become more aware of sex discrimination and take concerted action to see it ended, equality may come much more quickly. The evidence seems to suggest the women's movements have been successful in achieving this aim. As recently as 1968, interviews with Minnesota residents found that only 27 percent believed that most women did not have equal opportunities for advancement in business.[174] No doubt due to the women's movement's targeting of employment discrimination, in just a little over ten years the change in awareness of the problem was dramatic. By 1979, one national poll found a majority of women believed they were discriminated against in business, in top government posts, and as doctors, lawyers, teachers, or other professionals. Moreover, only 55 percent felt that their salary treatment was equal to that of their male colleages. Only 52 percent responded that they believed they had an equal chance with male co-workers for promotion.[175]

Recognition appears strongest among those most attuned to the women's movement: the young, the college-educated, and working women. For instance, in 1976, 82 percent of all women with at least some college education and 91 percent of such women under thirty agreed with the statement, "Many qualified women can't get a good job; men with the same skills have much less trouble." Correspondingly, working women at all education levels were also more willing than full-time homemakers to agree with this statement.[176]

In addition to this growing awareness of discrimination, especially with respect to good jobs, there is also increased acceptance of the idea that women *should* have equal opportunities with men. While support for equal pay for equal work always has been high, the same has not always been true with respect to economic opportunities in general. In 1946, only 29 percent of all women and 22 percent of all men believed that "a woman should have an equal chance with men for any job in business or industry regardless of whether they have to support themselves."[177] By the mid 1970s, support for equal pay and equal opportunity had grown considerably. As early as 1974 among Northern working women, 85 percent agreed with the view that "women should have exactly the same job opportunities as a man."[178] While nearly two thirds of those interviewed in 1979 favored efforts to strengthen and change the status of women in society (an increase from 40% in 1970), how best to achieve this goal is a matter of debate.[179] Whereas virtually all women who see some improvement in the situation of women in the United States between 1971 and 1976 attribute this change at least in part to the efforts of women's organizations, the strategy of organized activity alone as a way of improving women's status receives only limited support.[180] Although this alternative is viewed by a majority as a more viable strategy than simply "being feminine," it is only considered as a second-best alternative compared to the option of each woman making "sure she gets the best training possible for what she wants to do."[181]

With respect to government actions to improve the position of women, nearly three-quarters of a national poll in 1978 agreed with a call for stricter enforcement of existing laws.[182] However, a 1979 poll found less than half of all those interviewed favored quotas or special efforts to hire and promote women.[183] An even larger proportion rejected *preferential* treatment of women in getting jobs, getting into college, or getting into professional schools.[184]

Thus, while the movement may have convinced many women that they are discriminated against, disagreement on remedies to redress discrimination and some potent cultural barriers remain. Because such views do not appear to be changing as rapidly as those with respect to awareness of discrimination, a second set of proposed changes has been offered by feminists. Many of these in the short run are designed to make the burden of the mother and homemaker roles of women workers easier and more compatible with full-time, year-round careers. One area of special concern has been with the lack of adequate, affordable daycare. If a woman with children decides to work, whether or not she is the head of her household, daycare is an ever present problem—in both social and economic terms. For many mothers, leaving their children in the care of others is a guilt-inducing situation, having been socialized that their place is with their children, particularly in the formative years. Although many Western European nations provide either free day-care centers or child-rearing subsidies for working mothers, the United States does not.[185] In 1971, Congress passed a law to begin federal funding of day-care centers that would be available to all regardless of their economic status. However, President Nixon vetoed this bill, and an override effort was unsuccessful. In the Reagan era of social welfare cuts, it is unlikely that a similar bill could be passed in either house although an increased tax credit for childcare was enacted.[186]

Most privately operated day-care centers charge between 45 and 80 dollars per week per child. For a woman with three children, this is a costly investment, particularly since her salary is likely to be low. Private, in-home care is even more expensive. Because federal law mandates that domestics or regular sitters be paid $3.35 an hour, in-house arrangements easily could cost over $600 a month for a woman employed eight hours a day. This amount obviously puts private care out of the price range of most working women— even those whose husbands are gainfully employed. Given that the median weekly income of women in the United States in 1982 was $240 for full-time workers and $86 for part-time workers, the "average" woman, *before taxes* would make only slightly more than her hired sitter.[187]

Since the issuance of the first Report of the President's Commission on the Status of Women in 1963, government support of adequate daycare has been a priority item for many women's rights groups.[188] The failure of Washington officials to act in this area other than to grant a tax credit for a proportion of day-care expenses and some minimal provisions for day-care funds for poor women and those in government training or employment programs[189] has led women to resort to a variety of other measures: forming co-ops, leaving their children with relatives, or leaving their children unattended have been solutions for many, as revealed in Table 6–7.[190] By far, however, the most frequent arrangement involves a jostling of schedules so that one parent is available to watch the children.[191] A 1977 study reported that 11.6 percent of dual-income families worked different shifts, a solution that undoubtedly makes family life difficult for many.[192] While government-sponsored but not controlled daycare is the overwhelming choice of most women workers,[193] licensed child-care facilities are scarce. Although by March 1978, 29.7 million children under age eighteen had mothers in the labor force,[194] there were only 1.6 million slots in licensed centers, fewer openings than there were in 1945.[195] Given that the average annual cost per child for

TABLE 6-7

Arrangements Made for the Daytime Care of Children 3 to 13 Years Old, by Age of Child, Labor Force Status, and Marital Status of Mother: October 1974 and February 1975

(Numbers in thousands. Civilian noninstitutional population)

| Age of child and labor force status and marital status of mother | Total | Care in own home | | | | Care in someone else's home | | | | | $n=$ |
		Child's parent	Child cares for self	Other relative	Non-relative	Relative	Non-Relative	Day care center	Other	Not reported	
PERCENT DISTRIBUTION											
Children 3 to 13 years old........	100.0	80.5	4.5	5.1	1.4	2.9	3.1	0.8	0.2	1.5	40,765
3 to 6 years old..................	100.0	80.9	0.1	3.5	1.3	5.1	6.1	1.6	—	1.3	13,758
7 to 13 years old.................	100.0	80.3	6.7	5.9	1.5	1.8	1.6	0.4	0.4	1.6	27,007
Mother in labor force	100.0	63.6	9.2	8.7	2.7	5.5	6.8	1.6	0.4	1.5	17,555
3 to 6 years old..................	100.0	58.0	0.4	6.8	2.8	11.3	14.9	3.7	—	2.1	5,308
7 to 13 years old.................	100.0	66.1	13.1	9.5	2.6	3.0	3.2	0.7	0.6	1.3	12,247

Mother employed	100.0	61.1	9.9	9.4	2.9	5.8	7.3	1.7	0.4	1.5	16,046
3 to 6 years old	100.0	54.0	0.4	7.4	3.2	12.2	16.6	4.1	—	2.1	4,658
7 to 13 years old	100.0	64.0	13.8	10.2	2.7	3.2	3.5	0.8	0.6	1.3	11,388
Mother employed full time	100.0	50.1	12.9	12.3	3.6	7.3	9.1	2.4	0.6	1.7	10,323
3 to 6 years old	100.0	41.4	0.7	9.0	4.0	15.2	21.0	6.0	—	2.7	2,917
7 to 13 years old	100.0	53.5	17.7	13.7	3.4	4.2	4.4	1.0	0.8	1.3	7,406
Mother not in labor force	100.0	94.3	0.7	2.0	0.3	0.8	0.2	0.1	0.1	1.4	22,498
3 to 6 years old	100.0	96.1	—	1.3	0.2	1.0	0.4	0.1	0.1	0.8	8,255
7 to 13 years old	100.0	93.3	1.1	2.4	0.4	0.6	0.2	0.1	0.1	1.8	14,243
Marital status of mother	100.0	80.5	4.5	5.1	1.4	2.9	3.1	0.8	0.2	1.5	40,765
Married, husband present	100.0	83.4	3.9	4.0	1.2	2.5	2.8	0.6	0.2	1.4	33,467
Separated, divorced, or widowed	100.0	67.7	7.4	9.6	2.2	4.2	4.6	1.7	0.6	1.9	5,960
Never married	100.0	69.6	3.8	11.2	1.3	7.8	2.6	1.3	0.3	1.8	625

Note: Date for children 3 to 6 years old obtained from February 1975 Current Population Survey; data for children 7 to 13 years old obtained from October 1974 Current Population Survey.

— Represents zero or rounds to zero.

Source of data: U.S. Bureau of the Census, *Current Population Reports*, Series P-20, No. 298, "Daytime Care of Children: October 1974 and February 1975," U.S. Government Printing Office, Washington, D.C. 1976, p. 6.

these kinds of arrangements is $2,500, government inaction in this area certainly has made employment more difficult for those with primary responsibility for childcare.[196]

Recently some courts have ruled that Title IX requires colleges and universities to provide daycare for the children of students or face a cutoff of federal dollars for discriminating against females.[197] Since the absence of suitable day-care facilities has been held to discriminate against female students, it is possible, but unlikely, that a successful suit could be brought by women employees whose employer failed to provide for childcare. Some employers already have acted to provide daycare, particularly in situations where they find it difficult to retain female workers. Some hospitals, for example, provide free childcare for nurses on the 3 to 11 o'clock shift. Unions, too, are recognizing this problem as more and more women become members.[198] Thus far, however, only one union, the Amalgamated Clothing and Textile Workers, has sponsored day-care facilities for its members.[199]

Part of the reason for the absence of a large-scale, comprehensive child-care program in the United States is political—day-care centers have been characterized by a vocal minority as a "communist plot" to destroy the American family. The establishment of child-care facilities is viewed by many as a first step in *requiring* all women to work—thereby robbing females of their free choice whether or when to enter the work force. Others see it as further facilitating the breakup of the American family.

In some political debates, government-sponsored day-care centers have been taken out of the realm of options and instead have been portrayed by opponents as a true public bad/good. Some of those opposed to the ERA tried to argue that ratification of the amendment would *require* the federal government to sponsor day-care centers and eventually *require* all women to work to support themselves. Conservatives who opposed the 1971 child-care legislation set the stage for these conclusions when Sen. James Buckley (C-New York) characterized the bill as one that "threatens to destroy parental authority and the institution of the family."[200] By portraying daycare as something that would force a change in the life-styles of all women as well as rob them of control over their children,[201] opponents of daycare effectively utilized the concept of a true public bad. As we pointed out in Chapter 2, it is much easier to mobilize opposition to an idea or a law if it appears that all will be affected. Little organized opposition has arisen to most laws prohibiting sex discrimination, but day-care is another issue entirely. Having masterfully been characterized by its opponents as life-style threatening, many politicians, mindful of the power of some conservative groups, have been unwilling to vote in favor of it. This may be especially true for the Reagan administration, which relied heavily on the support of conservative groups for its election victory. Thus, the prospects for future extension of government-sponsored daycare seem dim even though 75 percent of all women and 66 percent of all men favor the establishment of additional day-care centers.[202]

Another proposal urges employers to make greater use of flexitime, a system whereby employees may clock in early and work late in any configuration as long as they work forty hours a week.[203] Allowing employees to choose their starting and finishing times permits one parent to stay home until the children go to school and the other, by starting early, can be home when the children return. Use of flexitime is common in Europe, and the federal government has switched to this system in many of its agencies.[204] Although flexitime and/or compressed workdays, i.e., four 10-hour days, are still experimental in the few businesses that use them, some studies have reported positive results where they are used. One study undertaken by the Business and Professional Women's Foundation found "substantial reductions in tardiness, absenteeism, and turnover," and increased productivity.[205]

The use of part-time employees in all occupations, including the professions, also can help women if safeguards are taken to assure that part-time employment is not viewed with less prestige.[206] Many women with small children would like to work but only on a part-time basis.[207] Part-time work during the child-rearing years may allow a woman to continue her professional interests, or at least hold her own if not move up the ladder in her business or profession. But as we have noted, part-time work can in many jobs result in little career progress. Indeed, the fact that one-third of all women employed in 1981 worked only part time compared to only 14 percent of all men helps explain the inability of women to make progress in the marketplace.[208]

There must also be statutory changes if these programs are to be implemented. Employers, for example, may incur substantial economic penalties for using part-time employees. The Social Security system treats all workers as full time, therefore requiring larger employer contributions for two part-time workers each making $10,000 a year than for one earning $20,000 a year. It should be noted, however, that most part-time employees are not covered by other employer-paid benefits (e.g. retirement plans, health insurance).

Another proposal calls for job sharing. In this situation, two persons hold the same position, but each works only part time. One particularly interesting version of job sharing is the hiring of the husband-wife teams who share an academic appointment. Studies of these couples, however, indicate possible drawbacks. More specifically, couples found hostility from administrators who viewed their part-time work as evidence of lack of commitment, and both spouses report less-than-perfect relations with colleagues.[209]

While all the above proposals are usually introduced as measures to help women workers, the eventual hope is that changing attitudes will result in both spouses taking advantage of the increased flexibility to combine work, marriage, and family that would result from the adoption of these policies. One large and growing segment of the female population, however, seems destined to have to take advantage of these options without a husband's help—the single mother. If these new measures are only adopted or used by women, however, the impact on the status of women (and women's jobs) in the marketplace may be quite negative. The "special treatment" may well produce the same results that "protective" legislation of the early twentieth century did.

Another problem faced by married women workers is the marriage penalty found in the current tax system. Although changes were made in 1982 to reduce the penalty paid by married couples, women's earnings continue to cause a couple increased tax liability.[210]

To summarize, while legal, cultural, preparational, and discrimination barriers have diminished considerably in the last few decades, women still face some serious hurdles in their efforts to achieve equality. Paralleling the situation in politics, in this situation these barriers loom largest for those positions with the most prestige and greatest economic rewards. Just as in the political arena, many of the changes that are needed before these barriers are eliminated are tied to life-styles and the traditional views of childcare and a woman's role in that process. As will be detailed in Chapters 7 and 8, changes are coming in the family that are likely to affect women's place in the labor force. While law and new kinds of work can advance the status of some women, attitudinal changes also are necessary before women can enjoy greater equality in the work force.

NOTES

1.   Unless otherwise indicated, the data analyzed in this chapter were made available by the Inter-University Consortium for Political and Social Research. The data for 1977 and 1978 are from the General Social Surveys, conducted by the National Opinion Research Center at the University of Chicago. The data for 1972 and 1976 are from the American National Elections Studies. They were originally collected by the Center for Political Studies of the Institute for Social Research, the University of Michigan, under a grant from the National Science Foundation. Neither the original collectors of the data nor the Consortium bears any responsibility for the analyses or interpretations presented here.

2.   Elizabeth Cady Stanton, Susan B. Anthony, and Matilda Joslyn Gage, eds., *History of Woman Suffrage*, vol. I, 1848–1861 (Rochester, N.Y.: Charles Mann, 1887), p. 71 (hereafter HWS I).

3.   This legislation often became the rationale for many firms not to hire women for certain jobs. In defending itself against a 1970 discrimination suit challenging its hiring practices, AT&T, for example, claimed certain protective legislation requirements made it impossible for it to hire women for craft jobs that led to management positions. See Margaret J. Gates, "Occupational Segregation and the Law," in Martha Blaxall and Barbara Reagan, eds., *Women and the Workplace: The Implications of Occupational Segregation* (Chicago: University of Chicago Press, 1976), p. 66.

4.   National Advisory Council on Women's Educational Programs, *Title IX: The Half Full, Half Empty Glass* (Washington, D.C.: Government Printing Office, 1981), p. 27.

5. William H. Chafe, *Women and Equality: Changing Patterns in American Culture* (New York: Oxford University Press, 1977), pp. 100–101.

6. See Marianne A. Ferber and Helen M. Lowry, "Women: The New Reserve Army of the Unemployed," in Blaxall and Reagan, eds., *Women and the Workplace*, pp. 213–232.

7. Valerie Kincade Oppenheimer, *The Female Labor Force in the United States: Demographic and Economic Factors Governing its Growth and Changing Composition* (Berkeley: Institute of International Studies, 1970), pp. 136–139.

8. For a good discussion of various economic theories of sex discrimination, see Francine D. Blau and Carol L. Jusenius, "Economists' Approaches to Sex Segregation in the Labor Market: An Appraisal," in Blaxall and Reagan, eds., *Women and the Workplace*, pp. 181–199 and Mary Huff Stevenson, "Wage Differences between Men and Women: Economic Theories," in Ann H. Stromberg and Shirley Harkess, eds., *Women Working: Theories and Facts in Perspective* (Palo Alto, Calif: Mayfield, 1978), pp. 89–107.

9. Gary Becker, *Human Capital: A Theoretical and Empirical Analysis, with Special Reference to Education* (New York: National Bureau of Economic Research, 1964). For discussion of the evidence against this model, see Isabell V. Sawhill, "The Economics of Discrimination Against Women: Some New Findings," *Journal of Human Resources* 8 (1973):383–396.

10. For a statement of this model, see Stevenson, "Wage Differences," in Stromberg and Harkess, *Women Working*, p. 92. See also, Edmund S. Phelps, "The Statistical Theory of Racism and Sexism," *American Economic Review* 62 (1972):659–661.

11. Blau and Jusenius, "Economists' Approaches to Sex Segregation," in Blaxall and Reagan, eds., *Women and the Workplace*, p. 195.

12. Sharlene J. Hesse, "Women Working: Historical Trends," in Karen Wold Feinstein, ed., *Working Women and Families* (Beverly Hills, Calif.: Sage Publications, 1979), pp. 38–39.

13. Robert W. Smuts, *Women and Work in America* (New York: Columbia University Press, 1959), pp. 119–121.

14. There is some evidence of high career aspirations among young women. See, for example, data presented in Frank Stricker, "Cookbooks and Law Books: The Hidden History of Career Women in Twentieth-Century America," in Nancy F. Cott and Elizabeth H. Pleck, eds., *A Heritage of Her Own: Toward a New Social History of American Women* (New York: Simon and Schuster/Touchstone Books, 1979), p. 480.

15. The acceptability of single women working was apparently so universal that most questions addressed the propriety of married women working only.

16. Most of the material that follows on attitudes in the 1930s through the 1960s is from Oppenheimer, *The Female Labor Force*, pp. 39–55 and Hazel Erskine, "The Polls: Women's Role," *Public Opinion Quarterly* 35 (Summer 1971):275–290.

17. Oppenheimer, *The Female Labor Force*, p. 53.

18. Erskine, "The Polls," p. 282.

19. Leila J. Rupp, "Woman's Place Is in the War: Propaganda and Public Opinion in the United States and Germany, 1939–1945," in Carol Ruth Berkin and Mary Beth Norton, eds., *Women of America, A History* (Boston: Houghton Mifflin, 1979), p. 345.

20. Ibid., p. 346.

21. Ibid., p. 347.

22. Erskine, "The Polls," p. 284.

23. Rupp, "Women's Place Is in the War," in Berkin and Norton, eds., *Women of America,* p. 351.

24. Erskine, "The Polls," pp. 286–287.

25. William H. Chafe, *The American Woman: Her Changing Social, Economic, and Political Role, 1920–1970* (New York: Oxford University Press, 1972), pp. 176–177. One Southern senator noted that the Congress should "force wives and mothers back to the kitchen" to ensure that there would be jobs available for returning veterans.

26. Erskine, "The Polls," p. 283.

27. Ibid., p. 284.

28. Ibid.

29. Alfreda P. Iglehart, *Married Women and Work* (Lexington, Mass.: Lexington Books, 1979), pp. 31 and 34. See also, Oppenheimer, *The Female Labor Force,* p. 49.

30. In 1949, for example, 79 percent of the public responded affirmatively when asked if they thought it was all right for women to work for the first few years of married life if not doing so would mean the women would have to postpone their weddings. Erskine, "The Polls," p. 285.

31. Chafe, *The American Woman,* pp. 178–179 reports that in New York, 80 percent, and in Detroit, 75 percent of the working women interviewed by the Women's Bureau at the end of the war wanted to continue to work.

32. Iglehart, *Married Women,* p. 27.

33. Oppenheimer, *The Female Labor Force,* chap. 5.

34. Erskine, "The Polls," p. 283.

35. 1978 data from the National Opinion Research Center, General Social Surveys. Figures compiled by the authors.

36. 1977 data from the National Opinion Research Center, General Social Survey. Figures compiled by the authors. Data from 1945 drawn from Erskine, "The Polls," p. 284.

37. This question was asked in the 1976 American National Election Study. In the 1972 American National Election Study, in response to this question, 45 percent favored laying-off women first.

38. The data on careers and achievement outside the home are contained in the 1977 General Social Survey. Figures compiled by the authors.

39. *The 1980 Virginia Slims American Women's Opinion Poll,* conducted by the Roper Organization, p. 12.

40. Reported in Deborah Durfee Barron and Daniel Yankelovich, "Today's American Woman: How the Public Sees Her," The Public Agenda Foundation, December 1980, p. 64.

41. Karen Oppenheim Mason, John Czajka, and Sara Arber, "Change in U.S. Women's Sex-Role Attitudes, 1964–1974," *American Sociological Review* 41 (August 1976):585–587 and 1977 General Social Survey data. Figures for 1977 compiled by the authors.

42. Frank L. Mott, *Women, Work and Family* (Lexington, Mass.: Lexington Books, 1978), p. 13.

43. This, however, was an increase from the 12.2 percent of all professional women who were married in 1910. Stricker, "Cookbooks and Law Books," in Cott and Pleck, eds., *A Heritage of Her Own,* p. 486.

44. Oppenheimer, *The Female Labor Force,* pp. 46 and 55.

45. Iglehart, *Married Women,* pp. 65–68.

46. Ibid., p. 72.

47. Mason et al., "Change in U.S. Women's Sex-Role Attitudes," pp. 585–587.

48. Iglehart reports that in 1976, only 29 percent of working mothers (and the same percentage of housewives) indicated they frequently felt inadequate as a parent in contrast to 1957 figures of 53 percent for working mothers and 31 percent for housewives. *Married Women,* p. 68.

49. *The 1980 Virginia Slims American Women's Opinion Poll,* p. 12.

50. "The Superwoman Squeeze," *Newsweek,* May 19, 1980, p. 74.

51. Barron and Yankelovich, "Today's American Women", p. 61.

52. Stricker, however, suggests that a much greater career orientation and a desire to combine marriage and career existed among professional women in the 1920s through 1940s than reported previously.

53. Constantina Safilios-Rothschild, *Sex Role Socialization and Sex Disrimination: A Synthesis and Critique of the Literature* (Washington, D.C.: The National Institute of Education, 1979), p. 43.

54. Ibid., pp. 44–46.

55. *The 1980 Virginia Slims American Women's Opinion Poll,* p. 12.

56. Ibid., pp. 10 and 13.

57. Iglehart, *Married Women and Work,* p. 27.

58. A. Regula Herzog, Jerald G. Bachman, and Lloyd D. Johnston, "High School Seniors' Preferences for Sharing Work and Family Responsibilities Between Husband and Wife," *Monitoring the Future Occasional Paper Series* #3 (Ann Arbor, Michigan: Institute for Social Research, 1979), pp. 7–8.

59. Ibid., p. 12.

60. Ibid., p. 9.

61. Iglehart, *Married Women and Work,* p. 31. See also, Joan E. Crowley, Teresa E. Levitin. and Robert P. Quinn, "Seven Deadly Half-Truths About Women," *Psychology Today,* March 1973, p. 94 and Mary Lindenstein Walshok, "Occupational Values and Family Roles: Women in Blue Collar and Service Occupations," in Feinstein, ed., *Working Women and Families,* p. 74. She notes that among blue-collar women, economic motives for working are often phrased in terms of the independence and self-worth that come from earning one's own money.

62. Crowley et al., "Seven Deadly Half-Truths," pp. 95–96 and Patricia Gurin, "The Role of Worker Expectancies" in Phyllis A. Wallace and Annette M. LaMond, eds., *Women, Minorities, and Employment Discrimination* (Lexington, Mass.: Lexington Books, 1977), p. 22.

63. *The 1980 Virginia Slims American Women's Opinion Poll,* pp. 10 and 27.

64. Edward H. Clarke, *Sex in Education,* a book written during the 1870s quoted in Smuts, *Women and Work in America,* p. 114.

65. Ibid., p. 112, quoting Mary Putnam Jacobi, perhaps the first prominent woman physician in America, in 1891.

66. Erskine, "The Polls," pp. 387–388.

67. Quoted in Chafe, *The American Woman,* p. 177.

68. See Sheila Tobias, "The Mathematics Filter," *National Forum* (Fall 1981):17–18.

69. Ibid., p. 17. Tobias reports that women with mathematics abilities often end up as math majors and not in well-paying fields like engineering.

70. Louis Harris, *The 1972 Virginia Slims American Women's Opinion Poll,* conducted by Louis Harris and Associates, Inc., 1972, p. 34.

71. Connie De Boer, "The Polls: Women at Work," *Public Opinion Quarterly* 41 (1977):275.

72. Ibid.

73. The 1972 question was phrased, "In general, women in our society have not been as successful as men in business, politics and leadership posts, in our country. I'll read some reasons why some people think this is so. 'Men are born with more drive and ambition.'" In 1976 the question asked was, "Which statement do you agree with? 'Men have more of the top jobs because they are born with more drive to be ambitious and successful than women,' or 'Men have more of the top jobs because our society discriminates against women.'" Questions from the 1972 and 1976 National Elections Studies. Figures compiled by the authors.

74. Eighty-two percent of young, college-educated women fully reject the idea men have more top jobs because of more drive and ambition. Only 79 percent of the men agreed with them. Figures compiled by the authors.

75. *The Gallup Poll,* (October 19, 1953).

76. *The 1980 Virginia Slims American Women's Opinion Poll,* p. 11.

77. Ibid. and *The Gallup Poll:* 1976, p. 708.

78. De Boer, "The Polls: Women at Work," p. 274 and Safilios-Rothschild, *Sex Role Socialization and Sex Discrimination,* p. 49–53. See also, Carol Ireson, "Girls' Socialization for Work," in Stromberg and Harkess, eds., *Women Working,* p. 182.

79. For discussions of such studies and possible solutions, see Gaye Tuchman, "The Impact of Mass-Media Stereotypes Upon the Full Employment of Women," in Ann Foote Cahn, ed., *Women in the U.S. Labor Force* (New York: Praeger, 1979), pp. 249–268. See also, Susan Knell and Gerald Winer, "Effects of Reading Content on Occupational Sex Role Stereotypes," *Journal of Vocational Behavior* 14 (1979):78–87 and Harry F. Waters, "Life According to TV," *Newsweek,* December 6, 1982, pp. 136–140.

80. Safilios-Rothschild, *Sex Role Socialization and Sex Discrimination,* p. 51. For a discussion of the factors leading to occupation innovation, see Sandra Schwartz Tangri, "Determinants of Occupational Role Innovation Among College Women," in Martha Tamara Shuch Mednick, Sandra Schwartz Tangri, and Lois Wladis Hoffman, eds., *Women and Achievement: Social and Motivational Analyses* (Washington, D.C.: Hemisphere Publishing, 1975), pp. 255–273 and Mary Anne Orcutt and W. Bruce Walsh, "Traditionality and Congruence of Career Aspirations for College Women," *Journal of Vocational Behavior* 14 (1979):1–11.

81. For a good overview of girls' socialization for work and success on the job both, see Ireson, "Girls' Socialization for Work," in Stromberg and Harkess, eds., *Women Working,* pp. 176–200 and Lois Wladis Hoffman, "Early Childhood Experiences and Women's Achievement Motives," in Mednick et al., *Women and Achievement,* pp. 129–150.

82.   Safilios-Rothschild, *Sex Role Socialization and Discrimination*, pp. 43 and 49–50.

83.   Matina S. Horner, "Toward an Understanding of Achievement-Related Conflicts in Women," in Mednick et al., *Women and Achievement,* pp. 206–220. See also, Gurin, "The Role of Worker Expectancies," in Wallace and LaMond, eds., *Women, Minorities and Employment Discrimination,* p. 21 and Ireson, "Girls' Socialization for Work," in Stromberg and Harkess, eds., *Women Working,* pp. 183–189.

84.   Safilios-Rothschild, *Sex Role Socialization and Discrimination,* pp. 28–35 and 45. See also, Thelma Alper, "Where Are We Now? Discussion of Papers Presented in the 1975 AERA Symposium of Sex Differences in Achievement Motivation and Achievement Behavior," *Psychology of Women Quarterly* 1 (Spring, 1977):294–303.

85.   Safilios-Rothschild, *Sex Role Socialization and Discrimination,* p. 37.

86.   Ibid., p. 38.

87.   Ibid., p. 41.

88.   Verbal report of ongoing research by Dr. Brenda Majors, The State University of New York at Buffalo (April, 1981).

89.   Safilios-Rothschild, *Sex Role Socialization and Discrimination,* pp. 43, 44, and 52–53.

90.   Ibid., pp. 36, 44, and 48. See also, Linda J. Trigg and Daniel Perlman, "Social Influences on Women's Pursuit of a Nontraditional Career," *Psychology of Women Quarterly* 1 (Winter 1976):138–150.

91.   Safilios-Rothschild, *Sex Role Socialization and Discrimination,* pp. 44–45 and 52.

92.   Waters, "Life According to TV," pp. 136–137.

93.   "Groups Fighting Sexist, Racist Books Called 'Censors,'" *PEER Perspectives* 6 (March 1980), p. 2. See also, Judith Stacey, Susan Bereard, and Joan Daniels, eds., *And Jill Came Tumbling After: Sexism in American Education* (New York: Dell Publishing, 1974).

94.   Pamela Ann Roby, "Vocational Education" in Cahn, ed., *Women in the U.S. Labor Force,* pp. 217–220 and Anita M. Mitchell, "Facilitating Full Employment of Women Through Career Education," in Cahn, ed., *Women in the U.S. Labor Force,* pp. 195–202.

95.   Thomas J. Donahue and James W. Costar, "Counselor Discrimination Against Young Women in Career Selection," *Journal of Counseling Psychology* 24 (November 1977):481–486.

96.   As Susan Gilbert of Wider Opportunities for Women (WOW) has noted, the women in these programs are headed for "dead-end, $4-an-hour jobs" rather than faster-growing craft and technical jobs that pay from $6 to $10 an hour. Quoted in Bailey Morris, "Women Avoid High-Paid Jobs, Report Shows," *Buffalo Evening News,* September 19, 1980, p. 1–13.

97.   Roby, "Vocational Education," in Cahn, ed., *Women in the U.S. Labor Force,* pp. 214–215 and Safilios-Rothschild, *Sex Role Socialization and Discrimination,* p. 53.

98.   See Gurin, "The Role of Worker Expectancies," in Wallace and LaMond, eds., *Women, Minorities and Employment Discrimination* and Glenna D. Spitze, "Role Experiences of Young Women: A Longitudinal Test of the Role Hiatus

Hypothesis," in *The Journal of Marriage and Family* 40 (August 1978):471–479.

99.   Oppenheimer, *The Female Labor Force,* pp. 13–33 and 104.

100.   Ibid.

101.   Nijole V. Benokraitis and Joe R. Feagin, *Affirmative Action and Equal Opportunity: Action, Inaction, Reaction* (Boulder, Colorado: Westview Press, 1978), pp. 72–73.

102.   A survey of employers in 78 business firms that train Wisconsin state-registered apprentices found that two-thirds of the men would not consider placing a women in *any* apprenticeship program. One-half of them gave as the reason for their beliefs the unsuitable (dirty, heavy, etc.) conditions of the trade. These comments are especially interesting because women worked in many of these places in *unskilled* jobs under the same "dirty" conditions. Norma Briggs, "Apprenticeship," in Cahn, ed., *Women in the U.S. Labor Force,* pp. 227–228.

103.   For examples of how attitudes influence hiring decisions in government, business, and academia, see Benokraitis and Feagin, *Affirmative Action,* pp. 32–39, 72–82, and 133–154.

104.   Francine D. Blau, *Equal Pay in the Office* (Lexington, Mass.: Lexington Books, 1977), chap. 4.

105.   Lynn Langway with William D. Marbach and Donna M. Foote, "Boiling Point in the Steno Pool," *Newsweek,* December 3, 1979, pp. 99–100. See also, Helen Dimos, "Getting Mad and Doing Something About It," *Ms.,* May 1980, pp. 44–49 for a report on the efforts of the National Commission on Working Women to hold a conference to air the problems of women in the low-paying jobs.

106.   Smuts, *Women and Work,* pp. 119–120 and Oppenheimer, *The Female Labor Force,* pp. 51–55.

107.   De Boer, "The Polls: Women at Work," p. 275.

108.   In 1979, however, the U.S. Supreme Court upheld the use of separate seniority lists for blacks and whites when entrance into a training program was in issue and blacks historically had been shut out of skilled jobs at Kaiser Aluminum. See *United Steel Workers of America* v. *Kaiser Aluminum,* 443 U.S. 193 (1979).

109.   Sally Hilsman Baker, "Women in Blue-Collar and Service Occupations," in Stromberg and Harkess, eds., *Women Working,* p. 352. See also, Benokraitis and Feagin, *Affirmative Action,* pp. 88–93.

110.   "First Woman is Elected to Labor Council," *Buffalo Evening News,* August 21, 1980, pp. 1–10.

111.   Dimos, "Getting Mad and Doing Something About It," p. 49.

112.   Baker, "Women in Blue-Collar and Service Occupations," in Stromberg and Harkess, eds., *Women Working,* pp. 355–363.

113.   For example, 11 percent of all women apprentices were in training to be barbers and beauticians—the only trade program where more than half the apprentices were women. Briggs, "Apprenticeship," in Cahn, ed., *Women in the U.S. Labor Force,* pp. 225–226.

114.   Baker, "Women in Blue-Collar and Service Occupations," in Stromberg and Harkess, eds., *Women Working,* pp. 361 and 365–366.

115.   Laura Berman, "'Women in Men's Jobs,' The Going is Rough," *Buffalo Evening News,* November 18, 1979, F-6.

116. Barbara M. Wertheimer, "Search for a Partnership Role: Women in Labor Unions Today," in Jane Roberts Chapman, ed., *Economic Independence for Women: The Foundation For Equal Rights* (Beverly Hills, Calif.: Sage, 1976), pp. 183–210.

117. Laurily Keir Epstein, ed., *Women in the Professions* (Lexington, Mass.: Lexington Press, 1975) and Michelle Patterson and Laurie Engelberg, "Women in Male-Dominated Professions," in Stromberg and Harkess, *Women Working*, pp. 266–292.

118. See Martha S. White, "Women in the Professions: Psychological and Social Barriers to Women in Science," in Jo Freeman, ed., *Women: A Feminist Perspective*, (Palo Alto, Calif.: Mayfield, 1975), pp. 231–232. See also, Benokraitis and Feagin, *Affirmative Action*, pp. 77, 91–92, and 150–152 and Patterson and Engelberg, "Women in Male-Dominated Professions," in Stromberg and Harkess, *Women Working*, pp. 283–296.

119. Catherine MacKinnon, *Sexual Harassment* (New Haven: Yale University Press, 1980).

120. Claire Safran, "Sexual Harassment: The View From the Top," *Redbook Magazine*, March, 1981, p. 49. She reports the results of a survey of men and women executives who subscribe to *Harvard Business Review*. An earlier study of readers of *Redbook* found nearly 90 percent of the women who responded had experienced sexual harassment and virtually all (92 percent) thought the problem was a serious one. See also, Karen Lindsey, "Sexual Harassment on the Job," *Ms.*, November, 1977, pp. 47–51 and 74–78.

121. Safran, "Sexual Harassment: The View From the Top," p. 48.

122. Ibid., p. 49.

123. Ibid., p. 50.

124. Ibid., pp. 50–51.

125. "Sexual Harassment Costly to U.S.," *Buffalo Evening News*, April 29, 1981, III-42.

126. According to the U.S. Merit System Protection Board, 30 percent of female federal workers and 9 percent of the males reported experiencing sexual harassment. Ibid.

127. United States Department of Labor, Bureau of Labor Statistics, *Perspectives on Working Women: A Databook* (Bulletin #2080) (October 1980), p. 3. Figures for 1982 were derived from United States Department of Labor, Bureau of Labor Statistics, "Education Level of Labor Force Continues to Rise" (August 10, 1982). Unless otherwise noted, 1982 data are first-quarter figures.

128. *Perspectives on Working Women: A Databook*, p. 22 and "Education Level of Labor Force Continues to Rise," Table 4.

129. *Perspectives on Working Women: A Databook*, p. 23.

130. "Education Level of Labor Force Continues to Rise," Table 4. Among women whose husbands were not present, 60 percent were in the labor force in 1982.

131. See Ralph E. Smith, *Women in the Labor Force in 1990* (Washington, D.C.: The Urban Institute, 1979), pp. 51–55 for a discussion of several of these studies and the evidence for causal direction of attitudes on employment.

132. United States Department of Labor, Bureau of Labor Statistics, "Employment in Perspective: Working Women," (Fourth Quarter/Annual Summary, 1982), p. 1.

133. "Women-Led Families Rise," *The New York Times,* December 3, 1980, p. C-15; *Perspectives on Women: A Databook,* p. 30; and "Education Level of Labor Force Continues to Rise," p. 2 and Table 5.

134. *Perspectives on Women: A Databook,* p. 28, and "Education Level of Labor Force Continues to Rise," Table 4.

135. "Education of Labor Force Continues to Rise," Table 6 and *Perspectives on Working Women: A Databook,* p. 28.

136. Frank L. Mott and David Shapiro, "Pregnancy, Motherhood and Work Activity," in Mott, ed., *Women, Work and Family,* pp. 42–43.

137. Smith, *Women in the Labor Force in 1990,* chap. 2.

138. Agnes Farris, "Commuting," in Robert and Rhona Rapoport with Janice Bumstead, eds., *Working Couples* (New York: Harper/Colophon Books, 1978), pp. 100–107.

139. George Masnick and Mary Jo Bane et al., *The Nation's Families: 1960–1990* (Cambridge, Mass.: Joint Center for Urban Studies of MIT and Harvard University, 1980), p. 84.

140. Ibid., pp. 84–85.

141. *Perspectives on Working Women: A Databook,* p. 25.

142. Ibid., pp. 28–29.

143. Ibid., p. 25.

144. Ibid., p. 20.

145. "U.S. Birth Rate Is Off Sharply, Census Shows," *Buffalo Evening News,* February 8, 1981, p. A–5. See also, Karl E. Taeuber and James A. Sweet, "Family and Work: The Social Life Cycle of Women," in Juanita M. Kreps, ed., *Women and the American Economy: A Look to the 1980s* (Englewood Cliffs, N.J.: Prentice-Hall, 1976), pp. 31–60.

146. Carolyn Shaw Bell in "Working Wives and Family Income," in Chapman, ed., *Economic Independence for Women,* pp. 239–261 estimates that a working wife contributes a third or more of her family's income in 44 percent of all such families. See also, discussion in Chapters 7 and 8.

147. *National Survey of Working Women: Perceptions, Problems and Prospects.* Survey conducted by the National Commission on Working Women. (Washington, D.C.: Center for Women and Work, 1979), p. 4.

148. Mason et al., "Change in U.S. Women's Sex-Role Attitudes," p. 586.

149. Mary Corcoran, "The Structure of Female Wages," *The American Economic Review,* Proceedings of the 90th Annual Meeting of the AERA, New York (December 1977):165–167 and Beth Niemi, "Geographic Immobility and Labor Force Mobility: A Study of Female Unemployment," in Cynthia B. Lloyd, ed., *Sex Discrimination and the Division of Labor* (New York: Columbia University Press, 1975), p. 74.

150. Lester C. Thurow, "Why Women Are Paid Less Than Men," *The New York Times,* March 8, 1981, p. 3.

151. Mary Corcoran and Greg Duncan, "Work History, Labor Force Attachment and Earning Differences Between the Sexes, *The Journal of Human Resources* 14 (Winter 1979):10.

152. Eileen Appelbaum, *Back to Work: Determinants of Women's Successful Re-entry* (Boston: Auburn House Publishing Co., 1981), chaps. 3 and 6.

153. United States Department of Labor, Bureau of Labor Statistics, "Employment in Perspective: Working Women," (Second Quarter, 1982), p. 1.

154. Weekly rates are from Ibid., Table 1; the year-round figures are from "Education Level of Labor Force Continues to Rise," Table 3.

155. Diane Pearce and Harriette McAdoo, *Women and Children: Alone and in Poverty* (Washington, D.C.: National Advisory Council on Economic Opportunity, 1981), p. 2. Reprinted by the Women's Research and Education Institute.

156. Interview with Dorothy Riding and Tish Sommers, C.B.S. Morning News (August 11, 1982).

157. For a discussion of the problems faced by older women, see The Women's Studies Program and Policy Center at George Washington University in conjunction with The Women's Research and Education Institute of the Congresswomen's Caucus, *Older Women: The Economics of Aging* (Washington, D.C., October, 1980).

158. Sara E. Rix and Anne J. Stone, *Impact on Women of the Administration's Proposed Budget* (Washington, D.C.: The Women's Research and Education Institute, 1982).

159. Nancy S. Barrett, "Women in the Job Market: Unemployment and Work Schedules," in Ralph E. Smith, ed., *The Subtle Revolution: Women at Work* (Washington, D.C.: The Urban Institute, 1979), p. 46; Ruth G. Blumrosen, "Wage Discrimination, Job Segregation and Women Workers," *Women Rights Law Reporter* 6 (Fall/Winter 1979–80):19; Blau and Jusenius, "Economists' Approaches to Sex Segregation in the Labor Market," in Blaxall and Reagan, eds., *Women and the Workplace*, pp. 183–185; and Blaxall and Reagan, *Women in the Workplace* (entire book).

160. Blau, *Equal Pay in the Office*, chaps. 3–5.

161. Ibid., p. 1.

162. Rosabeth Moss Kanter, *Men and Women of the Corporation* (New York: Basic Books, 1977) and Joan Acker, "Issues in the Sociological Study of Women's Work," in Stromberg and Harkess, eds., *Women Working*, pp. 149–151.

163. Patricia Gurin, "The Role of Worker Expectations in the Study of Employment Discrimination," in Wallace and LaMond, eds., *Women, Minorities and Employment Discrimination*, pp. 22–23 and Acker, "Issues," in Stromberg and Harkess, eds., *Women Working*, pp. 150–151.

164. Heidi Hartmann, "Capitalism, Patriarchy, and Job Segregation by Sex," in Blaxall and Reagan, eds., *Women and the Workplace*, pp. 137–169. The whole section in Blaxall and Regan on the historical roots of occupational segregation, pp. 87–179, are recommended.

165. William H. Chafe, "Looking Backward in Order to Look Forward: Women, Work, and Social Values in America," in Kreps, ed., *Women and the American Economy*, pp. 12–14.

166. Nancy D. Perlman and Bruce J. Ennis, *Preliminary Memorandum on Pay Equity: Achieving Equal Pay for Work of Comparable Value* (Albany, N.Y.: Center for Women in Government, April 1980), p. 13.

167. Ibid., pp. 21–25.

168. Pat Swift, "Reagan May Deal Setback to Women, Minorities," *Buffalo Evening News*, February 12, 1981, p. II-20.

169. Appelbaum, *Back to Work*, pp. 118–125 argues that the automation of clerical jobs will reduce jobs in this sector by 20 to 30 percent and that any new jobs to run these computers may well become male positions. Only the poor economy and, we might add, the rise of the single-parent family suggest the rate of employment for

women will remain high in the decades ahead.

170.   Michael J. Carter and Susan Boslego Carter, "Women's Recent Progress in the Professions or, Women Get a Ticket to Ride After the Gravy Train Has Left the Station," *Feminist Studies* 7 (Fall, 1981):475–480.

171.   Ibid., pp. 480–486.

172.   Ibid., pp. 488 and 491.

173.   Ibid., pp. 488–489 and 491–492.

174.   Erskine, "The Polls," p. 285.

175.   *The 1980 Virginia Slims American Women's Opinion Poll*, p. 11. *The 1972 Virginia Slims American Women's Opinion Poll*, pp. 5–6, reported that 50% of the women and 36% of the men, respectively, thought women were discriminated against in getting jobs in professions.

176.   Data from the 1976 American National Election Study. Figures compiled by the authors.

177.   Erskine, "The Polls," p. 286.

178.   Mason et al., "Change in U.S. Women's Sex-Role Attitudes," p. 586.

179.   *The 1980 Virginia Slims American Women's Opinion Poll*, p. 6.

180.   Gallup Opinion Poll, pp. 693–696. Overall, 45 percent of the women sampled thought a "great deal" of the improvement in women's status in the last five years was due to the efforts of women's organizations. An additional 39 percent felt a "fair amount" was attributable to such organizations.

181.   The following question was asked in the 1976 American National Election Study, "Which of these statements do you agree with?"

"The best way to handle problems of discrimination is for each woman to make sure she gets the best training possible for what she wants to do," OR "Only if women organize and work together can anything really be done about discrimination." Only 22 percent of the women questioned chose the second alternative. The question on the other strategy regarding "being feminine" was phrased, "Which of these statements do you agree with?" "Women can best overcome discrimination by pursuing their individual career goals in as feminine a way as possible," OR "It is not enough for a woman to be successful herself; women must work together to change law and customs that are unfair to all women." Overall, 53 percent of all women chose the second alternative.

182.   Barron and Yankelovich, "Today's American Woman," p. 73.

183.   Ibid., p. 74.

184.   Ibid.

185.   In Sweden, for example, the government provides daycare for all children. It also will pay up to 90 percent of either parent's salary for one year after the birth of a child so that one parent can stay home to care for the newborn. For an excellent review of different national policies on daycare and other parental policies, see Carolyn Teich Adams and Kathryn Teich Winston, *Mothers at Work: Public Policies in the United States, Sweden and China* (New York: Longman, 1980).

186.   The tax code provides for a tax credit for childcare dependent on family income. Those earning $10,000 or less can get a credit of up to $1,400 for two or more children. The credit then declines as family income increases. Thus, the maximum credit for families earning $28,000 a year with two children is $980.

187.   United States Department of Labor, Bureau of Labor Statistics, "Earnings of Workers and Their Families" (Third Quarter 1982, November 1982), Tables 4 and 6.

188.   Jill Norgen, "In Search of a National Child Care Policy: Background and Prospects," *The Western Political Quarterly* 34 (1981):127–142.

189.   Ibid and U.S. Civil Rights Commission, *Child Care and Equal Opportunity for Women* (Washington, D.C.: Government Printing Office, 1981), pp. 16–36 and 40–42.

190.   For an excellent summary of this problem, see Mary Jo Bane et al., "Childcare Arrangements for Working Parents," *Monthly Labor Review* 102 (October 1979):50–55.

191.   Ibid., p. 51.

192.   Ibid., noting Joseph Pleck and Michael Rustad, "Works Impact on the Family Study: Preliminary Results on Two-Earner Couples, Joint Distribution of Job Schedules," unpublished ms. 1979.

193.   Results of a 1978 *Family Circle* survey of 10,000 working women reported in "The Superwoman Squeeze," p. 73.

194.   Elizabeth Waldman et al., "Working Mothers in the 1980's: A look at the statistics," distributed by the United States Department of Labor, 1980.

195.   "Superwoman Squeeze," p. 72.

196.   Ibid., p. 73. See also, U.S. Civil Rights Commission, *Child Care and Equal Opportunity for Women.*

197.   *De la Cruz,* v. *Tormey,* 522 F.2d 45 (9th Cir. 1978), cert. denied, 99 S.Ct. 2416 (1979).

198.   See "Women in Labor Organizations: Their Ranks Are Increasing," *Monthly Labor Review* 101 (August 1978):8–14.

199.   "Superwoman Squeeze," p. 79.

200.   *U.S. Congressional Record,* September 9, 1971, S. 14010.

201.   See Nadine Brozan, "White House Conference on the Family: A Schism Develops," *The New York Times,* Jan. 7, 1980, p. D–8.

202.   *The 1980 Virginia Slims American Women's Opinion Poll,* p. 13.

203.   Barrett, "Women in the Job Market," in Smith, ed., *The Subtle Revolution,* p. 89.

204.   Federal Employees Flexible and Compressed Work Schedules Act of 1978.

205.   Barrett, "Women in the Job Market," in Smith, ed., *The Subtle Revolution,* p. 90.

206.   This will be a difficult stereotype to overcome. For example, some law firms are now creating permanent associates positions for persons who choose not to work the long hours required before one becomes a partner; however, some fear that those who take these positions will be regarded as second-class attorneys. The same problem often holds true in academia. A large proportion of those in part-time teaching positions are females. Traditionally these positions are low-paid and carry no benefits and no possibility of tenure.

207.   In March, 1976, 35 percent of married women with children under the age of six worked on a part-time basis. According to Barrett, "nearly half of all women" who worked part time gave "taking care of the home" as the reason for not working full time. "Women in the Job Market," in Smith, ed., *The Subtle Revolution,* p. 83.

208.   United States Department of Labor, Bureau of Labor Statistics, "One in Five Persons in Labor Force Experienced Some Unemployment in 1981," (July 20, 1982), Table 3.

209.   William Arkin and Lynne R. Dobrofsky, "Job Sharing," in Rapoport and Rapoport, eds., *Working Couples,* pp. 122–137.

210.   For an excellent account of the inequities in the tax system and recent changes, see James A. Duran and Elizabeth C. Duran, "The Marriage Tax," *Social Policy* 11 (March–April 1981):21–24.

PART THREE

Family and Lifestyle Rights

The changes sought by the three women's movements under the general classifications of sexual, marital, and reproductive rights are the most controversial of all the issue areas discussed thus far. More than political or employment rights, the changes sought under these classifications are most likely to be perceived as public bads by the greatest number of people.

We have placed the discussion of these issues near the end of this book because efforts to change traditional practices in this arena often had to be postponed until greater political and economic rights were obtained.[1] Without political rights, women had little chance of gaining or maintaining economic and social rights. Without economic opportunities to earn a living wage outside the home, few women had any options in life other than to marry and to remain at home under the "protection" of their husbands. This was especially true when women had little or no control over reproduction. Without the ability to limit the number or timing of the arrival of children, women were made even more dependent on men for their livelihood and that of their children. And, a woman's options to living in a patriarchal family were further limited with the arrival of children.

Given the lack of political and economic rights, it is not surprising that women were reluctant to challenge the institution of marriage and/or make demands for any significant change in its structure. Without any alternative life-style options, loss or even threatened loss of this institution was a public bad that would have plunged almost all women into the depths of poverty and to the bottom of the political underclass. As a result, early efforts in this arena often were limited to attempts to gain for women control over reproduction—a prerequisite to any other changes in family structure.

In a very important way, therefore, the achievement, if only partial, of political and economic rights has made *possible* attempts to reform the traditionally male-dominated institution of marriage. Not surprisingly, this battle in the mid-twentieth century has again involved the issue of a woman's right to control reproduction.

As should be clear from earlier discussions, economic opportunities and political power of women still are not equal to those of men, and in fact, many women remain dependent on the marital institution. Thus, real or imagined threats to this institution can be very disturbing and without an economic backup, many more women would slip below the poverty level.

To this perceived threat to the family, an additional complication—sexuality—can be added. Sexual identity has been intimately linked to gender, and one's gender and associated roles, in turn, have been intimately linked to roles within the traditional family. In turn, roles in the family have defined gender role behaviors.[2] Thus, challenges to the traditional family pose a serious threat to sexual identity. So, too, does talk of homosexuality, lesbian rights, and associated issues like test-tube babies that appear to alter society's understanding of human sexuality radically.

Thus, the changes proposed or those that have already occurred in those areas are grave public bads in the eyes of many. Given this, it is not surprising that a vocal, well-organized, well-financed, and in the early 1980s, politically powerful, anti movement has arisen to prevent these perceived public bads from being fully adopted. Moreover, this movement, threatened by changes in family and gender roles, appears to recognize the connection between economic and political power and change in the family. Thus, the "New Right's" plans include an effort to roll back rights in all three areas. The outcome of the struggle between these two social movements may hold the key to the future of the women's movement as further discussed in Chapters 7 and 8.

NOTES

1.   The ideas of much of the following discussion draw heavily on Barbara Easton, "Feminism and the Contemporary Family," in Nancy F. Cott and Elizabeth H. Pleck, eds., *A Heritage of Our Own: Toward a New Social History of Women* (New York: Simon and Schuster/Touchstone Books, 1979), pp. 555–577. We do not touch on Easton's discussion of the need for love in this section, but see Chapter 8. See also, Betty Friedan, *The Second Stage* (New York: Summit Books, 1981), pp. 83–123.

2.   For an excellent discussion of these issues as they relate to the rise of the New Right, see Rosalind Pollack Petchesky, "Antiabortion, Antifeminism, and the Rise of the New Right," *Feminist Studies* 7 (Summer 1981): 206–246. See also Betty Friedan, *The Second Stage,* pps. 86–87. Her discussion of the "personhood of women" seems to accept, at least somewhat, the link between motherhood and one's being a woman. According to Friedan, "To deny the part of one's being as woman that has, through the ages, been expressed in motherhood—nurturing, loving softness, and tiger strength— is to deny part of one's personhood as woman." Ibid., p. 86.

7 The Struggle for Rights in the Family

INTRODUCTION

According to Carl N. Degler, the period around 1830 signaled the development of what he terms the "modern family."[1] This social change in the institution of marriage was characterized by:

1. marriages based on mutual affection and not parental arrangement;
2. "separate spheres" for the sexes in which "a woman's life was physically spent in the home and with the family, while the man's life was largely outside the home, at work"[2];
3. a focus on the importance of childrearing; and,
4. smaller families.[3]

In the "modern family," a woman's place was indisputably in the home. As the keeper of her family, a wife was regarded as the moral superior of her husband,[4] although this "superiority" did not necessarily carry over into their interpersonal relations or into laws concerning a woman's place in the family. Relegation of women to the home also put married women in a position of near-complete economic dependency on their husbands, which was further exacerbated by laws that treated women, at best, as no better than children.

In this chapter, we examine the laws and the social policies relating to marriage, the family, and reproduction, which have affected the "modern family." Our focus will be on the efforts of the various women's movements to seek changes in each of these areas. Many of the alterations sought by the three women's movements involve changes in the power relationship of marriage and women's role within that institution and in the case of reproductive freedom, women's role within society at large. Given the nature of these changes—many of which are pure public goods that would directly or indirectly affect all—the movements' attempts to produce life-style changes have resulted in vocal opposition, and, in the case of the current women's movement, a strong countermovement.

THE WOMAN'S RIGHTS MOVEMENT

The Pre-Civil War Period

During the Seneca Falls convention in 1848, several charges were levied against the laws and practices that subjugated women to male superiority in family matters. Included in the Declaration of Sentiments were accusations that men had:

> made [her], if married, in the eye of the law, civilly dead.
> taken from her all right in property, even to the wages she earns.
> ...compelled [her] to promise obedience to her husband, he becoming, to all intents and purposes, her master—the law giving him power to deprive her of her liberty, and to administer chastisement.
> framed the laws of divorce, as to what shall be the proper causes, and ...to whom the guardianship of the children shall be given...in all cases, going upon a false supposition of the supremacy of man, and giving all power into his hand.
> created a different code of morals for men and women.[5]

After enumerating these inequities, those in attendance voted on a series of resolutions in which they vowed to work for an end to most of these discriminatory practices.

Historically, many of the problems attacked above stemmed from women's legal inferiority within the marital relationship that could be traced to the English common law, which was later adopted by the colonists. Under common law, the existence of a legal doctrine, coverture, meant that upon marriage women lost all legal capacity. A married women ceased to be a person in the eyes of the law because her legal identity merged with that of her husband. An expert commentator on the common law described the system as follows:

> By marriage, the husband and wife are one person in law; that, the very being or legal existence of the woman is suspended during the marriage, or at least is incorporated or consolidated.[6]

Thus, coverture, which was based in part on biblical teachings,[7] had far-ranging legal and social consequences. Under the doctrine, married women had no right to contract, be sued in their own names, or to own property.[8] But perhaps the greatest effect of coverture was in the simple issue of control: as it evolved, coverture produced and legitimized almost total male domination over women. A married woman lost claim to her name, her assets, and even her children. A man as the sole legal guardian of his offspring, could, by will, transfer their custody to someone other than his wife.

In exchange for this loss of her rights, a married woman was guaranteed the support of her husand and "dower rights," a one-third share of her husband's estate, *if* he died intestate (without a will). However, the support requirement was basically unenforceable because no one could/would tell a man how to provide for his wife.[9] This of course is not to say that men regularly failed to support their wives. However, when they did not, or died and left a will bequeathing no assets to their wives, these women had no legally enforceable way to gain economic assistance for themselves or their families.

Therefore, just prior to the Seneca Falls convention, many women had lobbied the New York state legislature for the enactment of reforms for some of these laws.[10] Their efforts ultimately led to the passage of the Married Woman's Property Act of 1848. This law gave women the right to control property they acquired by "inheritance, gift, bequest or devise," although they continued to be denied control over their wages and earnings, custody of their children, and the right to divorce drunken or abusive husbands.[11]

Encouraged by the passage of the 1848 law and the apparent widespread support among women for other reforms, as evidenced by the large turnout at Seneca Falls, women continued to press for additional statutory changes. In the many woman's rights conventions that were regularly held throughout New York and adjoining states, Elizabeth Cady Stanton and other leaders continued to call for marriage reform. In 1853 and 1854, woman's rights advocates carried out extensive statewide petition drives to persuade the New York legislature to enact liberalized child custody and property control reforms.[12] On February 20, 1854, the petitions signed by 5,931 men and women were presented to members of the New York State Assembly.[13] This activity, one orchestrated by Susan B. Anthony and borrowed from the abolitionists, led the Select Committee to consider the women's request but no legislation was enacted.[14]

The effort to enact reform legislation persisted under Anthony's careful leadership. A series of conventions were held across the state and petitions sent to legislators at the beginning of each subsequent session. This work eventually paid off: in 1860, a law guaranteeing civil rights for married women was enacted in New York. It gave women control of their inheritances and wages and allowed them to make contracts and sue in their own names. And for the first time, women were given joint custody of their children, and a widow was permitted to inherit at least a third of her husband's estate, regardless of whether he left a will to the contrary.[15]

While these efforts for expanded rights for married women were being made, calls also were raised for basic changes in the institution of marriage, especially the reform of divorce laws. As early as 1852, Elizabeth Cady Stanton, as President of the New York Women's Temperance Society, shocked many of its members when during its convention she urged from the podium:

> Let no woman remain in the relation of wife with a confirmed drunkard. Let no drunkard be the father of her child.... Let us petition our State government so to modify the laws affecting marriage and the custody of children that the drunkard shall have no claim on his wife or child.[16]

The "radical" nature of Stanton's demand—only one state at the time allowed a woman to divorce her husband on grounds of drunkenness—led supporters of temperance to distance themselves from Stanton's demands. It appears that even temperance supporters did not want to complicate the drinking issue with a more controversial one—divorce—although it was clear that many unhappy marriages were the result of drinking problems. A drunken husband could spend all of his wages, sell his and/or his wife's property, or apprentice his children to work for others, all without consulting his wife. Even so, many temperance workers feared that their goals would be harder to achieve if they were allied with calls for other kinds of reform.

The disfavor of temperance advocates, however, did not deter Stanton's advocacy of liberalized divorce laws. In 1853 she wrote to Anthony, "It is in vain to look for the elevation of women so long as she is degraded in marriage."[17] Stanton, Anthony, and several of the other later leaders of the National Woman Suffrage Association (NWSA) believed that little change could come in women's status unless their position in marriage were improved. Holding to the view of female moral superiority, they believed that divorce reform was necessary to assure that marriage was kept to a high standard.[18] Even some conservative supporters of woman's rights believed that marriage laws were so central to women's lives that they had to be discussed. In 1859, Lucy Stone wrote to Stanton, "I wish you would call a convention to discuss divorce, marriage, infanticide, and their kindred subjects."[19]

Even though Stone and others like her recognized the problem, many believed it was far too controversial to mix with other reforms sought during this period. Consequently, when Stanton introduced a series of resolutions concerning these controversial subjects at the 1860 National Woman's Rights Convention, many in attendance were horrified.[20]

When others challenged the propriety of a discussion of divorce noting that "the laws bore equally" on the sexes and that women had "no special ground for complaint,"[21] Anthony emotionally closed the heated debate that arose, noting:

> Marriage has ever been a one-sided matter, resting most unequally on the sexes. By it man gains all; woman loses all; tyrant law and lust reign supreme with him; meek submission and ready obedience alone befit her.[22]

Although the text of this debate was published, the resolutions were defeated.[23]

The uproar that arose at the convention and subsequently in the national and state presses surprised Stanton. In her autobiography she wrote, "So alarming were the comments on what had been said that I began to feel that I had inadvertently taken out the underpinning from the social system."[24]

Because divorce reform can be viewed as a public bad to many, this reaction of the general public is not surprising. Although laws such as the New York Married Women's Property Act gave women joint custody of their children, these laws were generally viewed as strengthening women's proper role—motherhood. By assuring that a woman be allowed to control her property to assure her children were fed or have joint guardianship of her children, legislators simply were expanding upon society's traditional views of women's sphere. Also, on a more practical level, some legislators felt that their daughters needed protection from wandering or shiftless husbands, who under the system of coverture, could dispose of all assets that a woman received from her family.[25] Divorce, however, was viewed by many as a public bad, which would result in radical, far-ranging changes in the social order. It was characterized by opponents as potentially destructive of the family, and thus became far more controversial.

While the issue of altering divorce laws may have been radical, at least some women spoke out in favor of reform.[26] This was not the case with the issue of birth control. In 1856, Lucy Stone aptly captured woman's rights advocates' consensus about birth control. In writing about her concern for "moral reform" in marriage, she noted, "It is very little to me to have the right to vote, to own property, etc., if I may not keep my body and its uses my absolute right. But, we are not ready for that question."[27] Similar sentiments were expressed by Stanton earlier in 1853 in a letter written to Anthony:

> The right idea of marriage is at the foundation of all reforms. ... A child conceived in the midst of hate, sin, discord, nurtured on abuse and injustice cannot too much bless the world or himself. Man in his lust has relegated long enough the whole question of sexual intercourse. Now let the mother of mankind, whose prerogative it is to set the bounds to his indulgence, rouse up and give this matter fearless thorough examination.[28]

While it is clear that Stanton was very concerned with limiting childbirth, even she did not generally speak out publicly concerning birth control.

One controversial issue that Stanton involved herself in, however, concerned dress. In the early 1850s, many women active in the fledgling woman's movement adopted a new kind of wearing apparel—a loose tunic-type knee-length dress worn over "pantelettes."[29] In many respects, the clothing worn by most women during this period exemplified the constraints placed on them by society. From the early 1800s to around 1890, women wore corsets "made of silk or cotton and ribbed with several dozen whalebone or steel stays which were girded to the female body from the chest to the hips."[30] These corsets were laced very tightly, particularly during the era of the "hourglass figure" and often made breathing difficult. A metal or loose hoop skirt, measuring four or five feet in diameter then was worn over the corset. Both of these articles of clothing severely restricted movement.

Firmly believing that changing a woman's apparel was closely related to changing her way of life, Anthony, Stanton, the Grimké sisters, Lucy Stone, and Amelia Bloomer, among others, adopted what came to be called the "Bloomer" costume. Women who wore bloomers immediately became the targets of public ridicule—they were denounced from the pulpit and ostracized in their communities. Even Stanton, who had adopted the costume for health reasons and convenience sake, abandoned it believing that other goals of the movement were too critical to sacrifice for comfort. Anthony and others, however, continued to eschew dresses for several years but were finally persuaded by Stanton to go back to more conventional garb. The adoption of unconventional dress early in the development of the movement added fuel to claims of woman's rights opponents who charged that these women were trying to undermine women's traditional role in the family. Newspaper comments similar to the one reprinted below were not uncommon:

> We saw, in broad daylight, in a public hall in the city of New York, a gathering of unsexed women—unsexed in mind all of them... publicly propounding the doctrine that they should be allowed to step out of their appropriate sphere, and mingle in the busy walks of every-day life, to the neglect of those duties which both human and divine law have assigned to them.
>
> They violate the rules of decency and taste by attiring themselves in eccentric habiliments, which hang loosely and inelegantly from their forms, making that which we have been educated to respect, to love, and to admire, only an object of aversion and distrust.[31]

Thus, by the 1860s, the woman's movement had attained some of its objectives including property law reforms and inheritance and child custody laws. Yet, the movement failed in other areas. For example, not only did it fail to obtain uniform divorce law and the acceptance of less-restrictive clothing but also its position on these issues created external and internal controversy.

The Civil War and Beyond

Between 1861 and 1865, agitation for woman's rights was virtually abandoned as supporters devoted their full energies to the war effort.[32] Nevertheless, woman's rights were not forgotten by its advocates. It was during the war that women came to see the tremendous importance of the vote, which ultimately led many advocates of woman's rights to shift their emphasis toward the more narrow goal of suffrage.[33] Stanton and Anthony were quick to recognize that certain legislative actions were largely attributable to the fact that women had abandoned their pressure activities on the legislators. For example, in 1862, the N.Y. State legislature amended or repealed many of the laws that women across the state had campaigned for long and hard. For instance, it amended an act that had given men and women joint guardianship of their children and replaced "it with a species of veto power," over the actions of their husbands.[34] The legislature also repealed laws that guaranteed widows control of their property and the care of their minor children.[35] Therefore, Stanton and Anthony came to realize how temporary legislative gains could be without the vote with which to threaten recalcitrant legislators. This factor, coupled with the demands being made for Negro suffrage served to focus attention on the ballot, thereby detracting from many of the other reforms proposed at Seneca Falls and later conventions. So marked was this change in emphasis, that "after the War feminist activists began to refer to themselves as the woman suffrage movement rather than the women's rights movement."[36] (We, however, will continue to use the term woman's rights movement to refer to the activities that took place circa 1848 to 1870.)

Although there was this change in short-term goals, some movement leaders, notably Stanton, continued to believe that familial rights were of far greater importance than suffrage.[37] *The Revolution,* for example, regularly published editorials concerning marriage and its impact on women's status. The excerpt below is illustrative of their theme:

> Woman's chief discontent is not with her political, but with her social, and particularly her marital bondage. The solemn and profound question of marriage ... is of more vital consequence to woman's welfare, reaches down to a deeper depth in woman's heart, and more thoroughly constitutes the core of the woman's movement, than any such superficial and fragmentary question as woman's suffrage.[38]

While NWSA leaders believed that family reforms were important, the major goal of their efforts toward the end of this period was for the ballot as detailed in Chapter 3.

After the war, however, some woman's rights supporters found themselves entangled in issues, not necessarily of their creation, that diverted their full attentions from suffrage. Involvement in these issues often also brought additional unneeded controversy to the movement. For example, in March 1867, even before NWSA was founded, the New York City Police Commissioner requested the city's medical examiner to devise a plan whereby all prostitutes would be periodically examined for evidence of venereal disease.[39] Anthony immediately organized a large number of women to fight this proposal. She acted because she believed that this kind of semiofficial sanction of prostitution would strengthen the double moral standard attacked in the Declaration of Sentiments and reinforce the notion that women were "chattel to be exploited by men's lust."[40]

Later, in 1872, members of both the AWSA and NWSA, led by Frances Willard and Dr. Elizabeth Blackwell, undertook a concerted lobbying effort against an American Medical Association plan, similar to the New York City proposal, which called for the periodic examination of prostitutes for venereal disease. Willard and Blackwell wrote articles in women's papers as well as medical journals urging the rejection of the proposal because legal sanction of prostitution would weaken the family.[41] The medical profession ultimately was forced to abandon this suggestion and accept what the women wanted— at least some semblance of one high moral standard for all.[42]

Prostitution, the double moral standard, and marriage were regularly discussed by only a small segment of those who supported woman's rights. That segment's associations with suffrage, however, led opponents regularly to link suffrage with far more radical calls for change. During a period in which a "refined" woman was forced to refer to chair legs as "stems,"[43] the mere mention of the marriage relationship or the double moral standard, let alone the call for reform, was highly controversial and regarded by most as beyond the bounds of propriety.

Thus, NWSA's formalized support of these controversial reforms coupled with Stanton's regular proclamations on these topics, led many woman suffrage advocates to affiliate with the more conservative AWSA. Lucy Stone, for example, firmly believed that Stanton's and Anthony's demands were ideas whose time had not yet come and to press for them then was only foolhardy. Stone did not necessarily disagree with their ideas; she simply believed that the public was unwilling to accept them in that era. Her own life-style bears witness to the fact that she was not a traditionalist. When she married Elizabeth Blackwell's brother in 1855, she insisted on retaining her maiden name as a protest against what she and her husband viewed as restrictive and archaic marriage laws. She viewed her action, however, as a personal protest, and it is clear that she believed most marital reforms would have to be gained by individuals acting alone or not be secured until after woman suffrage. Because she believed that suffrage was attainable while the other reforms espoused by NWSA were not, Stone was instrumental in the creation of AWSA as an alternative. In fact, it was specifically founded to "avoid all side issues and devote itself to the main issue of suffrage."[44] This philosophy attracted a large number of members to AWSA and some state groups formerly affiliated with the NWSA switched their allegiance to the newer organization.[45]

Her distress and that of other AWSA members over NWSA goals and tactics became even more acute in 1871 when Stanton and Anthony invited Victoria Woodhull to speak at a NWSA meeting. The press attention given to Woodhull's address and her vocal advocacy of free love, which she defined as "an inalienable, constitutional, and natural right to love whom I may, to love as long or as short of a period as I can, to change that love everyday if I please,"[46] almost overnight bound together the issues of suffrage and free love.

Although neither Stone nor Anthony favored free love, some NWSA members stated their support of the concept publicly. That, plus the association's welcoming of Woodhull, when added to its other demands for change, had a profoundly negative impact on its image and, correspondingly, its success, as discussed in Chapter 3. Public furor over the perceived scope of change advocated by some supporters of woman's rights was so great that AWSA felt the need to publicly disassociate itself from the idea of free love and announce its denunciation of its potential ramifications.

According to historian William C. O'Neill, "The Woodhull affair... despite its grotesque and accidental features, marked a decisive turning point in the history of American feminism."[47] It made suffrage a laughing matter and associated the movement with immorality and advocacy of the breakdown of the family. Even though this image was cast in the minds of many, only a small number of woman's rights advocates actually advocated free love.

Birth Control and Voluntary Motherhood. Public disfavor about these kinds of discussions including that of free love, and concern with a perceived general decline in morals ultimately led the U.S. Congress to pass the Comstock Act in 1873. This act prohibited the use of the U.S. mails for distribution of any "obscene" materials. It specifically labeled as obscene, "the dissemination of any pornography, abortion devices and any drug, medicine, article or thing designed adapted or intended for preventing conception."[48] It also "branded as smut" and therefore "obscene" many essays that urged abstinence as a method of family planning.[49]

Prior to passage of the Comstock Act, and as early as the 1830s, a number of handbooks and guides written by physicians were published that contained instructions or urgings concerning family planning. While many authors advocated abstinence but often misjudged the safe period, thus revealing a very real misunderstanding of the menstrual cycle, others advocated douches, condoms, or more unusual methods including "intercourse on an inclined plane so as to avoid dislodging the egg from the ovary," or dancing or horseback riding over a rough road after intercourse.[50] Showing this lack of knowledge concerning the menstrual cycle, one author advised, "If intercourse is abstained from until ten or twelve days after cessation of the menstrual flow, pregnancy will not occur." Another advised women to wait eight days from cessation of their periods.

Proponents of the act, including Anthony Comstock, believed that this kind of information could only lead to moral decay and abortion.[51] He was particularly enraged by the ideas advocated by Woodhull and her sister, Tennessee Clafin, in their weekly newspaper. In it, ideas and/or information that Comstock viewed as obscene regularly appeared.[52] It is interesting to note that Comstock, a moral reformer, was joined by both free lovers and woman's rights advocates in his distaste for birth control. Even Clafin wrote, "The means [women] resort to for... prevention is sufficient to disgust every natural man."[53]

While moral reformers and most woman's rights advocates did not necessarily agree with Clafin's rationale for her opposition to artificial birth control, many of them were in accord with the concept of "Voluntary Motherhood," a woman's right to limit her family size by natural means.[54] They and free lovers believed that contraceptive devices were "a standing reproach upon, and a permanent indictment against, American women."[55] Distaste for artificial birth control, "the washes, teas, tonics and various sorts of appliances known to the initiated,"[56] stemmed from two sources. In keeping with the notion of "romantic love" that pervaded this era, women believed use of contraceptive devices destroyed the love act. But perhaps more important, they feared an increase in marital infidelity.[57] In this era when a woman's identity, livelihood, and status depended on a stable marriage, threats to that institution were perceived as public bads to be avoided at all cost. This is not to say, however, that these women wished to have children every year. Stanton, who herself had eight chidren and did not become active in the woman's movement until many of them were grown, believed that before women could gain full equality, they had to have control over their bodies. A staunch supporter of voluntary motherhood, Stanton frequently addressed "women only" audiences during the suffrage campaign. At those meetings she regularly talked about the need for women to limit the size of their families, in order to improve their overall status.[58]

While the claims for voluntary motherhood by Stanton, woman's rights advocates, and moral reformers were made to protect the family, their association with others brought condemnation from the press and the pulpit. The controversial changes sought by Stanton and some of her followers, while they presented good copy for news editors, were never supported by enough women actually to be considered a public good. Thus it was difficult for the NWSA branch of the woman's rights movement to secure change. In fact, although women were able to secure positive changes in property rights and divorce reform laws before and during the Civil War, afterwards little progress was made in these areas.

THE SUFFRAGE MOVEMENT

While most women in the suffrage movement eventually came to view divorce reform, at least in personal terms, as strengthening the family because divorce laws generally held men to a single moral standard, they did not take a public stand on the issue.[59] Calls for reform by some socialist or radical feminists, including Charlotte Perkins Gilman[60]—many of whom were attacked in the press for their own divorces—occurred during this period.[61] The advocates of divorce reform generally were associated with the several, smaller radical movements that developed during the suffrage era.

For example, although followers of the Women's Peace Movement,[62] the birth control movement, and the isolated "radical feminist" movement[63] often worked for suffrage, they generally were more concerned with familial change. And, in spite of their small size, the birth control and radical feminist movements in particular were responsible for most of the changes in or advocacy of familial change that occurred in this era. One of the most important and influential of these advocates of change was Gilman.

From 1895 to World War I, the philosophies of Gilman, a radical feminist, were the most widely reported of the feminists. In *Women and Economics,* published in 1898, she urged radical changes in the family and childcare so that women would not have to take a secondary place in the economic sphere, which she believed was at the heart of women's inequality.[64] Her calls for professional daycare and communal living arrangements with central kitchens[65] were taken by critics of the vote as the logical consequences of women suffrage. The changes proposed by Gilman as well as those of Emma Goldman, a proponent of free love and radical socialism,[66] and Margaret Sanger, the leading advocate of birth control in the United States, were not favored by others in the suffrage movement. Indeed, they were viewed by most as public bads and thus faced tremendous opposition.

Birth Control in the Suffrage Era

An exceptionally controversial issue during the suffrage movement era was birth control. Margaret Sanger first advocated that birth control clinics be set up and contraceptive devices dispensed by nonphysicians. As noted earlier, the Comstock Act was passed in 1873 with the blessing of woman's rights supporters. While it barred dissemination of birth control information through the mails, many educated, middle-class women used artificial forms of contraception by the 1900s. The idea of birth control, however, was embarrassing to many, and it was not a widely discussed topic among most women or women's groups.[67] Beginning around 1900, however, Emma Goldman began to call for birth control. Having worked as a nurse in New York slums, she believed that for many, the only way out of poverty was family planning. It was not, however, until Margaret Sanger took up the issue that birth control began to receive extensive publicity.

Like Goldman, Sanger was a nurse with strong ties to the socialist movement. She was appalled at the heartache and death faced by many poor women who found themselves pregnant every year, and she resolved to find some safe method of contraception to remedy their problem. Consequently, she spent over a year searching for this information in American medical libraries.[68] When it became clear that this information was unavailable in the United States, at Goldman's urging Sanger traveled to Europe to learn more about the contraceptive devices available there.

On her return, she began publication of *The Woman Rebel,* a feminist paper. In it she explained the kinds of contraceptive devices available, called on women to limit the size of their families, and urged them to revolt against patriarchal society.[69] Checking for dissemination of birth control information, enforcers of the Comstock Act read the pages of *The Rebel* carefully, and eventually, Sanger was indicted for violating the act.[70] Sanger, however, did not give up her crusade for birth control. In fact, before fleeing to Europe in 1914 to avoid a possible 45 year prison sentence, Sanger prepared a pamphlet containing detailed contraceptive information, which her friends later surreptitiously released after her departure.[71] In her absence, a group of women, headed by Mary Ware Dennett, a past executive secretary of NAWSA, founded the National Birth Control League (NBCL), a call for whose creation had first appeared in *The Woman Rebel.*

When Sanger returned from Europe, she and Dennett clashed over goals as well as over who would lead the NBCL. They also sharply disagreed on strategy. Dennett believed in total repeal of laws like the Comstock Act; Sanger, doing an about-face, abandoned her previously held more radical views.[72] She now believed that to be successful, the issue of birth control had to be isolated from more controversial socialist ideas.[73] Consequently, she adopted a conservative strategy, seeking only a change in anticontraceptive laws to allow physicians to fit birth control devices. This more reactionary tactic made her goals more acceptable to physicians, a powerful political group, and to many suffragists who distrusted Dennett, who by then was the field secretary of the American Union Against Militarism and supporter of the peace movement.[74]

The arguments Sanger consequently put forth in support of birth control closely paralleled those made earlier by suffragists during their educated suffrage phase. When a new organization, the American Birth Control League (ABCL) was founded by Sanger in 1921 out of her dissatisfaction with Dennett, birth control was offered as a social reform, not a woman's issue. Appealing to racists and nativists, the preamble to the Principles of the ABCL read:

> Everywhere we see poverty and large families going hand in hand. Those least fit to carry on the race are increasing most rapidly. People who cannot support their own offspring are encouraged by Church and State to produce large families.

In addition to this great evil we witness the appalling waste of women's health and women's lives by too frequent pregnancies.[75]

Although the ABCL was far more acceptable to most than the NBCL, Sanger still faced an uphill battle because birth control was an issue far more controversial than suffrage. Even after ratification of the Nineteenth Amendment, Sanger was unable to attract the support of many women's organizations to her largely separate movement.[76]

Hostility to Sanger and birth control was evidenced by the General Federation of Women's Clubs' refusal even to discuss a birth control resolution at its national meeting. A similar action also was taken by the League of Women Voters. In fact, the only women's organization to go on record publicly in support of the ABCL's activities was the National Women's Trade Union League. At its 1922 meeting, it passed a resolution calling for an end to laws "that withhold contraceptive information from the women of the working classes, while it is in most cases readily available to the well to do."[77] Even the liberal National Woman's Party refused to adopt a resolution favoring birth control, fearing it would confuse public perceptions of its goal—an equal rights amendment—that had nothing to do with birth control. In fact, the NWP leaders took great pains to disassociate their goals with any ideas that could be considered to be antifamily.

The failure of many of the major women's groups to support the birth control movement is not surprising. It was vehemently objected to by many ministers and priests and even suffragists. In declining to be a sponsor of the ABCL, Carrie Chapman Catt, President of NAWSA, wrote to Sanger, "Your reform is too narrow to appeal to me and too sordid."[78] Even many socialists believed that an association with birth control made their economic radicalism less acceptable. In fact, many rejected birth control, and some even adopted the argument put forth in the woman's rights era, namely, that artifical contraception only reinforced the double moral standard.[79] Thus, declining support from conservative feminists and isolation from many radicals and socialists largely account for the relative lack of progress by the birth control movement during this period.

Educated Motherhood

While rejecting most of the reforms suggested by radical feminists like Gilman and Sanger, women in the suffrage and progressive movements worked for some changes that would benefit the position of women in their role as mothers. One of the first of these issues to which these women turned their attention was the seriously high infant and female childbirth mortality rates in the United States. In fact, after woman suffrage was won, one of the first issues that most suffragists turned their attention to was remedying that problem. Concern for the high number of birth-associated deaths was a natural response for the women who had sought the vote based on their claims as mothers. Stressing the idea of "educated motherhood,"[80] they called for federal legislation to give money to the states to set up clinics where expectant women and young mothers could be taught preventive health care.

As early as 1916 and 1917, the U.S. Children's Bureau conducted extensive studies of infant and childbirth mortality and found that death rates in the United States for these causes were among the highest in the western world. Bureau studies also revealed that 80 percent of the expectant women in the U.S. received no medical care or advice during their pregnancies.[81] This report prompted Rep. Jeanette Rankin (R-Montana), who had close ties to women in both the suffrage and progressive movements, to introduce a bill in 1919 calling for "federal grants to states willing to conduct health conferences, establish pre-natal care centers and otherwise extend maternal aid."[82] This legislation was clearly reflective of the philosophy of educated motherhood that had the support of most suffragists. Programs funded by the bill would teach women how to be better mothers as well as how to raise healthy children. Thus, in many ways, these proposals perpetuated the idea of woman's "separate sphere," by aiding her efforts to be a better mother.

Women's groups including the League of Women Voters immediately endorsed this proposal and were able to persuade the Democratic, Farm-Labor, Socialist, and Prohibition parties to include calls for federal dollars for a pre- and post-natal care program in their party platforms.[83] And, although the Republican party platform did not include support for this kind of legislation, Warren Harding, the Republican nominee for President, went on record in support of the then-pending bill.[84]

During 1920 and 1921, the Women's Joint Congressional Committee (WJCC) and each of its constituent organizations put their concerted efforts behind passage of the Sheppard-Towner Maternity Act, a bill that embodied many of the proposals behind the idea of "educated motherhood." Florence Kelley, Executive Secretary of NCL, headed the WJCC subcommittee especially created to push for passage of the bill. Under her leadership, most major women's groups urged their members to write to and visit their representatives in Congress. Thousands of letters were received and one senator's secretary remarked, "I think every women in my state has written to the Senator."[85]

Kelley, whose childhood life was overshadowed by her mother's grieving for five children she lost in childbirth, worked tirelessly for passage of the bill.[86] Believing that "of all the activities in which [she had] shared during more than forty years of striving, none was... of such fundamental importance as the Sheppard-Towner Maternity Act,"[87] she was thrilled when the nation's women's magazines took up the cause. A *Good Housekeeping* article entitled, "Herod is not Dead," which urged readers to work for passage of the law that could guarantee a lowered infant mortality rate, was typical of the many pieces written that year.[88]

Just as NWP clashed with the dominant women's rights groups of the suffrage era over strategy for the vote, they also strongly opposed the ideology behind the Sheppard-Towner Maternity Act.[89] While never challenging traditional marriage itself—in fact, the NWP was on record as "dedicated to finer homes and better marriages"[90]—it believed passage of this law would legally sanction the treatment of women as "mothers not persons." This, NWP leaders believed, would simply reinforce the entire notion of "separate spheres" as women would be singled out for special treatment solely on account of their reproductive capacity. This kind of treatment was at odds with the Party's support of an equal rights amendment.[91] However, neither equal rights for women nor the idea that women should be anything other than mothers first, was particularly popular in the 1920s. Thus, when those representing a majority of women asked, "Why does Congress wish women and children to die?"[92] the Sheppard-Towner Maternity Act (STMA) was finally enacted in 1921.

The Maternity Act called for money "to be paid to the several states for the purpose of cooperating with them in promoting the welfare and hygiene of maternity and infancy." Two sections of the act prohibited any state or federal official from entering "any home" over parental objection and also reassured opponents nothing in the law should "be construed as limiting the power of a parent." It specifically authorized appropriation of $1,480,000 for fiscal year 1921 and less each year for the next five years.

The WJCC was elated over this victory. Antisuffrage forces, however, saw passage of the act as an additional opportunity to stop the women's rights cause. In fact, according to Vose, "The Sheppard-Towner Maternity Act led quite directly to the [formation of] the Sentinels of the Republic," a group composed largely of persons who had been involved in the antisuffrage movement.[93] It believed that the STMA was an unwarranted invasion of the family by the federal government. To stop implementation of the act, it filed suit in federal court challenging the constitutionality of its provisions.[94]

Florence Kelley, using tactics that had served her well when she had directed much of NCL's maximum hour litigation, immediately contacted several state attorneys general to urge them to submit friend of the court briefs in support of the constitutionality of the law.[95] Several did and the Supreme Court ultimately dismissed the lawsuit holding that a federal taxpayer's interest in the monies spent by Congress was too remote to afford a plaintiff adequate standing to challenge the provision.[96] Thus, the Court disposed of the case without ever reaching the actual constitutionality of the issue.

Suffrage opponents were not the only forces to attack the STMA. Shortly after its passage, even some initial supporters of the act began to attack it. For example, the Daughters of the American Revolution (DAR) denounced it in 1927. In arguing against renewed funding for the STMA, which it labelled "a Bolshevik device to destroy the family,"[97] the DAR disassociated itself from WJCC and its legislative activities. This kind of charge was representative of the many attacks made against former suffragists involved in the peace movement. Kelley, the major organizer behind the Maternity Act, was regularly villified during this period for her membership in the Women's International League for Peace and Freedom. Her part in the act's passage thus made the real reasons for it suspect in the eyes of many. The kind of charges that were being leveled at the Maternity Act, WJCC, and its individual members caused the General Federation of Women's Clubs to withdraw from WJCC by 1928. WJCC was further crippled when the membership of the National League of Women Voters, one of its constituent associations, fell to less than 100,000 members.[98]

Given the declining membership of WJCC, regular attacks on the purposes of the Maternity Act, and recognition by politicians that women did not vote as a bloc, it is not surprising that funding for the act was not continued when it came up for a vote in Congress in 1928.[99]

Conclusion

The failure of women in the postsuffrage era to consolidate or expand the reforms they had obtained is traceable to several problems.

First, opponents of birth control and the Sheppard-Towner Maternity Act, relying on many Americans' belief in a growing Communist threat were able to link proponents with what they termed "Bolshevik" activities. They characterized both birth control and federal spending for maternal care as leading to a breakdown of the traditional family and charged that supporters of these reforms were part of a conspiracy to destroy America.[100] This was especially devastating in the birth control area because of Goldman's[101] and Sanger's early ties to socialism. Success was further made improbable at that time because of public perceptions of the suffrage movement and its peripheral groups. Moreover, birth control was linked by some to abortion, and its proponents as well as other reformists were characterized as socialists, communists, and even free-lovers, which militated against broad-based support.

Probably just as important to the failure to maintain gains as the controversies that arose over birth control, the Maternity Act, and the loyalty to the United States of some women who supported far-ranging reforms was the generally apathetic nature of women during this period. At first, the move away from many restrictions on women was characterized by the healthy and athletic "Gibson Girl" of the 1890s who "wore a tailored suit or dark shirt and a simple blouse or 'shirtwaist.'"[102] The young woman symbolized by the Gibson Girl was a reflection of the growing awareness of the restrictions dress placed on women and the ill health that often accompanied the restrictive clothing earlier attacked by Stanton, Anthony, and Bloomer. But, by the 1920s, even the "Gibson Girls" seemed old-fashioned as dress and other changes reached their zenith with the dawn of the "flapper" era. Flappers were said to lead wild lives, smoke, and wear short skirts.[103]

Flappers were revolutionary but not a part of the suffrage movement, although they often personified the kinds of changes that suffrage opponents feared. They were linked by women's magazines to obscene dancing, Bolshevism, birth control, loose morals, and indecent attire. As dress and notions about women's abilities and even sexuality began to change, it is clear that few young women sought or even supported the kinds of changes advocated by radicals or even reformers. Lillian Hellman, a playwright, who viewed this phenomenon firsthand, described the prevailing ethos:

> By the time I grew up the fight for emancipation of women, their rights under the law, in the office, in bed, was stale stuff. My generation didn't think much about the place or problems of women, were not conscious that the designs we saw around us had so recently been formed, or that were still part of that formation.[104]

These middle-class young women, with their own concerns, were not as interested as their older sisters and mothers in continued work for the reforms advocated by the progressives. And although it appears that some relied on the contraceptive devices popularized by Sanger, few took an active part in securing further rights. Must had what they had wanted, which ultimately led to an undersupply of the public goods attained by the reformers of this period.

Particularly after World War I, most Americans sought a return to tranquility. As progressivism and Americans' desire for reform declined, so too did radical women's chances for success. When conservatives linked reforms with a spreading Communist plot, it is easy to understand how legislative gains were lost. These reforms, particularly the STMA, were viewed as public goods by a declining number, while a vociferous minority began to characterize them as public bads.

THE CURRENT WOMEN'S MOVEMENT

Many of the reforms sought during the first woman's rights movement, as well as those pursued by radicals such as Gilman and Sanger during the suffrage movement, were adopted during the current women's rights movement. Reproductive freedom, characterized by Margaret Sanger's fight for birth control, was expanded to include abortion. Changes also were made in laws concerning women's status within the family, and further legislation is advocated by many women's rights groups as the agenda for change has expanded during this era.

Women from both branches of the movement have been active in the areas of family rights and reproductive freedom. In fact, those in the younger branch probably have done more to change the institution of marriage and the family than women in the older branch, which was not the case in the other issue areas discussed in Chapters 3 and 5. Another phenomenon that has occurred concerns the older branch's growing acceptance, and indeed advocacy of, changes first advocated by those in the younger branch. This has led to a movement fairly united in purpose although not necessarily in tactics as we describe below. However, because the combined forces of both branches of the movement had lobbied and continue to lobby for change in the family and reproductive freedom, a strong anti movement has arisen to fight for the status quo and against what its followers believe to be the pure public bads advocated by the women's movement.

The Younger Branch

As noted in Chapters 3 and 5, women in the younger branch of the movement have declined to play a significant role in the drive for greater political and economic rights. With the call "the personal is political," however, radical feminists have challenged all aspects of the sexual relationship between men and women. Identifying this relationship as one of the key manifestations of the unequal division of power between the sexes, women in the younger branch have targeted all of its facets—from marriage through male control of reproduction—for change.[105] These feminists have located the source of women's oppression in the sex role system and its related institutions. Although some of the early feminists—politicos—believed that liberation would come with the overthrow of the capitalist system, most quickly rejected this analysis as incomplete. Noting the persistence of sexual inequality even in socialist systems like the Soviet Union, they argued that one must go beyond the economic class system to understand and eventually to overcome women's inequality.

Early feminist writings including the *Redstockings' Manifesto* identified men as the source of oppression in the following terms:

> We identify the agents of our oppression as men. Male supremacy is the oldest, most basic form of domination. All other forms of exploitation and oppression (racism, capitalism, imperialism, etc.) are extensions of male supremacy: men dominate women, a few men dominate the rest. All power structures throughout history have been male-dominated and male-oriented. Men have controlled all political, economic and cultural institutions and backed up this control with physical force. They have used their power to keep women in an inferior position. *All men* receive economic, sexual, and psychological benefits from male supremacy. *All men* have oppressed women.[106]

The solution of the Redstockings, a New York based, militantly activist group, to this problem was to develop a female, class awareness among *all* women, regardless of their social class, race, or other characteristics. Once this was accomplished, they believed that women, as a class, would lead a revolution to overthrow male supremacy.[107]

Their primary technique to develop this kind of awareness, borrowed from civil rights and Chinese Communist movements, was consciousness-raising groups. In these, a small group of women—generally fewer than fifteen—gather together to focus on a given topic (their relationship with men, for example). Then, through discussions, they try to see how their individual and common experiences are the product of the same cultural system. The rise of such groups became one of the most important of the feminists' strategies for change and was later adopted by some organizations, most notably NOW, in the older branch.[108]

While the Redstockings' development of the consciousness-raising strategy was important, subsequent ideological developments in the younger branch tended to move away from the Redstockings' antimale focus to a broader analysis of the source of women's oppression. In 1970, Kate Millet identified the source as the patriarchal system more generally. She noted that it resulted in members of each sex being socialized into what society viewed as their appropriate roles—men the aggressor and oppressor, women the underling caste or class.[109] Other feminists also went beyond the position of identifying individual men as the enemy to the view that it was the sex role system more broadly that was the core of the problem. One group, The Feminists, for example, called for complete elimination of male and female roles.[110]

It was not only elimination of sex roles but also the end of institutions that perpetuated those roles—heterosexual relations, love, marriage, and the nuclear family—that were demanded by women in the younger branch. To replace these sex role based institutions, these women argued for new structures that would allow women and men to be equal and free of sex role stereotyping. Shulamith Firestone, for example, a leading New York City feminist and author of *The Dialectic of Sex,* painted a future of cybernetic socialism in which reproduction was to be done by artificial means, the nuclear family would be replaced by communelike "households," and both men and women would share parenting and other domestic roles, although most tasks would be performed by machines[111]—a future very similar to that earlier proposed by Gilman. Other feminists challenged what they termed the "myth of the Vaginal Orgasm,"[112] male control over reproduction, birth control, and women's health more generally.[113] Socialist feminists also included on their list of required changes the abolition of the present capitalist economic system to facilitate familial change.[114] Recently, violent, antifemale pornography also has come under attack by feminists.[115]

Before proceeding with a discussion of the strategies adopted by radical feminists to achieve their goals, we should note that in terms of the public goods notion introduced in Chapter 2, what these women were seeking were pure public bads in the eyes of the vast majority of the American public. If the changes being advocated were indeed adopted, all women and men would be forced to abandon their present life-styles. Some feminists perceived correctly, that to call for the end of such universally recognized "goods" as heterosexual sex, love, marriage, or the family would only alienate the vast majority of women and men and probably harm the cause more than help it. Indeed these women were at least partially right. Resistance to the "Women's Liberation Movement" has generally been directed to the fear that marriage, the family, etc. would be destroyed if the movement should succeed. However, organized opposition did not develop early on to these pronouncements because few people believed these radical goals were likely to be implemented. Thus, efforts to stop them were not deemed necessary.

Even women themselves in the younger branch realized a revolution destroying the sex role system and its supporting institutions was not around the corner. Consequently, the strategies they adopted were aimed more at preparing the groundwork for that day and solving the more immediate problems of individual women. Only a few groups demanded that their members start living the new life-style immediately.[116]

The main strategies to prepare for an eventual end to the sex role system were directed at awakening women with respect to their downtrodden position as a class and the need to take action to change the system. The most innovative method developed to accomplish this awakening, the consciousness-raising group, was a very successful technique in bringing home to individual women their common plight. One participant's reaction to the influences of these sessions was as follows:

> In consciousness raising I saw women who recognized there was no such thing as a personal way of solving their problems so long as male supremacy in all its formal and informal forms still existed. Here were women looking for solutions based on their collective experience.... They were talking about their personal experiences and analyzing them in terms of social structures rather than in terms of their own weaknesses.[117]

While the aim of the originators of this method was to prepare women to take action to rectify their common oppression, it soon became evident that as a prelude to action such groups were of only limited value. Only a few such small groups were able to transform themselves into action groups. Those that were successful, however, have become the model for local self-help centers.

Demonstrations were another strategy used by radicals to make women aware of their position. Generally, the protests were directed against specific events or things that embodied or represented women's inferior or menial roles. One early, well-publicized demonstration occurred at the 1968 Miss America Pageant. While the goal of this protest was to show all women and the public at large that beauty pageants harmed *all* women by treating them as sex objects, the negative coverage the radicals received in the press may have hurt the cause more than helped it. Judith Hole and Ellen Levine, however, attribute the formation of several women's groups around the country to the publicity women's issues received as a result of this event.[118] Similar demonstrations were held at bridal fairs in 1969 by WITCH—the Women's International Terrorist Conspiracy from Hell—and other women's groups. Additionally, "Whistle-ins," which exposed men to the same humiliation as women, and sit-ins, most notably one that was held at the *Ladies Home Journal* office, which resulted in a several page spread on women's concerns in a subsequent issue, also were standard methods of raising the consciousness of women both inside and outside of the movement.[119]

Other radical feminists organized "speak-outs"—public testimonies by women who had experienced particular problems—concerning the difficulty of obtaining an abortion, an experience of being raped and having to go through the legal system that "blamed the victim," prostitution, marriage, and motherhood.[120] In fact, many of the "speak-outs" on abortion were part of a systematic effort to influence state legislators to adopt legislation legalizing abortion.

One of the most controversial issues to be raised by the radical feminists was the topic of sexual preference. Many in the radical branch have argued that rejection of the sex role system requires rejection of relationships with men. Their argument that commitment to women required a commitment to choose women for sexual relations resulted in pressure on many women to adopt a lesbian way of life. While the split over the issue was often intense, eventually, both as a direct result of many radical feminists going into the older branch of the movement and the indirect result of the influence of feminist ideas on the older branch, even such reform groups as NOW have come out in favor of lesbian rights.[121] However, there was much original dissension over this that probably hurt the movement, at least in terms of meeting its immediate goals. Indeed, the perceived threat to traditional values posed by homosexuals led Phyllis Schlafly and others in the New Right to link the issue of sexual preference with the ERA, which in turn further confused the issue and perhaps provided some with a major reason to fight the amendment rather than forming a separate movement to combat homosexuality. Thus, the association of this issue with the feminist movement resulted in considerable controversy especially outside the movement where the linkage between liberation and lesbianism was already being made by some who opposed efforts to change women's position in society.

Outcomes of the Radical Feminists' Efforts. The ability of the radical feminists to achieve their ultimate goals has been limited. Still, the influence of their ideas on society should not be underestimated, and the view that the sex role system limits the ability of women to take an active role outside the home has become widely accepted. The influence of these ideas on the older branch has been particularly important. Many of the issues taken up in the 1970s by the liberal feminists have their roots in the younger branch. Reproductive rights, legalized abortion, and lesbian rights to name but a few ideas supported by NOW had their origins in the radical branch of the movement. Zillah Eisenstein argues that the inherent logic of liberal feminism will push it even further in the direction of radical feminists in questioning established social and economic institutions.[122]

In addition to their legacy of ideas, the radical feminists can also claim at least partial victory in their efforts to win for women control over their own bodies. Many of the self-help health books and clinics and the abortion and birth control counseling centers owe their start, if not their development, to the radicals. A similar claim can be made for other of the "women helping women" centers. The vast proliferation of such groups (one directory lists 690 battered women and rape victim services, 179 career counseling centers, 199 displaced homemaker programs, 568 women's centers, and 89 women's health centers)[123] is partial testimony to the impact of the women's liberation branch of the movement. In many communities today, these self-help centers have come together with groups of the liberal branch to form women's networks. The ability of these networks to persist and continue to provide needed services for individual women may become even more crucial in the years to come if the present move to dismantle federal programs in these areas continues.

While the proliferation of ideas and women's centers represents the positive developments to come out of the radical branch, not all of the efforts of the radical branch have had beneficial results. As noted earlier, for example, the small groups on the local level have not always been successfully activated for larger political efforts. Thus while they have supplied some of the needed public goods—health care, daycare, etc.—these efforts generally have resulted in an undersupply of the good sought. Without national policies in these areas, only those women aware of such services and living in communities where they are available have benefitted. The vast majority of women have not.

The other negative aspect of the radical feminist efforts has been the backlash their demands has generated. The statements of the anti movement make clear that they fear that the goals of the radicals may be achieved. The failure of the anti movement to distinguish between radical and liberal feminists' goals, moreover, has resulted in the anti movement attacking almost all efforts to improve women's status under the mistaken assumption that all such changes threaten the social structure as they know it and from which they derive their status. We will return to the development of the anti movement later in this chapter.

The Older Branch

Being far more conservative in nature, most women in the older branch initially tried to disassociate themselves from the tactics and ideology of the younger branch. The women who founded NOW in 1966 strongly supported both marriage and the family but thought that some changes needed to be made in society so that women could more easily pursue careers while continuing to be good wives and mothers.

Their demands for reasonable pregnancy leaves without loss of seniority, tax-deductions for child-care expenses, and establishment of child-care centers all reflect concern with the family. Although radical feminists also advocated child-care centers, they viewed them as but a first step toward eliminating sex role stereotypes about parenting. In contrast, NOW and other older-branch women saw them as simply facilitating women's entrance into the work force and allowing them to combine their societal roles more easily.

It is not surprising that older-branch women, most of whom at least initially were working women, were very concerned with laws or practices that negatively affected working wives. Childcare is but one example. Other inequities attacked by those in the rights branch included the marriage tax penalty and disrimination in the social security system, as discussed in Chapters 5 and 6.

They also were very concerned with the position of women more generally within the marriage institution. While unswerving in their belief in the family, older-branch women agreed that wives should be treated as equal partners within the institution of marriage. Like Elizabeth Cady Stanton, they viewed inequalities in marriage as at the heart of the problems faced by women. Thus, they called for reforms both in marriage and in the law's treatment of married women both during and upon the dissolution of a marriage.

Among the many legislative changes sought and won by rights branch advocates were the Equal Credit Opportunity Act, partial elimination of the marriage tax penalty, and tax credits for child-care payments. These laws were necessary largely because of the discrimination faced by married women or those with children. But, it should be noted that these laws were *national* and did not remedy many of the other problems in state laws or social practices that contribute to women's inferior status within the family.

One of the more obvious, albeit subtle, forms of discrimination that occurs upon marriage, concerns a woman's loss of identity. Although a woman no longer legally ceases to exist when she marries, she does lose some of her identity when she takes the last name of her husband. Particularly in the past, many women suffered adverse legal consequences for this change. Continued credit in her own name (even as Mrs. Mary Smith Jones) was denied because most creditors preferred to open one account for the family in the husband's name.

Since Lucy Stone's marriage to Henry Blackwell in 1855, a small number of women have followed her lead and have chosen not to adopt the surname of their husbands, although several state laws have made this difficult. While few states actually require a woman to change her name upon marriage, some have laws concerning the issuance of driver's licenses, etc., mandating that a married female applicant must use her husband's last name regardless of what name the woman uses in other situations. Additionally, until the mid-1970s, the U.S. Passport Office refused to issue passports in a woman's maiden name—*even* if it was the only name she was known by. While pressure from a variety of women's rights groups forced the Office to end this practice, the refusal of some states to grant women driver's licences in their own names was twice upheld by the U.S. Supreme Court.[124]

In terms of our public goods notion, the small number of women who choose to retain their maiden names often seeks a legal name change through relatively inexpensive court proceedings to avert these kinds of bureaucratic problems. Thus, should they live in a state where they are likely to experience difficulties about their name, the court order can be produced and the problem solved. These actions by a privileged class lead to an undersupply of the public good. The problem is solved for the individual woman but not for others in the class. This phenomenon was further exacerbated by a 1972 Supreme Court decision in which the Court specifically recognized the availability of judicial proceedings for those who wish to retain their maiden names.[125] In essence, the Justices affirmed the privileged nature of the right by recommending the name change procedure.

Women's rights groups, however, did target one area for change that had its roots in the dependency notions and loss of identity suffered by women when they changed their names: credit discrimination. Although "hormones, birth control and wedding rings are not matters of credit," most banking institutions considered all three as rationale for routinely denying credit to women prior to 1974.[126] Members of NOW, WEAL, and the National Women's Political Caucus, among others presssured Congress to conduct hearings concerning blatantly discriminatory banking practices, which included outright refusal to extend credit to a woman in her own name, halving a woman's salary for purposes of determining a couple's credit worthiness, and inquiring into a woman's method of birth control. Largely due to these women's groups' efforts, Congress passed the Equal Credit Opportunity Act in 1974, which prohibits credit discrimination on the basis of sex or marital status.[127]

Efforts to change discriminatory bank practices, which were rooted in notions about traditional familial roles, were clearly facilitated by common recognition of the problem. In fact, a poll conducted in 1974 had revealed that 57 percent of the women sampled believed that women suffered from credit discrimination.[128] Thus, unlike other reforms, there was some agreement on the need for change, and it was a problem capable of a national solution—the level where women's rights activists best function.

Many other legal rights within marriage, however, are of low saliency and occur at the state level, which have made it difficult for women's rights groups to mobilize their supporters to seek changes in existing laws. For example, some states continue to discriminate against married women in terms of their ability to convey land, to make contracts, or to engage in business. Thus, often the best resource has been to go to court to seek judicial invalidation of discriminatory statutes. For example, in *Reed* v. *Reed,*[129] the United States Supreme Court ruled that an Idaho law that favored males over females as administrators of estates was unconstitutional.

Although the courts often remain as a last resort, the problem in changing laws or enacting new ones is exacerbated by the local or state nature of familial laws. While many national organizations have studied family issues or have task forces to suggest reforms in these areas, family laws are state in nature. Thus, to be viable, efforts to change these laws must be made at the state level. Organizations such as WEAL, for example, historically have not had strong state affiliates. Other organizations that do have strong affiliates, including NOW, BPW, and the League of Women Voters, have made inroads to reform, but progress in individual states has not been uniform. Progress also has been hampered when some have perceived proposed change as pure public bads. This has led many of the women active in the anti-ERA, antiabortion, and Moral Majority movements also to oppose these reforms. These anti groups appear to be best organized on the local or state level. They regularly can rally hundreds of women to descend on state legislators who see them as representative of their constituents' wishes. This, coupled with the conservative nature of many state legislatures, has made women's rights' efforts for change in this area a difficult task. There are signs, however, that women's rights groups have recognized these problems and are now organizing at the grass-roots level and even assisting the efforts of state and local office-holders, as noted in Chapters 3 and 4. They now realize that family law reforms often are difficult to attain because of the necessity for strong state organizations—and forming such organizations is a task that since the time of the suffrage drive has proven very difficult.

To get around the "state problem," several women's rights branch oragnizations, however, have concerned themselves with national solutions to issues including divorce, alimony and child support, child custody, and homemaker rights. As early as 1963, the Commission on the Status of Women suggested the elimination of laws discriminating against women in the marriage relationship and in the dissolution of marriage.[130] Later, NOW drafted an Equal Rights Divorce Reform Bill, which calls for a greater recognition of a woman's economic contribution to marriage and a right to an equal division of the couple's property.[131] And, in 1977, at the National Women's Conference, which was supported by the U.S. government as part of the United States International Year of the Woman observance, over 20,000 women came together (2,000 of them as state delegates) to adopt a 26-plank National Plan of Action, which was submitted to then President Carter in March 1978. As part of the Conference's recommendations concerning homemakers, federal and state lawmakers were urged to enact the economic provisions contained in the Uniform Marriage and Divorce Act, a proposed law supported by the American Bar Association.[132] In documenting the need for such provisions, its report to the President noted in 1977, in Georgia, if a house was titled in a husband's name, it "belonged only to him, even if the wife was the wage earner and made all payments."[133] Further, "in Arkansas, a husband could dispose of all property, even jointly owned, without his wife's consent."[134]

Even in community property states, where property accrued during marriage is considered joint property of the marriage partners, a husband generally has legal control of those assets during the marriage.[135] Thus, while in terms of older-branch philosophy, a woman's services are to some extent recognized in community property states, control places women in an inferior position in the marriage relationship.

However, general calls for divorce reform have been met with great hostility by anti groups, who often blame escalating divorce rates and breakup of the family on the women's rights movement. In fact, the very name of the Eagle Forum, a large, anti-ERA group founded by Phyllis Schlafly, was selected because "the eagle is almost the only creature that keeps one mate for a lifetime."[136]

Alimony and Child Support. While all states have laws allowing alimony,[137] the presiding judge has tremendous discretion in awarding such payments. Alimony is awarded in less than 15 percent of all divorces, and only "7 percent of divorced men actually make such payments."[138] While child support payments are far more common, they seldom cover even half a child's expenses and are very difficult to collect.[139]

NOW in particular has urged the adoption of divorce laws that would improve the standard of living for a divorced woman and her children.[140] Several of its state affiliates have rigorously lobbied their state legislators to see NOW-supported legislation enacted. In 1978, the Delaware NOW successfully lobbied for a bill that allowed divorced persons to collect alimony until they reached financial independence.[141] Its sponsor said the bill was drafted to assist those women who "after 20, 30 years of raising children" found themselves without the skills necessary to get a job outside of the home.[142] These kinds of "retraining" awards are favored by most older-branch movement members. The Delaware statute, for example, recognizes that a woman who has devoted herself to her family on a full-time basis needs to be reschooled and thus gives her an opportunity to get training so that she may become self-sufficient.

NOW, other women's rights groups, and the Children's Legal Defense Fund also are asking Congress to pass national legislation as part of the Women's Economic Equity Act. This proposal would allow the Justice Department to conduct a study of state laws and jurisdictional problems and then make recommendations back to Congress concerning the desirability of legislation to solve child support, alimony, and property settlement enforcement problems.[143]

The kinds of self-sufficiency that women can attain, even when court orders are enforced, are likely to result in vastly reduced life-styles given women's salaries and the kinds of positions that will be available to the older women. In fact, the plight of older women has been of particular concern to NOW and other rights-branch members. This has led directly to NOW's support of legislation recognizing the contribution of homemakers to the household unit.

Calls for Recognition of Homemakers and Abolition of Stereotypes. The absence of equality in the marriage and the low value placed on women's services within the marriage and upon its breakup led NOW to propose what it calls a "Bill of Rights for Homemakers" (see Appendix C). State chapters of NOW have lobbied their respective state legislators to get various facets of the proposal enacted into law. In February 1978, largely at the urgings of the Massachusetts NOW Legislative Task Force, state alimony laws were reformed so as to call attention to the contributions of homemakers in assessing division of property or alimony awards.[144]

In addition, NOW and other rights-branch groups were instrumental in passage of federal pension reforms that recognize the contribution of divorced wives. NOW, from almost the beginning of the current women's rights movement, has been at the fore of many of the efforts to recognize the services of homemakers. This became particularly true in the mid-1970s when it appeared that NOW needed to expand its organizational base and, in particular, to appeal to the numerous nonworking women who believed that the women's movement was only for those who were employed outside of the home. It also was around this time that leaders of the movement began to realize that few women could successfully manage a home and a career without a support system. It was also the period in which NOW elected a full-time homemaker as its president. Calls for daycare and tax credits for childcare continued under Eleanor Smeal's leadership, but NOW and other movement organizations began to call for additional legislation to assist women, particularly those who had bought into the "feminine mystique," and after raising their families found themselves out of work, either because of widowhood or divorce.

In fact, in 1975, the Alliance for Displaced Homemakers was cofounded by the chair of NOW's Task Force on the Elderly to assist older women who found themselves "displaced homemakers."[145] As originally coined, the term "displaced homemakers" referred to women past middle age who found themselves out of work either through the deaths of their husbands or when they were "fired" by their husbands when the men secured divorces. Generally these women had been out of the labor force so long that they, in effect, needed to be trained to be trained. Unlike men, who upon the loss of their jobs still have their skills and past work experience to fall back on, many of these women had little or nothing in the way of skills or even esteem necessary to seek other employment. Their resulting un- or underemployment often was exacerbated by the inadequacy or absence of alimony awards received by these women, while many men often receive unemployment or disability insurance. Concerted efforts by NOW, the Alliance, and the Displaced Homemaker's Network effectively drew publicity to the plight of the estimated 3 million plus displaced homemakers in America, many of whom for the first time in their lives found themselves living below the poverty level.[146] After extensive lobbying, California and Maryland were the first states to establish centers in which these women could be trained to find jobs. After the success of these programs was demonstrated, in 1978 the U.S. Congress provided monies for the funding of additional pilot programs, but the likelihood of continued funding appears almost nonexistent.[147]

The kind of help sought by rights groups, however, transcends funding centers. Several women's rights organizations have lobbied Congress for increased widows benefits and revised inheritance tax laws to assist displaced homemakers under the rubric of the Women's Economic Equity Act, discussed in Chapter 5. Pressure for revision of inheritance tax laws, in particular, is indicative of the philosophy of those in this branch of the movement concerning the importance of equality within marriage and recognition of women's services within that institution. Prior to 1981, under federal inheritance tax laws, a woman was required to pay taxes on any inheritance she received upon her husband's death in excess of $100,000. NOW and other groups argued that these laws should take into account what a woman had done to help her spouse amass his estate. Largely because of tradition and the difficulty in ascertaining the value of a woman's services, little progress was made in this area until 1981 and the passage of the Reagan tax bill. Ironically, although the nontaxable portion of the estate was raised to $600,000, this was probably done more to help the wealthy than to appease women's rights supporters.[148] Not yet passed but still high on the list of priorities of several groups, including NOW, is legislation allowing employers to earn a year tax credit if they hire displaced homemakers.[149]

Thus, in the area of the family, the women's rights branch of the movement has made many advances in legal rights, but many changes still need to be made before true equality is a reality. While legal changes have been made, much of the inequality that continues to exist within the family is directly attributable to attitudes and not laws. While those in the younger branch have been targeting sex role stereotypes, it is only since the late 1970s that women in the rights branch have moved to accept this view. Although most still seek legal equality for women within the family, they now agree that sex roles are at the center of the problem. As Gloria Steinem has put it:

> "Help out" is the clue. Until we reach a point where everybody who lives in a house is responsible for it and until we pursue the logic of children being raised by both parents, the majority of women who work outside the home as well as in it will have an enormously unfair burden.[150]

Reproductive Freedom. In addition to marital issues, women in the current movement have been concerned with related issues of reproductive rights. According to Gloria Steinem, "reproductive freedom signifies an individual's basic human right to decide whether or not to have children," while the phrase rejected by feminists, "population control" "legitimizes some external force or power over women's lives."[151] To remove this "external force," radical branch women, often with the help of those in the rights branch have pressed for improved methods of contraception. They also have lobbied for education and availability of contraceptives for teenagers to remedy the national problem of teenage pregnancy, which has reached epidemic proportions. Additionally, they have started feminist-run health clinics, so as not to have to rely on male physicians and written self-help books, including *Our Bodies, Our Selves,*[152] with the goal of giving women information about and control over their own bodies. All of these activities have created misconceptions about the goals of the movement and have generated tremendous controversy.

Abortion. During the 1820s, the first laws prohibiting abortion began to appear in the United States.[153] Prior to that time, no states prohibited abortion. States began to enact statutes outlawing abortion except when necessary to protect the life and health of mothers because surgery was crude and dangerous at this time. Thus, most commentators believed that these statutes were enacted solely to protect women's health and were not motivated by moral or religious concerns.[154]

During the times of both the first woman's rights and suffrage movements, although even birth control was very controversial, it is clear that women procured illegal abortions.[155] But even radicals, including Elizabeth

Cady Stanton and Margaret Sanger, preferred not to get involved in any move to change existing abortion laws, and Sanger publicly denounced abortion.[156] In fact, Planned Parenthood, founded by Sanger, did not support repeal of abortion laws until 1970.[157]

It was not until the 1960s that many came to recognize the need for changes in restrictive state abortion laws. During this decade, a number of events occurring almost simultaneously led to the creation of an abortion movement in the United States. Abortion first became an issue of public debate in 1962 when Sherri Finkbine, a Phoenix, Arizona television personality, sought to have an abortion after she realized that she had taken Thalidomide, a drug proven to cause hideously disfiguring fetal abnormalities. For the first time in history, abortion received prominent national attention when Finkbine was forced to fly to Sweden to secure an abortion, having been unable to secure a legal one in the United States. As her plight was broadcast in minute detail,[158] attention also was turned to the scientific advances that had lessened the medical risks associated with abortion. Furthermore, and in part based on Finkbine's experience, the American Law Institute (ALI) redrafted its model penal code. As adopted, it called for the legalization of abortion in three situations:

1. When continuation of pregnancy would gravely impair the physical or mental health of the mother,

2. When the child might be born with a grave physical or mental defect,

3. When pregnancy resulted from rape, incest, or other felonious intercourse, including illicit intercourse with a girl below the age of sixteen.[159]

The importance of these proposed changes was graphically illustrated to American women when a German measles epidemic occurred in 1963 and 1964. If a woman contracts measles during the first three months of her pregnancy, there is a high probability that the fetus will be deformed. Thus, as more and more pregnant women found themselves exposed to the measles and unsuccessfully sought legal abortions, public concern over abortion reform increased. However, even though over 20,000 children were born with deformities directly traceable to measles, concern and publicity still were inadequate to forge an abortion movement.

Taken together, however, these factors prompted several individuals to become increasingly concerned with abortion reform. During the 1950s, for example, Lawrence Lader had researched and written a book about Margaret Sanger.[160] By the mid-1960s, his studies convinced him that abortion reform was necessary. As he traveled and spoke around the country, he began to advocate abortion reform and to refer women to physicians who would risk performing the illegal procedures. Around the same time, Patricia Maginnis, a California woman who had undergone three illegal abortions, began to advocate total repeal of all abortion laws—a radical proposal that went far beyond the ALI Model Code. To call attention to the issue, she used a tactic that Sanger had used earlier: she leafleted the streets with abortion information that included the names of Mexican physicians who would perform the procedure. After the press began to cover this activity, she was arrested for distributing lewd and obscene literature. Her arrest and subsequent hearing generated much-needed free publicity for her cause and the organization she founded to work for abortion law repeal, the Society for Humane Abortion.[161]

In 1964, two additional groups were formed to address the abortion issue. The Association for the Study of Abortion was created to provide information about abortion. Its founders believed that much of the public apathy concerning the issue was attributable to the lack of factual information available to those in professions where they might have been confronted with abortion problems. The Parent's Aid Society also was founded in 1964.[162] Its founder, long-time birth control proponent Bill Baird, established the Society to assist women locate qualified abortionists.[163]

The isolated actions of Lader and Maginnis and the founding of two other prochoice groups, even when coupled with news accounts of the horrors of illegal, back-alley abortions and the birth of deformed children, would not have been enough to start a movement without the infusion of potential supporters provided by both branches of the current women's movement. In fact, the first formal call for the repeal of restrictive abortion laws can be traced to the Bill of Rights for Women adopted by the National Organization for Women at its first annual convention. The last section demanded:

> The right of women to control their own reproductive lives by removing from the penal codes laws limiting access to contraceptive information and devices and by repealing penal laws governing abortion.[164]

This provision was passed over the strong opposition of some in attendance who believed that abortion was not a civil rights issue. Other dissenters believed that NOW's association with abortion would bring unnecessary unfavorable publicity to the organization, which in turn would make other more attainable goals increasingly difficult to achieve.

NOW's public support of abortion, however, added the members and even some of the leaders necssary for the start of a real movement for change. For example, soon after NOW's Declaration in late 1967, other "rights"-oriented organizations also began to follow suit. In 1968, the Citizens Advisory Council on the Status of Women called for the repeal of all restrictive abortion laws as did the American Civil Liberties Union.

Women from both branches became increasingly active in campaigns not to reform but instead to repeal restrictive state laws. In 1969, several members of the New York NOW chapter founded New Yorkers for Abortion Law Repeal to press for liberalization of the state's abortion law. Also formed in 1969 was the National Association for the Repeal of Abortion Laws which later was to become the National Abortion Rights Action League (NARAL).[165] Lader was instrumental in the founding of NARAL as were many NOW members, including Betty Friedan. NARAL, as the largest and most important abortion movement organization, viewed the proposed New York law as a political symbol around which to rally support for repeal of abortion laws.[166]

While both groups relied on conventional lobbying techniques to secure passage of the New York law, those in the radical branch relied on more controversial tactics. When hearings were held on the proposed legislation, radicals picketed the meeting and others "invaded the hearing itself,"[167] challenging New York State Legislative Committee's right to waste time considering abortion reform when repeal was the only answer. They argued that women alone could be experts on abortion and questioned why only one woman, a nun, was allowed to testify before the Committee.[168] Later, many of these women participated in a counterhearing held by the Redstockings in New York where twelve women spoke out for abortion as a radical woman's issue.[169]

Largely on account of pressure from women in both branches of the movement and over the vehement protest of the Catholic Church, Governor Nelson Rockefeller signed into law the abortion reform provision in 1970. The New York statute, which legalized abortions performed by licensed physicians during the first twenty-four weeks of pregnancy, thus became the most liberal abortion law in the country. The publicity generated by the efforts of pro- and antiabortion forces during the New York campaign led several organizations to join the "repeal" movement. Planned Parenthood, the Board of Trustees of the American Medical Association, the YWCA, and Church Women United all voiced their support for an end to abortion restrictions.

While this victory in New York fueled the prochoice movement, it also provided the catalyst for the antiabortion movement. The Catholic Church had always played a central role in the abortion controversy. Unlike most Protestants, who believe that "life" begins at quickening or most Jews, who believe that life begins at birth, Catholic doctrine teaches that life begins at conception. Therefore, many Cahtolics, a sizeable portion of the American populace, believe that abortion at anytime is murder. Thus by 1972, pressure from right to life forces, heavily supported by the Catholic Church, led the New York state legislature to repeal the 1970 law, but this action was vetoed by the Governor.

Repeal advocates also experienced other legislative setbacks because of the efforts of the right to life movement. In Michigan and North Dakota, for example, proposals for abortion law reform were put to the voters and overwhelmingly rejected.[170] Increasingly, those in the rights branch in particular, but not exclusively, began to believe that the courts were their best resource if change was to be accomplished.

Consequently, between 1969 and 1971, scores of cases were brought by attorneys and/or abortion rights groups generally on behalf of physicians who performed abortions and later on behalf of women who sought abortions but because of restrictive state statutes were unable to secure them. For example, in 1970, the United States Supreme Court decided *United States* v. *Vuitch*.[171] In *Vuitch*, a physician had been prosecuted for performing an abortion in violation of a D.C. statute that prohibited abortions except when they were necessary to protect the mother's life or health. The Supreme Court rejected the District Court's finding that the statute was unconstitutionally vague, and concluded that "health" as used in the statute, should be interpreted to include *both* mental and physical health. Thus, while the Court did not find the statute unconstitutional, the Justices, in effect, added to the legal rationale for allowing abortions to be performed by physicians.

Against this setting and growing support for change among women's rights groups, the U.S. Supreme Court agreed to hear two more cases involving abortion rights, *Roe* v. *Wade*[172] and *Doe* v. *Bolton*.[173] *Roe* v. *Wade* involved a pregnant woman's challenge to a Texas law that prohibited abortions except to save a mother's life. Because Roe's pregnancy was not life-threatening, she was advised to seek an abortion out of state but she did not have the money to do so. Thus, she alleged that the Texas law deprived "women and their physicians of rights protected by the 4th, 5th, 9th, and 14th Amendments" and that she was deprived of "the fundamental right...to choose when and where to bear children."

Unlike the Texas law, the Georgia statute challenged in *Doe* v. *Bolton* by local ACLU attorneys on behalf of Planned Parenthood and several doctors, nurses, clergy, and social workers was based on the ALI's Model Penal Code. Doe's lawyers alleged that the Georgia law was an undue restriction of personal and marital privacy and a denial of equal protection of the laws.

These abortion cases marked the first major national confrontation of pro- and antiabortion forces because they involved a woman's right to an abortion. Amicus curiae briefs in support of *Roe* and *Doe* were filed by several physicians' groups and organizations representing the rights branch of the women's movement (the American Association of University Women, the YWCA, NOW, Planned Parenthood, and the Professional Women's Caucus) as well as representatives of the radical branch (New Women Lawyers). While not as numerous, antiabortion groups also filed amicus curiae briefs in large numbers. Among these were Americans United for Life, Women for the Unborn, and Women Concerned for the Unborn Child.

These cases were first argued before the Court in late 1971 and reargued in October 1972.[174] On January 22, 1973, the Supreme Court handed down its momentous decision. While the Justices did not adopt the view that abortion was totally a private matter as urged by radical women, seven Justices concluded that a woman's constitutional right to privacy was more important than state regulation of abortion as codefied in the Texas and Georgia statutes. In *Roe*, the Justices divided pregnancy into trimesters and found different rights in each. The Court held that during the first trimester, a woman in consultation with her physician had an absolute right to obtain an abortion free from state interference. In the second trimester, the Court found that the "State in promoting its interest in the health of the mother, may, if it chooses, regulate the abortion procedure in ways that are reasonably related to maternal health." In the last trimester of pregnancy, the Justices concluded that the states, to promote the interests of "potential human life," could regulate or prohibit abortions, except when they were necessary to preserve the "life or health of the mother."

While this decision was met with enthusiasm by women in the abortion and women's movements, it provided the catalyst for major organizational efforts of the antiabortion movement. In fact, in the aftermatch of the abortion cases, several antiabortion organizations were formed. For example, the National Right to Life Committee (NRTLC) was founded in 1973 directly "in response to" the Court's abortion decisions.[175] From its inception, NRTLC's ultimate goal has been a constitutional amendment that would give full legal rights of personhood to the fetus from the moment of conception.[176] Since 1973 it has been closely allied to the Roman Catholic Church, which has provided it with an important source of members and considerable financial support. For example, the NRTLC has an agreement with the Church in New York which allows "it to collect money from parishioners after Sunday Mass."[177]

Catholic bishops themselves also organized in 1973 to work for passage of a constitutional amendment banning abortion.[178] Both the bishops and the NRTLC are funded by individual Catholic dioceses, which contribute one percent per parishioner to the organization. This money is then used in part to establish local *citizens'* antiabortion groups.[179] In fact, the Catholic Church was not content to limit its support to financial aid. In 1975, the National Conference of Catholic Bishops unanimously approved the *Pastoral Plan for Pro-Life Activities*, a detailed political document for reversing or limiting *Roe* and *Doe*.[180]

The moral issues underlying the abortion debate and opponents' depiction of abortion as murder immediately made the controversy front-page news across the country, providing free publicity to the growing movement. In addition, just as the women's movement had provided an organizational base for prochoice forces, antiabortion advocates were helped when Phyllis Schlafly, herself a Catholic, publicly attacked the Court's decision, perhaps even sensing an opportunity to help her own cause. For example, shortly after the Court's decision, she announced:

No one else had ever seen abortion there for a hundred years, and abortion was clearly *not* intended by those who ratified the 14th Amendment. How much easier it will be to find an absolute, government-financed right to abortion in ERA![181]

As a consequence of statements like these, an almost symbiotic relationship between the two movements developed. Schlafly charged that *Roe* and *Doe* were but examples of the havoc that would occur to traditional values if the ERA were ratified. And, antiabortion supporters blamed the decision on the increasing decline in morals and destruction of the family personified by the women's rights movement.

Given the phenomenal growth of the antiabortion movement and the publicity attendant upon its activities, it is not surprising that by September 1973, the ACLU reported, "At least 188 anti-abortion bills have been introduced in 41 states."[182] These proposed laws included provisions regulating clinics, requiring parental or spousal consent, requiring waiting periods, and even the viewing of aborted fetuses before a patient could give her consent for the procedures. Generally, these laws or regulations were enacted at the suggestion or with the support of NRTLC members. The enactment of this kind of legislation immediately placed prochoice advocates on the defensive. All around the country, they were forced to expend large sums of money and considerable energy to challenge the constitutionality of these laws.[183] And, while they were defending the rights guaranteed by *Roe* and *Doe,* right to lifers continued to lobby the U.S. Congress.

Fervent in their belief that the Court's decision not only threatened a public good, but in fact, destroyed it, antiabortion individuals deluged their members of Congress with antiabortion letters, which often contained photos of fetuses at various stages of development. Immediately after the abortion decisions, in response to this well-organized political activity, several conservative members of Congress called for passage of various constitutional amendments to overrule the Supreme Court's abortion decisions. While the text of these proposals has varied, generally they have called for constitutional recognition that human life begins at conception.

While early efforts to secure a constitutional amendment were unsuccessful, in 1976 Congress finally passed legislation (generally referred to as the "Hyde Amendment") prohibiting the use of medicaid funds for abortions in all but three circumstances:

1. where the mother's life was in danger;

2. where two physicians certified that a woman would suffer "severe and long lasting damage;" or

3. where the pregnancy was the result of rape or incest as reported to the proper authorities.

Thus, by 1977, the then-cohesive antiabortion movement began to deal both the abortion and women's rights movements severe setbacks.

To some extent the successes of the Right to Life movement were directly attributable to the women's rights movement. Prior to 1973, both radical and rights branch women had largely relied on the courts to expand abortion rights. By 1973, although most women's movement organizations agreed on the need for reproductive freedom, the issue still had not been sufficiently defined. Groups calling for repeal at times only meant reform, and those supporting repeal often disagreed on the role male physicians should play in the procedure. Also, many organizations believed abortion rights had been won and thus turned their attention to the ratification of the ERA. They were additionally hurt when right to lifers labeled them as "murderers" and depicted abortion as antifamily. By redefining abortion as a moral and not a medical issue, those opposed to abortion placed prochoice advocates on the defensive, which created further difficulties.

Although the ACLU specifically created a Reproductive Freedom Project (RFP) in 1974 to "ensure compliance with last year's Supreme Court decision on abortion,"[184] most women were caught off guard by the success of Henry Hyde, the sponsor of the medicaid restrictions, and state groups that lobbied to see all types of restrictions and conditions placed on women's access to an abortion. For example, although the RFP successfully challenged a Missouri law that required informed written consent prior to an abortion and was joined by an amicus curiae brief from NOW, the Supreme Court upheld various recordkeeping requirements of the law.[185]

With the passage of the Hyde Amendment, however, some women's rights groups turned their attentions to medicaid funding and went to court to block implementation of the Hyde Amendment. Initially, they charged that Medicaid's refusal to pay for abortions was unconstitutional because it discriminated against poor women.

This argument, however, was dealt a stunning blow in 1977 by a series of Supreme Court decisions. In three separate challenges by women's rights groups and Planned Parenthood to state medicaid programs that financed childbirths but not abortions, the Court concluded that these practices did not violate a woman's constitutional right to secure an abortion even though some women could not afford them.[186] As a result of these decisions, the number of publicly funded abortions has declined precipitously.[187]

These losses in 1977 and their resultant consequences acted to mobilize women's rights groups just as *Roe* and *Doe* did for the right to life movement. While new groups were not created, the ACLU immediately launched a "Campaign for Choice" and was supported by most other women's rights groups. At the National Women's Conference in Houston in the same year, over the strenuous objections of right to life supporters, the delegates also accepted a resolution opposing "the exclusion of abortion…from Federal, State, or local funding of medical services."[188]

In an effort to implement this resolution, NARAL, which serves as the major clearinghouse of abortion issues, began a grass-roots campaign modeled after the NRTLC and founded NARAL-PAC to raise money for prochoice candidates. Again, however, this was a reactive move designed to counter the growing political forces of the antiabortion movement.

Even before prochoice losses in 1976, prolife forces ran their own political candidate for President, Ellen McCormack on the Pro-Life party ticket. This allowed her to receive several hundred thousand dollars in federal matching campaign funds, and more important, secured access to television advertising that could be used for highly controversial campaign spots including vivid pictures of in utero fetuses. McCormack received few votes in state primaries and blamed this on NARAL, whose leaders had challenged her eligibility for federal matching funds, thereby delaying her campaign.

While McCormack also fared poorly in the general election, she received over five percent of the vote in New York state, which then entitled the Pro-Life party to a place on the ballot in subsequent years. Because New York allows a candidate to run on more than one party line, many a conservative politician has run for office as a Republican or Democrat, as well as on the Pro-Life party line. For example, in 1980, now N.Y. Senator D'Amato received a substantial number of votes on the Pro-Life party line. And D'Amato was not the only candidate who was assisted by prolife support in 1980. Conversely, several liberal senators, including Birch Bayh and George McGovern who were targeted by right to life forces for their prochoice stands on abortion or related legislation, were defeated.[189] Even prior to the 1980 election, although prochoice advocates were able to convince the Democratic party to include planks supporting *Roe* and *Doe* as well as medicaid funding of abortions, the Republican platform endorsed by Reagan included a call for a constitutional amendment to ban abortions and the selection of only federal judges who took stands consistent with the platform.

The political clout of right to life forces, however, has yet to be completely tested. Although since 1977, most women's organizations in both branches of the movement have supported a right to choose, only recently have their members come to realize what they view as a public good, reproductive freedom, is being seriously challenged.

In fact, while conservatives first began calling for a constitutional amendment to outlaw abortion in 1973, it was not until the Reagan election that the spectre of an amendment and its full ramifications were realized by women's rights groups. As most human life amendments have been proposed, it is generally conceded that they would also outlaw common methods of birth control, including intrauterine devices and some forms of birth control pills. In 1981, Planned Parenthood ran a full page advertisement in newspapers around the country proclaiming, "In 1982 if you have a miscarriage, you could be prosecuted for murder."

This kind of advertisement was designed to alert women to the potential loss of a public good and thereby raise the consciousness of potential movement members or supporters. Thus, while prochoice supporters are still trying to attract sympathizers and to publicize the potential of a human life amendment, amendment supporters have clearly defined its scope, i.e., "to prevent murder," and therefore may have an advantage in terms of the emotionalism of the issue. Additionally, they have been assisted by several organizations of great wealth and membership, including the Catholic and fundamentalist churches.

While the prochoice movement has attracted widespread support among women's rights organizations, even many women's rights advocates disagree about the issue[190] or see it as a private one that they do not want to advocate publicly. Other potential abortion rights advocates now are in their thirties. Many of these women have delayed childbearing and now are more concerned with getting pregnant than having abortions. In addition, women affected by medicaid cutoffs are poor and have always constituted a difficult group to mobilize, particularly for leaders of the women's rights movement.

The differences in the zealousness of the supporters of the two movements have translated into more victories than defeats for the right to life movement. While right to lifers were outraged at the appointment of Sandra Day O'Connor to the bench and charged that her votes as a legislator revealed her to be "proabortion," they have persuaded Congress to tighten the Hyde amendment's restrictions on abortion by abolishing payments for abortions on account of rape or incest. The strong organization and fervently held and often religious beliefs of the right to life movement also allow it to produce thousands of letters to members of Congress on a few days notice of important bills, and, as the 1980 elections revealed, turn out one-issue voters. In 1980, in particular, its supporters forced prochoice advocates into a defensive posture by defining abortion as a "bad" by resorting to the use of vivid photographs, etc. Many members even wear lapel pins designed to look like tiny feet—the feet of an aborted fetus.

Thus far, the right to life movement has suffered few losses since *Roe* and *Doe*. But on September 15, 1982, an 18-month effort in the Senate to restrict or reverse abortion rights was defeated first by a liberal filibuster and then when the proposals were tabled by a forty-seven to forty-six vote. The defeated bill, as proposed by Sen. Helms, declared it a finding of Congress that life begins at conception and encouraged state legislatures to pass restrictive abortion laws, which would then be entitled to an expedited review by the U.S. Supreme Court.[191] This kind of legislation, however, is expected to be reintroduced in the near future as well as an amendment to the Constitution to ban abortion altogether.

Once serious debate begins on a human life amendment, statutes limiting abortions, and/or legislation to curb the jurisdiction of the federal courts to decide abortion-related issues, supporters of reproductive freedom *must* attempt to frame the issue in their terms.[192] Just as ERA opponents defeated that amendment through charges of what the amendment could do, the prochoice movement must also depict a human life amendment in particular as a public bad in order to defeat it. Because the amendment as proposed also outlaws several forms of artificial birth control, including the intrauterine device (IUD), they must argue that abolition of popular forms of birth control in addition to abortion would necessitate sweeping life-style changes for women and men who prefer to plan their families. Learning from their opposition, prochoice leaders should argue that families would be torn apart by successive pregnancies when parents could not afford to feed and clothe their children adequately. Cries of "reproductive freedom" are too nebulous to forge a successful movement. To win, prochoice advocates will have to learn from the lessons of the ERA further discussed in Chapter 9 and be fully aware of the potential power of the New Right.

THE NEW RIGHT

They may have to learn these lessons soon because not only reproductive rights but the whole spectrum of gains won by women in the last decade are being threatened by the development of a new and powerful force—the New Right. The New Right is a well-organized, well-financed social movement that counts among its accomplishments the election of Ronald Reagan and the defeat of a number of liberal senators in 1980. The development of this movement rather neatly follows the pattern for anti movements that we outlined in Chapter 2. More specifically, it has a solid organizational base in the antiabortion movement as devevloped around the conservative wing of the Catholic and fundamentalist Protestant churches. This base has supplied the meeting places, the communication networks, the leaders, and the private incentives for followers, including the salvation of one's own soul by saving the souls of the unborn.[193] The New Right has expanded on the base by relying heavily on (1) the recruitment of born-again Christians who follow media preachers, including Jerry Falwell whose "Old Time Gospel Hour" once had an estimated audience of 15 million viewers[194] and (2) a direct-mail campaign.[195] This base, if fully mobilized, could present a tremendous political force. In fact, a prominent New Right direct-mail solicitor, Richard A. Viguerie, estimates its potential to be 85 million Americans.[196] The real and potential supporters of this movement have been drawn in by the fear that the ways of life on which their identity and status have been built (e.g., the father-led nuclear family, the male-minister and male-priest led churches) are threatened by existing and/or proposed changes suggested by the liberals and feminists.[197] According to one leader of the New Right,

> There are people who want a different political order....Symbolized by the women's liberation movement, they believe that the future for their political power lies in the restructuring of the traditional family, and particularly in the *downgrading of the male or father role in the traditional family.*[198] [emphasis added]

They are mobilized to act because they see the extent to which the traditional nuclear family has already been weakened (Viguerie cites the high divorce rate, the large number of illegitimate births, and the high employment rate of married women with children), and they are fearful of what the future without this type of family will be like. They believe action is needed now before it is too late.[199]

The New Right's plan of action is to return to the "private" those "personal" issues made political by the women's movement. Included on the New Right's "hit" list are abortion, sex education, and domestic violence services. For example, it opposes the Domestic Violence Bill ("an unwarranted federal intrusion into family matters"), test-tube baby research, and equal educational opportunities for women.[200]

The New Right's program with respect to women is probably best exemplified by its support and sponsorship of the Family Protection Act. This 50-plus page bill is a laundry list of provisions whose professed goal is to return things to the situation prior to the women's movement. According to one spokesperson of the New Right, this legislation is "pro-family, pro-God and a reaffirmation of the traditions and morals on which this nation was built."[201] Some of the more relevant provisions of this act are as follows:[202]

1. prohibit federal law from superseding any state law concerning spouse abuse and domestic relations;

2. prohibit Legal Services lawyers from handling "any proceedings or litigation seeking to obtain or arising out of a divorce," which opponents assume would also act as a limitation on assisting clients in the collection of alimony and child support. Additionally, Legal Services would be prevented from handling abortion-connected and homosexual rights cases;

3. prohibit federal funds from being used to "promote" educational materials which "do not reflect a balance between the role of men and women, do not reflect the different ways in which men and women live, and do not contribute to the American way of life as it has been historically understood";

4. allow local educational agencies to limit or to prohibit the intermingling of sexes in any sport or other school-related activities; and

5. repeal the Women's Educational Equity Act.

Because the scope of the act is so broad, it was referred to several committees in both Houses of Congress.[203] Additionally, portions of the bill are now being introduced separately or implemented through budget cutbacks in social service and educational programs.[204] And, it may be difficult to mobilize on so many fronts to defeat these actions.

A supporter of the bill, Senator Paul Laxalt, has stated quite clearly the problem that the bill poses for its opponents: "For years we have been debating on the terms of those who want to remake society. Now those groups will have to explain why they oppose the traditional idea of the family."[205] Our next chapter will discuss what the structure of the traditional family has been and how it has changed in the last two decades. The success or failure of the New Right and its Family Protection Act may help shape its future.

CONCLUSION

Collectively, the issues of reproductive freedom and changes within the family itself differ significantly from others discussed in Chapters 3 and 5. Unlike their actions in other areas of legal rights, for example, the radical branch of the current women's movement has played a major role in publicizing and forcing acceptance of both issues. This has led the rights branch to adopt many radical branch ideas facilitating cohesion between the branches yet fueling external opposition to many of the movement's goals. Because abortion, birth control, and changes within the traditional family, including calls for lesbian rights, are perceived as public bads and thus differ from many other issue areas targeted by the current movement, they have generated significant opposition that may have a lasting impact on the rights already secured by women.

Another key to women's rights activists' abilities to maintain even current levels of reproductive freedom is the U.S. Supreme Court. During its 1982 term, for example, the Court heard several cases involving state restrictions on abortion, including stringent parental consent and waiting period require- ments. While it is unlikely that the Court will uphold the numerous state laws under challenge, a change in the composition of the Court (if liberal Justices are replaced by Reagan appointees), may force women's rights activists to rely more heavily on state legislatures for rights. This will necessitate far greater political mobilization at that level. Thus, even though substantial legal changes have occurred in the expansion of reproductive freedom, given organized opposition and the political climate, the women's movement will have to devote substantial activity and resources to maintain current rights.

NOTES

1. Carl N. Degler, *At Odds: Women and the Family in America from the Revolution to the Present* (New York: Oxford University press, 1980), chap. 1.
2. Ibid., pp. 8–9.
3. Ibid., p. 9.
4. Ibid., p. 26.
5. Elizabeth Cady Stanton, Susan B. Anthony, and Matilda Joslyn Gage, eds., *History of Woman Suffrage,* vol. I, 1848–1861 (Rochester, N.Y.: Charles Mann, 1887), pp. 70–71 (hereafter HWS I).
6. *Blackstone's Commentaries,* quoted in Leo Kanowitz, *Women and the Law: The Unfinished Revolution* (Albuquerque: The University of New Mexico Press, 1969), p. 35.
7. See, for example, Gen. 2:22–23: "And Adam said, this is now bone of my bones, and flesh of my flesh; she shall be called Woman, because she was taken out of a man...and they shall be one flesh."
8. In fact, under coverture, all property that a woman owned prior to her marriage fell under the control of her husband.
9. Barbara Allen Babcock et al., *Sex Discrimination and the Law: Cases and Remedies* (Boston: Little Brown and Co., 1975), p. 592.
10. For an analysis of the results of these efforts, see ibid., pp. 592–599. See also, Virginia Sapiro, "Research Frontier Essay: When Are Interests Interesting? The Problem of Political Representation of Women," *American Political Science Review* 75 (September 1981):701–716.
11. Ellen Carol DuBois, *Elizabeth Cady Stanton/Susan B. Anthony: Correspondence, Writings and Teachings* (New York: Schocken Books, 1981), pp. 4–5.
12. For a discussion of the similar activities that occurred in seven states, including Ohio, Massachusetts, and Kansas, see HWS I, generally.
13. HWS I, p. 612.
14. Ibid., p. 618.
15. Ibid., pp. 686–687.
16. Quoted in Ida Husted Harper, *The Life and Work of Susan B. Anthony,* vol. I (Indianapolis and Kansas City: Bowen Merrill Co., 1899), p. 67.
17. Quoted in Degler, *At Odds,* p. 175.
18. Ibid.
19. Quoted in Nelson Manfred Blake, *The Road to Reno: A History of Divorce in the United States* (New York: MacMillan, 1962), pp. 88–89.
20. See Elizabeth Cady Stanton, *Eighty Years and More: Reminiscences 1857–1897* (1898; reprint of T. Risher Unwin ed., New York: Schocken Books, 1971), pp. 215–226. Barbara Easton has suggested women were reluctant to attack marriage

because men's power was so great in that institution that there would be no possibility of success. Barbara Easton, "Feminism and the Contemporary Family," in Nancy F. Cott and Elizabeth H. Pleck, eds., *A Heritage of Her Own: Toward a New Social History of American Women* (New York: Simon and Schuster/Touchstone Books, 1979), pp. 555–561.

21. Stanton quoting Wendall Phillips in *Eighty Years*, p. 219.

22. Ibid.

23. Stanton, Lucretia Mott, and Ernestine Rose, however, received the permission of those in attendance at the 1860 National Woman's Rights Convention to testify before a New York State Committee on divorce reform, although the organization itself refused to support it. Judith Papachristou, *Women Together: A History in Documents of the Women's Movement in the United States* (New York: Alfred A. Knopf, 1976), p. 40.

24. Stanton, *Eighty Years*, p. 225.

25. HWS I, pp. 63–64.

26. See Harper, *Susan B. Anthony*, vol. I, pp. 185–205.

27. "Lucy Stone to Elizabeth Cady Stanton, October 22, 1856," Theodore Stanton and Harriet Stanton Blatch, eds., *Elizabeth Cady Stanton as Revealed in Her Letters, Diaries and Reminiscences*, vol. II (New York: Harper, 1922), pp. 67–68.

28. Ibid., p. 49. "Elizabeth Cady Stanton to Susan B. Anthony, March 1, 1853."

29. Edward T. James, ed., *Notable American Women: 1607–1950, A Biographical Dictionary*, vol. I (Cambridge: The Belknap Press of Harvard University Press, 1971), s.v. "Amelia Boomer."

30. Carol Hymowitz and Michaele Weissman, *A History of Women in America* (New York: Bantam Books, 1978), p. 70.

31. Quoted in HWS I, pp. 556–557.

32. And, Papachristou notes, in *Women Together*, that both Anthony and Stanton questioned the wisdom of this action, p. 47. However, they founded the Women's National Loyal League to press for an amendment to ban slavery. In fact, "petitions by the hundred thousand" were sent to Congress by League members supporting the amendment, HWS I, p. 747.

33. Ellen Carol DuBois, *Feminism and Suffrage: The Emergence of an Independent Women's Movement in America, 1848–1869* (Ithaca: Cornell University Press, 1980), p. 54.

34. HWS I, p. 747.

35. Ibid.

36. DuBois, *Feminism and Suffrage*, p. 54.

37. William L. O'Neill, ed., *The Woman Movement: Feminism in the United States and England* (Chicago: Quadrangle Books, 1969), p. 27.

38. Quoted in ibid., p. 27.

39. James Reed, *From Private Vice to Public Virtue: The Birth Control Movement and American Society Since 1830* (New York: Basic Books, 1978), pp. 35–36.

40. Quoted in ibid., p. 36.

41. Lois Banner, *Women in Modern America* (New York: Harcourt Brace Jovanovich, Inc., 1974), p. 16.

42. Reed, *Vice to Virtue*, p. 36.

43. Hymowitz and Weissman, *A History of Women*, p. 70.

44. Quoted in Papachristou, *Women Together*, p. 73.

45. Karen O'Connor, *Women's Organizations' Use of the Courts* (Lexington, Mass.: Lexington Books, 1980), chap. 3.

46. Quoted in Johanna Johnston, *Mrs. Satan* (New York: Putnam, 1967), pp. 118–119.

47. O'Neill, *Woman Movement*, p. 29.

48. Banner, *Women in Modern America*, p. 17.

49. Reed, *Vice to Virtue*, p. 37. The inadequacies of birth control methods and lack of knowledge about fertile periods may have contributed to the lack of popularity of birth control. For example, one popular pamphlet on birth control counseled women to refrain from sex at all times except the middle of the menstrual cycle. For a discussion of the issue, see Charles Knowlton and Robert Dale Owen, *Birth Control and Morality in Nineteenth Century America, 1859–1878* (1878; reprint ed., New York: Arno Press, 1972), p. 34.

50. Degler, *At Odds*, p. 216. The following quotation and information in the paragraph are also found in Degler, *At Odds*, p. 214.

51. Reed, *Vice to Virtue*, p. 36.

52. Hymowitz and Weissman, *A History of Women*, p. 173.

53. These sentiments appeared in a book written by Tennessee Clafin in 1873 as quoted in Linda Gordon, *Woman's Body, Woman's Right: Birth Control in America* (New York: Penguin Books, 1977), p. 97.

54. Ibid., p. 95.

55. Quoted in Gordon, *Woman's Body, Woman's Right*, p. 97.

56. Ibid.

57. Ibid., pp. 97–98.

58. Degler, *At Odds*, p. 204.

59. See contra, Elizabeth Cady Stanton and others, *Woman's Bible*, 2 vols. (New York: European Publishing Company, 1895 and 1898) where she discusses this and other controversial issues.

60. See, for example, Charlotte Perkins Gilman, *The Home, Its Work and Influence* (1903; reprint ed., New York: Source Books, 1970) and *Human Work* (New York: Phillips and Co., 1904). See also, *Herland* (New York: Charlton Co., 1914) for Gilman's futurist view of female society.

61. Banner, *Women in Modern America*, p. 109. The charge by the press that feminism and divorce were linked was fueled by statistics that revealed that from 1890 to 1920, the divorce rate increased two-and-one-half times. Papachristou, *Women Together*, p. 113. For a discussion of this problem, see William L. O'Neill, "Divorce as a Moral Issue: A Hundred Years of Controversy," in Carol V.R. George, ed., *"Remember the Ladies." New Perspectives on Women in American History* (Syracuse: Syracuse University Press, 1975), p. 138.

62. See Marie Louise Degen, *The History of the Woman's Peace Party* (Baltimore: Johns Hopkins University Press, 1939), p. 20.

63. Banner, *Women in Modern America*, pp. 102–104. She dicusses Gilman and other like-minded reformers as "radicals."

64. Charlotte Perkins Gilman, *Woman and Economics* (1878; reprint ed., New York: Source Book, 1970).

65. In a few places these new reforms were taken up if only briefly. See Betty Friedan, *The Second Stage* (New York: Summit Books, 1981), pp. 288–293. See also, Banner, *Women in Modern America,* p. 103.

66. For more about Emma Goldman, see Richard Drinnon, *Rebel in Paradise: A Biography of Emma Goldman* (Chicago: University of Chicago Press, 1961) and Emma Goldman, *Living My Life* (New York: Alfred A. Knopf, 1931).

67. Papachristou, *Women Together,* p. 191.

68. Reed, *Vice to Virtue,* pp. 83–84. For a more detailed account of Sanger's activities, see Lawrence Lader, *Margaret Sanger and the Fight for Birth Control* (Boston: Beacon Press, 1955). See also, by Margaret Sanger, *My Fight for Birth Control* (New York: Farrarr, 1931), and *Women and the New Race* (New York: Truth Publishing, 1921).

69. Reed, *Vice to Virtue,* p. 87.

70. Ibid., p. 88.

71. Ibid.

72. Sheila M. Rothman, *Woman's Proper Place* (New York: Basic Books, Inc., 1978), p. 221.

73. In limiting herself to one issue, Sanger noted, "The other pioneers have made the same mistake; they have not concentrated on the one object to the exclusion of everything else." Quoted in Reed, *Vice to Virtue,* p. 96.

74. James, ed., *Notable American Women,* vol. I, s.v. Mary Dennett, p. 646.

75. *The Birth Control Review,* December 1921, p. 18.

76. Gordon, *Woman's Body, Woman's Right,* p. 221.

77. Mary Ware Dennett, *Birth Control Laws: Shall We Keep Them, Change Them, or Abolish Them?* (New York: Frederick H. Hitchcock, 1926), p. 192.

78. Quoted in Gordon, *Woman's Body, Woman's Right,* p. 238.

79. Ibid., p. 242.

80. Rothman, *Woman's Proper Place,* p. 221.

81. Reported in U.S. Congress, Senate Committee on Public Health and National Quarantine, Protection of Maternity and Infancy, hearings, 66th Cong., 2nd Sess., on S. 3259, May 12, 1920, pp. 7–8.

82. Clement E. Vose, *Constitutional Change* (Lexington, Mass.: Lexington Books, 1972), p. 262.

83. J. Stanley Lemons, *The Woman Citizen: Social Feminism in the 1920s* (Urbana: University of Illinois Press, 1973), p. 155.

84. Vose, *Constitutional Change,* p. 262.

85. Quoted in Lemons, *Woman Citizen,* p. 155.

86. Josephine Goldmark, *Impatient Crusader* (Urbana: University of Illinois Press, 1953), p. 93.

87. Ibid.

88. "Herod is Not Dead," *Good Housekeeping,* LXXI, December, 1920, p. 4.

89. The NWP was not against the act itself. However, it believed that the orientation of the proposed legislation should be changed so that pregnancy would not be treated as something that made women unique. Rothman, *Woman's Proper Place,* pp. 157–158.

90. William L. O'Neill, *Everyone Was Brave* (Chicago: Quadrangle, 1969), p. 303.

91. Rothman, *Woman's Proper Place,* p. 157.

92. U.S. Congress, House Committee on Interstate and Foreign Commerce, Public Protection on Maternity and Infancy, hearings, 66th Cong., 3rd Sess., on H.R. 10925, Dec. 20–29, 1920, pp. 27–29.

93. Vose, *Constitutional Change,* p. 265.

94. Ibid., p. 267.

95. Ibid., p. 268.

96. *Frothingham* v. *Mellon,* 262 U.S. 447 (1923).

97. Quoted in Papachristou, *Women Together,* p. 197.

98. Ibid., p. 196.

99. Rothman argues that any chances at all for WJCC success were dashed when the American Medical Association (AMA) came out solidly against funding extension. In the early 1920s, although the AMA had been against the act, few physicians were interested in the bill. In the 1920s, doctors had not yet come to see their mission as preventive medicine; thus, they failed to view the clinics funded by the act as threatening. Once, however, the medical profession became involved in prevention, many doctors came to see these prenatal clinics as opening the floodgates to socialized medicine. Thus, they successfully lobbied against further funding of the programs begun by the STMA. In essence, because the act allowed women to seek medical assistance from clinics, private physicians saw the act as a public bad that threatened their livelihood. *Woman's Proper Place,* pp. 142–147.

100. Papachristou, *Women Together,* p. 199.

101. Goldman, in fact, was deported for her socialist ties in 1919.

102. Banner, *Women in Modern America,* p. 20.

103. Ibid., p. 149.

104. Lillian Hellman, *Unfinished Woman: A Memoir* (Boston: Little Brown, 1969), p. 35.

105. For an excellent discussion of the radical feminist positions and activities in this area, see Alix Kates Shulman, "Sex and Power: Sexual Bases of Radical Feminism," *Signs* 5 (Summer 1980):590–604.

106. *Redstockings Manifesto* in Robin Morgan, ed., *Sisterhood is Powerful: An Anthology of Writings from the Women's Liberation Movement* (New York: Vintage Books, 1970), p. 534.

107. Ibid., pp. 533–536.

108. Gayle Graham Yates, *What Women Want: The Ideas of the Movement* (Cambridge, Mass.: Harvard University Press, 1975), pp. 103–106.

109. Kate Millet, *Sexual Politics* (Garden City, N.Y.: Doubleday, 1970).

110. Judith Hole and Ellen Levine, *Rebirth of Feminism* (New York: Quadrangle Books, 1971), pp. 142–144 and "The Feminists: A Political Organization to Annihilate Sex Roles," in Anne Koedt, Ellen Levine, and Anita Rapone, eds., *Radical Feminism* (New York: Quadrangle Books, 1973), pp. 369–370.

111. Shulamith Firestone, *The Dialectic of Sex: The Case for Feminist Revolution* (New York: Bantam Books, 1970).

112. Anne Koedt, "The Myth of the Vaginal Orgasm," in Leslie B. Tanner, ed., *Voices from Women's Liberation* (New York: New American Library/ Mentor Books, 1970), pp. 158–166.

113. For a discussion of these writings, see Shulman, "Sex and Power," pp. 596–601 and Yates, *What Women Want,* pp. 77–116. Many of the original documents

are reprinted in Tanner, ed., *Voices from Women's Liberation* and Morgan, ed., *Sisterhood is Powerful.*

114. Zillah R. Eisenstein, ed., *Capitalist Patriarchy and The Case for Socialist Feminism* (New York: Monthly Review Press, 1979), pp. 5–40.

115. Irene Diamond, "Pornography and Repression: A Reconsideration," *Signs* 5 (Summer, 1980):688–691 and Laura Lederer, ed., *Take Back the Night: Women On Pornography* (New York: Bantam Books, 1980).

116. The Feminists, however, limited the membership of married women to only one-third of its members. "The Feminists," in Koedt et al., eds., *Radical Feminism,* p. 374.

117. Quoted in Barbara Susan, "About My Consciousness Raising," in Tanner, ed., *Voices from Women's Liberation,* p. 241.

118. Hole and Levine, *Rebirth of Feminism,* pp. 123–124. It was at this demonstration that supposed "bra-burning" took place, which earned women liberationists the nickname "bra burners." This "event," however, never occured.

119. For a discussion and listing of some of these events, see Shulman, "Sex and Power," pp. 594–596 and Hole and Levine, *Rebirth of Feminism,* pp. 126–128.

120. Ibid.

121. See Shulman, "Sex and Power," p. 596 and Yates, *What Women Want,* pp. 108–110.

122. Zillah R. Eisenstein, *The Radical Future of Liberal Feminism* (New York: Longman, 1981), pp. 192–197 and 201–253.

123. Reported in *Ms.,* September 1981, p. 18.

124. In 1972 and again in late 1976, the Court upheld the right of Alabama and Kentucky to mandate a woman's use of her husband's surname when applying for a driver's license. Although there was no organized women's rights group activity in the Alabama case, the Kentucky suit was brought by a NOW member with NOW support. Thus, at this writing a woman's right to retain her maiden name is clearly a right largely determined by state law, and the Supreme Court appears unwilling to become involved in the issue of sex discrimination found in the Kentucky/Alabama-type statutes.

125. *Forbush* v. *Wallace,* 405 U.S. 970 (1972).

126. Testimony of Betty Furness before the Subcommittee on Banking and Currency of the House of Representatives, 1973, quoted in Joyce Gelb and Marian Lief Palley, "Women and Interest Group Politics: A Case Study of the Equal Credit Opportunity Act," 5 *American Politics Quarterly* (July 1977):336.

127. Gelb and Palley, "A Case Study," provides an analysis of these lobbying efforts for the Credit Act.

128. Noted in ibid., p. 336.

129. 404 U.S. 71 (1971).

130. *Report of the President's Commission on the Status of Women,* 1963, pp. 46–48.

131. Karen DeCrow, *Sexist Justice* (New York: Vintage Books, 1975), pp. 201–203.

132. *What Women Want,* from the Official Report to the President (New York: Simon and Schuster, 1979), p. 129 (hereafter, *What Women Want*).

133. Ibid.

134. Ibid.

135. Kanowitz, *Women and the Law,* pp. 64–67.

136.   Babcock et al., *Sex Discrimination and the Law*, p. 693.

137.   In 1978 in *Orr* v. *Orr*, 440 U.S. 268, the United States Supreme Court ruled that Alabama's law, which allowed women but not men to sue for awards of alimony, was impermissible discrimination. Thus, states have moved to change their laws to comply with the Court's decision.

138.   *What Women Want*, p. 178.

139.   For a detailed analysis of the problems of enforcing child-support awards, see David L. Chambers, *Making Fathers Pay: The Enforcement of Child Support* (Chicago: University of Chicago Press, 1979). Some studies have found that only 25 percent of all eligible women actually receive child support. And, in 1975, 60 percent of those who did receive child support got less than $1,500. Black and Hispanic women, in particular, are less likely to be awarded child support by the court (71 percent of all white women but only 44 percent of Hispanic and 29 percent of black women are awarded child payments by the court). The amounts of the award are similarly skewed, with white women getting $2,800, Hispanic women $1,320, and black mothers $1,290 per year. (Only 5 percent of all unmarried mothers ever get any child support money.) Similarly, less than half of all divorced women (in 1979) received any property settlement upon divorce. The median value of property received was $4,650. Diane Pearce and Harriett McAdoo, *Women and Children: Alone and in Poverty* (Washington, D.C.: National Advisory Council on Economic Opportunity, 1981), Reprinted by the Women's Research and Education Institute. pp. 4–5.

140.   Additionally, the National Women's Conference Report urged state courts to consider the standard of living a child enjoyed before the divorce in determining support awards and also recommended strong enforcement of maintenance orders by state attorneys.

141.   *NOW Times*, April–May 1978, p. 12.

142.   Ibid.

143.   Women's Research and Education Institute, *Study of Enforcement of Alimony and Child Support* (Washington, D.C., 1982), p. 27.

144.   *NOW Times*, February 1978, p. 13.

145.   Rae André, *Homemaker: The Forgotten Workers* (Chicago: University of Chicago Press, 1981), pp. 186–228.

146.   For a discussion of this problem, see Pearce and McAdoo, *Women and Children*.

147.   André, *Homemakers*, pp. 218–229.

148.   It should be noted that the 1982 tax cut bill also contained a provision to reduce the tax penalties paid by married couples.

149.   As proposed within the comprehensive Women's Economic Equality Act, employers would be entitled to a $3,000 first year and $1,500 second year credit. The Women's Research and Education Institute, *Tax Credits for Hiring Displaced Homemakers* (Washington, D.C., n.d.), p. 14.

150.   "Gloria Steinem Examines the Women's Decade: Wins, Losses and Changes in Her Life," *People*, June 23, 1980, p. 32.

151.   *What Women Want*, introduction by Gloria Steinem, p. 16.

152.   Boston Women's Health Book Collective, *Our Bodies, Ourselves* (New York: Simon and Schuster, 1971).

153.   Connecticut passed the first law restricting abortion in 1821.

154. Lawrence Lader, *Abortion* (Boston: Beacon Press, 1966), p. 88 and Hole and Levine, *Rebirth of Feminism*, p. 280.

155. Gordon, *Woman's Body, Woman's Right*, pp. 49–60.

156. Lawrence Lader, *Abortion II—Making of the Revolution* (Boston: Beacon Press, 1973), p. 20.

157. Hole and Levine, *Rebirth of Feminism*, p. 290.

158. Lader, *Abortion*, pp. 10–17 and Hole and Levine, *Rebirth of Feminism*, p. 283.

159. Reported in Lader, *Abortion*, pp. 145–146.

160. Lawrence Lader, *Margaret Sanger and the Fight for Birth Control* (Boston: Beacon Press, 1955).

161. Lader, *Abortion*, pp. 147–148.

162. Ibid., p. 148.

163. Hole and Levine, *Rebirth of Feminism*, p. 284.

164. National Organization for Women, *NOW Bill of Rights*, Washington, D.C., 1967.

165. Betty Friedan, *It Changed My Life: Writings on the Women's Movement* (New York: Dell, 1977), pp. 166–176.

166. Hole and Levine, *Rebirth of Feminism*, pp. 296–297.

167. Ibid., p. 296.

168. Ibid.

169. Ibid., p. 297. This kind of protest is illustrative of the "Zap Action" by groups of younger-branch women who banded together on an ad hoc basis to demonstrate or to testify against restrictive abortion laws—one of the earliest and most enduring concerns of radical feminists.

170. Ibid., p. 298.

171. 402 U.S. 62 (1971).

172. 410 U.S. 113 (1973).

173. 410 U.S. 179 (1973).

174. For an interesting account of the Court's handling of the abortion cases, see Bob Woodward and Scott Armstrong, *The Brethren: Inside the Supreme Court* (New York: Simon and Schuster, 1979), pp. 165–178.

175. Constance Balides et al., "The Abortion Issue: Major Groups, Organizations and Funding Sources," in Howard and Joy Osofsky, eds., *The Abortion Experience* (New York: Harper and Row, 1973), p. 513.

176. Deirdre English, "The War Against Choice—Inside the Antiabortion Movement," *Mother Jones*, February/March 1981, p. 17.

177. Ibid., p. 20.

178. Robert N. Lynch, "The National Committee for a Human Life Amendment, Inc.: Its Goals and Origins," *Catholic Lawyer* 20 (Autumn 1974):303.

179. English, "The War Against Choice," p. 20.

180. Frederick S. Jaffe, Barbara L. Lindheim, and Phillip R. Lee, *Abortion Politics: Private Morality and Public Policy* (New York: McGraw Hill, 1981), chap. 6.

181. Quoted in Carol Felsenthal, *The Sweetheart of the Silent Majority: A Biography of Phyllis Schlafly* (Garden City, N.Y.: Doubleday & Co., 1981), p. 239.

182. Quoted from *Civil Liberties* in Lee Epstein, "The Impact of the ACLU Reproductive Freedom Project," paper delivered at the 1981 Annual Meeting of the

Midwest Political Science Association.

183. See Eva R. Rubin, *Abortion, Politics and the Courts* (Westport, Conn.: Greenwood Press, 1982).

184. For more detailed discussions of the RFP, see Epstein, "ACLU" and Rubin, *Abortion, Politics and the Courts.*

185. *Planned Parenthood* v. *Danforth*, 428 U.S. 52 (1976).

186. *Maher* v. *Roe*, 432 U.S. 464 (1977); *Beal* v. *Doe*, 432 U.S. 438 (1977); and *Poelker* v. *Doe*, 432 U.S. 519 (1977).

187. Barbara Hayler, "Abortion," *Signs* 5 (Winter 1979):319. See also, Jon R. Bond and Charles A. Johnson, "Implementing a Permissive Policy: Hospital Abortion Services after *Roe* v. *Wade*," *American Journal of Political Science* 26 (February 1982):1–24.

188. *What Women Want*, p. 160.

189. Marjorie Randon Hershey and Daniel M. West, "Single-Issue Groups and Political Campaigns: Six Senatorial Races and the Pro-Life Challenge in 1980," paper presented at the 1981 Annual Meeting of the Midwest Political Science Association.

190. In fact, several organizations, including Feminists for Life, exist.

191. The bill also would have cut off funds to all hospitals and health care providers that had anything to do with abortion, including research and counseling.

192. During 1982, several amendments were proposed to limit abortion. One, the Paramount Life Amendment (H.J. Res. 104 and S.J. Res. 19), defined the fetus as a person and would prohibit all abortions except to save the life of a mother. Another, the Human Life Federalism Amendment (S.J. Res. 110 and H.J. Res. 504), proposes to overturn *Roe* v. *Wade* and allows states or the Congress to limit, restrict, or prohibit abortions.

193. Rosalind Pollack Petchesky, "Antiabortion, Antifeminism, and the Rise of the New Right," *Feminist Studies* 7 (Summer, 1982), pp. 212–217; Richard A. Viguerie, *The New Right: We're Ready to Lead* (Falls Church, Va.: The Viguerie Company, 1980), pp. 161–162; and Andrew H. Merton, *The Right to Life Movement and its Threat to Abortion* (Boston: Beacon Press, 1981).

194. Petchesky, "Antiabortion, Antifeminism, and the New Right," pp. 215–217 and Viguerie, *The New Right*, pp. 162–163. One group noted by Viguerie, the Christian Voice, has enlisted 37,000 clergymen from 45 denominations. With a budget of $3 million it plans to distribute radio and TV tapes of messages by Senators Helms and Hatch.

195. Viguerie, *The New Right*, pp. 120, 127–128. The Viguerie Company, alone, has a mailing list of 4½ million individuals who have indicated an interest in New Right candidates.

196. Ibid., p. 162.

197. Petchesky, "Antiabortion, Antifeminism, and the New Right," pp. 221–222. Among the many liberal measures on his antifamily list, Viguerie cites (1) the 1962 and 1963 Supreme Court decisions on prayer, (2) the Elementary and Secondary Education Act of 1965, (3) the Coleman study on the benefits of school desegregation, (4) the Congressional passage of the ERA, and (5) the 1973 Supreme Court decision on abortion. Viguerie, *The New Right*, pp. 202–203.

198. Paul Weyrich, quoted in Petchesky, "Antiabortion, Antifeminism, and the New Right," p. 232. Viguerie places on his antifamily-movement list "women's libbers

who want a different political and cultural order." Viguerie, *The New Right,* p. 210.
199. Ibid., p. 195.
200. Viguerie, *The New Right,* pp. 197–198. See also, Linda Gordon and Allen Hunter, "Sex, Family and the New Right: Anti-Feminism as a Political Force," *Radical America* 11 (November 1977):12–15.
201. Viguerie, *The New Right,* p. 231.
202. The following provisions and accompanying discussion are drawn from an analysis of the Family Protection Act of 1981 by the Women's Research and Education Institute (July 1981). The provisions listed are only part of a long list of iter s in the bill which also includes (among other things) provisions to return prayer to school; provisions to inform parents if children seek birth control information (put in to force in 1983); a number of tax breaks for nonworking wives (but not those that do), for married couples who have or adopt children, and for taking care of one's elderly relatives; and provisions to obtain allotments for armed forces dependents. For a more detailed account of the New Right's lobbying efforts on behalf of the Family Protection Act, see Janet K. Boles, "Social Movements as Political Entrepreneurs: The Family Protection Act and Family Impact Policy," paper delivered at the 1982 Annual Meeting of the American Political Science Association.
203. Patricia Marks, "Legislative Update," *Women's Political Times,* September 1982, p. 11.
204. For example, reductions in Women's Educational Equity Act programs and less stringent enforcement of existing antidiscrimination provisions all are attempts to carry out the spirit of the proposed legislation. See "A Retreat on Civil Rights?" *Newsweek,* September 27, 1982, pp. 62–63 and "Every Man for Himself," *Time,* September 7, 1981, pp. 6–9.
205. Quoted in Viguerie, *The New Right,* p. 200.

8   Women's Place in the Family

INTRODUCTION

The review presented in Chapter 7 of the political struggle for women's rights as they relate to marriage, the family, and sexuality helps set the stage for an examination of the extralegal position of women in these areas. As we saw in our discussion of political and employment rights, new laws alone are rarely sufficient to bring about full equality. The situation is little different with respect to the status of women in the family. Indeed, the absence of full legal rights in this realm serves to buttress a situation that is far from parity.

The progress of women in these areas has been further hindered by the nature of many of the proposed new rights. Advocates of change to improve or to expand the opportunities of women both within and outside the family often encounter staunch opposition because such rights are perceived as direct threats to the family. Hence, they are considered pure public bads. This has been particularly true for the goals of the more radical branch of the current women's movement. Even the more modest reforms sought by the women's movements in the nineteenth and early twentieth centuries and the older branch of the movement today have been characterized by some as threats to motherhood and the sacred institution of the traditional family.

One result of these interpretations of the changes sought by these movements has been the development of organized opposition to proposed reforms. Currently, for example, groups such as the National Pro-Family Coalition have been organized to oppose virtually all of the changes sought by the modern women's movement. Such opposition movements or the absence

322

of laws, however, are only part of the explanation for the slow progress of women in this realm. The other barriers we identified in the political and economic arenas, including cultural stereotypes about the "ideal" marriage, lack of preparation by women to ask for or to bring about change, and discrimination or at least reluctance to change by men, also have hampered efforts to expand the rights of women in the family. In the sections to follow we will focus on these barriers. Our concern will be with how they have been modified over time, how they have prevented or delayed changes, and what the prognosis for the future is with respect to the barriers and women's rights vis-à-vis marriage and the family.

We focus first on the most immediate barrier, cultural stereotypes concerning women's role in the family and a woman's right to control her reproductive capabilities. Change in public attitudes, as we have seen in our discussion of the progress of women in politics and the marketplace, is usually the critical and the most important barrier to equality. We have chosen to concentrate on several attitudinal dimensions that seem most important in understanding the position of women within the family. The first of these is the public's perception concerning the place of marriage in an individual's life. We will be concerned with social attitudes about the nature of the marriage relationship as well as the perceived ideal role of each spouse concerning marital and family tasks, including housework, childrearing and decision-making. Because of the importance of the parental role on the status and progress of women both outside and within marriage, our special focus will be on attitudes toward the role of mother and the rights or acceptability of individual women's desire to limit or reject this role.

ATTITUDINAL CHANGE

The process of social change is a complex mixture of attitudinal and behavioral transformation. As the chapters on the activities of women in politics and in the marketplace made clear, it is often difficult to tell which comes first or what the interplay between practice and ideology actually is at any time. The same holds true with respect to women's rights within the family. Some key outside events often have played a critical part in setting the stage for or introducing alterations in sex roles. The influence of advocates of new ideas about the family and women's rights in that institution, however, seems to have been equally important, if not more so, in fostering changes in public opinion. Data from the 1950s and early 1960s, for example, reveal that employment of wives outside the home had little impact on traditional beliefs about women's role, the division of labor, or the authority structure of the family. More recently, however, some dramatic shifts in the public's attitudes toward marriage, the family, and role-sharing have occurred. Yet, as we shall examine, the life-style patterns in the average American family have not always kept pace with these new views. Thus, at the end of the chapter we shall try to suggest why practices and ideologies have diverged and what the prospects are for their convergence in the near future.

Attitudes Toward Marriage and the Family

Much of our data about popular stereotypes concerning the importance and nature of marriage before the advent of public opinion polls are based on actual marital practices. Alternatively, we can look at what popular writers of the time were saying or ordinary men and women were writing in their personal correspondence concerning their feelings about marriage. There are, of course, problems with either approach. Given these limitations, however, we can draw some conclusions about the nature and importance of marriage and the family in the first few decades of our nation's existence.

Pre-Twentieth Century America.[1] In colonial times, marriage was perceived as a virtual necessity and ideal goal for most men and women. Divorce was infrequent and most marriages lasted until death. While all were expected to marry, the decision about whom to marry was only secondarily, if at all, based on mutual attraction. Rather, the primary basis for marriage was economic survival of the individuals or their families. Accordingly, parental control over the timing and choice of partner was quite strong until perhaps the mid-eighteenth century.[2] Additionally, the nature of the marital relationship and the cultural attitudes about the appropriate locus of authority, division of labor, and domestic relations strongly favored a male-dominated union. However, the scarcity of women relative to men, the need for workers to grow food and deliver rudimentary services, and the Protestant faith of the colonists created a situation of somewhat greater equality between the sexes than was present at that time in many parts of the Old World.[3]

In fact, the nature of farm life and the need for both spouses to contribute to the survival of the family unit led to a greater sharing, or at least equal division, of other family roles. One factor contributing to this role-sharing was the barren existence of most early colonial homes. This meant that there was little housekeeping for either spouse as we now know it.[4] Furthermore, the lesser importance of children, probably because of the high child and infant mortality, tended to reduce the parental role. The decisions that had to be made about childrearing were assumed to be the joint endeavor of both mother and father or if anything, the father's alone to make. Indeed, the importance of the father is reflected in the guides to parents written in this period. Few mentioned the mother, stressing instead the father's role.[5]

Motherhood, in general, was less important than it was to become in Post-Revolutionary America. While all women were expected to marry, the

Protestant faith, especially the Calvinist strain, took a more "relaxed" attitude toward limiting children than did Catholicism. Abortion before "quickening" (or in the science of the day, before "life") was apparently quite acceptable.[6] In sum, the status of women in marriage differed in several aspects from what many have assumed. Women were freer to take on responsibilities outside the home and less emphasis was placed on parental and homemaker roles.

In at least one respect, however, a double moral standard existed: only married women, not married men, could be found guilty of adultery and summarily divorced or punished.[7] In the family decision-making process, as well, the husband-father was universally recognized as the ultimate authority. Women were cautioned that the "proper attitude of a wife toward her husband was 'a reverend subjection.'"[8] Thus, a married woman could expect little in the way of deference from her spouse. Given this curious mixture of pluses and minuses it is not surprising that there is disagreement among scholars, historians, and feminists whether the developments with respect to marriage that occurred after this early period were a step forward or backward.[9]

In the years after the American Revolution the nature of marriage began to change as the "modern family" emerged.[10] As noted by Carl N. Degler, the characteristics contributing to the rise of (what he terms) the modern family did not arise simultaneously. Rather, they began to evolve in the late-1700s and did not reach their ultimate development until the mid-twentieth century. He traced the emergence of the modern marriage to a number of phenomena including: the American Revolution, the Enlightenment, Protestantism as practiced in the states, the moral reform movement of the late eighteenth-early nineteenth centuries, and the new emphasis in the early nineteenth century on the child and childhood.[11] Others have attributed the changes in the marriage relationship to the growth of cities and to the Industrial Revolution.[12]

Whatever the source of the new "ideal" marriage as described in popular literature, letters, and practices of the time, this change altered the position of women within the family. A new emphasis on love or mutual attraction rather than economic necessity meant that not marrying and/or divorcing became increasingly more acceptable options to an unhappy marriage.[13] The early nineteenth century, for example, saw publication of the first advice books for young girls and, in fact, many contained at least some support for women who chose not to marry.[14]

For those who married, the changed emphasis on the goals of marriage from economics to affection meant that romantic love, perhaps long an ideal, now became the sought-after basis for marriage. The nature of this early version of companionship, however, was strongly conditioned by the inequality of the sexes and thus was overwhelmingly patriarchal.[15] A woman was expected to obey, revere, and submit to her husband's will. One minister characterized the duties of a wife as those of:

counsellor and friend of the husband; who makes it her daily study to
lighten his cares, to soothe his sorrows, and to augment his joys; who, like a
guardian angel, watches over his interests, warns him against dangers,
comforts him under trials; and by her pious, assiduous, and attractive
deportment, constantly endeavors to render him more virtuous, more
useful, more honourable, and more happy.[16]

There is little reference during this period to any reciprocal emotional support
from husband to wife. Indeed, it is unlikely that the stringent sex-segregated
lives of men and women made it possible for either spouse to understand or
support each other fully.[17]

Another facet of marriage—mutual sexual satisfaction—also changed as
a result of the sharpened role divisions that were present at the height of the
Victorian era. The sexual needs of men and women were viewed as quite
distinct. Men had a sex drive; women had only maternal urges. Only toward
the end of the nineteenth century was there a growing awareness of female
sexuality.[18]

In terms of performance of marital/family tasks, the parting of work and
home that accompanied the Industrial Revolution meant that increasingly
"separate spheres" of activity were assigned to men and women. With respect
to family decision-making, the husband was supreme and women were
regularly reminded that they were to be submissive to their husbands.[19]

While major family decisions were left to the husband, the wife had more
say in "her spheres," including care of the home. During the nineteenth
century, housekeeping became an art and by the beginning of the twentieth
century a science. Many women's magazines dedicated to helping women
learn and perfect their skills in this area were founded during this period.[20] It is
clear that men were not expected to have anything to do with this new and
growing set of domestic chores.

The division of sex roles with respect to parenthood was almost as sharp.
The highest goal for a woman was to be a mother. Indeed, motherhood came
to be the only way a woman could gain any status in the community or
authority in the family. The assumed greater religiousness, patience, and
moral superiority of women—all tenets of what Welter calls the new cult of
true womanhood—made them ideal for raising children. Equation of
parenthood with motherhood also was conditioned by the growing absence of
the father from the home as more and more men went "out" to work. The view
that motherhood was indeed the sole purpose of women and the maternal
instinct universal may have reached its apex in the second half of the
nineteenth century when both abortion and birth control information were
outlawed.[21]

An effort by some feminists to gain some restrictions on motherhood,
labeled "Voluntary Motherhood," was itself firmly grounded in the promotherhood ideology. Limiting the number of children was viewed as only a

step in improving a woman's ability to perform her role as mother. Only a few radicals, like Elizabeth Cady Stanton, went so far as to question the primacy of the motherhood role for all women,[22] although it should be noted that restricting or limiting one's sexual activity may have helped increase a woman's power within her marriage.[23]

Thus, the Industrial Revolution and the sharpening of sex roles it produced in the economic arena had a profound impact on the position of women in the "ideal" family. The narrowing of a woman's roles in life to those of wife, mother, and housewife, when juxtaposed with the man's role as breadwinner left women in a dependent and secondary position except in those areas assigned exclusively to women.

The Changing Sexual Scene and its Impact on Marriage: 1900–1940. In many ways, the ideal marital relationship and the accompanying sharp division of sex roles that developed during the nineteenth century remained relatively stable for at least the next fifty years. In one important area, however, a significant change occurred. As early as 1910, there began to develop a growing recognition that women had sexual needs above and beyond the desire to have children.[24] The ramifications of this view were profound. The double moral standard was challenged, although far from abolished, and the "flapper" became the epitome of the new change in women's sexuality.

Many theories about the source of these changes in attitudes and behavior have been offered. Some see the prime moving agent as the suffrage movement, although suffrage leaders themselves generally were intensely moralistic. Others have identified the growth of cities with their accompanying independence of young women from their families and the employment of young women as the critical factors. Additionally, writers view the anonymity, independence from family, and community standards as associated with urbanization and work away from home as key factors in the change with World War I as having an important catalytic effect.[25]

The growing awareness of equal sexual needs of men and women affected the marriage relationship in several ways. Notions of companionship and romantic love ideals were strengthened because both men and women expected greater satisfaction of their physical needs.[26] Another area that benefitted from the change in attitudes toward sexuality was the dissemination of birth control information. The decline in the prudery of women made discussion of such topics more open and the spread of information somewhat easier. The expectation that sexual relations were not solely for procreation added to the desire for such information. Although public resistance to birth control was still intense and its advocacy often illegal as discussed in Chapter 7, there is considerable evidence that more and more women wanted such information. A 1937 poll, for example, found 79 percent of all women believed in limiting the number of births.[27] There was still, however, an almost universal assumption that all women would become mothers. The option of childlessness often did not exist as a choice. If anything, the push for birth control in this era reflected increased demands on mothers. Specifically, the popularization of such movements and theories as eugenics and Freudian psychology increasingly stressed the impact a mother had on the mental and physical development of her children. Her treatment of and behavior toward her children were identified as critical factors in predicting their future success or failure. The role of the father in the development of his children received but scant mention. Friedan and others have noted that the spread of these new ideas on child development from the 1920s on increased the burden and duties of motherhood beyond what was expected of women in earlier eras.[28] A related corollary of Freudian psychology—that women must have children to be fulfilled—also contributed to the "baby boom" that occurred in the 1950s when economic conditions were much better.

In other areas of the marital relationship there was little evidence of significant change. The ideal division of labor and sex roles between spouses, for example, remained intact. Housework continued to be seen as the responsibility of women alone. Indeed, the importance associated with this aspect of a woman's role intensified. The domestic science movement, originating out of a conference held in 1899, urged women to apply the principles of business and science to their homemaking jobs. New and higher standards were introduced.[29] Reflecting this emphasis on housework, colleges in the 1920s created home economics courses for the purpose of training women for their future "occupation."[30] Women's magazines also took up the theme. Articles in such periodicals as the *Ladies Home Journal* and *McCalls* in the 1920s and 1930s stressed the triple "joys" of being a wife, a mother, and a homemaker. Even women who went to college, unlike their counterparts in previous generations, were more likely to express a desire to forego a career for marriage and motherhood. The Depression and the shortage of jobs only strengthened the effort to define a woman's place in life as in the home.[31] In fact, as the nation entered World War II, popular perceptions of the appropriate division of labor and roles in the family were probably as strong as ever. In theory, if not always in practice, husbands continued to be the main breadwinners and wives remained the primary parent and homemaker. While alteration in public attitudes about female sexuality may have increased somewhat, the "ideals" of companionship and shared decision-making in at least some families were largely unattainable given the absence of any significant changes in public opinion about other aspects of marriage and the relative gap in economic resources between husbands and wives.

The Changing Economic Scene and Its Impact on the Family: The First Phase: 1940–1970. World War II and the movement of large numbers of married women into the workplace might have been expected to alter public perception of the ideal marriage. However, several aspects of this new phenomenon restricted the impact of women working on views about the marriage relationship. First, the jobs that these women took often failed to threaten their husbands' economic superiority. Even though the wife's salary may have allowed the family to move up the economic ladder, the larger wage gap between marital partners presented little challenge to the prevailing ethos of the male as head of the house. Second, many or most women in the 1950s who went to work saw their jobs as extensions of their mother and wife-helper roles. Third, because most of the wives who went to work were over thirty-five with only school-aged or older children, it may have been easier to add their new duties outside the home to their mother and wife roles.[32]

Rather than alter public perception of the ideal marriage, the immediate post-War era saw an increased emphasis on these role divisions within the family, a phenomenon Betty Friedan labeled the "feminine mystique"—the notion that a woman's fulfillment in life could only come through her total commitment to and adoption of, the roles of mother, wife, and homemaker.[33] Even though more and more wives were joining the labor force, the media and other authority figures in the 1950s were nearly united in the view that the happiness of a woman, the preservation of the family, and the continuation of our society required that a woman remain at home. Interviews with wives living in the Chicago area in the late 1950s and early 1960s found considerable agreement with these ideals. Among nonworking women especially, the triple roles of mother, homemaker, and wife loomed large. Almost all full-time homemakers identified their most important role as that of mother. Being a wife and/or a housewife were close seconds. Among working women, the same three roles dominated, the motherhood role taking on somewhat lesser importance because these women were older than most of the full-time homemakers questioned. Only a small percentage of women listed any roles outside the family as important.[34]

When asked to rank the most important roles for the man of the family, breadwinner was ranked first by 64 percent of the women while husband was so ranked by only 14 percent. Fatherhood was assigned first by just 9 percent. No women listed the breadwinner role as an important one for women. The main economic function of a woman continued to be one of "supporting" her husband's career by providing a happy home, encouraging him, and entertaining his business associates or perhaps taking a "temporary job."[35] Similarly in many marriages of the 1950s and early 1960s, equal sharing of household tasks was rejected or at least not expected by wives.[36]

Male dominance in decision-making also was supported by a majority of men and women in the prewomen's movement era. A poll of married women taken in Detroit found only a third disagreed with the following statement: "Most of the important decisions in the life of the family should be made by the man of the house." Working women and better-educated women were only slightly more likely to reject this view. Support for male authority was not merely reflective of views of an older generation of women. Indeed, there actually was a slight tendency for younger women to be more willing to assign the decision-making power to the husband.[37] Thus, the movement of married women into the labor force in the 1950s and early 1960s seems to have had little, if any, impact on cultural stereotypes about women's roles in life or the structure of the ideal family.

The Women's Movement and the Position of Women in the Family: 1970–Present. As recounted in previous chapters, one of the main goals of both the rights and the radical feminist branches of the movement was the abolition of the stereotype that a woman's place was solely in the home. Paralleling this objective, and partially as a result of it, was the fact that the massive flow of married women into the work force continued unabated. More important, the married working wife became the working mother of young children. The resultant social changes began to have a massive effect on attitudes toward marriage and women's and men's roles in society and in the family. While it may have been possible in the 1950s to combine a "job" and motherhood, especially when children were older, the new working woman soon discovered the burden of the two roles, especially if she wanted a "career," difficult if not impossible to manage.[38] The conflict between the traditional roles of women and the new roles—careerist and breadwinner— has yet to be resolved, but it is clear to many that combining the two is not as simple as Friedan supposed when she wrote twenty years ago, "It is not as difficult as the feminine mystique implies, to combine marriage and motherhood and even the kind of lifelong personal purpose that once was called 'career.'"[39] By 1979 Friedan, referring to her misplaced optimism, noted:

> We told our daughters that they could—and should—have it all. Why not? After all, men do. But the "superwomen" who are trying to "have it all," combining full-time careers and "stretch-time" motherhood, are enduring such relentless pressures that their younger sisters may not even dare to think about having children.[40]

As noted in Chapter 6, feminists in the women's movement have suggested two approaches to solving the conflict between the traditional and new roles of women. One involves a change in the economic arena to make jobs and careers more amenable to the demands of raising a family and taking care of a home. Initially, these changes were advocated to make the mother role easier, but more recently they have been suggested as methods to help the father perform his role as well. The realization that these reforms alone often are not sufficient has led to a related strategy for coping with the conflict: structural changes in the family itself. What is being advocated is a change in attitudes and practices with respect to sharing of roles, responsibilities, and domestic tasks by husbands and wives, fathers and mothers. The extent to which the latter ideology has been adopted is our next topic.

Attitudes Toward Marriage: Post 1970. In the mid-1950s nearly every woman believed that to find fulfillment in life she had to get married. By the early 1980s, it appears that this view may be declining in popularity, although the desire to get or be married remains strong. According to a 1979 poll, more than 90 percent of all women still favor marriage over alternative life-styles.[41] Marriage, however, is no longer seen as a necessity. Surveys in the late 1970s and early 1980s found large majorities of Americans agreeing that remaining unmarried can be a valid and positive choice as compared to the 1950s, when 80 percent felt that not being married was an unnatural state for either sex.[42] Among some young women, a career outside the home may even be replacing marriage as a life goal. A 1979 study of adolescent women living in New York City, for example, found "getting married" was considerably less important to them than "getting a job I enjoy." Only 25 percent viewed marriage as important while nearly 90 percent stressed the importance of getting a good job.[43]

Disillusionment with the rewards and fulfillment of marriage also is reflected in the noticeable decline in positive attitudes toward marriage among married women. The drop has been particularly significant among full-time homemakers. In 1957, nearly 40 percent of a national sample of housewives had only positive things to say about marriage. By 1976, just slightly more than 25 percent of such women were so upbeat. The decline among working married women was smaller but still downward. Thirty-five percent of them gave only positive comments about marrige in 1957. By 1976, the figure had dropped to 30 percent. Interestingly, in 1976 majorities of full-time housewives and working wives mentioned the restrictive nature of marriage in discussing its impact.[44]

There also is a growing acceptance of divorce when a marriage is unsuccessful. Between 1970 and 1979, the percentage of women who believed that divorce was an acceptable solution to an unsuccessful marriage rose from 52 to 62 percent with only 22 percent objecting to divorce under all circumstances.[45]

The changing view of marriage, however, is accompanied by a fear among a large segment of the population that marriage itself is threatened. More than 66 percent of all women responding to a national study in 1979, for example, felt that the institution of marriage had weakened over the past ten years.[46]

Attitudes Toward Motherhood. In the past, motherhood ranked second only to marriage as a woman's goal in life. Today, however, many women no longer identify motherhood as the route to happiness or the primary role in life for all women. Eighty-two percent of women questioned in 1979 disagreed with the statement that children are essential for a full and happy marriage.[47] Similarly, a 1976 national poll of adults found that nearly 66 percent of those interviewed rejected the statement, "By nature women are happiest when they are making a home and caring for children." More than 80 percent of the young, college-educated men and women denied the validity of this basic tenet of the feminine mystique.[48] Even childlessness as an ideal life-style is gaining popularity among some groups of women. A 1976 survey of 18- to 34-year-old women, for example, revealed that close to 15 percent of women with at least one year of college expect never to have a child.[49]

Polls, moreover, continue to show that among those desiring a family, the ideal number of children has declined dramatically since the 1950s. In 1980, more than half of all adults chose two as the best number and those wanting four children dropped to 12 percent from its high point of 49 percent in 1949.[50] Additionally, most of the public believes that trends toward smaller families will continue.[51]

Even mothers today evidence some reservations about their role. In 1976, for example, 60 percent gave ambivalent, neutral, or negative first comments when asked about the impact of having children on a woman's life. Additionally, more than 80 percent of the women interviewed made at least some reference to the restrictive nature of children on a woman's life.[52] The rate of change in attitudes among certain groups of women is often dramatic. For example, John Scanzoni reports that from 1971 to 1975, the percent of young, married women in one sample group agreeing with the view that "a woman's greatest reward and satisfaction come through her children" went from 61 to 45 percent.[53] There were also parallel declines in the perceived sacredness of the mother role and in the attitude that a mother should place the interests of her children above her own personal interests.[54]

Finally, as earlier noted in Chapter 6, among women especially, the notion that children do not need a full-time mother in the home is becoming increasingly accepted. This change in attitudes toward the "joys of motherhood" may be traceable to the growing desire of women to have a career outside the home and the recognition that this is made more difficult, if not impossible, when one has children.

The more flexible attitude toward the mother role also is observed in opinion polls concerning birth control. In 1978, 72 percent of a national sample of adults expressed positive attitudes toward birth control, and in 1977, 81 percent thought birth control information should be available to teenagers.[55] These figures, however, may decline if the leaders of the New Right and related groups are successful in convincing the public that sex education, at least in public schools, threatens the family and contributes to teenage pregnancy.[56]

On the question of abortion, the complex nature of the issue and the presence of organized and vocal proponents and opponents have led to a heated debate and solidifying of opinion on both sides. While only a minority of the public—10 percent in a June 1981 ABC poll—disapproved of abortion in all circumstances, 34 percent qualified their approval of this practice favoring abortion only under certain circumstances. Forty percent, however, approved of abortions for any reason.[57] Not surprisingly, pollsters report that opposition is consistently strongest among those groups where we have previously seen evidence of resistance to new ideas about women's role in society—Southerners, frequent church attenders, the less well educated, and to some extent older citizens and Catholics.[58] Additionally, there was an association between opposition to abortion and support for other traditional, patriarchal views. One study found that those most opposed to abortion also objected to premarital sex, divorce, contraception, and sex education.[59]

While the New Right movement has had only marginal success in persuading the public of the need for a constitutional amendment banning abortion—61 percent opposed such an amendment in winter of 1982[60]—it has had success in convincing the Congress about the desirability of cutting off public monies to fund abortions for poor women. President Reagan's endorsement both of a constitutional amendment and of funding limitations may well increase the legitimacy of these viewpoints among some, but public opinion polls to date suggest this has not yet happened. Indeed, prochoice voters now seem as willing as antiabortion voters to vote against a candidate who takes a position opposite to them on this issue.[61] In fact, the defeat of attempts to limit abortion by Congressional law or constitutional amendment in 1982 may indicate an awareness of this trend on the part of politicians.

Nature of the Marriage Relationship: Division of Roles and Labor. Perhaps the most dramatic and important change in attitudes toward marriage and motherhood, however, is found in the type of marriage and motherhood young people, especially women, want today. By the end of the 1970s, few young women reported expectations of a traditional marriage in which the husband is the breadwinner and the wife stays home with the children. As early as 1973, only one-third of women under thirty expressed a desire for that kind of relationship as compared to nearly two-thirds of the women over fifty. Among the young, the favored life-style was a shared or partnership marriage where "husband and wife share responsibilities more—both work, both share homemaking and child responsibilities."[62] Surveys in the late 1970s especially among young and working women, indicate even further decline in preference for traditional forms of marriage.[63]

With respect to specific aspects of marriage, support for men helping out with housework, at least among women, has grown dramatically. Arland

Thornton and Deborah Freedman report that between 1962 and 1977 in one sample of married women, the percentage who believed a woman should expect help from her husband around the house increased from 46 to 62 percent. The more educated, younger, and/or working women were even more likely to favor this practice.[64] Scanzoni describes a similar trend between 1971 and 1975 in a sample of young married women. In this group, the percentage of women agreeing that a husband should share household tasks if the wife works climbed from 58 to 75. Additionally, over 90 percent of the women interviewed in 1975 believed that the parental role should be divided equally if the wife worked.[65] Interviews with blue-collar women in non-traditional jobs also revealed overwhelming support for a helping husband. More than 90 percent of these women rejected the statement that "a man who helps around the kitchen is doing more than expected," and close to the same figure opposed the view that "a wife should do the cooking and housecleaning and the husband should provide the family with money."[66] Not surprisingly, this sentiment about sharing tasks is stronger among women than men. A 1979 survey, for example, found that 80 percent of men aged eighteen to fifty thought that doing the wash was women's work; 75 percent felt the same way about cleaning the bathroom and fixing dinner.[67]

Closely associated with an increased desire to share housework with men is a marked decline in positive attitudes toward housework among women. When housewives were interviewed in 1957, 66 percent of a national sample gave positive responses to a question asking for their feelings about housework. By 1976, only half of all housewives in a similar sample responded favorably. Among college-educated housewives, the number giving positive responses dropped to 33 percent. Interestingly, half of those reporting negative attitudes were planning to work outside the home.[68] Working women, especially young professional women, were even more likely to downgrade housework and the housewife role.[69] The 1980 General Mills survey of American families reports similar results. It found only among full-time homemakers was the job of homemaking seen as having more advantages than disadvantages. Among women who worked at jobs outside the home, more than 50 percent saw more disadvantages to the traditional woman's role and only a third believed it had more advantages. Most men, especially those with working wives, saw more disadvantages than advantages to the job of homemaking.[70]

The decline in the status of housework and the housewife role is also reflected in the lower levels of "happiness" reported by full-time homemakers compared to working wives in the 1970s.[71] Myra Marx Ferree provides some evidence that part of this decline in satisfaction with the housewife role may be attributable to the growing trend for women to work at paid jobs. The isolation and lack of adult companionship make the life of the housewife seem comparatively lonely and dull. In one limited study, she found for women with children under six the more isolated the woman, the more likely she was to be dissatisfied with housework. For women with older children, however, the desire for a career, not isolation, was the most potent predictor of dissatisfaction.[72] But another explanation for the lower level of happiness among women in the home may be that some of them are unemployed women who would like to go back to work. One study found it was the latter group, and not housewives per se who are unhappy.[73]

Attitudes toward increased role sharing between men and women also are being extended to cover the breadwinner role. For example, only a third of the women interviewed by Scanzoni in the early 1970s identified the married man's chief responsibility as his job. Moreover, 55 percent of all working women felt it was their duty alone or the joint duty of husband and wife to provide for the family, rather than this being solely the husband's responsibility.[74] While the questions were not identical, this seems to represent a considerable change from what was found in the 1960s.

One of the roles assigned almost exclusively to the woman in the nineteenth century that most men and women now think should be shared is the parental role. In 1980, only 10 percent of all men and women living in families thought raising children should be the mother's responsibility.[75] As discussed below there are several barriers to complete parental role sharing. Additionally, in ranking roles, parenting is still perceived by a majority of the public as the woman's first responsibility relative to other roles (worker, political activist, etc.), while for men the breadwinner role is recognized as predominant. For example, as discussed in Chapter 6, if and when there are young children at home, the mother, and not the father, is expected to decrease or forego the breadwinner-worker's role to handle additional parenting responsibilities. For example, large majorities of the public believe that the mother should stay home when children are sick, shop for children's clothes, and take the children for checkups. Moreover, while a majority believed that both parents should share most other parental roles, with the exceptions of deciding on a child's allowance and teaching sports, few see the father alone having any significant role raising children.[76] Further evidence that old stereotypes about division of family roles are changing slowly can be found with respect to role reversal, where the husband stays home and the wife works. Once soundly rejected by all, this concept received verbal support from almost 50 percent of the adult women interviewed in 1979. Younger women, college graduates, those with high incomes, and those not living in the South were most in favor of this dramatic change.[77] No comparable question was asked of men but it is doubtful that so many would be as agreeable to such an arrangement. Hesitancy about role switching, for example, was reflected in a 1979 survey where only 40 percent of all men and women reported they would not lose respect for a male homemaker. While this represents an improvement from ten years earlier when only 20 percent of men and only 12.5 percent of the women responded in this way, it is clear that public attitudes toward completely interchangeable and hence equal roles for men and women with respect to family needs enjoy less than universal support.[78]

A similar change in attitudes is reflected in women's opinions on gender division of the family decision-making process. On the one hand, there appears to be some movement toward a belief that this process should be shared. For example, while in 1962 a majority of Detroit area wives believed that husbands should make the important family decisions, by 1977 these same women rejected this idea by nearly a two to one margin.[79] Similarly, by 1980 more than 75 percent of men and women living in families disagreed with the statement that "the person whose salary or wages are the most important to the family should make most of the big financial decisions" and with the proposition that the lesser wage earner should make most of the decisions about housework and family activities.[80]

Wholehearted agreement with joint decision making, however, may be tempered by some older views about who should have the final say in many matters. Seventy-five percent of all the young married women interviewed by Scanzoni in the mid-1970s agreed with the notion that "the husband should be the head of the family," even though most of these women favored shared decision making in family matters.[81] Thus, as with role sharing, the favored family pattern of decision making appears to have shifted from one of total role division between the sexes to some form of sharing but with each spouse still regarded as retaining a dominant role in areas that previously were his or hers alone.

Expressive Relationship. Probably the one aspect of marriage where there is the widest support for gender equality is the expressive area. Women today, reflecting an ideal begun during the nineteenth century, want their husbands to listen to their problems, give them emotional support, and satisfy their physical needs. The 1980 Virginia Slims poll found that "being in love," "being able to talk together about your feelings," "having a good sexual relationship," and "having your spouse understand and appreciate what you do every day" were all seen as very important by the majority of women and men. Women, however, more than men, rated these factors as very important.[82] There is some evidence that women who support equal roles for the sexes and women with higher education levels expect even more sharing and equal treatment than traditionally minded women.[83]

Thus, there have been some significant changes in cultural attitudes toward the marriage relationship in the decade of the 1970s. The source of this change is multifaceted but one of the most important factors appears to be the women's movement. By recognizing and advocating a woman's right to find fulfillment outside of the home, the proponents of the movement have caused many women to question and some to reject the feminine mystique. Additionally, by encouraging women to join the work force, the movement has led large numbers of people to recognize that changes in the family are necessary if women are able to combine a job and marriage successfully. Evidence of the women's movement's effectiveness in these attitudinal changes is indicated by the greater growth in egalitarian views among the women most attuned to the movement: the young, the college educated, and working women.

In recognizing the importance of the women's movement, we do not mean to ignore the fact that this change in attitudes has been made possible and further encouraged by the practice of the working wife and mother. Especially in the 1970s and early 1980s, the phenomenon of the working mother with young children has made the need for change in the family clearer and more pressing to larger numbers. The fact that employed women of all classes tend to be more egalitarian in their attitudes toward marriage is indirect support for the impact of work on women's views.

Although recent changes in attitudes have been great, one qualification about the extent of these changes is in order; there remains a considerable residue of the older belief system. Even many young, college-educated working women believe that a woman's primary role in life is motherhood and that her career should take second place to her husband's. Additionally, this residue of older beliefs is particularly strong in some significant elements of the population. Certain groups in the political process—most notably the Moral Majority and the New Right—have attempted to reinstitute old practices and beliefs. Its supporters and many women, especially housewives, think proposed changes in the family power structure are pure public bads. They believe that any alteration in the existing institutional structure will negatively affect everyone—both those who do as well as those who do not want any change. Members of these groups identify the traditional family as the basis of the social system and argue that any tampering with it or with traditional gender roles will bring down the whole culture. And, at least one segment of this opposition—the antiabortion movement—has had some success in halting and perhaps even reversing the trend in public opinion.

Organized opposition or cultural stereotypes about the roles of women, however, only partially explain why the position of women vis-a-vis the family has yet to become equal to that of men. Other barriers, developed in part as a result of these stereotypes, also have affected the position of women in the family. One of these barriers is the lack of preparation of women to assume or to bargain for greater equality.

PREPARATION OF WOMEN FOR AN EQUAL ROLE IN THE FAMILY

In attempting to explain the subordinate position of women in the family, many sociologists have focused on the inferior resources of wives. This lack of resources, or in our terminology, preparation, on the part of women to demand or to bargain for a more equitable role in the marriage relationship is partly traceable to the cultural stereotypes about women discussed above. For example, with respect to economic resources, one of the most direct results of the cultural stereotypes that the "proper" role for a woman was to marry and to devote her life to the roles of supportive wife, homemaker, and mother was, as we have seen in Chapters 4 and 6, that women have been ill-prepared until recently to do much else. In the past, this has generally meant that only a small minority of women was able to substitute a well-paying career as an option to marriage. In the early nineteenth century when few married women were allowed or expected to work outside the home, not having any alternative means of support meant married women were placed in a dependent position on their spouses for their existence. Later, when large numbers of women entered the work force, the low wages of women relative to men still left young women with few options except living at home or getting married. Even in the post-1940 era when married women went to work in large numbers, their meager salaries meant most had little choice but to stay married or face economic hardship. In the marriage relationship itself, the resultant relative distribution of economic resources between spouses has tended to place the wife in a poor bargaining position compared to her husband in marital disputes or attempts to equalize tasks or jobs around the house. As detailed in Chapter 6, this uneven distribution of preparation for well-paying jobs outside the home has only begun to change. Additionally, where economic resources of spouses are more evenly distributed, the position of the wife in the marital union seems to rise only marginally.

Traditionally, there have been other more visible differences in the resources of men and women. One of the most obvious is the greater physical strength of men—a resource that, at times, has been used to intimidate women. A recent study conducted by the Department of Justice suggests that marital violence is common—8.7 percent of the women reported severe physical abuse while 21 percent reported being the victims of frequent slappings, etc.[84] Additionally, most women have not been as well-prepared as men to bargain or to negotiate. Because women often are reluctant to engage in conflict, getting a husband to help around the house and with childcare may be difficult. Traditionally, women have been socialized to be unwilling or unable to engage in that kind of discussion.[85] Similarly, because of their early training to assume a passive, reactive role, women have tended to be worse bargainers than men. Many women find themselves unable to negotiate successfully with husbands who started developing related skills during boyhood. There is evidence, however, that women who adopt more egalitarian views and who work outside the home gain internal psychological resources that aid them in negotiating with their spouses in family disputes.[86]

Historically, two other resources for negotiating also have been unevenly distributed between spouses. First, the greater educational attainment of husbands relative to their wives tended until recently to give the man greater prestige with which to bargain for higher status in the family. Closely related to this, historical stereotypes about the mental and logical abilities of women have led many women to doubt their abilities to present their side of the argument in family discussions.

For the woman who did not question her own intelligence, the messages of marriage manuals and popular women's magazines was clear—let the husband be the final authority in family matters. In the mid-1800s, a wife was reminded:

> She is in a measure dependent. She asks for wisdom, constancy, firmness, perseverance, and she is willing to repay it all by the surrender of the full treasure of her affections.[87]

Betty Friedan's review of stories in women's magazines popular in the 1950s reveals that the message in most was the same as it had been 100 years earlier. Women, almost all of whom were wives in the stories, were "swallowed in an image of such passive dependence that they want[ed] men to make the decisions, even in the home."[88] Thus, the woman who read these stories and followed their advice could hardly have been expected to develop the independence and decision-making abilities that would allow her to be an equal partner in the decision-making process. Even some modern marriage manuals, including Marabel Morgan's *The Total Woman,* are often little more than "how-to-books" on keeping a husband happy.[89]

Furthermore, evidence from research on childhood socialization indicates girls are trained to this dependence very early in life. Constantina Safilios-Rothschild's review of several studies reports that virtually all find that girls are not encouraged to be independent; rather, obedience and conformity are stressed. Additionally, while girls are "overhelped" with schoolwork and other tasks, boys are forced to be independent and accomplish tasks on their own.[90] Thus, with this kind of training it is not surprising that in many families today as in the past, the husband is placed in charge of deciding important family matters.

There is evidence, however, that young girls growing up today may be developing more independence than those in previous generations. The presence of a working mother, for example, seems to encourage independence.[91] Additionally, early socialization to dependence is not necessarily irreversible, although a recent popular book, *The Cinderella Complex: Women's Hidden Fear of Independence,* has received much publicity because it makes the argument that such dependence in women is not easily eliminated.[92]

Furthermore, it should be noted that in at least two areas, housework and childcare, girls and women may actually have been overtrained to "take charge." The resulting difference in skills has been used by many men as their rationale for not sharing equally in these tasks. Additionally, the higher standards of women in certain homemaking tasks may act as stumbling blocks. In the past and even today, many women find it easier to do the jobs themselves rather than to try to train unwilling husbands. Some have also argued that some women may be reluctant to give up the little authority they have in a marriage. According to feminist Robin Morgan, "Motherhood is the one area where *we're* raised to have some power, and sure, we're ambivalent about sharing it."[93]

In other dimensions as well, women have been overtrained and men undertrained. For example, the ideal of a companionship marriage has as one of its key elements the goal of mutual affection and understanding; yet, as we know from an examination of popular literature and socialization studies, girls and women are better educated to listen, help, and provide emotional support to others than are boys and men.[94] Some have even argued that the greater emotional needs of women that develop as a result of this early training leave many women in a poor bargaining position with their husbands.[95]

Thus, until very recently, as a result of cultural stereotypes that defined their roles in a very narrow fashion to wife and mother and disparaged their abilities to do anything else, women have not always been as well prepared as men to assume, to negotiate for, or to demand an equitable division of all family roles. Nor might we add, as a result of these stereotypes, have more than a few women probably wanted a complete sharing of all aspects of family life. Our review of cultural stereotypes suggests some of these barriers may be changing, especially among young, educated women attuned to the women's movement, but the depth of some of the beliefs means change will not come quickly. Even if women do become ready to demand an equitable, shared marriage and a chance to develop as an individual both inside and outside that union, their success in achieving that goal will be limited unless they can overcome yet another important barrier—the attitudes, prejudices, and simple unwillingness to change on the part of men.

DISCRIMINATION BY MEN IN THE FAMILY

In discussing the apparent reluctance of men to share in all facets of marriage, we need to distinguish among the several aspects of this phenomenon. While concrete evidence on the different perceptions of male and female roles in marriage is scant prior to the advent of public opinion polls, in the present era men have shown a greater tendency to cling to traditional views about marriage and family life. For example, men are more conservative on such issues as the impact of a working mother on her child's development or the need for husbands and wives to share tasks around the home. While young adults of both sexes are more supportive of egalitarian marriages than were those of previous generations, a considerable gap in male-female attitudes in this area is still particularly strong in just those groups of the population most likely to be wrestling with the problem of putting these beliefs into practice—young adults. Among teenagers as well, boys tend to be more traditional in their views about role and task sharing, decision making, and working mothers.[96] For example, a survey of teenagers by General Mills found 49 percent of the boys but only 35 percent of the girls felt the person whose salary was the most important to the family should make most of the decisions.[97] Additionally, Mirra Komarovsky's studies of young males warn us that even when the attitudes of young men appear egalitarian on the surface, further probing often reveals significant qualifications in just how much their attitudes have really changed. She found that many of the college men she interviewed who were in agreement with the position that it was appropriate for a mother of preschool aged children to take a full-time job qualified their support by adding "provided, of course, that the home was run smoothly, the children did not suffer, and the wife's job did not interfere with the husband's career." Similarly, support for sharing in housekeeping tasks often was tempered by excluding specific jobs like "doing the laundry" or "changing diapers."[98]

These hidden qualifications and mixed emotions are apparently widespread throughout the male population. A 1979 survey of men aged eighteen to fifty, for example, found 82 percent approved of a mother working but at the same time, 80 percent also felt the ideal woman should be, first and foremost, a good mother.[99] The extent of the paradox in male attitudes is perhaps best exemplified in this quotation from a male college senior, "I believe that women should have equal opportunities in business and the professions, but I still insist that a woman who is a mother should devote herself entirely to her children."[100] Thus, this lag by men and the numerous qualifications in their support for change may present a serious stumbling block for putting changing views into practice.

Even among men who might want to share certain family responsibilities, many may have found that their own socialization has hampered their efforts. For example, the lack of training on the part of men for simple household tasks may inhibit their ability to share full responsibility. This may change in the future as more mothers start expecting boys and girls to perform the same jobs around the home. Evidence that this already has begun can be found in a 1979 national poll that reported that between 1974 and 1979, the proportion of women who thought boys should mend clothes and be responsible for doing the laundry rose sharply.[101]

Similarly, there has been a growing trend in the popular culture—magazine articles, books, and movies—to stress the joys of traditional female tasks like cooking and the responsibilities and rewards of fatherhood.[102] Surveys are finding, moreover, that men today are very concerned with spending time with their families even at the expense of their jobs. Large majorities of married men say that their families, marriages, or children are important factors in their decisions about hours worked, commuting distances, promotions, on-the-job travel, and transfers. In addition, only with respect to hours worked was there greater than a 10 percent difference between the importance of family to the job decisions of employed men and women.[103] Men are not always allowed, however, to take these factors into consideration. Employers place greater demands on men because they inaccurately believe that men are much more willing than women to sacrifice time with their families for their jobs. The inaccuracy of employer perceptions is reflected in a 1980 poll that found while 72 percent of all men and 77 percent of all women reported that they take their families into consideration in deciding the amount of on-the-job travel they will accept, interviews with executives in large corporations found only 34 percent believed that this was a consideration for men. In contrast, 64 percent said they believed it was an important consideration for women.[104] As long as such misperceptions persist, it will be harder for men than women to take advantage of such things as paternity leave or part-time work. According to one professional who was also a father, "Look, my boss would think I was nuts if I asked for six months off. Her [his wife's] company expects her to leave, so why should I rock the boat."[105]

One other area where men may find it easier to achieve parity with women is in their ability to express their emotions and give comfort and support. Men's liberation groups have long sought this as a goal. Increasingly, the popular media is picking up the theme. However, years of childhood socialization and the pressure on men from other men to be "macho" will not make this change easy.[106]

While men, thus, may be moving in the direction of wanting and being able to establish more equitable family arrangements, alteration of old practices will not come quickly or easily. Unlike the reforms with respect to employment or even politics, where women could exercise their rights without requiring much in the way of sacrifice from males, new proposals with regard to family life require men to relinquish some of their power and leisure that they have enjoyed in the past. For many men, movement from a position of dominance to one of joint authority is difficult if not impossible. Interviews with male college seniors, for example, have found many reluctant to even consider marrying a woman whose career would equal theirs in status or a woman who would put her career ahead of theirs.[107] Efforts to split household and child-rearing tasks may encounter even more resistance. No one likes to do many of the jobs involved in running a home and raising children. Therefore, not surprisingly, many men refuse or attempt to avoid helping with certain tasks. Even egalitarian men in dual-career families, fully recognizing and agreeing with the need to divide the burdens, may need prodding to get them to contribute their fair share. According to one male from a dual-career family on his own failures in this area,

What are the lessons of this saga of a well-intentioned male? One is that equality or communality is not won once and for all, but must continually be striven for. Backsliding and easy accommodation-to-the-male-is-less-troublesome are likely to occur unless there is, at least occasionally, effort to bring about or maintain true communality rather than peaceful adjustment.

What follows is that women must struggle for equality—that it will not easily be won or re-won. A male is not likely to bestow it—in more than surface ways.[108]

Thus, barriers to equitable sharing of all roles in the family with the possibility of individual development on the part of all members have been and continue to be strong. Therefore, we should not expect to find complete equality in all spheres of married life. The next sections explore how barriers that have evolved have shaped and continue to influence family life and the ability of individual women and men to develop both inside and outside that institution.

IMPACT OF CULTURAL ATTITUDES, LACK OF PREPARATION, AND DISCRIMINATION ON THE POSITION OF WOMEN IN THE FAMILY

Marriage and Divorce Rates

During the colonial period, cultural standards and the economic needs of both men and women combined to result in virtually all men and women getting married. Unlike their Western European counterparts, women settlers in the New World married at a relatively young age.[109] Beginning in the eighteenth and nineteenth centuries, however, the new emphasis on marrying "for love" and the drive for autonomy on the part of women resulted in a gradual increase in the number of women who remained single.[110] Yet, the absence of economic alternatives for most women kept this figure low. In the early twentieth century, this pattern was reversed. With the exception of the Depression years, the percentage of women never marrying as well as the age at which women actually married, fell steadily until 1960.[111] For example, among women born in 1930, fewer than 9 percent were single at age thirty.[112] Degler traces this increase in marriage rates to the growing acceptablity of divorce and birth control, both of which made escape from an unhappy marriage or too many children easier.[113] The growing popularity of companionship marriage and public perceptions of the necessity of marriage for a full and happy life also contributed to this trend.

Starting in the mid-1960s, however, the age of women first marrying and the percent of men and women not marrying again rose. This change was reflected in the dramatic drop in the number of married couples. While in 1960, 75 percent of all households in the United States consisted of married couples, by 1981, the figure had fallen to 59.8 percent.[114] Paralleling this decline has been the rise in the number of single-person households. For example in 1960, single-person households comprised 13.1 percent of all households; in 1981 they comprised 23 percent.[115] These figures do not really indicate that the institution of marriage is dying, but they do suggest some of the new ideas about marriage and women's roles are having an impact on the institution.

The lesser role marriage plays in many young women's lives and the increased availability of well-paying jobs seem to be causing many women to postpone or delay marriage until they are much older than women in previous generations. Between 1960 and 1979, the percentage of women aged 20–24 who had never been married doubled. Similar trends are evident in the next older group of women, those aged 25–29, among whom 21.8 percent remained single in 1981—a figure that was more than double the 1960 figure.[116] A recent study predicts this trend to delay marriage will continue and by 1990, it is projected that 28 percent of all women and 46 percent of all men will still be single between the ages of 25 and 29.[117]

Many of the women who postpone marriage do so to finish their educations or start careers.[118] The expectation of most demographers and sociologists is that these women eventually will marry. But, others have pointed out that some may never do so, especially if they perceive that conflicts await them should they try to combine marriage and career.[119] Still others argue that traditionally minded men may be unwilling to marry the "modern" young women.

It also should be noted that the single woman of today is quite unlike her past counterparts. Almost all work or attend school. And, an increasingly large percentage—65 percent of those 25–29 and 91 percent of those 30–34— maintain their own households.[120] This practice is, of course, in sharp contrast to the status of the single woman in earlier periods. By establishing their own independent lives and proving that they can "take care" of themselves without men, these women may come to believe that marriage is *not* necessary or that at least they deserve and can command an equal role with their husbands in any future marriage.

Another indicator of the trend away from marriage is reflected in the phenomenal growth of the number of couples that live together without benefit of marriage. While the total is still small—1,808,000 in 1981—they represent a significant change from previous marital practices and, indeed, a 246 percent increase since 1970.[121]

Even when women get married they are much less likely today than those in previous generations to stay married. Since the mid-nineteenth century, the national divorce rate has risen almost every year. The rate of increase dramatically accelerated—rising from 9.2 divorces per 1,000 married women in 1960 to 23.3 per 1000 in 1981.[122] Additionally, these figures are expected to continue to climb through the 1980s. The result is that one out of three couples who married in 1980 can expect to get divorced.

The most important reason for the increase in divorce appears to be the failure of many unions to live up to the ideal of companionship marriage.[123] As early as the nineteenth century, both men and women grew to expect affection and companionship in their marriage. Thus, divorce became a more acceptable solution when these were missing.[124] Today even larger numbers of both men and women think a good marriage should involve a satisfactory sexual relationship, romance, and sharing of activities and friends. Both sexes also want understanding spouses. Many believe that an absence of these things may be grounds for divorce.[125] High expectations and the growing acceptability of abandoning a marriage that fails to meet them coupled with liberalized divorce laws all contribute to the higher divorce rates. Financial independence may be another important factor in the breakup of many marriages. More specifically, some studies have found an association between employment of the wife and greater frequency of divorce. This association appears to be largely a function of the fact that having a job, or the prospect of one, especially if it pays well, provides the means by which a woman can establish an economic existence independent from her husband.[126]

Finally, the high divorce rate may simply be the result of the longer life-span of men and women in the late twentieth century. Whereas in the past most marriages ended shortly before or after the last child reached maturity or with the death of one of the spouses, today with increased longevity, marriages have the potential to last fifty years or more. The strain this long time together produces on a couple is seen by at least one researcher as the prime cause of divorces.[127]

Whatever the source of the increase in divorce rates, they are not without significant social impact on the family and the life-styles of women. For example, the cultural stereotype that the responsibility for childcare should remain with the mother means that in almost all divorces where there are children the mother gets custody. The result is a burgeoning number of single-parent families headed by women. In 1960, only 7.4 percent of all families with children under eighteen were headed by mothers alone. By 1982, the proportion of female-headed families (most with children) out of all families was nearly 17 percent. By contrast, two-parent families only increased by 8.1 percent in the decade of the 1960s and actually declined by 3.1 percent in the 1970s.[128] Among certain groups, most notably blacks, female-headed families now account for more than 40 percent of the families.[129] The result is that almost 20 percent of children under eighteen live in families headed by women. One study even projects that 50 percent of all children today can expect to live part of their lives in single-parent families.[130]

Increased divorce rates alone are not solely responsible for this rise in single-parent families. Another factor has been the growth in the number of never-married women with children. Between 1970 and 1978, the percentage of one-parent families headed by divorced women rose from 29 to 38 percent, while those attributable to never-married women with children climbed from

7 to 15 percent. In the same time period, families headed by widows declined from 20 to 12 percent.[131] Ross and Sawhill see the phenomenon of the female-headed families as one of the most significant changes of the past two decades.[132]

One of the attributes of these families is their low quality of life. Studies consistently find them at the bottom of the scale on every measure of economic well-being. For example, in 1978, the percent of white, female-headed families with children under eighteen years of age below the poverty level was 33.5 percent, 58.8 percent for black families, and 68.9 percent for Spanish origin families.[133] Preliminary 1982 figures suggest that the trend is continuing to rise. Overall, 32.7 percent of all female-headed families were below the poverty level—up from 31.4 percent in 1978.[134] Part of the reason for this low standard of living is the result of the failure of fathers to support their children. The Urban Institute reports that 40 percent of all absent fathers contribute nothing to their children's support, while the payments of the other 60 percent average less than 2,000 dollars per year. As one commentator on the situation noted, "The poverty among female-headed families resulting from lack of child support will not decrease unless there is real change in the societal context that condones and even encourages the absent father's neglect of his financial responsibilities to his children."[135]

Even in couples without children or those where the children are grown, divorce is often harder on women. This is particularly true for the individual who accepted the myth of the feminine mystique and devoted her life to being a good wife and mother. The displaced homemaker, both with and without children, often is left to fend for herself without the experience or training necessary to obtain a job by which she can support herself and/or her children. More generally, older women, whether divorced or widowed, frequently find themselves alone without any immediate family members to help support them. The result is often extreme poverty. In the mid-1970s, 28 percent of all women over 65 and living alone were well below the poverty line. In fact, 61 percent of black women in this group lived in poverty. Because of inadequate or no pension coverage, the lives of these women often are bleak. Projected growth in the numbers of the elderly population and Reagan budget cutbacks will only make these problems worse.[136]

The situation for middle-aged women is little better. As the former president of NOW, Eleanor Smeal has noted, "The harsh reality is that women in midlife, whether married, divorced, widowed or single, find that their opportunities for employment and security are severely limited, and their futures precarious and uncertain."[137] The delay or avoidance of marriage by younger women may, in part, reflect their growing awareness of this plight of their mothers and grandmothers.

Thus, the institution of marriage, at least as reflected in divorce, age of marriage, and marriage rates, has undergone significant changes over time.

Most recently, in part as a result of the women's movement, the increased acceptability, desirability, and feasibility of women having a life of their own separate from marriage has contributed to a rise in the numbers of unmarried women, the age of marriage, and the divorce rate. But, as the still high marriage figures indicate, the idea of radical feminists to abolish the institution has been adopted by only a few. As we shall see below, the aims of the more moderate feminists to reform the institution also are achieving less than complete success.

Motherhood

Changing practices in marriage over time are closely related to attitudes and behavior with respect to childbearing and childrearing. One of the most enduring cultural stereotypes with respect to women is stress on the importance of the mother's role in defining, shaping, and giving meaning to a woman's life. Interestingly, however, this emphasis on motherhood has not been accompanied by a rise in the birthrate. Except for the brief post World War II period, the number of children born to an average adult woman in the United States has declined almost every decade since 1800.[138] The apparent paradox of a declining birthrate and an increase in the importance of the motherhood role has been explained as a combination of several interrelated factors. Degler argues that the rising consciousness of women in the nineteenth century as individuals was an important factor in this decline in the birthrate. He claims:

> Women have always had a reason for limiting children that men have not, but that reason could motivate behavior on a large scale only when women became self-conscious about themselves as individuals—that is, when they began to see themselves as beings separate from their husbands and their families.[139]

Perhaps more important than a sense of self, however, was the realization that if women were going to perform their roles as mothers successfully, fewer children would make their task easier.[140] Thus, it is not surprising that in the first half of the nineteenth century, abortion and crude forms of birth control were used by women to limit births. But, in the Victorian era, abortion and dissemination of birth control were outlawed and the single acceptable method of birth control became abstinence. The prudery and denial of female sex drive in this period also were parts of the effort by women to limit the number of children they bore.[141] The existence of laws that required a wife's submission to her husband's sexual demands and the normal sex drive of both spouses, however, resulted in the widespread failure of abstinence, and many women regularly found themselves pregnant.

The renewed realization of female sexuality in the early twentieth century led to an increase in discussions and information about more efficient birth

control methods, making family planning easier.[142] The temporary reversal in
the birthrate in the 1940s through the early 1960s (the baby boom) seems best
explained by the delay in childrearing that accompanied the 1930's Depression
and World War II and the reemphasis on family and motherhood that
characterized the feminine mystique.[143] The desire to be a mother and to have
a large number of children was very strong. Fertility jumped dramatically in
the postwar years to an average 3.76 children per woman. Blood and Wolfe
found in the 1950s that for women the opportunity to have children was the
second most valuable aspect of marriage.[144]

A closer look at the importance of motherhood to women, however,
reveals that there were some recognized drawbacks to the role. The birth of the
first child, in particular, had a sharp impact on sex roles, the division of labor,
and male superiority in family decision making. Lopata notes, "Childrearing,
as carried on by the new mother, produces more traditional feminine-
masculine role segregations than practically any other social relation in
modern American middle-class life."[145]

This sharpening of sex roles and the associated division of labor often
produced a negative impact on the marriage relationship. One study, for
example, found general satisfaction with marriage declined precipitously with
the birth of the first child.[146] In blue-collar marriages where husband's and
wife's lives were already quite distinctly divided along gender lines, the arrival
of a child may have given them something in common to share, but in
middle-class marriages where spouses previously had enjoyed a sharing or
companionship relationship, the decline in marital satisfaction was often
marked.[147] The mental and physical health of the new mother often suffered as
well. For the woman who had worked outside the home, the changes in her life
and marriage brought about by the sudden isolation from others and the
heavy burdens and responsibilities of her new role often resulted in the "tired
housewife syndrome," a debilitating physical illness in women found to be
particularly prevalent in mothers with young children.[148] Interestingly,
mothers who went out to work were less likely to believe that children
restricted their life-styles. This does not necessarily imply that the life of the
working mother was without problems. In addition to the long hours
associated with two jobs, many mothers who worked outside the home often
bore a burden of guilt about the lack of time they spent with their children and
their adequacy as parents.[149] One should not overestimate the negative side of
motherhood, but as Bernard, Friedan, and others have documented, for many
women, both those who worked and those who stayed home, this role often
failed to live up to all their expectations.

The changes in cultural stereotypes with respect to childbearing and
childrearing that accompanied the women's movement have contributed to
the alteration of the state of motherhood. One of the most important trends is
the growing practice of delaying the birth of the first child. Unlike the women
of the 1950s and early 1960s, today's young women are likely to remain

childfree until well into their twenties or thirties. One study found that nearly one quarter of all women born in 1950 had not had a child by the age of thirty, which was nearly double the percentage of women who were childfree at this age among women born between 1931 and 1940.[150] Similarly, while the overall birthrate in the U.S. increased from 3.1 million live births in 1973 to 3.7 million in 1981, birthrates of women over thirty in particular have increased as a proportion of first births by 73 percent since 1975.[151] Although there are several reasons for this delay, perhaps one of the most significant is the practice of many young women, especially college-educated, career-oriented women, to postpone childbirth to concentrate on the development of their careers.[152] As a result, in the early 1980s, talk of a "Baby Panic" was becoming more common as women who had postponed childbirth were entering their thirties and were faced with the prospect of a "now or never" situation. Norma Wikler, coauthor of a study on older mothers, "Up Against the Clock," has noted, "They have deferred and deferred and now they see that deadline approaching."[153] For other women, like those who "put-off" marriage, there is a growing realization that they waited too long or that they really do not want children after all. Caroline Bird quotes one twenty-eight-year-old reporter as saying:

> When I was growing up, I never questioned that I would one day have a child. But now I'm not so sure. I've found a job that I really like and I now can see what children mean—a lot of time, a lot of expense, a lot of frustration—and I am sure, too, a lot of satisfaction. But I can't see myself quitting my job and staying home with the kids.[154]

Rather than have no children at all, others, especially working women, choose to have only one or two children as compared to the three or four children had by women in the era of the feminine mystique. In fact, although in 1960, the average number of children per woman was 3.61, in 1981, it was 1.82.[155] Among young women interviewed in the late 1970s, 22 percent expected to have one or no children at all.[156] Researchers at the Joint Center for Urban Studies of Massachusetts Institute of Technology and Harvard University predict that as many as 40 percent of the women born in the 1950s will have no or only one child.[157]

There are numerous explanations for the rapidly declining birthrate of the 1960s. Some note the change in cultural stereotypes about the necessity of motherhood as well as the availability of options in which women can find fulfillment, most notably careers. Another important factor has been the development and regular use of new and more effective methods of birth control and the spread of information about these techniques.

One of the important results of the new small family is that women are devoting increasingly less time to motherhood. Today the typical woman can expect to spend only thirteen years with preschool children.[158] Unless there is a complete reversal in public attitudes toward family size, these figures suggest that motherhood in the future will loom as even less of an important role for most women. It might even be speculated that if the proportion of one's life devoted to a pursuit determines its relative importance, then the worker role might replace the mother role in the value hierarchy of *some* women. The growing practice of full- and part-time work among professional women with very young children may indicate this reversal in ordering has already occurred for some.[159] However, rather than replacing the mother role with the worker role, a more likely result will be an equal balancing of the two roles during the short period of time when one's children are young. As we shall see in the next section, this equal "balancing" is not really possible for many women because most husbands and fathers have not made much effort to share the domestic or parental role with their spouses and because of the inadequacy of available childcare. Indeed, one of the reasons for the decision to postpone, forego, or limit children or marriage altogether may be the realization on the part of many women that the job of taking care of the home and children continues to be, in most marriages, exclusively the woman's.

Task/Role Division

Until recently, the ideal, companionship marriage relied heavily on the notion of "separate spheres" for each spouse. Since the Industrial Revolution, the spouse "in charge" of taking care of the home has been the wife. Additionally, this ideal was almost uniformly implemented during the nineteenth and early twentieth centuries.[160] As we have indicated, even the entrance of large numbers of married women into the labor force did little to change perceptions of appropriate roles. In fact, the message of the feminine mystique was that in homemaking a woman would find her true happiness.

The combined strength of these role divisions was sharply reflected in the tasks each performed around the home in the late 1950s. While one study found that 40 percent of the women indicated that their husbands occasionally helped with cooking or the dishes, major responsibility for these tasks and making beds, straightening up the house, and doing the laundry were wives' jobs alone. And, with respect to childcare, it was the mother who had the prime and often sole responsibility. This same study found 66 percent of all fathers with young children needing care "helped," but only 14 percent were reported to "always help."[161]

The importance assigned to the housewife role by the feminine mystique and the associated necessity of doing all the housework resulted in many full-time homemakers devoting as much time and perhaps even more time to housekeeping tasks as their mothers and grandmothers. Studies found the typical full-time housewife spent fifty-five hours per week doing housework in the mid-1960s.[162] Commenting on these findings, Oakley, Friedan, and others have noted that the amount of time spent on housework was a function of amount of time available—the more time available the more hours spent.[163]

Examination of the impact of a wife going to work on the division of labor in the home produced rather ambiguous results. Blood and Wolfe reported some increase in sex role division of tasks, with husbands helping out their wives in some traditionally female areas but working wives doing fewer traditionally male tasks than nonworking wives.[164] Others discovered little or no difference in the division of household tasks in families with a working wife and those without. An examination of time usage in 1965–1966, for example, found husbands of employed women contributed no more time to housework than those with nonemployed wives.[165]

The leaders of the women's movement began to challenge traditional stereotypes about role division in the 1960s. As indicated earlier, it appears that many women, especially younger women, have adopted the view that home-making tasks should be shared by husbands and wives. However, studies of the actual division of labor in the home in the 1970s and early 1980s find only limited evidence that the desired equality in task sharing has been put into practice. Men today are probably doing more around the home than their forefathers, but the amount of time they contribute still is only a small proportion of that given by women.[166]

Depending on the study, one-quarter to two-thirds of all husbands in the United States report doing *no* housework at all. Among husbands who help, the average number of hours devoted to household tasks ranges from six to eleven per week.[167] Contrary to what might be expected given the rising support among women for the idea of task sharing, there is even some evidence that the actual amount of time spent on housework may have declined between 1965 and 1975.[168]

Even in families where both husbands and wives have professional careers, it generally is the wife who is responsible for most of the household chores.[169] Even if the husband does more and working wives cut back on the amount of housework they do, the number of hours a week a working wife devotes to home and job results in a much longer work week.[170] On the average, the work week of married women who are full-time housewives is fifty-six hours, of employed married men 62.5 hours, and of employed married wives seventy-one hours. In families where the working mother has young children, the wife's work week is eighty hours compared to sixty-five for her husband.[171] Not surprisingly, many working mothers complain that they have little time for themselves.[172] In commenting on the results of these time studies done in the late 1970s, sociologist Richard Berk has noted that it is often the younger, better-educated husbands who are the least helpful. "They talk endlessly about the ERA, women's rights and equality, but when the chips are down their wives will be doing everything at home."[173]

Among many young couples, role divisions often become exacerbated when children are born. Previous sharing of household tasks often is dramatically altered when women become mothers. Even though more men today care for their children than previously, the *responsibility* for child *care,* and not *play,* remains primarily the woman's. The failure of husbands to take on their fair share of domestic tasks, even in the face of overwhelming support for this practice among working wives, led Berk and Berk to conclude, in 1979, "It is still probably fair to say employed wives hold down two full-time jobs: one in the market and one in the household."[174]

The "helping out" by men that characterizes child and house care tasks is to be contrasted with the greater responsibility many women undertake in traditionally male roles. Not only do a majority of wives now work, but of those that do, many are making significant contributions to the family income. In 1982, the multiearner family composed of both spouses had an average weekly income of $590 compared with $399 for a family in which only the husband worked.[175] The wife's wages often mean the difference in which social class the family falls or its general living standard. It is estimated that without the income from a wife's salary, two-thirds of families with working wives would fall below a "comfortable" standard of living.[176] Of course, it should be noted that sexual barriers of one form or another *prevent* most women from earning a wage or salary comparable to their husbands'. This income inequality apparently becomes the basis in some families for the continuation of the assumption that the wife is merely "helping out" the husband in his breadwinner role. Furthermore, wives often help a husband with his role as breadwinner in many other ways than earning money. Many keep the family finances straight, entertain business associates, etc. The working wife generally can expect much less help from her husband with her paid job outside the home.[177]

Division of Authority in Marriage

Based on personal reports, husbands dominated the family decision making process in the nineteenth and early twentieth centuries. Even as late as the 1950s and early 1960s, the ideal of a male-headed household was reflected in most studies of family decision making. Blood and Wolfe's early study of authority patterns in the 1950s, which were based on wives' reports,[178] found that the balance of power favored the husband. The husband made most of the important economic decisions while wives' decision making tended to be limited to areas closely connected with their roles as mothers and housewives. Only with respect to decisions about where to go on a vacation or where to live was the primary pattern that of joint decision making. The locus of authority can perhaps be best seen in the contrast between two areas of family decision: what job a husband should take and whether or not the wife should work. With respect to the first, 90 percent of the wives reported that this was the husband's decision alone to make. Concerning work outside the home by the wife, however, in a third of the families, generally the husband made this decision.[179]

Several scholars have noted that one of the main causes of greater male authority was the husband's superior resources.[180] They discovered that when these resources were more equally distributed between husbands and wives in individual couples the result was more joint decision making. However, even in those families where a wife worked outside the home, the man generally had greater overall authority.[181] Thus, early research on authority seems to indicate that more than simply inadequate resources kept women in a secondary position.

While popular views about the appropriate division of authority in the family have changed, as noted, there is still a tendency to accord men the final say. Additionally, cultural stereotypes are not the only barrier with respect to equalizing authority patterns. Reluctance by men to give up the power and prestige they have traditionally enjoyed, their greater earning power, and the lack of readiness on the part of at least some women to share this role also present problems. Thus, it is not surprising that in 1980, 44 percent of men sampled reported that when it came right down to it, they were the main decision makers when it came to what the family could afford or not afford to spend on most things. Nearly a third of all women also recognized their husbands as the final authority on such questions. Few men (12 percent) or women (25 percent) believed that the wife had the final say.[182] Although most of the evidence suggests women who work have more power in family decision making than full-time housewives, especially in decisions about how the family's money is spent, men still dominate.[183] For example, in a 1980 study, only 25 percent of the housewives and 14 percent of the working women sampled reported their belief that the person who makes the most wages *should* make the important family decisions, but in fact, almost twice as many women in both groups reported that this *was* the actual practice in their families.[184] Perhaps most surprising is the persistent practice of many women to defer to their husbands' wishes with respect to their taking a job outside the home. Among women under twenty-four, one survey found that only 25 percent would work if their husbands objected.[185] Thus, as with role sharing generally, all three of the barriers discussed in the first part of this chapter continue to prevent a completely equitable division of family authority.

CONCLUSION

While there has been considerable progress in the direction of the creation of an equitable, equal institution of marriage, many of the traditional practices remain. Where barriers to change have been weakened or eliminated, progress toward equality has been great. However, where barriers remain strong or nearly intact—in the sharing of unpleasant or burdensome household tasks, for example—women may still find themselves having to shoulder more than their fair share. This lack of equality of the sexes with respect to all aspects of marriage is, of course, not without consequence for the position of women not only within but outside of the family. For example, the progress of women in two key areas, politics and the marketplace, are today considerably hampered by the division of roles in the family.

In making any prognosis for further change in the institutions of marriage and the family, we need to look at whether barriers we have identified as important are likely to weaken in the near future. With respect to the barrier of cultural stereotypes about the family and women's place in it, we have reason to expect the rapidity of the change in the decade of the 1970s will not be repeated in the 1980s. We make this projection based on two factors: (1) the formation of a number of active and well-financed associations and organizations dedicated to returning the ideal of the traditional marriage to its former place of importance, and (2) the growing fear among a large number of people that the changes in the family in the last few years have had some negative consequences. For example, in 1979, two-thirds of a national sample of women indicated they believed the institution of marriage had weakened in the past ten years and 49 percent throught that the institution of life-time marriage will vanish.[186] Such fears may well provide an opening wedge through which those opposed to further change will be able to convince many to resist any other alterations in family life lest the whole institution be lost. Indeed, in 1982, over 90 percent of those polled favored increased emphasis on traditional family ties.[187] At best, it seems that feminists groups should expect to encounter more resistance in the future to any proposed reforms in traditional family practices.

Our projection for the future on the question of the preparation of women to assume or demand a more equitable marriage relationship is more optimistic. The most progressive segment of the population is comprised of young, well-educated women. They are increasingly not only ready but also willing and able to assume an equal partnership with men in all spheres of life, including the family. In 1979, 64 percent of all women approved of efforts to strengthen and change the status of women in society.[188] This represented a 24 percent increase in support for change since 1970. Such enthusiasm for progress may well provide the basis by which to overcome the anti groups and the reservations of the general public. This is not to say that the decisions these young women have to make about their futures are easy or that the stress caused by trying to combine the roles of mother/ wife with that of worker is easily overcome. Indeed, studies indicate the psychological stress on young women today is taking its toll in terms of mental and physical health.[189]

Thus, a key group in the ultimate resolution of the question of whether the institution of the family will move forward to some new form or back to a more traditional one may well be men and more particularly, young married men. If the third barrier, resistance by men in the family to change is not eliminated or diminished, then reforms in the relationships between husband and wife, and father and mother cannot really be expected. According to Betty Friedan, "We will never bring about these changes [a restructuring of the institutions of home and work] unless fathers demand them too."[190] Whether fathers and husbands will demand and participate in reforms in the family remains to be seen. If they do not, it seems likely the forces opposed to change may well be expected to be victorious.

Thus, the future of women's position in the family and in all other spheres of life as well is dependent on a number of factors. The outlook is uncertain and the real possibility of return to more traditional practices should not be underestimated. As our discussion of the fight over the ERA in the next chapter will show, the forces opposed to further alteration in the position of women may well have the upperhand in the decades to come.

NOTES

1. For a discussion of the origins of marriage and marriage in a historical perspective, see Kathleen Gough, "The Origins of the Family," in Jo Freeman, ed., *Women: A Feminist Perspective* (Palo Alto, Calif.: Mayfield Publishing Co., 1975), pp. 43–63.

2. Carl N. Degler, *At Odds: Women and the Family in America from the Revolution to the Present* (New York: Oxford University Press, 1980), pp. 9–10.

3. John Demos, "Husbands and Wives," in Jean E. Friedman and William G. Shade, eds., *Our American Sisters: Women in American Life and Thought* (Boston: Allyn and Bacon, 1973), pp. 32–33. See also, Mary Beth Norton, "Colonial America to 1800: The Myth of the Golden Age," in Carol Ruth Berkin and Mary Beth Norton, eds., *Women of America, A History* (Boston: Houghton Mifflin, 1979), pp. 37–47 for a discussion challenging this notion of women's position in the colonial era.

4. Ann Oakley, *Woman's Work: The Housewife, Past and Present* (New York: Vintage Books, 1976), pp. 23–24.

5. Degler, *At Odds*, p. 73.

6. Linda Gordon, *Woman's Body, Woman's Right: A Social History of Birth Control in America* (New York: Viking Press, 1976), pp. 18 and 48–49. See also, Degler, *At Odds*, pp. 240–241.

7. Demos, "Husbands and Wives," in Friedman and Shade, eds., *Our American Sisters*, pp. 36–41.

8. Quoted in ibid., p. 31.

9. Carl Degler sees the postcolonial period and the new companionship marriage that developed at this time as a change for the better for women, at least in the short run, *At Odds*, p. 28. For a somewhat different opinion, see Oakley, *Woman's Work*, pp. 32–52 and Jessie Bernard, *The Future of Motherhood* (New York: Dial Press, 1974), pp. 9–16.

10. Degler, *At Odds*, pp. 8–9.

11. Ibid., Chapters I, IV, VIII, and whole book generally.

12. See Barbara J. Berg, *The Remembered Gate: Origins of American Feminism* (New York: Oxford University Press, 1978), pp. 60–74; Oakley, *Woman's Work*, pp. 32–52; and Bernard, *The Future of Motherhood*, pp. 9–16, but see also, Heidi Hartmann, "Capitalism, Patriarchy, and Job Segregation by Sex," in Martha Blaxall

and Barbara Reagan, eds., *Women and the Workplace: The Implications of Occupational Segregation* (Chicago: University of Chicago Press, 1976), pp. 137–169.

13. Degler, *At Odds,* pp. 151–152, 166, and 168.

14. Ibid., p. 161.

15. Michael Gordon, *The American Family: Past, Present, and Future* (New York: Random House, 1978), pp. 201–209.

16. Quoted in Barbara Welter, "The Cult of True Womanhood: 1820–1860," in Friedman and Shade, eds., *Our American Sisters,* p. 112.

17. Studies during the 1950s and 1960s indicate the greater the extent of gender differences in life-styles the less likely is the development of real companionship. See Mirra Komarovsky, *Blue-Collar Marriage* (New York: Random House, 1964).

18. Gordon, *The American Family,* pp. 203–209 and Carroll Smith-Rosenberg, "Sex as Symbol in Victorian Purity: An Ethnohistorical Analysis of Jacksonian America," in John Demos and Sarane Spence Boocock, *Turning Points: Historical and Sociological Essays on the Family* (Chicago: University of Chicago Press, 1978), pp. S212–S247.

19. Welter, "The Cult of True Womanhood," in Friedman and Shade, eds., *Our American Sisters,* pp. 102–103.

20. Ibid., p. 107; Oakley, *Woman's Work,* pp. 49–55; and Joann Vanek, "Housewives as Workers," in Ann H. Stromberg and Shirley Harkess, eds., *Women Working: Theories and Facts in Perspective* (Palo Alto, Calif.: Mayfield Publishing Co., 1978), pp. 392–399.

21. Gordon, *Woman's Body, Woman's Right,* pp. 23–24, 52–59, and 65. Abortion was not completely eliminated, and many women continued to receive illegal abortions. Many more practiced some form of birth control.

22. Ibid., p. 104. Degler, *At Odds,* pp. 279–282.

23. See Daniel Scott Smith, "Family Limitation, Sexual Control, and Domestic Feminism in Victorian America," in Nancy F. Cott and Elizabeth H. Pleck, eds., *A Heritage of Her Own: Toward a New Social History of Americian Women* (New York: Simon and Schuster/Touchstone Books, 1975), pp. 231–239.

24. Gordon, *Woman's Body, Woman's Right,* chap. 9.

25. Erwin O. Smigel and Rita Seiden, "The Decline and Fall of the Double Standard," in Friedman and Shade, eds., *Our American Sisters,* pp. 286–288.

26. Ibid., pp. 285–291.

27. Reported by Gordon, *Woman's Body, Woman's Right,* p. 320.

28. Betty Friedan, *The Feminine Mystique* (New York: Dell Publishing, 1963). See also, Bernard, *The Future of Motherhood,* pp. 76–84.

29. Joann Vanek, "Housewives as Workers," in Stromberg and Harkess, eds., *Women Working,* pp. 396–397.

30. William H. Chafe, *The American Woman: Her Changing Social, Economic and Political Role, 1920–1970* (New York: Oxford Press, 1972), pp. 103–104.

31. Ibid., pp. 102–104 and Lois Scharf, *To Work and To Wed: Female Employment, Feminism, and the Great Depression* (Westport, Conn.: Greenwood Press, 1980).

32. For the few working mothers with young children, the problems engendered by the new economic role were often intense. Day-care facilities were limited, and the

double burden of work and being the primary parent often resulted in neglect of one or both roles. Ibid., pp. 159–171 and 186–187.

33. Friedan, *The Feminine Mystique.*

34. • Even a forced choice among various roles which included worker and career woman found these two options among the very least important roles. Working women did not even rank them highly. Helena Znaniecki Lopata, *Occupation: Housewife* (New York: Oxford Press, 1971), pp. 48–53.

35. Ibid., pp. 91 and 95. Of course, the many women who were joining the work force to help out would ultimately make their jobs permanent.

36. Arland Thornton and Deborah Freedman, "Changes in the Sex Role Attitudes of Women, 1962–1977: Evidence from a Panel Study," in *American Sociological Review* 44 (October 1979):833.

37. Ibid., 833–835. Similarly in Komarovsky's blue-collar couples, a majority of men and women supported the notion of male dominance in family matters. Komarovsky, *Blue-Collar Marriage,* pp. 225–226.

38. For a discussion of difference between a career and a job as it relates to conflict with motherhood, see Bernard, *The Future of Motherhood,* p. 186.

39. Friedan, *The Feminine Mystique,* p. 330.

40. Betty Friedan, "Feminism Takes a New Turn," *The New York Times Magazine,* November 16, 1979, p. 94.

41. *The 1980 Virginia Slims American Women's Opinion Poll,* conducted by the Roper Organization, p. 15.

42. Reported in Gloria Steinem, "In the Middle of the Backlash Some Cheerful Words About Men," *Ms.,* June, 1981, p. 45.

43. "Youth Values and Adolescent Sexuality," *American Educator* 3 (Winter 1979):5.

44. Alfreda P. Iglehart, *Married Women and Work* (Lexington, Mass.: Lexington Books, 1979), p. 63. A 1973 survey found one-quarter of all women cited "you give up too much" as a reason *not* to marry. *The Virginia Slims American Women's Opinion Poll,* volume III, conducted by the Roper Organization, 1974, p. 41.

45. *The 1980 Virginia Slims American Women's Opinion Poll,* p. 19.

46. Ibid., p. 17.

47. Ibid., p. 18. Caroline Bird in *The Two-Paycheck Marriage* (New York: Rawson, Wade Publishers, 1979), pp. 229–230 reports that only 59 percent of all first year college men and women in 1977 saw "raising a family" as one of the things in life they thought was important to do.

48. Data from the 1976 American National Election Study conducted by the Center for Political Studies at the University of Michigan. Figures compiled by the authors.

49. Kristen A. Moore and Sandra L. Hofferth, "Women and Their Children," in Ralph E. Smith, ed., *The Subtle Revolution: Women at Work* (Washington, D.C.: The Urban Institute, 1979), p. 128.

50. *Gallup Opinion Index,* Report #176 (March 1980), p. 19.

51. Shelley, Yankelovich and White, Inc. 1980 survey reported in Deborah Durfee Barron and Daniel Yankelovich, "Today's American Woman: How The Public Sees Her," The Public Agenda Foundation, December 1980, p. 28.

52. Iglehart, *Married Women and Work,* p. 64. In 1976, Ann Landers found 70 percent of all readers who wrote her in answer to a question would *not* have children again if they could choose. Noted in Bird, *Two-Paycheck Marriage,* p. 183.

53. John Scanzoni, *Sex Roles, Women's Work, and Marital Conflict* (Lexington, Mass.: Lexington Books, 1978), pp. 7 and 16.

54. Ibid., pp. 15 and 18.

55. Data reported in Barron and Yankelovich, "Today's American Woman," pp. 27 and 111.

56. Dena Kleinman, "Parents' Groups Purging Schools of 'Humanist' Books and Classes," *The New York Times,* May 17, 1981, pp. 1 and 52 and Richard A. Viguerie, *The New Right: We're Ready to Lead* (Falls Church, Va.: The Viguerie Co., 1980), pp. 208–209.

57. ABC Poll reported in GARAL (July/August, 1981):3. See also, E.J. Dionne, Jr., "Abortion Poll Not Clear Cut," *The New York Times,* August 18, 1980, p. 18. This article makes the point that when the question about a constitutional abortion amendment focuses on protecting the life of the unborn child, support for an amendment increases.

58. The Gallup Opinion Index #178 (June, 1980), p. 6. See also, Lucky M. Tedrow and E.R. Mahoney, "Trends in Attitudes Toward Abortion: 1972–1976," *Public Opinion Quarterly* 43 (Summer 1979):185–188.

59. Donald Granberg, "Pro-Life or Reflection of Conservative Ideology? An Analysis of Opposition to Legalized Abortion," *Sociological and Social Research* 62 (April 1978):414–429.

60. Lisa Cronin Wohl, "Public Opinion Bombshell: Prochoice Majority Vows to Vote," *Ms.,* July/August, 1982, pp. 70–73.

61. Ibid., p. 70.

62. *The Virginia Slims American Women's Opinion Poll,* vol. III, p. 31.

63. Interviews with high school seniors in 1977 indicated a preference for a marriage in which both husband and wife worked. "Young People Look at Changing Sex Roles," in *ISR Newsletter,* Spring, 1979, p. 31. *The 1980 Virginia Slims American Women's Opinion Poll* found that by 1980, more than half of *all* women favored a shared marriage, p. 15.

64. Thornton and Freedman, "Changes in Sex Role Attitudes of Women," pp. 833 and 837–838.

65. Scanzoni, *Sex Roles, Women's Work, and Marital Conflict,* p. 17.

66. Mary Lindenstein Walshok, "Occupational Values and Family Roles: Women in Blue-Collar and Service Occupations," in Karen Wolk Feinstein, ed., *Working Women and Families* (Beverly Hills, Calif.: Sage Publications, 1979), p. 79.

67. Bernice Kanner, "She Brings Home the Bacon and Cooks It," *Ms.,* March, 1980, p. 104.

68. Iglehart, *Married Women and Work,* pp. 44, 49, and 57. In 1957 there was no relationship between attitude about housework and desire for outside work.

69. Christine Bose, "Social Status of the Homemaker," in Sara Fensternmaker Berk, ed., *Women and Household Labor* (Beverly Hills, Calif.: Sage Publications, 1980), p. 84. See also, Jessie Bernard, *The Future of Marriage* (New York: World Publishing, 1972), p. 43.

70. *The General Mills American Family Report, 1980–81: Families Strengths*

and Strains At Work. Survey conducted by Louis Harris and Associates (General Mills Inc., 9200 Wayzata Boulevard, Minneapolis, Minnesota, 55440), pp. 34-35.

71. For example, while the reported difference in the percentage of full-time housewives and working women who report they are "very happy" is only 10 percent, (40 and 50 percent respectively), this difference was lower in 1957. Iglehart, *Married Women and Work*, p. 73. At least one study claims to find no difference in happiness of full-time homemakers and workers, James D. Wright, "Are Working Women Really More Satisfied? Evidence from Several National Surveys," *Journal of Marriage and the Family* 40 (May 1978):301-313.

72. Myra Marx Ferree, "Satisfaction with Housework: The Social Context," in Berk, ed., *Women and Household Labor*, pp. 90-91 and 105-106.

73. Angus Campbell, "Changes in Psychological Well-being During the 1970s of Homemakers and Employed Wives" in Dorothy G. McGuigan, ed., *Women's Lives: New Theory, Research and Policy* (Ann Arbor, Mich.: University of Michigan Press, 1978), pp. 294-295.

74. Scanzoni, *Sex Roles, Women's Work and Marital Conflict*, pp. 17 and 72.

75. *The General Mills American Family Report, 1980-81*, p. 43. Interestingly, interviews with leaders of the National Pro-Family Coalition and the Eagle Forum found a third felt this way in sharp contrast to the public's view and that of feminist leaders among whom only 2 percent felt raising children should be the woman's job. Ibid., p. 44.

76. *The General Mills American Family Report, 1976-77* data reported in Barron and Yankelovich, "Today's American Woman," p. 82.

77. "Male Role Switch to Kitchen Approved by 50 percent of Females," Women Poll Survey reported in *The Buffalo Courier-Express*, October 21, 1979, p. E-5.

78. *The 1980 Virginia Slims American Women's Opinion Poll*, p. 17.

79. Thornton and Freedman, "Changes in Sex Role Attitudes of Women," p. 833. Change was somewhat greater among the more educated women, women employed in 1962, younger women, and nonfundamental Protestant women. See pp. 837-838.

80. *The General Mills American Family Report, 1980-81*, p. 43.

81. This figure represents an improvement over the early 1970s when 85 percent thought the husband should be the head of the household. Scanzoni, *Sex Roles, Women's Work and Marital Conflict*, p. 17.

82. *The 1980 Virginia Slims American Women's Opinion Poll*, pp. 15-16. These attitudes have remained virtually unchanged since 1974. See *The Virginia Slims American Women's Opinion Poll*, vol. III, p. 45. The only exception is with respect to "having a good sexual relationship." In 1974, 77 percent of all women thought this was very important while in 1979 only 68 percent felt this way. The figure for men remained unchanged at 75 percent.

83. Bird, *Two-Paycheck Marriage*, p. 43.

84. Figures from U.S. Department of Justice, "A Survey of Spousal Violence Against Women in Kentucky," reported in Barbara R. Bergmann, "The Economic Risks of Being a Housewife," *American Economic Association Papers and Proceedings*, 71 (May 1981), p. 82.

85. Bird, *Two-Paycheck Marriage*, p. 89.

86. Scanzoni, *Sex Roles, Women's Work and Marital Conflict*, pp. 27, 124-125,

and 140–145. There is also evidence that the characteristics of a woman's job may influence her ability to negotiate with her spouse. Joan Spade, "Understanding the Interaction of Work and Family in Dual-Worker Families," unpublished manuscript, SUNY at Buffalo, August, 1982.

87. Quoted in Welter, "The Cult of True Womanhood," in Friedman and Shade, eds., *Our American Sisters*, p. 103.

88. Friedan, *The Feminine Mystique*, p. 43.

89. Marabel Morgan, *The Total Woman* (Old Tappan, N.J.: Rewell, 1973).

90. Constantina Safilios-Rothschild, *Sex Role Socialization and Sex Discrimination: A Synthesis and Critique of the Literature* (Washington, D.C.: The National Institute of Education, 1979), p. 35.

91. Ibid., pp. 31–38.

92. Colette Dowling, *The Cinderella Complex: Women's Hidden Fear of Independence* (New York: Summit, 1981).

93. Quoted in "The Superwoman Squeeze," *Newsweek,* May 19, 1980, p. 74.

94. Florence Denmark, "Growing Up Male," in Eleanor L. Zuckerman, ed., *Women and Men: Roles, Attitudes and Power Relationships* (New York: The Radcliff Club of New York, 1975), pp., 91–92 and Ellen Ross, "'The Love Crisis': Couples Advice Books of the Late 1970s," *Signs* 6 (Autumn 1980), pp. 109–12.

95. Komarovsky, *Blue-Collar Marriage,* p. 227 and 230–231. See also, Bernard, *The Future of Marriage,* pp. 51–53 and Nancy Chodorow, *The Reproduction of Mothering: Psychoanalysis and the Sociology of Gender* (Berkeley: University of California Press, 1978).

96. A. Regula Herzog, Jerald G. Bachman, and Lloyd D. Johnston, "High School Seniors' Preferences for Sharing Work and Family Responsibilities Between Husband and Wife," *Monitoring the Future Occasional Paper Series* #3 (Ann Arbor, Michigan: Institute for Social Research, 1979), p. 20. See also, chapter 6, table 6-3, and table 6-4.

97. *The General Mills American Family Report, 1980–81,* p. 75. See also, Alan E. Bayer, "Sexist Students in American Colleges: A Descriptive Note," *Journal of Marriage and Family* 37 (May 1975):391.

98. Mirra Komarovsky, "Cultural Contradictions and Sex Roles: The Masculine Case," *American Journal of Sociology* 78 (January 1973):878–883.

99. Kanner, "She Brings Home the Bacon," p. 104.

100. Komarovsky, "Cultural Contradictions and Sex Roles," p. 882.

101. *The 1980 Virginia Slims American Women's Opinion Poll,* p. 19. In 1979, 4 out of 5 mothers thought boys should be as responsible as girls for doing the laundry, and 56 percent thought boys should mend clothes. This represents an increase from 3 out of 5 and 39 percent in 1974.

102. One of the most popular movies in 1979 was *Kramer vs. Kramer,* the story of a father who tries to gain legal custody of his son. See also, S.M. Miller, "The Making of a Confused, Middle-aged Husband," in Constantina Safilios-Rothschild, ed., *Toward a Sociology of Women* (Lexington, Mass.: Xerox College Publishing, 1972), p. 255 and Betty Friedan, *The Second Stage* (New York: Summit Books, 1981), chap. 4.

103. *The General Mills American Family Report, 1980–81,* p. 39. Fifty-five percent of all men and 71 percent of all women cite family as important in determining hours worked. See also, Safilios-Rothschild, *Sex-Role Socialization and Discrimina-*

tion, p. 28 and Joseph H. Pleck, *The Myth of Masculinity* (Cambridge, Mass.: The MIT Press, 1981), pp. 141 and 151–152.

104. *The General Mills American Family Report, 1980–81*, p. 41. Similar discrepancies were reported with respect to all of the questions on the impact of family on work conditions. Interviews with labor leaders found that they too underestimated the importance of family in men's job decisions. See also, Laura Lein, "Male Participation in Home Life: Impact of Social Supports and Breadwinner Responsibility on the Allocation of Tasks," *The Family Coordinator* 28 (October, 1979), 489–496; Jane Hood and Susan Golden, "Beating Time/Making Time: The Impact of Work Scheduling on Men's Family Roles," *The Family Coordinator* 28 (October, 1979), 575–582; Friedan, *The Second Stage*, pp. 133–136 for a discussion of studies on changing male attitudes toward their family roles; and *Ms.* (October, 1982), where the whole issue is devoted to changes in male attitudes and behavior.

105. Quoted in "The Superwoman Squeeze," p. 79.

106. Pleck, *The Myth of Masculinity*, pp. 148–150.

107. Komarovsky, "Cultural Contradictions and Sex Roles," pp. 878–884; Friedan, *The Second Stage*, p. 145; and Robert Brannon, "Inside the Men's Movement," *Ms.*, October, 1982, pp. 40–44.

108. Miller, "The Making of a Confused, Middle-aged Husband," in Safilios-Rothschild, ed., *Toward a Sociology of Women*, p. 250. For an interesting discussion of strategies that may be used to bring about change in men's role in the family, see John Scanzoni, "Strategies for Changing Male Family Roles: Research and Practice Implications," *The Family Coordinator* 28 (October, 1979), 435–444.

109. Degler, *At Odds*, pp. 7–8.

110. Ibid., p. 152.

111. George Masnick and Mary Jo Bane, *The Nation's Families: 1960–1990* (Cambridge, Mass.: Joint Center for Urban Studies of MIT and Harvard University, 1980), p. 31.

112. Ibid.

113. Degler, *At Odds*, p. 176.

114. "U.S. In Profile—Latest Report," *U.S. News & World Report*, October 25, 1982, p. 13.

115. Ibid.

116. Masnick and Bane, *The Nation's Families*, p. 33 and "U.S. in Profile," p. 13.

117. Masnick and Bane, *The Nation's Families*, p. 37.

118. Sandra L. Hofferth and Kristin A. Moore, "Women's Employment and Marriage," in Smith, ed., *The Subtle Revolution*, pp. 106–108.

119. Other reasons for the possible nonmarriage of these women include rejection of the wife role and the unavailability of suitable potential spouses of equal or greater age and status. See Bernard, *The Future of Marriage*, pp. 34–35; Karl E. Taeuber and James A. Sweet, "Family and Work: The Social Life Cycle of Women" in Juanita M. Kreps, ed., *Women and the American Economy: A Look to the 1980s* (Englewood Cliffs: Prentice-Hall, 1976), pp. 44–47; and Hofferth and Moore, "Women's Employment and Marriage," in Smith, ed., *The Subtle Revolution*, p. 102.

120. Masnick and Bane, *The Nation's Families*, p. 51.

121. Current Population Reports—*Marital Status and Living Arrangements* (March 1981), Bureau of the Census, p. 6.

122. "U.S. in Profile," p. 13.

123. Degler, *At Odds,* pp. 166–175.

124. Ibid.

125. *The Virginia Slims American Women's Opinion Poll,* vol. III, pp. 45 and 56.

126. Frank L. Mott and Sylvia P. Moore, "The Causes and Consequences of Marital Breakdown," in Frank L. Mott, ed., *Women, Work and Family* (Lexington, Mass.: Lexington Books, 1978), pp. 113–135. See also, Heather L. Ross and Isabell V. Sawhill, *Time of Transition: The Growth of Families Headed by Women* (Washington, D.C.: The Urban Institute, 1975), pp. 39–62.

127. "Increased Longevity Ends Marriage, Study Claims," *Buffalo Evening News,* May 27, 1981, p. 8. This is a report of a study by Dr. Holger Stub of Temple University.

128. United States Department of Labor, Bureau of Labor Statistics, "Education of Labor Force Continues to Rise" (August 10, 1982), p. 1 and "Single-Parent Families up 80 Percent in 1970s, Census Reports," *Atlanta Journal and Constitution,* August 17, 1980, p. 14a.

129. "Women Led Families Rise," *The New York Times,* December 3, 1980, C-15.

130. "Education of Labor Force Continues to Rise," Table 6 and Diana Pearce and Harriette McAdoo, *Women and Children: Alone and In Poverty* (Washington, D.C.: National Advisory Council on Economic Opportunity, 1981). Reprinted by the Women's Research and Education Institute, p. 4.

131. "Single-Parent Families Up 80 Percent in 1970s," p. 15a.

132. Ross and Sawhill, *Time of Transition: The Growth of Families Headed by Women.*

133. Pearce and McAdoo, *Women and Children: Alone and In Poverty,* p. 2.

134. "Poverty Increasing in U.S., Report Says," *Buffalo Evening News,* August 19, 1982, p. A-10.

135. Diana Pearce, "Women, Work and Welfare: The Feminization of Poverty," in Karen Wolk Feinstein, ed., *Working Women and Families* (Beverly Hills, Calif.: Sage Publishers, 1979), p. 110.

136. *Older Women: The Economics of Aging* (Washington, D.C.: The Women's Studies Program and Policy Center at George Washington University and the Women's Research and Education Institute, October 1980), p. 12. See also, Margaret Gates, "Homemakers into Widows and Divorcées: Can the Law Provide Economic Protection?" in Jane Roberts Chapman and Margaret Gates, eds., *Women into Wives: The Legal and Economic Impact of Marriage* (Beverly Hills, Calif.: Sage Publications, 1977), p. 217; William D. Spector, "Women's Retirement Income," in Feinstein, ed., *Working Women and Families,* p. 247; and Sara E. Rix and Anne J. Stone, *Impact on Women of the Administration's Proposed Budget* (Washington, D.C.: The Women's Research and Education Institute, April 1982), pp. 17–20.

137. Quoted in Patricia McCormick, "A 'Homemaker's Bill of Rights' Tackles Real Problems of Midlife," *Buffalo Evening News,* May 31, 1979, p. II-25.

138. Degler, *At Odds,* p. 181.

139. Ibid., p. 189.

140. Ibid., p. 201.

141. Gordon, *Woman's Body, Woman's Right,* pp. 101–111.

142. There is some limited evidence that sexual relations within marriage improved in this era. Smigel and Seiden, "The Decline and Fall of the Double

Standard," in Friedman and Shade, eds., *Our American Sisters,* pp. 284–291.

143. Sandra Stencel, "The Changing American Family," in Sandra Stencel, ed., *Editorial Research Reports on the Changing American Family* (Washington, D.C.: Congressional Quarterly, 1979), p. 8.

144. Robert O. Blood, Jr. and Donald M. Wolfe, *Husbands and Wives: The Dynamics of Married Living* (Glencoe, Illinois: Free Press, 1960), pp. 117–118 and Lopata, *Occupation: Housewife,* pp. 200 and 205.

145. Lopata, *Occupation: Housewife,* p. 200.

146. Bernard, *The Future of Marriage,* p. 63.

147. Lopata, *Occupation: Housewife,* pp. 198–199 and Ann Oakley, *The Sociology of Housework* (Bath, Gr. Br.: Pitman Press, 1974), pp. 149–150.

148. Lopata, *Occupation: Housewife,* pp. 189–199 and Bernard, *The Future of Marriage,* p. 47.

149. Iglehart, *Married Women and Work,* pp. 64 and 67–68.

150. Stephanie J. Ventura, "Trends in First Births to Older Mothers, 1970–79," *Monthly Vital Statistics Report* 31 (May 27, 1982), p. 1 and Masnick and Bane, *The Nation's Families, 1960–1990,* p. 47.

151. "At Long Last Motherhood," *Newsweek,* March 16, 1981, p. 86. Ross M. Stolzenberg and Linda J. Waite, "Age, Fertility Expectations and Plans for Employment," *American Sociological Review* 42 (October 1977):769–783; "U.S. in Profile," p. 13; and Ventura, "Trends in First Births to Older Mothers," p. 1.

152. Ventura, "Trends in First Births to Older Mothers," p. 1, reports nearly half of all first time mothers over 30 had four years of college.

153. Quoted in "At Long Last Motherhood," p. 86.

154. Bird, *Two-Paycheck Marriage,* pp. 158–159. Most of the popular women's magazines in the early 1980s had at least one article on how late in life it was still safe or not so safe to have a baby.

155. "U.S. in Profile," p. 13. The 1981 rates, however, were up from those of 1976, which were 1.77 births per woman.

156. Masnick and Bane, *The Nation's Families,* pp. 42–43. See also, Moore and Hofferth, "Women and Their Children," in Smith, ed., *The Subtle Revolution,* pp. 128–131.

157. Masnick and Bane, *The Nation's Families,* p. 143.

158. Hofferth and Moore, "Women's Employment and Marriage," in Smith, ed., *The Subtle Revolution,* pp. 102–103.

159. Frank L. Mott and David Shapiro, "Pregnancy, Motherhood, and Work Activity," in Mott, ed., *Women, Work and Family,* pp. 40–44 and Masnick and Bane, *The Nation's Families,* p. 82.

160. Vanek, "Housewives as Workers," in Stromberg and Harkess, eds., *Women Working,* pp. 393–399 and Norton, "The Myth of the Golden Age," in Berkin and Norton, eds., *Women of America,* pp. 37–38.

161. Lopata, *Occupation: Housewife,* pp. 113–122.

162. Vanek, "Housewives as Workers," in Stromberg and Harkess, eds., *Women Working,* p. 401.

163. Friedan, *The Feminine Mystique,* chap. 10 and Oakley, *Sociology of Housework,* p. 111.

164. Blood and Wolfe, *Husbands and Wives,* p. 65.

165. Vanek, "Housewives as Workers," in Stromberg and Harkess, eds., *Women Working,* p. 402.

166. For reviews of the new findings, see Joann Vanek, "Household Work, Wage Work, and Sexual Equality," in Berk, ed., *Women and Household Labor,* pp. 275–291. See also, Hofferth and Moore, "Women's Employment and Marriage," in Smith, ed., *The Subtle Revolution,* pp. 111–116.

167. Ibid., p. 112, although see also, Joseph H. Pleck, "Men's Family Work: Three Perspectives and Some New Data," *The Family Coordinator* 28 (October 1979): 481–488.

168. John P. Robinson, *How Americans Use Time: A Social Psychological Analysis of Everyday Behavior* (New York: Praeger, 1977), p. 151.

169. See, for example, Richard A. Berk and Sara Fensternmaker Berk, *Labor and Leisure at Home: Content and Organization of the Household Day* (Beverly Hills, Calif.: Sage Publications, 1979), p. 123; Bird, *Two-Paycheck Marriage,* pp. 84–99; Julia A. Ericksen, William L. Yancey, and Eugene P. Ericksen, "The Division of Family Roles," *Journal of Marriage and the Family* 41 (May 1979):301–313; and Michael Berger, Martha Foster, and Barbara Strudler Wallston, "Finding Two Jobs," in Robert Rapoport and Rhona Rapoport with Janice Bumstead, eds., *Working Couples* (New York: Harper Colophon, 1978), pp. 30–31.

170. There is even some evidence that shows that a working wife allows more leisure time for her husband. Vanek, "Household Work, Wage Work, and Sexual Equality," in Berk, ed., *Women and Household Labor,* p. 277.

171. Ibid.

172. *The General Mills American Family Report, 1980–81,* p. 19. Sixty-three percent of all working mothers but only 40 percent of working fathers report they do not have enough time for themselves.

173. Quoted in Pat Swift, "NOW Looks at Feminism and the Family," *Buffalo Evening News,* June 7, 1979, p. II–21.

174. Berk and Berk, *Labor and Lesiure at Home,* p. 231.

175. United States Department of Labor, Bureau of Labor Statistics, "Earnings of Workers and Their Families: Third Quarter 1982" (November 8, 1982), Table 1. See also, Carolyn Shaw Bell, "Working Wives and Family Income," in Jane Roberts Chapman, ed., *Economic Independence for Women: The Foundation for Equal Rights* (Beverly Hills, Calif.: Sage, 1976), pp. 246–255, where she reports that in 1977 women's salaries accounted for 25 percent of the family's income.

176. Masnick and Bane, *The Nation's Families,* pp. 94–95.

177. Helena Z. Lopata, Debra Barnewolt, and Kathleen Norr, "Spouses' Contributions to Each Other's Roles," in Fran Pepitone-Rockwell, ed., *Dual-Career Couples* (Beverly-Hills, Calif.: Sage Publications, 1980), pp. 120–123.

178. For a review of this and some of the other common measures of power in the family, see Stephen J. Bahr, "Effects on Power and Division of Labor in the Family," in Lois Wladis Hoffman and F. Ivan Nye, eds., *Working Mothers* (San Francisco: Jossey-Bass, 1974), pp. 167–172. There are many criticisms of their measures. Rarely is any discussion given to the relative importance of one decision-making area over another. In one study, the questions about where to take a vacation and whether the wife should work were considered equally important. Blood and Wolfe, *Husbands and Wives,* pp. 2–23. Also, the process by which decisions are arrived at has received only

scant examination as has the process by which it is agreed who shall make the decisions in the various issue areas in the first place.

Several authors have begun to study the process of decision making. See, for example, Scanzoni, *Sex Roles, Women's Work and Marital Conflict,* especially chaps. 4 and 5. For further discussion and criticism of these measures, see Dair R. Gillespie, "Who Has the Power? The Marital Struggle," in Freeman, ed., *Women: A Feminist Perspective,* pp. 64–87.

179. Blood and Wolfe, *Husbands and Wives,* p. 21. In blue-collar marriages, Komarovsky reported that male authority, as measured by outcomes of marital disagreements, the view of an outside observer, and the decision making power of each spouse, was even more marked. Forty-five percent of all the working-class marriages she studied fell in the male-dominant category. The lower the education level, the more skewed was the division of authority in the direction of the husband. In the few couples where the wife had more authority, she tended to hide her power, at least in public, and to cling to the view that it would have been better if the man were in control. Komarovsky, *Blue-Collar Marriage,* pp. 221–234.

180. Ibid., pp. 225–231 and Blood and Wolfe, *Husbands and Wives,* pp. 12–13.

181. Blood and Wolfe, *Hubands and Wives,* p. 40. See also, Bahr, "Effects on Power and Division of Labor in the Family," in Hoffman and Nye, eds., *Working Mothers,* pp. 173–177 for a review of studies that indicate the extent of and limits upon the increase in a wife's power if she works.

182. *The General Mills American Family Report, 1980–81,* p. 46.

183. Judith Long Laws, "A Feminist View of Marital Adjustment," in Alan S. Gurman and David G. Rice, eds., *Couples in Conflict: New Directions in Marital Therapy* (New York: Jason Aronson, 1975), pp. 85–89. See also, Hofferth and Moore, "Women's Employment and Marriage," in Smith, ed., *The Subtle Revolution,* pp. 116–118.

184. *The General Mills American Family Report, 1980–81,* pp. 43 and 45.

185. Frank Mott, "Introduction and Overview," in Mott, ed., *Women, Work and Family,* p. 14.

186. *The 1980 Virginia Slims American Women's Opinion Poll,* pp. 17 and 33.

187. The Gallup Report, #197 (February 1982), p. 6.

188. Ibid.

189. Friedan, *The Second Stage,* pp. 76–78.

190. Quoted in "The Superwoman Squeeze," p. 78. See also, Friedan, *The Second Stage,* especially chaps. 3, 6, and 8.

9   Conclusion—The Women's Movement and the Equal Rights Amendment: What's Ahead?

INTRODUCTION

Our discussion of the various women's movements' attempts to gain greater political, employment, educational, and intrafamily rights has revealed that while each movement contributed to progress, often that progress was followed by a period of entrenchment. In fact, at times, rights won for women often have disappeared or at best, been severely curtailed as was the case in the era immediately preceding the current women's movement. Thus, now that the unifying issue of the current women's movement—the Equal Rights Amendment—has failed to gain ratification, it remains to be seen if the current movement, unlike those in the past, can be sustained.

HISTORY OF THE EQUAL RIGHTS AMENDMENT

An amendment to the constitution to guarantee to all women equal rights was first proposed by the National Woman's Party (NWP) shortly after passage of the Nineteenth Amendment. According to William H. Chafe, "No issue divided women's organizations more than the Equal Rights Amendment to the Constitution."[1] As submitted to the Congress in December 1923 by Daniel Anthony (R-Kansas), Susan B. Anthony's nephew, the proposed amendment read, "Men and women shall have equal rights throughout the United States and every place subject to its jurisdiction."[2] The NWP's introduction of the amendment immediately split the already faltering suffrage movement into three distinct coalitions: (1) "hard core feminists;" (2) "social feminists;" and (3) antifeminists.[3] NWP leaders, as spokeswomen for "hard core" feminists, rejected pleas from the "social feminists" to work for causes such as peace, birth control, and social reform. Instead, they saw these efforts as diverting their energies from the ultimate goal—equality—and thus a waste of time.

In contrast, the social feminist League of Women Voters believed that women should continue to work for legislation to better their roles as wife and mother and not for equal rights. Thus, it was instrumental in the creation of the Women's Joint Congressional Committee and urged its members to work for the enactment of legislation including the Cable and Sheppard-Towner Maternity Acts. The National Consumers' League, another social feminist organization, continued in its efforts to see maximum hour and minimum wage legislation for women and children enacted by the legislatures of the states. The NCL, in particular, found itself forced to take a public stand against the amendment because of the clear indications that the ERA, as written, would have negated all protective legislation for women—legislation that it believed imperative to the health and well-being of female workers.

The split in the ranks of the coalition that earlier had brought about passage of the Nineteenth Amendment was well-publicized and clearly had an impact on the U.S. Supreme Court as well as on elected officials who soon began to recognize that women lacked political clout. Additionally, inter-organizational disputes concerning the role of women and the ERA continued into the 1930s. In spite of these divisions and the continuing militant tactics of the NWP—in many ways a model for those used by the radical branch of the current movement—pro-ERA efforts appeared to be effective. A sub-committee in the House of Representatives endorsed the ERA in 1936 and in fact, according to William C. Chafe, some members of Congress were willing to vote for the amendment in 1937 just to keep peace. Later in 1938, the Senate Judiciary Committee reported the amendment to the floor. And, in 1940, the Republican party added support of the amendment to its platform.[4]

Largely because of continuing pressure by the NWP, the ERA was introduced every session of Congress between 1923 and 1971.[5] Beyond simple introduction of the amendment, however, treatment of the ERA by Congress was mixed. For example, the House of Representatives held hearings on the ERA in 1948 but failed to do so again until 1971 largely because of the refusal of the House Judiciary Committee Chair, Emanuel Celler (D-New York), to schedule hearings for an amendment to which he was personally opposed. The ERA was better received in the Senate. After its original introduction, hearings on the ERA were held during several Senate sessions and in 1950 and 1953, the Senate passed the proposed amendment. On both of those occasions, however, the Senate version included a rider guaranteeing that protective legislation for women would not be affected.[6]

It was not until the rise of the current women's movement, particularly the rights branch, that the ERA was seriously discussed. In fact, the President's Commission on the Status of Women, which some say was formed by President Kennedy to diffuse "the present troublesome and futile agitation over the ERA," failed to recommend ratification of the amendment.[7] The sole advocate of the ERA on the commission, Marguerite Rawalt, however, was successful in persuading other commission members to temper their rejection of the need for an ERA by the inclusion of the word "now" in the commission report: "We conclude that a constitutional amendment need not *now* be sought,"[8] which paved the way for a later recommendation to the president.

Even five years later, however, the concepts inherent in the amendment still were not greeted enthusiastically by many women's groups. In fact, when NOW endorsed the ERA in 1967, some of its members resigned in protest voicing fears similar to those earlier noted by social feminists and many existing women's groups: the amendment would negate protective legislation.[9]

In 1970, however, the Citizens Advisory Council on the Status of Women reported to Richard Nixon its belief that an amendment was necessary, thus rejecting the earlier recommendation of the original Commission on the Status of Women.[10] Included in its report was a legal analysis of such an amendment by Mary Eastwood, a Justice Department attorney and one of NOW's founders, just prior to that group's public support of the amendment.[11]

Eastwood's analysis included a section on the ERA's impact on protective legislation in which she concluded that where benefits were given to women, they would be extended to men. According to Eastwood, an attorney, the only kinds of protective legislation that would be voided by the ERA were those that restricted women's access or rights to certain positions. This analysis then was entered into the Congressional Record on March 26, 1970 by Martha Griffiths (D-Michigan), a longtime ERA supporter.

Later that year, on June 11, Griffiths used a discharge petition to force the amendment out of the House Judiciary Committee where it had been blocked since 1948 by Rep. Celler.[12] Finally, on August 10, 1970, on the first occasion that the full House ever had to vote for the ERA, after eloquent presentations concerning the effects of the ERA by Reps. Griffiths, Edith Green, and Margaret Heckler, it passed on a 350 to 15 vote.

A somewhat different pattern emerged in the Senate. In May 1970, prior to the House vote, the Senate Subcommittee on Constitutional Amendments held hearings chaired by Birch Bayh (D-Indiana). At these hearings several representatives from the AFL-CIO testified in opposition to the amendment while *no* women's groups spoke against it.[13] A similar pattern emerged when new hearings were held by the full Senate committee, after the House vote— most of those who testified, including the John Birch Society, the AFL-CIO, and National Council of Catholic Women, spoke against the amendment.[14] A rider proposed by Sam Ervin (D-North Carolina), which prohibited the drafting of women into the armed forces and also contained language limiting the ERA's impairment of protective legislation[15] had substantial support, but, nevertheless, after a tremendous effort on the part of women's organizations,[16] on March 22, 1972, the Senate accepted the ERA by a vote of 84 to 8.

Interestingly, the hearings that were held during the two-year period in which the Congress considered the amendment ultimately gave both supporters and opponents fuel for their arguments. Constitutional law experts differed on the need for an amendment as well as on its legal consequences.

Women's rights groups, however, generally were in total agreement for the need for the ERA by 1972. Just as suffrage had been viewed by many women as leading to full equality, the ERA was viewed as a necessary first—and the most far-ranging—step toward full equality in all spheres of life. Because while opponents argued that women had achieved a variety of expanded rights through legislation and judicial decisions, women's rights advocates realized that without an amendment, these gains could be lost at anytime as the composition of legislatures or of the courts changed.

Thus, they believed that the following amendment as proposed by Congress was essential:

Sec. 1.   Equality of rights under the law shall not be denied or abridged by the United States or by any State on account of sex.

Sec. 2.   The Congress shall have the power to enforce, by appropriate legislation, the provisions of this article.

Sec. 3.   This amendment shall take effect two years after the date of ratification.

They believed it was necessary because extensive discrimination was:

directly attributable to governmental action both in maintaining archaic discriminatory laws and in perpetuating discriminatory practices in employment, education and other areas. The social and economic cost to our society, as well as the individual psychological impact of sex discrimination, are immeasurable. That a majority of our population should be subjected to the indignities and limitations of second class citizenship is a fundamental affront to personal human liberty.[17]

To end this discrimination, a national amendment was sought. It was believed that this approach would be far easier than the state-by-state approach of attempting to change thousands of discriminatory state and national laws.[18]

While there was general agreement about the concepts of equal educational, employment, and political opportunity that would be absolutely guaranteed by the amendment,[19] controversy over the impact of the ERA on familial relations, including alimony, child support, divorce laws, and military service, were present from the beginning. The sweeping language of Section 1 of the proposed amendment led opponents, including Professor Paul Freund of Harvard University, to testify that women might be *required* to work outside the home in order to contribute *equally* to their families' support.[20] It was also argued that discrimination on the basis of sexual preference would be unconstitutional,[21] women would no longer be exempt from compulsory military service, and that the power of the states would be further diminished in the federal system.[22]

While eventually the first two fears subsided,[23] the notion of compulsory military service for women, which would be required under the amendment,[24] and the authority of the states to legislate in the area of domestic relations, which also would be curtailed,[25] proved roadblocks to ratification particularly as the amendment went to the states for approval. In fact, once it was sent to the states for ratification, the real battle over the ERA began in earnest. At first it looked to the amendment's supporters that victory would be easy. The Court's rulings striking down most protective legislation as unlawful under the Civil Rights Act of 1964 helped to bring into the ERA camp most of the liberal feminists and labor groups that had not initially supported the cause.[26] Even some radical feminists who saw little to be gained from a constitutional change supported the amendment, perceiving it to be a symbol and a possible tool to facilitate additional rights.[27] Additionally, research demonstrated that there was growing national support for efforts to improve the status of women. For example, early polls on the ERA found favorable response clearly outnumbered negative.[28]

Given the amendment's support in Congress and in the public, it is not surprising that between March 1972 to January 1973, twenty-eight states quickly moved to ratify the amendment.[29] These early victories, however, were not an indication of an easy road ahead. In fact, the states that did not ratify the amendment initially often had political cultures that resisted innovative legislation and expanded women's rights.[30] Additionally, most supporters of the amendment failed to recognize growing grass-roots opposition. For example, in March of 1973, Martha Griffiths confidently predicted that "ERA will be part of the Constitution before the year's out."[31]

This kind of confidence when coupled with the women's movement's disorganization resulted in increased ratification effort difficulties. Unlike the Nineteenth Amendment ratification effort, in which a single national umbrella organization, NAWSA, had developed a plan complete with state organizations in place *before* the suffrage amendment passed Congress, the groups who sponsored the ERA had no such plan or organizational structure,[32] both of which became increasingly important in the wake of growing local and state opposition. While a national ERA Ratification Council was formed by thirty supporting groups soon after the amendment's passage in Congress, it had no staff, no materials, and only a minimal budget.[33] Indeed, it was April 1973 before the Council even appointed a committee—the ERA Action Committee—to develop a national ratification strategy. This committee—composed of representatives from NWP, Common Cause, the League of Women Voters, and Business and Professional Women's Clubs (BPW)—formulated a plan of action but held only one meeting after May 1973.[34]

A second attempt to form a national organization, Operation Task Force, was made in summer 1973. This group, composed of representatives from NOW, the National Women's Political Caucus, the League of Women Voters, Common Cause, the American Civil Liberties Union, the American Association of University Women, the United Methodist Women, and a number of unions, was only slightly more active than the ERA Ratification Council. In fact, the total sum of money spent by all Task Force organizations in 1973–1974 was only $200,000.[35]

Given that a seven-year time limit for ratification was attached to the ERA, these national efforts wasted valuable time. A study funded by BPW, however, which recommended a more organized and well-financed national headquarters for coordinating state campaigns and soliciting money resulted in the founding of ERAmerica in January 1976. But this organization, like those before it, relying as it did on member organizations for help, soon turned out to be relatively poor and powerless.[36] Thus, without a strong national coordinating organization, actions to ratify the ERA relied almost exclusively on the efforts of individual groups, particularly NOW, BPW, and the League of Women Voters as well as ad hoc state coalitions. Not only did each of these groups pursue different strategies but all sought to become the leader in the ratification effort, which according to Janet Boles, can be divided into three clearly delineated stages.[37]

During the first stage of the effort, 1972–1977, NOW, the League, and BPW participated nearly equally in traditional forms of lobbying, including sponsoring letter and telegram campaigns, giving expert testimony, and support pro-ERA candidates. During this period, state groups were reactive and were created or mobilized only in response to anti-ERA activity. While pro-ERA groups were able to defeat some state legislators who opposed ratification, only five states ratified the ERA after 1973.

Therefore, by 1977, NOW adopted different tactics "which marked the ascendancy of NOW as the leading proponent of the ERA"[38] in the second stage of the ratification effort. NOW's rise to the forefront of the ERA ratification effort was triggered by the adoption of two campaigns. First, NOW called for an economic boycott of states where ratification had not yet occurred. Generally, this boycott took the form of having large national associations cancel or threaten to cancel conventions scheduled in cities located in unratified states.[39] Second, given the impending deadline for ratification—March 1979—Rep. Elizabeth Holtzman (D-New York) introduced a resolution to extend the ratification deadline an additional seven years at the urging of NOW. NOW, the NWPC, and many other groups relied on intensive traditional lobbying and, as suffragists had done earlier, sponsored a march on Washington, D.C. that attracted over 100,000 participants. In fact, during the 1979 march, many dressed in white as suffragists had done long before in their quest for an amendment. These well-planned efforts of the current women's movement ultimately led Congress to approve a thirty-nine month extension period for ratification over the objections of opponents.

It is interesting and important to note that both of these strategies were national in nature and thus quite unlike the "Winning Plan" devised earlier by Carrie Chapman Catt. In fact, the then-President of NOW, Eleanor Smeal, justified the necessity of a *national* campaign saying that "this is an unratified country. We communicate as a nation...our states are economically inter-dependent [and][o]ur opposition is national."[40] This kind of determination to pursue a national strategy in the wake of growing anti-ERA and New Right strength in nonratified states' legislatures is interesting given that the amendment could not be ratified without the approval of the states.[41] Nevertheless, NOW continued its national campaign, although, according to Boles, it was not until the third stage of the ratification effort, which began in late 1979, that NOW fully devoted itself to implementation of this new national plan of action. In fact, by 1982, NOW was receiving over a million dollars a month for amendment ratification and had formed several political action committees to elect pro-ERA candidates,[42] while a variety of other traditional and nontraditional strategies were employed. For example, "ERA missionaries" went door-to-door seeking support in unratified states and pro-ERA entertainers went on television to gain support and more publicity. Additionally, a variety of forms of violent protest occurred, including instances of women chaining themselves to Republican headquarters, hunger strikes, and vandalism.

All of these tactics came too late and generally occurred at the wrong level of government. Thus, even in states such as Illinois, which were the targets of massive pro-ERA efforts, few votes were changed and the amendment was finally defeated on June 30, 1982 when the time period for ratification expired. This lack of coordinated effective effort, however, was probably just one of several factors contributing to the defeat of the amendment. In fact, had it not been for the activities of anti-ERA groups, like the New Right with its close ties to state legislators and corporate interests, the amendment's chances of passage would have been far greater.

THE ANTI-ERA FORCES

The anti-ERA movement did not have to be particularly large or well organized to achieve its aim. In fact, as we shall see, it can be characterized as a privileged movement in the Olson sense. In other words, the efforts of a relatively few persons with only one recognized leader helped to prevent the amendment's adoption. Interestingly, Phyllis Schlafly, the leader of the Stop ERA movement, as late as 1971, did not even object to the then proposed amendment. Schlafly, who in 1971 was caught up in her concern for the national defense and other conservative causes, believed that the "ERA was something between innocuous and mildly helpful."[43] In December of that year, however, a close friend urged her to argue against the amendment in a debate to be held in Connecticut. Schlafly declined the invitation but was persuaded by her friend to read at least some background information on the proposed amendment.

Once Schlafly studied the ERA and its legislative history, she immediately set out to stop ratification.[44] Because the House of Representatives already had accepted the amendment and Senate passage was assured, she decided to focus on the states to stop ratification there. Schlafly believed that she "had found enough seriously wrong with ERA to stop it, or at least stall it, for an awfully long time, if only [she] could get the message out."[45]

In February 1972, she devoted an entire issue of her newsletter, *The Phyllis Schlafly Report,* to the ERA. In it she described what she believed to be its detrimental impact on women and the family. *The Report,* which she started in 1967, regularly addressed issues, including foreign policy, nuclear warheads, and pornography. It had a sizeable conservative readership that gave her a base from which eventually to launch a countermovement. Largely because of the response to her anti-ERA issue of the newsletter, Schlafly founded STOP ERA in October of 1972 with herself as chair. Subsequently, she personally appointed state chairs in 45 states, who served at her pleasure.[46] STOP ERA itself had no members and Schlafly regularly referred to it as a movement.[47] And, because Schlafly created her *own* organization, she was able to exercise considerable control over the direction of the movement in sharp contrast to the efforts of pro-ERA leaders.

Schlafly's undisputed leadership also assisted growth of the movement by providing additional publicity, much of it free. The women's rights movement was never totally in agreement on goals or tactics concerning ERA passage and the movement itself had many leaders. Schlafly, however, as the self-appointed leader of the anti-ERA movement, was generally its sole spokesperson. Therefore, when the press desired an anti-ERA comment or reaction, Schlafly, always accessible to the press, was regularly consulted. Thus, as early as 1973, most reports of antiamendment activity contained a quote from, or reference to Schlafly, giving her the publicity that was necessary to expand the base of her countermovement.

Boles has noted that even though most of those in the media favored the ERA, by featuring the arguments of the opponents alongside those of the proponents, the message of the former received wider support than it might ordinarily have received.[48] On other occasions, it was the stated opposition, neutrality, or less than wholehearted support on the part of elected officials that provided the necessary resources for the countermovement. In this respect, the positions of the Republican platform and President Reagan on the ERA no doubt greatly increased the legitimacy and hence the number of supporters and chances for success of the opposition forces.

It appears that the anti-ERA movement initially built primarily on two often interlocking, preexisting organizational structures: the religious right (fundamentalist, Mormon, and to a lesser extent, antiabortion groups supported by the Roman Catholic Church) and the political right (most notably the John Birch Society, the American party, and the Schlafly wing of the Republican party). Studies of countermovement participants found that both the religious and political right groups often provided the core for state anti-ERA leaders and followers. Kent L. Tedin et al., for example, found that 98 percent of those active in the movement to rescind the ERA in Texas were church members and 66 percent belonged to fundamentalist denominations.[49] The corresponding percentages for pro-ERA activists were 48 and four. Additionally, the belief that religion was important in one's everyday life ranked second only to conservative beliefs in distinguishing between the pro- and anti-ERA forces, with antis considerably more likely to rank religion as important.

Others who have studied the supporters of the anti-ERA movement in the South report similar evidence of the close association between being a member of a fundamentalist church and working against the amendment.[50] In fact, during the last stage of the ratification effort, media preachers of the New Right, including the Rev. Jerry Falwell, worked hard to mobilize their listeners and other fundamentalist Christians to oppose the ERA.

For many Southern women, the church and the church-connected women's associations have provided the prime source of social contact outside the family. In addition to the private rewards such as friendship, it is possible that the private negative aspects of not working against the ERA in some small communities also motivated some women to act. Besides followers, the churches supplied many anti-ERA leaders and some private incentives for those leaders. In fact, the number of evangelical ministers at the forefront of all the New Right movements is very reminiscent of the importance of ministers in the civil rights and abolition movements.[51]

The fundamentalist churches and the conservative right also furnished the communications network—speeches from the pulpit, church bulletins— by which to spread the message of the movement and mobilize new supporters.[52] A good example of the way churches aided the organizational effort is suggested by Tedin, who reports that trips to the Texas state capital, Austin, to lobby to rescind the ERA were organized by women's church groups.[53] In Utah, Nevada, and several other states the Mormon church lent much the same organizational support.[54] For example, it bussed large numbers of women to meetings where delegates for both the National

Women's Conference and White House Conference on Families were to be selected. Fourteen thousand men and women attended the Utah meeting to select delegates to the National Women's Conference at the call of the Mormon Relief Society, whose leaders urged them to "stand up for 'correct principles,'" including defeat of the ERA.[55]

The vehemence of the Mormon Church's opposition is reflected in its treatment of Sonia Johnson. When she, an active member in the Mormon Church, spoke out in favor of the ERA in Congress and began organizing Mormons for the ERA, the Church hierarchy moved quickly to excommunicate her. The political and religious right, however, often went beyond simply providing the followers, leaders, and communications network for the countermovement. During the ratification period, many ERA supporters charged that groups, including the John Birch Society and the conservative Manion Trust Fund, directly funded some of the costs of establishing anti-ERA organizations where preexisting organizational bases were small or nonexistent.

Another source of financial support appears to have come from those businesses that benefit by keeping women in the home or that profit from sexual stereotyping. According to Kathleen Teague, a Virginia Stop ERA co-"chairman," Jay Van Andel, founder of Amway, a company that employs thousands of housewives to sell its products at home parties, is "one of Phyllis's big donors."[56] Leaders of NOW and other women's rights groups also have charged that the insurance industry, which profits from the maintenance of gender-based actuarial tables, has been an important source of Stop ERA financial support as well as a potent lobbyist against the amendment.[57] In fact, in at least one key state, Illinois, campaign contributions from these interests may have provided one of the key elements in the final defeat of the amendment.[58]

In the case of organizational and financial support from men in both the political and religious right, the rationale for such help probably reflected self-interest as well as altruistic motives. It is likely that they saw the probability of success for their own group or movement's goals enhanced by the victory of the anti-ERA forces. This is certainly true for the leaders of the Right to Life movement and, in fact, this is often admitted by those active in that cause. For example, the National Conference of Catholic Bishops rejected the advice of the Ad Hoc Committee on Women in Church and Society, which urged the endorsement of the ERA, on the grounds that such support would hurt the antiabortion movement.[59] It should be noted, moreover, that the STOP ERA movement did not attempt to disassociate itself with the antiabortion movement and in fact encouraged the link between the two issues. Immediately after the U.S. Supreme Court ruled against restrictive state abortion laws in 1973, Schlafly noted to her supporters, "How much easier it will be to find an absolute, government-financed right to abortion in ERA!"[60] Linking the two issues clearly helped the STOP ERA movement attract new supporters, particularly among Catholics.

This conservative base, however, would not necessarily have led to a countermovement were it not for the nature of the ERA (as characterized by its opponents). Countermovements are most likely to form when the change or good sought threatens some existing pure public good(s). These perceptions are more likely to develop if the results thought to accompany the proposed new law or change are ambiguous, uncertain, and universal in their impact on the affected group and/or are characterized by opponents of the change as having such attributes.

The ERA, as its opponents were quick to point out, was easily open to interpretation. The uncertainty surrounding its effects was recognized by even many proponents, who concluded that the final interpretation of the results of the amendment would be determined by the Supreme Court,[61] the branch of government most distrusted by many conservatives. Additionally, much of the anti-ERA opposition stemmed from the second section of the proposed amendment, empowering Congress "to enforce, by appropriate legislation, the provisions" of the amendment. Sen. Ervin charged that Section 2 "would virtually reduce the states of this union to meaningless zeros on the nation's map."[62] Fears that Congress would pass legislation of the kind enacted pursuant to the Fourteenth Amendment and deprive states of their right to regulate domestic relations was abhorrent to conservatives who believed that less was better in terms of federal government regulation. Thus, when Schlafly made state legislators who stood to lose the most aware of this provision and coupled her states' rights plea with an account of what potential changes could occur should the amendment be ratified, her efforts produced almost immediate results. In fact, from 1974 to 1981 no states ratified the amendment.

The language of Section 1 guaranteeing "equality of rights" also encouraged the perception that the amendment would have a broad, universal, inescapable impact on all women. Many of its opponents pointed out that they favored equal rights for women, but that the ERA, because of its language, would eliminate some good as well as bad practices, and, therefore, was an inappropriate method to achieve this goal. Phyllis Schlafly, for example, said she would accept a revised ERA that would guarantee women special rights, allow for differences between men and women, and not deprive women of existing rights.[63]

The sweeping promises of supporters about the benefits of the ERA, especially in the beginning, may actually have encouraged the view that the amendment would have a widespread impact on all women. After the period for ratification of the ERA was extended, proponents attempted to reduce ambiguity about what the amendment would achieve and to narrow the claims made for the ERA—but such backtracking proved to be futile.

The uncertainty surrounding the outcome and breadth of the ERA was fully taken advantage of by its opponents. Schlafly charged that the ERA would mean:

1. private schools would have to be coed;
2. all sports, including contact sports, would be coed;
3. all persons would pay the same income tax regardless of their income;
4. government-funded abortions;
5. homosexual school teachers;
6. women forced into combat;
7. men refusing to support their wives;
8. taking away a woman's right to her home and support of her children;
9. legalizing homosexual marriages; and
10. allowing homosexuals to adopt children.[64]

Others have stated that it would legalize unisex toilets and pornography.[65] The ambiguity surrounding the amendment encouraged many to view it as a threat to existing pure, public goods. As the ERA was portrayed by opponents, the traditional family, the institution of marriage, and the right of a wife to be supported by her husband would be jeopardized by ratification. Phyllis Schlafly, in answer to the question of who would profit from the ERA, wrote in an often reprinted quotation, "Women will lose, families will lose, society will lose."[66]

Opponents often characterized the ERA as universal in impact—women would be unable to choose the amount of the new good they wanted; rather, all women would be forced to accept an equal amount of the good (bad). They would be drafted. They would *have* to work because their husbands no longer would be required to support them. And, their virtue as women would be threatened when they and their daughters were forced to share public toilets with men. STOP ERA and its followers also claimed that women would not be able to choose the amount of the old, threatened goods they might wish to continue to consume. As they interpreted and publicized the amendment, *all* women would lose previously enjoyed goods including dependence on their husbands for economic support, child support if divorced, the joy of family life, and an ordered society.[67] The fear that such things might be lost was probably enhanced by the fact that many women already saw facets of the traditional family on the decline, at least in part as a result of the women's movement. For example, in 1977, the CBS/*New York Times* poll found 47 percent of all women and 42 percent of all men believed the women's movement was a major cause of family breakdown, while only 20 percent of women (15 percent of men) thought the movement had created a better family structure. Additionally, and perhaps most importantly, Phyllis Schlafly and many conservatives believed that the women's rights movement "is inescapably wrapped up in the lesbian movement...the cause for the rising divorce rate...and a radical anti-family group."[68] These beliefs simply gave credence to the view that the ERA was a pure public bad.

Association of the women's movement and its efforts to gain ratification of the ERA with these "bads" led many housewives, especially those who were older or part of the middle class, to support the STOP ERA movement because, as presented, they clearly had the most to lose if the ERA was passed.[69] Studies of supporters find these women enjoyed their status as housewives and full-time homemakers and were fearful the ERA would eliminate this good as well as another—their economic security—by making women work or by taking away jobs from their husbands.[70] Many anti-ERA proponents, in fact, believed in the principles of equal pay and equal opportunity but feared the ERA's impact on the family. Compounding this problem was the public's perceptions that the women's movement was unconcerned with homemakers.

The fears of these women were enhanced by the fact that large majorities of them already believed that some related goods had been lost. Perhaps the prototypical example of this type of supporter was the movement's leader— Phyllis Schlafly. In an interview in *The New York Times,* she recounted her poor childhood, her struggle to put herself through school, and her salvation from the life of hard work via marriage to a wealthy man.[71] Quoting Schlafly on the advantages of the present threatened "good" whereby the husband is obliged by law to support his wife, she expressed her belief, "The law is beautiful. He [man] is liable. She is not. Is that fair? Sure. That's the beautiful way men treat women in this country."[72] On another occasion, Schlafly, taking target at the preference of some women for the term, Ms., noted, "I've worked too hard for the "r" in my name. Don't take it away."[73] In *Power of the Positive Woman,* written by Schlafly in 1977, she charged that "the ultimate goal of women's liberation is independence from men and the avoidance of pregnancy and its consequences. [Thus] lesbianism is logically the highest form of ritual in women's liberation."[74] Repeated depiction of feminists as antimen, antifamily, etc. effectively publicized the nebulousness of the proposed amendment. By drawing suspicion to amendment supporters, as well as to the proposed amendment itself, which was open to interpretation as even its supporters admitted, Schlafly was able to stop ratification and yearly increase opposition to the amendment.

Thus, the ERA was described by opposition leaders as a pure, public bad that threatened existing goods. This characterization generated the greatest concern among women who had the most to lose if the threatened goods were eliminated. Where these women were members of a preexisting organizational base—or where such organizational structure could be supplied by outside resources—the crisis that galvanized them to form a countermovement was the approaching victory of the ERA. Schlafly's first frontal attack on the amendment came in 1972, the same year she organized STOP ERA. Later, in 1975, she formed the Eagle Forum as an alternative to NOW. These two groups, along with assistance from conservative religious and political groups, and business interests, were able to stop ratification of the amendment by the initial March 22, 1979 deadline.

By 1978, ERA advocates realized that they would not be able to secure sufficient states for ratification. Therefore, while only three states short of ratification, they lobbied Congress, where they and not the anti-ERA supporters were best-organized, to extend the time period for ratification by an additional seven years. After a long and emotional debate, Congress agreed in October 1978 to their request to lengthen the time period for ratification by thirty-nine months, rejecting at the same time a provision that would have allowed state legislatures to rescind their prior approval. Both of these actions were met with indignation and charges of foul play from STOP ERA members who believed that Congress was changing the rules in the middle of the game. The anti-ERA forces also contended the extension was unconstitutional, an issue that the U.S. Supreme Court later declined to address.[75]

THE DEFEAT AND BEYOND

Even the extension did not make it possible for women's rights advocates to persuade the required number of state legislatures to ratify the amendment. In fact, not a single state ratified the amendment during the extended ratification period. This was in spite of the fact that women's rights groups devoted most of their energies and resources to ratification in target states like Illinois. Boycotts of states that did not ratify the ERA, lobbying, and television campaigns simply could not stop the growing conservative trend in this country. In fact, according to Mark R. Daniels, Robert Darcy, and Joseph W. Westphal, although Americans initially "strongly favored the amendment" at levels of "two to one," by 1980 support declined to its lowest level. They believed that this decline was directly attributable to Ronald Reagan's transformation of the ERA into a partisan issue and the Republican party's removal of its support.[76] Thus, this withdrawal of support "may have led many Americans to conclude that something was wrong with the ERA."[77] By July 1981, however, the partisan nature of the ERA appeared to be receding and in July 1982, shortly after the amendment was defeated, 61.5 percent of the public supported the ERA as revealed in Table 9-1. The victory of ERA opponents—never a majority of the population—thus signaled yet another victory for the New Right over the desires of the majority of the public.

Additionally, the countermovement's growth and its success in defeating the ERA bring with it the real possibility that the prowomen's movement and its other goals will be subject to the same fate. Schlafly, for instance, is quoted

TABLE 9-1

Support and Opposition to the ERA by American Public

Year	Favor	Oppose	Don't Know		n
1974	73.6	21.1	5.2	100%	(2822)
1975	58.3	23.7	18.0	100%	(2762)
1976	56.7	24.5	18.8	100%	(2798)
1977	65.5	26.5	8.0	100%	(1000)
1978	58.0	31.0	11.0	100%	(1010)
1980	52.3	28.3	19.4	100%	(2780)
1981	55.5	28.1	16.4	100%	(2740)
1982	61.5	23.4	15.1	100%	(1506)

Source of data: Mark R. Daniels, Robert Darcy, and Joseph W. Westphal, "The ERA Won—At Least in the Opinion Polls," 15 *PS* (Fall 1982): 579. Reprinted with permission.

as saying, "I see the defeat of the amendment as a tremendous defeat for the other goals of the women's lib movement."[78] Even if Schlafly's threat to attack other causes of the women's movement proves to pack only a limited punch, one might conjecture that defeat of the ERA will affect the movement in the same way success in obtaining the vote affected the cause of suffrage. More specifically, the broad-based, diverse coalition that united behind the ERA, like the one that supported the Nineteenth Amendment, may falter as to the next step. If the leaders of the various organizations cannot reach an accord on other issues but rather choose to pursue their own individual limited goals, their opportunity to achieve the ultimate target of full equality may be lost once again as it was in the 1920s.

While the ERA was reintroduced in Congress shortly after its defeat, quick passage is unlikely. Given this, a number of short-term strategies are being proposed. For instance, the leaders of several women's rights groups have told their followers, "Don't get mad. Get even. Vote." Several organizations, notably NOW and NWPC, even mounted a national campaign to elect prowomen's rights women and men to office and to exact revenge from those who sabotaged the ERA effort.[79] And, in some areas their efforts in the 1982 elections were quite successful. For example, support of women voters and women's groups was credited for the victory of Mario Cuomo over Louis Lehrman in the 1982 New York gubernatorial race.[80] Additionally, of the 1,166 women who ran for stage legislature in November 1982, 918 were elected.[81]

While the object of electing more women to office is indeed very important, this goal alone is not sufficient to assure that gains for the women's movement will continue to be forthcoming. Indeed many of the women who ran for office do not support key women's rights issues. Moreover, electing more women to office will not necessarily work to the benefit of the women's movement unless there is agreement on a common set of goals.

The split in the 1920s between social feminists working for protective legislation and the NWP for the ERA may once again be developing in the present women's movement. On one side are radical feminists who fear a capitulation to the New Right/Moral Majority especially over the issue of reproductive freedom. Naomi Weisstein, a founding member of the Chicago Women's Liberation Union, for instance, has warned:

> I sense an attack of cold feet on the abortion issue.... The retreat takes several forms: a softening of rhetoric, an apologetic tone, a kind of walking-on-eggs approach to coalition building....
>
> If we show how anti-abortion is the symbol and substance of the right-wing campaign to cancel everybody's right to choose how they will live their sexual and personal lives, legions will be ready to be brave in defense of their liberty."[82]

Weisstein may be right but some in the center and liberal wings of the movement are arguing for a broader coalition and/or more specific, limited reforms.[83] There is a real possibility that these more short-term, limited reforms will repeat the errors of the social feminists when they secured for women "protective legislation." For example, the changes proposed for the workplace, including increased availability of flexitime or 4-day work weeks, may only reinforce the notion that women are second-class workers. While there is rather widespread agreement that such options would help families cope with the stress of two working parents, such programs could later be construed as protective legislation by future feminists.[84] The problem with such limited, optional reforms, however, is that they will only benefit a minority. Moreover, unless *both* men and women, husbands and wives, fathers and mothers take advantage (or are allowed to take advantage) of such alterations in the workplace, the ability of women to attain an equal role in politics, on the job, or in the family will be severely hampered.

Betty Friedan sees the need to convince men and women both to share in the roles of worker, spouse, and parent as a key goal in the second stage of the women's movement. Although, as she discusses in *The Second Stage*, she is unwilling to go as far as radical feminists, she believes changes in gender roles and in the family are necessary: "I believe that feminism must, in fact, confront the family, albeit in new terms, if the movement is to fulfill its own revolutionary function in modern society.... Locked into reaction against women's role in the family of the past, we could blindly emulate an obsolete narrow male role ... not understanding that the power and the promise of the future lie in transcending that absolute separation of the sex roles, in work *and* family."[85] While for Friedan this prospect and how to achieve it may seem obvious, necessary, exciting, and unavoidable, for large segments of the

public already fearful that change in the family structure in the last ten years
seriously threatens the institution, further alteration of the family and
male/female roles may seem like pure public bads (not goods) they can live
without. Indeed, as noted, the public reports overwhelming support for the
idea of more emphasis on the traditional family. Thus, it is imperative that the
women's movement find a strategy for itself that allows it to avoid the label of
antifamily. Today, the women's movement still has the upper hand. The polls
show widespread support for the movement's long-term goal of equal rights
for women. Virginia Sapiro reports that most people appear to believe the
trend for the future is toward increased rights for women and numerous
studies still indicate an ideological coherence among movement women
concerning the main issues.[86] Even conservative women favor key concepts of
equal pay, equal educational opportunities, and participation of women in
public affairs. The challenge for the movement, then, is to find a way to
maintain this support and mobilize it to work for and support further reforms.

Thus, the future of the women's movement and its goal of full equality
for all women and men in the last decades of the twentieth century appear to
be at the crossroads. There are strong reasons to believe that more changes in
the status of women will be forthcoming, but the forces opposed to further
alterations in the status quo also are growing stronger. The next five years
may well determine whether improvements in the opportunities and status of
women will continue to be forthcoming or whether, like the periods following
the first two movements, we once again enter an era of stagnation or decline.

NOTES

1.   William H. Chafe, *The American Woman: Her Changing Social, Economic
and Political Role, 1920–1970* (New York: Oxford University Press, 1972), p. 112.

2.   In 1943, the language of the proposed amendment was changed to: "Equality
of rights under the law shall not be denied or abridged by the United States or by any
state on account of sex."

3.   William L. O'Neill was the first to use the first and second terms. According to
him, the social feminists sought suffrage to bring about a variety of social reforms. We
have added the third term, antifeminists, to refer to a sizeable group of women who
were against any changes concerning women's status in society, including suffrage.
Everyone Was Brave: The Rise and Fall of Feminism in America (New York:
Quadrangle Books, 1969).

4.   Chafe, *The American Woman,* pp. 130–131.

5.   Groups also supporting the proposed amendment during this period included
the National Federation of Business and Professional Women's Clubs, the General
Federation of Women's Clubs, and the National Association of Women Lawyers. See
Catherine East, "The First Stage: ERA in Washington, 1961–1972," *Women's
Political Times,* September 1982, p. 7.

6.   This rider was viewed as crucial because of the substantial opposition to the
ERA by many traditionally "liberal groups," including the ACLU, the National
Council of Negro Women, and the Americans for Democratic Action. Other groups

opposing passage included the NCL, the American Association of University Women (AAUW), and the National Council of Jewish Women. Ibid.

7.   This failure is not surprising given that most commission members were drawn from organizations that opposed the amendment—particularly labor unions and the AAUW.

8.   For a more comprehensive discussion of Rawalt's role on the commission, see East, "First Stage," p. 7.

9.   Judith Hole and Ellen Levine, *Rebirth of Feminism* (New York: Quadrangle Books, 1971), p. 68.

10.   It should be noted that President Nixon appointed strong supporters of the ERA to the council, which led to this recommendation.

11.   Also adding impetus to the drive for the ERA was Nixon's creation of a Task Force on Women's Rights and Responsibilities, which was chaired by a strong feminist. The task force's mission was to recommend legislation for administration support and transmission to Congress. The resulting report, "A Matter of Simple Justice," urged the president to support the ERA and other legislation to improve the status of women. For an excellent "insider's" account of this period, see East, "First Stage," pp. 7–10.

12.   During this period, members of Congress were lobbied by the hundreds of women who were in Washington, D.C. to celebrate the 50th anniversary of the Women's Bureau. Members also were inundated with telegrams from BPW members who were holding their convention in Hawaii.

13.   According to East, a particularly dramatic moment in the three-day hearings occurred when a woman, who had been a plaintiff in a lawsuit that ultimately led to invalidation of several state protective legislation laws, criticized her union's position on the ERA. "First Stage," p. 8.

14.   Testifying for the ERA were the National Federation of Republican Women and the Coalition of American Nuns.

15.   The proposed rider severely weakened potential equality by exempting from judicial scrutiny any laws "designed to promote the health, safety, privacy, education, or economic welfare of women, or to enable them to perform their duties as homemakers and mothers."

16.   See East, "First Stage," pp. 9–10, for a discussion of new House hearings on the ERA and rejection of proposed changes in the amendment that would have reauthorized protective legislation or exempted women from the draft.

17.   U.S. Congress, Senate Committee on the Judiciary, *Equal Rights for Men and Women* 92d Cong. 2d sess., 1972, S. Rep. 92-689, p. 7 (hereafter cited as *Senate ERA Report*).

18.   Thus, after the amendment was defeated, the director of the ACLU's Women's Rights Project noted, "We still have no broad legal policy that any governmental sex discrimination is unacceptable." Quoted in Jane Perlez, "Ratification Defeat Leaves Rights on Uneven Path," *The New York Times,* June 26, 1982, p. E-5.

19.   See California Commission on the Status of Women, *Impact ERA: Limitations and Possibilities* (Millbrae, Calif.: Les Femmes Publishing, 1976).

20.   Freund continues to believe that an ERA is unnecessary and has said that the 10-year struggle "diverted energy" from other more potentially productive avenues of ending sex discrimination. Perlez, "Ratification Defeat," p. E-5.

21.   East, "First Stage," p. 9. For similar conclusions about the ERA, see Rex E.

Lee, *A Lawyer Looks at the ERA* (Provo, Utah: Brigham Young University Press, 1980). It should be noted that Mr. Lee is the Solicitor General of the United States—the individual charged with representing the U.S. government before the U.S. Supreme Court.

22. Lee, *A Lawyer*, chaps. 6 and 8–10.

23. For a thorough analysis of the impact of the ERA on these areas, see Barbara Allen Babcock et al., *Sex Discrimination and the Law: Cases and Remedies* (Boston: Little Brown and Co., 1975), pp. 129–190; Barbara Brown et al., *Women's Rights and the Law: The Impact of the ERA on State Laws* (New York: Praeger, 1977); and Barbara Brown et al., "The Equal Rights Amendment: A Constitutional Basis for Equal Rights for Women," *Yale Law Review* 80 (April 1971):871–985.

24. See U.S. Commission on Civil Rights, *The Equal Rights Amendment*, pp. 19–21; *Senate ERA Report*, p. 13; and Kathleen Carpenter, "Women in the Military and the Impact of the Equal Rights Amendment," unpublished testimony before the Illinois House Judiciary Committee, April 30, 1980.

25. See U.S. Commission on Civil Rights, *The Equal Rights Amendment*, pp. 22–23; Ruth Bader Ginsburg, "Some Thoughts on Judicial Authority to Repair Unconstitutional Legislation," *Cleveland State Law Review* 28 (1979):301; and Brown et al., *Women's Rights and the Law.*

26. Janet K. Boles, *The Politics of the Equal Rights Amendment* (New York: Longman, 1979), pp. 41–42.

27. Zillah R. Eisenstein, *The Radical Future of Liberal Feminism* (New York: Longman, 1981), pp. 232–236. Many radical feminists initially rejected the ERA because they failed to perceive it as good for working-class women. See Hole and Levine, *Rebirth of Feminism*, p. 68.

28. See Chapters 4 and 6. In 1972, 48 percent of all women in a national sample reported they favored efforts to strengthen or change the status of women in society. Louis Harris, *The 1972 Virginia Slims American Women's Opinion Poll*, conducted by Louis Harris and Associates, Inc., 1972, p. 2.

29. Janet K. Boles, "Systematic Factors Underlying Legislative Responses to Woman Suffrage and the Equal Rights Amendment," *Women & Politics* 2 (Spring/Summer, 1982), pp. 14 and 17, found that if the ERA was considered in 1972 or before the mobilization of opposition in 1973, chances for state passage were greatly enhanced.

30. Ibid., pp. 11 and 15 and Ernest H. Wohlenberg, "Correlates of Equal Rights Amendment Ratification," *Social Science Quarterly* 60 (March 1980): 676–684.

31. Quoted in Carol Felsenthal, *The Sweetheart of the Moral Majority: The Biography of Phyllis Schlafly* (Garden City, N.Y.: Doubleday & Co., 1981), p. 235.

32. Boles, *The Politics of the Equal Rights Amendment*, p. 62.

33. Ibid.

34. Ibid., pp. 62–63.

35. Ibid., p. 63.

36. Ibid., pp. 64–65.

37. Janet K. Boles, "Building Support for the ERA: A Case of 'Too Much, Too Late,'" *PS* 15 (Fall 1982):572–577. The authors would like to thank Catherine Rudder, the editor of *PS*, for allowing us to see this and other ERA articles before they were published.

38. Ibid., p. 574.

39. Among the associations participating in the NOW boycott were: American Association of University Professors; American Association of University Women; American Baptist Churches, USA; American Civil Liberties Union; American Federation of Labor-Congress of Industrial Organizations (AFL-CIO); American Federation of State, County and Municipal Employees; Gay Pride Conference; International Ladies' Garment Workers Union; International Union of Electrical Radio and Machine Workers; United Auto Workers; United Farm Workers of America; United Methodist Church: Church & Society; United Presbyterian Church; and United Steelworkers of America. This boycott ultimately resulted in a major lawsuit upholding NOW's right to protest through the boycott strategy.

40. Quoted in "Organizations Supporting Equal Rights Amendment," *National NOW Times,* May 13, 1980, pp. 14–15.

41. In retrospect, this strategy was particularly fruitless given subsequent studies that have revealed growing concern on the part of state legislators about their loss of authority, which was not assuaged by the tactics pursued by NOW. See Deborah Borowski, "State Legislator Perceptions of Public Debate on the Equal Rights Amendment," paper delivered at the 1982 Annual Meeting of the American Political Science Association.

42. "NOW Starts $3 Million Election Drive," *Atlanta Constitution,* August 27, 1982, p. 2 and John Herbers, "Women Turn View to Public Office," *The New York Times,* June 28, 1982, p. 1 (con't. on p. 11).

43. Quoted in Felsenthal, *Sweetheart of the Silent Majority,* p. 240.

44. Diane Weathers, "Is Liberation Really Good for Women?" (an interview with Phyllis Schlafly), *Family Circle,* September 18, 1979, p. 62.

45. Quoted in Felsenthal, *Sweetheart of the Silent Majority,* p. 241.

46. Gail Sheehy, "Phyllis Schlafly," *The New York Times,* January 24, 1980, p. C-2.

47. Ibid.

48. Boles, *The Politics of the Equal Rights Amendment,* pp. 109–110.

49. Kent L. Tedin et al., "Social Background and Political Differences Between Pro- and Anti-ERA Activists," *American Politics Quarterly* 5 (July 1977):404.

50. See David W. Brady and Kent L. Tedin, "Ladies in Pink: Religion and Political Ideology in the Anti-ERA Movement," *Social Science Quarterly* 56 (March 1976):564–575; Wohlenberg, "Correlates of Equal Rights Amendment Ratification," 676–684; Kathleen M. Beatty and B. Oliver Walter, "Sex Related Issue Attitudes: The Effects of Religion and Situation," paper presented at the 1981 Annual Meeting of the Midwest Political Science Association, pp. 10–17; and Pamela Johnston Conover and Virginia Gray, "Political Activities and the Conflict Over Abortion and the ERA: Pro-Family versus Pro-Woman," paper delivered at the 1981 Annual Meeting of the Midwest Political Science Association, p. 26.

51. As Oberschall has pointed out, individuals with "movable skills" like those of ministers, writers, and intellectuals (he labels them the free professions) have almost always monopolized the leadership positions in prochange movements. He reasons this is because they carry their resources (communication skills) with them and hence have less to lose if the movement should fail and more to gain (leadership in the new order) if the movement succeeds than do other members of society (like people in

business, laborers) who are more dependent on someone else to provide their income and status. Anthony Oberschall, *Social Conflict and Social Movements* (Englewood Cliffs, N.Y.: Prentice Hall, 1973), pp. 146–157 and 167.

52. Boles, *The Politics of the Equal Rights Amendment,* pp. 69–70 and 109.

53. Tedin et al., "Social Background and Political Differences Between Pro- and Anti-ERA Activists," p. 407.

54. Richard A. Viguerie, *The New Right: We're Ready to Lead* (Falls Church, Va.: The Viguerie Co., 1981), p. 166, claims that Schlafly attributes Stop ERA victories in Florida, Nevada, and Virginia to help from the Mormon church.

55. *What Women Want,* from the Official Report to the President (New York: Simon and Schuster, 1979), p. 51.

56. Quoted in Jane O'Reilly, "Schlafly's Last Fling," *Ms.,* September 1982, p. 43. In reference to the amount of money, the same leader noted, "Oh, yes, we are talking big, big money."

57. "ERA Dies," *Time,* July 5, 1982, p. 29; Herbers, "Women Turn View," p. 11; and "Insurance Blamed in Sex Bias," *The New York Times,* June 2, 1982, p. 12.

58. Judson H. Jones, "The Effect of the Pro- and Anti-ERA Campaign Contributions on the ERA Voting Behavior of the 80th Illinois House of Representatives," *Women & Politics* 2 (Spring/Summer 1982):71–86.

59. Frederick S. Jaffe, Barbara L. Lindheim, and Philip R. Lee, *Abortion Politics: Private Morality and Public Policy* (New York: McGraw Hill, 1981), chap. 6.

60. Quoted in Felsenthal, *Sweetheart of the Silent Majority,* p. 239.

61. "What Equal Rights Amendment Could and Couldn't Do," *The New York Times,* May 29, 1982, p. 1.

62. *Congressional Digest* 56 (June/July 1977), p. 191.

63. *The New York Times,* July 14, 1978, p. 18.

64. List derived from Felsenthal, *Sweetheart of the Silent Majority;* Conover and Gray, "Political Activists;" and Suzanne Crowell, "Four Days in Houston—Watershed for Women's Rights," *Civil Rights Digest* 10 (Winter 1978):3–13.

65. John Hebers, "Equal Rights Amendment Is Mired in Confused and Emotional Debate," *The New York Times,* May 28, 1978, pp. 1 and 44.

66. *The Phyllis Schlafly Report,* July 1975, p. 4.

67. For a discussion of opponents' positions and counterarguments, see Ruth Bader Ginsberg, "Sex Equality Under the 14th and Equal Rights Amendments," *Washington University Law Quarterly* (Winter 1979):161–206; Carol G. Hochfelder, "Equal Rights ... Where Are We Now?" *Illinois Bar Journal* (June 1976):558–569; Brown et al., "The Equal Rights Amendment;" and Lee, *A Lawyer.*

68. Quoted in Felsenthal, *Sweetheart of the Silent Majority,* p. 479.

69. Tedin et al., "Social Background and Political Differences Between Pro- and Anti-ERA Activists," pp. 399–402; Susan Welch, "Support Among Women for the Issues of the Women's Movement," *The Sociological Quarterly* 16 (Spring 1975):223–224; and Boles, *The Politics of the Equal Rights Amendment,* pp. 83–84.

70. Joan Huber, Cynthia Rexroot, and Glenna Spitze, "A Crucible of Opinion on Women's Status: ERA in Illinois," *Social Forces* 57 (December 1978):555 and 559–560.

71. Sheehy, "Phyllis Schlafly," C-2.

72. Ibid.

73. *Biography News* 2 (July 1975):878–879.

74. Phyllis Schlafly, *The Power of the Positive Woman* (New York: Jove Publications, 1978), p. 12.

75. *NOW* v. *Idaho,* _____ U.S. _____ (1982).

76. Mark R. Daniels et al., "The ERA Won—At Least in the Opinion Polls," *PS* 15 (Fall 1982), p. 578.

77. Ibid., p. 578.

78. Quoted in Leslie Bennetts, "Feminist Drive Is Likely to Persist Even if Rights Amendment Fails," *The New York Times,* May 31, 1978, p. A-20.

79. See Demetra Lambros, "Caucus Indicts Twelve Who Roadblocked ERA," *Women's Political Times,* July 1982, p. 1.

80. Judy Mann, "Women's Vote," *The Washington Post,* November 5, 1982, p. B-1.

81. Figures from National Women's Political Caucus.

82. Naomi Weisstein, "Watch on the Right: Abortion Rights—Taking the Offensive," *Ms.,* September 1981, pp. 36 and 39.

83. See, for example, the discussion of the Women's Economic Equity Act in Chaps. 7 and 8 and "Holding Our Own Against a Conservative Tide," Ms. Roundtable with Lisa Cronin Wohl, Linda Gordon, Kathryn Sklar, Mary Lyndon Shanley, Elizabeth Higgenbotham, and Karen Burstein, *Ms.,* June 1981, pp. 50–53 and 86–89.

84. *The General Mills American Family Report, 1980–81: Families Strengths and Strains at Work.* Survey conducted by Louis Harris and Associates (General Mills Inc., 9200 Wayzata Boulevard, Minneapolis, Minnesota, 55440), p. 54. Majorities or near-majorities of working women and mothers think flexitime would help a great deal. Fewer men thought so.

85. Betty Friedan, *The Second Stage* (New York: Summit Books, 1981), p. 84.

86. Virginia Sapiro, "News From the Front: Intersex and Intergenerational Conflict Over the Status of Women," *The Western Political Quarterly* 33 (June 1980): 260–277 and Claire Knoch Fulenwider, *Feminism in American Politics: A Study of Ideological Influence* (New York: Praeger, 1980), chapters 3 and 4.

A   Declaration of Sentiments

When, in the course of human events, it becomes necessary for one portion of the family of man to assume among the people of the earth a position different from that which they have hitherto occupied, but one to which the laws of nature and of nature's God entitle them, a decent respect to the opinions of mankind requires that they should declare the causes that impel them to such a course.

We hold these truths to be self-evident that all men and women are created equal; that they are endowed by their Creator with certain inalienable rights; that among these are life, liberty, and the pursuit of happiness; that to secure these rights governments are instituted, deriving their just power from the consent of the governed. Whenever any form of government becomes destructive of these ends, it is the right of those who suffer from it to refuse allegiance to it, and to insist upon the institution of a new government, laying its foundation on such principles, and organizing its powers in such form, as to them shall seem most likely to effect their safety and happiness. Prudence indeed, will dictate that governments long established should not be changed for light and transient causes; and accordingly all experience hath shown that mankind are more disposed to suffer, while evils are sufferable, than to right themselves by abolishing the forms to which they were accustomed. But when a long train of abuses and usurpations, pursuing invariably the same object evinces a design to reduce them under absolute despotism, it is their duty to throw off such government, and to provide new guards for their future security. Such has been the patient sufferance of the women under this government, and such is now the necessity which constrains them to demand the equal station to which they are entitled.

The history of mankind is a history of repeated injuries and usurpations on the part of man toward woman, having indirect object the establishment of an absolute tyranny over her. To prove this, let facts be submitted to a candid world.

He has never permitted her to exercise her inalienable right to the elective franchise.

He has compelled her to submit to laws, in the formation of which she had no voice.

He has withheld from her rights which are given to the most ignorant and degraded men—both natives and foreigners.

Having deprived her of this first right of a citizen, the elective franchise, thereby leaving her without representation in the halls of legislation, he has oppressed her on all sides.

He has made her, if married, in the eye of the law, civilly dead.

He has taken from her all right in property, even to the wages she earns.

He has made her, morally, an irresponsible being as she can commit many crimes with impunity, provided they be done in the presence of her husband. In the covenant of marriage, she is compelled to promise obedience to her husband, he becoming, to all intents and purposes, her master—the law giving him power to deprive her of her liberty, and to administer chastisement.

He has so framed the laws of divorce, as to what shall be the proper causes, and in case of separation, to whom the guardianship of the children shall be given, as to be wholly regardless of the happiness of women—the law, in all cases, going upon a false supposition of the supremacy of man, and giving all power into his hands.

After depriving her of all rights as a married woman, if single, and the owner of property, he has taxed her to support a government which recognizes her only when her property can be made profitable to it.

He has monopolized nearly all the profitable employments, and from those she is permitted to follow, she receives but a scanty remuneration. He closes against her all the avenues to wealth and distinction which he considers most honorable to himself. As a teacher of theology, medicine, or law, she is not known.

He has denied her the facilities for obtaining a thorough education, all colleges being closed against her.

He allows her in Church, as well as State, but a subordinate position, claiming Apostolic authority for her exclusion from the ministry, and, with some exceptions, from any public participation in the affairs of the Church.

He has created a false public sentiment by giving to the world a different code of morals for men and women, by which moral delinquencies which exclude women from society, are not only tolerated, but deemed of little account in man.

He has usurped the prerogative of Jehovah himself, claiming it as his right to assign for her a sphere of action, when that belongs to her conscience and to her God.

He has endeavored, in every way that he could, to destroy her confidence in her own powers, to lessen her self-respect, and to make her willing to lead a dependent and abject life.

Now, in view of this entire disfranchisement of one-half the people of this country, their social and religious degradation—in view of the unjust laws just mentioned, and because women do feel themselves aggrieved, oppressed, and fraudulently deprived of their most sacred rights, we insist that they have immediate admission to all the rights and privileges which belong to them as citizens of the United States.

In entering upon the great work before us, we anticipate no small amount of misconception, misrepresentation, and ridicule; but we shall use every instrumentality within our power to effect our object. We shall employ agents, circulate tracts, petition the State and National legislatures, and endeavor to enlist the pulpit and the press in our behalf. We hope this Convention will be followed by a series of Conventions embracing every part of the country.

Source: Elizabeth Cady Stanton, Susan B. Anthony, and Matilda Joslyn Gage, eds., *History of Woman Suffrage,* vol. I, 1848–1861 (Rochester, N.Y.: Charles Mann, 1881), pp. 70–71.

B   Important Sections of Major Anti-Discrimination Provisions

EQUAL PAY ACT

No employer having employees subject to any provisions of this section shall discriminate, within any establishment in which such employees are employed, between employees on the basis of sex by paying wages to employees in such establishment at a rate less than the rate at which he pays wages to employees of the opposite sex in such establishment for equal work on jobs the performance of which requires equal skill, effort, and responsibility, and which are performed under similar working conditions, except where such payment is made pursuant to (1) a seniority system, (2) a merit system, (3) a system which measures earnings by the quantity or quality of production, or (4) a differential based on any other factor other than sex: Provided that an employer who is paying a wage rate differential in violation of this subsection shall not, in order to comply with the provisions of this subsection, reduce the wage rate of any employee.

EXECUTIVE ORDER 11375

The contractor will not discriminate against any employee or applicant for employment because of race, color, religion, *sex,* or national origin. The contractor will take affirmative action to ensure that applicants are employed, and that employees are treated during employment, without regard to their race, color, religion, *sex* or national origin. Such action shall include but not be limited to the following: employment, upgrading, demotion, or transfer; recruitment or recruitment advertising; layoff or termination; rates of pay or other forms of compensation; and selection for training, including apprenticeship. [emphasis added]

CIVIL RIGHTS ACT OF 1964

It shall be unlawful employment practice for any employer—

(1) to fail or refuse to hire or to discharge any individual or otherwise to discriminate against any individual with respect to his compensation, terms, conditions, or privileges of employment, because of such individual's race, color, religion, *sex* or national origin; or

(2) to limit, segregate, or classify his employees in any way which would deprive or tend to deprive any individual of employment opportunities or otherwise adversely affect his status as an employee, because of such individual's race, color, religion, *sex,* or national origin. [emphasis added]

BFOQ EXCEPTION TO THE CIVIL RIGHTS ACT OF 1964

Notwithstanding any other provisions of this subchapter ... it shall *not* be an unlawful employment practice for an employer to hire and employ employees ... on the basis of his religion, *sex,* or national origin in those certain instances where religion, *sex,* or national origin is a bona fide occupational qualification reasonably necessary to the normal operation of that particular business or enterprise. [emphasis added]

PREGNANCY DISCRIMINATION ACT OF 1978

The terms "because of sex" or "on the basis of sex" include, but are not limited to, because of or on the basis of pregnancy, childbirth, or related medical conditions; and women affected by pregnancy, childbirth, or related medical conditions shall be treated the same for all employment-related purposes, including receipt of benefits under fringe benefit programs, as other persons not so affected but similar in their ability or inability to work, and nothing in section 703(h) of this title shall be interpreted to permit otherwise. This subsection shall not require an employer to pay for health insurance benefits for abortion, except where the life of the mother would be endangered if the fetus were carried to term, or except where medical complications have arisen from an abortion: *Provided,* That nothing herein shall preclude an employer from providing abortion benefits or otherwise affect bargaining agreements in regard to abortion.

EEOC GUIDELINES ON SEXUAL HARASSMENT

Harassment on the basis of sex is a violation of Sec. 703 of Title VII. Unwelcome sexual advances, requests for sexual favors, and other verbal or physical conduct of a sexual nature constitute sexual harassment when (1) submission to such conduct is made either explicitly or implicitly a term or condition of an individual's employment, (2) submission to or rejection of such conduct by an individual is used as the basis for employment decisions affecting such individual, or (3) such conduct has the purpose or effect of unreasonably interfering with an individual's work performance or creating an intimidating, hostile, or offensive working environment.

C NOW Bill of Rights for Homemakers

I. ECONOMIC RIGHTS WITHIN MARRIAGE

In recognition of marriage as a truly equal partnership, homemakers shall be granted equal access to, and control over, all money acquired during the marriage

— through revision of Federal Income Tax forms and their interpretation, so that there is a clear indication that all income listed on a joint income tax return is co-owned;

— through abolition of gift taxes or interspousal transfers;

— through revision of state laws so that a homemaker has the right to obligate the family income through credit purchases, loans, and similar transactions;

— through evaluation and revision of state property laws so that the contributions of the wage-earner and the homemaker are given equal weight in determining ownership of marital property.

II. ECONOMIC RECOGNITION FOR HOMEMAKERS

In recognition of the fact that it is not the homemaker who benefits most from her unpaid labor, but it is the community and family and through them all of society, homemakers should be granted the recognitions and rights of paid, skilled workers

— through independent Social Security coverage in her own name, portable into and out of marriage and continuing as the homemaker leaves and re-enters the paid workforce, containing provision for disability and retirement benefits adequate to maintain a decent standard of living;

— through inclusion of the value of goods and services produced and provided by homemakers in the Gross National Product;

— through revision of welfare laws so that a low-income homemaker can remain at home with her family, rather than be forced to take a second, paying job;

— through development of flexible-time and part-time employment, and the development of adequate flexible-time and part-time child care facilities to make these jobs more available to parents of young children;

— through civil and criminal protection from spousal rape and domestic abuse;

— through providing the homemaker with a safe workplace; adequate housing regardless of income;

— through comprehensive review of current domestic relations laws to challenge and change those laws, statutes, procedures and codes that deprive homemakers of dignity, security and recognition;

— through recognition of the right to retire or change jobs.

III. ECONOMIC RIGHTS FOR HOMEMAKERS IN TRANSITION

In recognition of the fact that over one-third of all marriages now end in divorce; and that homemakers fare poorly in most states because division of property and recognition of entitlement is often inadequate and unjust; and that homemakers who are divorced have among the highest rates of unemployment and underemployment because of the lack of recent paid work experience; prejudice toward their marital status, age and sex discrimination, and the unwillingness to translate homemaking skills into marketable job skills; homemakers must be protected in divorce

— through equitable division of property which recognizes the unpaid contributions of the homemaker in acquiring and maintaining the family's assets;

— through maintenance (alimony) awards to compensate for the loss of educational opportunities, seniority, advancement, benefits, and accrued protections the homemaker would have had if the homemaker had been in the paid workforce during the years of homemaking;

— through vigorous enforcement of court-awarded maintenance;

— through comprehensive legislation and funded programs to offer divorced and displaced homemakers job-entry education, training, counselling and placement, and supportive services;

— through recognizing the right of homemakers to unemployment compensation;

— through award of an equitable share of pensions, annuities, legislative protection, and other retirement securities;

— through mandatory disclosure of assets of both parties of a divorce, including those sold or distributed in anticipation of a divorce.

In recognition of the special problems a homemaker faces when she is widowed, the homemaker must be protected from the unfair burdens that add to her grief

— through continuation of pensions, family insurance coverage, and other benefits;
— through abolition of interspousal inheritance taxes;
— through the right to continued access to the family savings accounts, checking accounts, securities and safety deposit boxes.

Source: National NOW Times, May 1979, p. 7. Reprinted with permission.

Index

399

regarding, 53; the right to vote,
43–63
Politicos, 71, 146, 288
Population control, 299
Pornography, 289
Power of the Positive Woman, 378
Preexisting associations: as a factor in
protest organization, 8, 15;
importance of, 8; and rise of anti
movements, 8; and the suffrage
movement, 9
Pregnancy discrimination, 180–82
Pregnancy Discrimination Act, 146,
182, 393–94
Preparation of women: for employment
outside the home, 228–31, 235–45,
246, 247, 254; for an equal role in
the family, 337–40, 354; for
political participation, 87–88,
94–95, 99, 113, 123, 129
President's Commission on the Status
of Women: and daycare, 249; and
development of the older branch
of the women's movement, 28, 176;
and discrimination in marriage,
295–96; and discrimination under
Social Security, 182; on education
for women, 188; on employment
rights, 169–70, 175, 179; on ERA,
368; and expansion of political
rights for women, 69–70; as
extragroup input, 8
Privileged group activity, and
attainment of rights, 6–7; examples
of, 6, 294; and the public good, 6
Privileged movement: anti-ERA forces
as, 372–73
Pro-America, 34
Professional Women's Caucus, 303
Progressive movement: and educated
motherhood, 283–85, 286–87; as a
factor in the development of the
suffrage movement, 19, 20, 21,
54–55; and working women, 157,
199 n.38.
Project on Equal Education Rights, 191
Pro-Life Party, 307
Prostitution, 278
Protective legislation. *See also* Antidiscrimination legislation: as a
barrier to equality, 210, 254, 381;
basis for, 149–50; and

disagreement among women
regarding, 159, 160–61, 162, 178,
179; during the Depression, 161;
during World War II, 165, 166–67;
the Equal Rights Amendment's
impact on, 368, 369, 370; and the
National Consumers' League, 158,
161–62
Protestantism, 325
Psychological involvement in politics:
differences between men and
women, 89–91, 111
Public bad, a: birth control as, 281;
definition of, 13; divorce as, 275;
divorce reform as, 275; lifestyle
rights as, 267, 268; protective
legislation as, 162; reform of
family law as, 295; Sheppard-
Towner Maternity Act as, 287;
suffrage as, 42, 53; and the
younger branch of the women's
movement, 290
Public good, a: definition of, 5, 14; as a
deterrent to group organization,
5–6; dimensions of, 13–14; and
privileged groups, 6; vs. public
bad, 13; as a source of
disagreement among women, 14
Public incentives, 8
Public opinion polls: on abilities of
women, 225–26, 227–28; on
abortion, 333, 358, n.57.; on
attitudes toward political
participation of women, 84–85,
86–87; on birth control, 327–28,
332; on credit discrimination, 295;
on divorce, 331; on the Equal
Rights Amendment, 370, 379, 380,
382; and gender differences on
voting issues, 100; impact on the
women's rights movement, 377–78;
on marriage, 331, 333, 334, 354; of
men regarding the role of women,
341; on motherhood, 332; on party
identification, 101; on role sharing,
335–36; on sex discrimination,
247–48; and sex roles, 360 n.101.;
on working women, 217, 217–18,
221–24, 248

Radical feminist, 71, 146, 281, 291, 292,
370, 381. *See also* Younger branch,